Pan-Asianism

ASIA/PACIFIC/PERSPECTIVES

Series Editor: Mark Selden

Crime, Punishment, and Policing in China
edited by Børge Bakken
Woman, Man, Bangkok: Love, Sex, and Popular Culture in Thailand
by Scot Barmé
Making the Foreign Serve China: Managing Foreigners in the People's Republic
by Anne-Marie Brady
Marketing Dictatorship: Propaganda and Thought Work in China
by Anne-Marie Brady
Collaborative Nationalism: The Politics of Friendship on China's Mongolian Frontier
by Uradyn E. Bulag
The Mongols at China's Edge: History and the Politics of National Unity
by Uradyn E. Bulag
Transforming Asian Socialism: China and Vietnam Compared
edited by Anita Chan, Benedict J. Tria Kerkvliet, and Jonathan Unger
China's Great Proletarian Cultural Revolution: Master Narratives and Post-Mao Counternarratives
edited by Woei Lien Chong
North China at War: The Social Ecology of Revolution, 1937–1945
edited by Feng Chongyi and David S. G. Goodman
Little Friends: Children's Film and Media Culture in China
by Stephanie Hemelryk Donald
Gender in Motion: Divisions of Labor and Cultural Change in Late Imperial and Modern China
edited by Bryna Goodman and Wendy Larson
Social and Political Change in Revolutionary China: The Taihang Base Area in the War of Resistance to Japan, 1937–1945
by David S. G. Goodman
Islands of Discontent: Okinawan Responses to Japanese and American Power
edited by Laura Hein and Mark Selden
Women in Early Imperial China, Second Edition
by Bret Hinsch
Civil Justice in China: Past and Present
by Philip C. C. Huang

Local Democracy and Development: The Kerala People's Campaign for Decentralized Planning
by T. M. Thomas Isaac with Richard W. Franke
Hidden Treasures: Lives of First-Generation Korean Women in Japan
by Jackie J. Kim with Sonia Ryang
Postwar Vietnam: Dynamics of a Transforming Society
edited by Hy V. Luong
The Indonesian Presidency: The Shift from Personal towards Constitutional Rule
by Angus McIntyre
Nationalisms of Japan: Managing and Mystifying Identity
by Brian J. McVeigh
To the Diamond Mountains: A Hundred-Year Journey through China and Korea
by Tessa Morris-Suzuki
From Underground to Independent: Alternative Film Culture in Contemporary China
edited by Paul G. Pickowicz and Yingjin Zhang
Wife or Worker? Asian Women and Migration
edited by Nicola Piper and Mina Roces
Social Movements in India: Poverty, Power, and Politics
edited by Raka Ray and Mary Fainsod Katzenstein
Pan-Asianism: A Documentary History, Volume 1, 1850–1920
edited by Sven Saaler and Christopher W. A. Szpilman
Pan-Asianism: A Documentary History, Volume 2, 1920–Present
edited by Sven Saaler and Christopher W. A. Szpilman
Biology and Revolution in Twentieth-Century China
by Laurence Schneider
Contentious Kwangju: The May 18th Uprising in Korea's Past and Present
edited by Gi-Wook Shin and Kyong Moon Hwang
The Inside Story of China's High-Tech Industry: Making Silicon Valley in Beijing
by Yu Zhou

Pan-Asianism

A Documentary History

Volume 2: 1920–Present

Edited by
Sven Saaler and
Christopher W. A. Szpilman

ROWMAN & LITTLEFIELD PUBLISHERS, INC.
Lanham • Boulder • New York • Toronto • Plymouth, UK

Published by Rowman & Littlefield Publishers, Inc.
A wholly owned subsidiary of The Rowman & Littlefield Publishing Group, Inc.
4501 Forbes Boulevard, Suite 200, Lanham, Maryland 20706
http://www.rowmanlittlefield.com

Estover Road, Plymouth PL6 7PY, United Kingdom

British Library Cataloguing in Publication Information Available

Library of Congress Cataloging-in-Publication Data

Pan-Asianism : a documentary history / edited by Sven Saaler and Christopher W.A. Szpilman.
p. cm. — (Asia/Pacific/perspectives)
Includes bibliographical references and index.
ISBN 978-1-4422-0596-3 (v. 1 : cloth : alk. paper) — ISBN 978-1-4422-0598-7 (v. 1 : electronic) — ISBN 978-1-4422-0599-4 (v. 2 : cloth : alk. paper) — ISBN 978-1-4422-0601-4 (v. 2 : electronic)
1. East Asia—History—19th century—Sources. 2. East Asia—History—20th century—Sources. 3. Regionalism—East Asia—Sources. 4. East Asians—Ethnic identity—Sources. 5. Nationalism—East Asia—History—Sources. 6. National characteristics, East Asian—Sources. I. Saaler, Sven, 1968– II. Szpilman, Christopher W. A., 1951–
DS504.5.P36 2011
950.4—dc22

ISBN 978-0-8108-9539-3 (pbk : alk. paper) 2010049256

™ The paper used in this publication meets the minimum requirements of American National Standard for Information Sciences—Permanence of Paper for Printed Library Materials, ANSI/NISO Z39.48-1992.

Contents

Preface and Acknowledgments

Pan-Asianism has been an ideology that has shaped the history of Asia over the past century and a half. It has been used both to express transnational aspirations to Asian regionalism and integration and to legitimize aggression and empire building. Whereas the former application makes Pan-Asianism highly relevant today in connection with various initiatives for regional integration, the latter has discredited Pan-Asianism to such an extent that for many years historians treated it as a taboo. The result is that there is no comprehensive book of materials on Pan-Asianism in English or, for that matter, in any Western language. This sad state of affairs has in effect hampered the study of modern Asian and Japanese history in which Pan-Asianism has played a decisive role. This book is intended to remedy this glaring gap. It is hoped that it will promote research into modern Asian history and throw some light on those many aspects of international relations in Asia that have remained underresearched because of shortage of easily accessible sources.

This project is the fruit of several years' collaboration by three dozen scholars on four continents. Several contributors to this project cooperated also on a collection of articles titled *Pan-Asianism in Modern Japanese History*, which was published in 2007. The preface to that volume stressed the need for further research on Pan-Asianism that would not be limited only to Japan but cover also the rest of Asia. For, although pan-Asian ideology was most frequently articulated in Japan, it had numerous and important advocates also in other Asian countries. For a number of practical reasons, however, it was necessary to limit the focus of the 2007 volume only to Japan. In recent years, however, Pan-Asianism as an academic field has shown rapid growth with a number of important publications on Pan-Asianism appearing in English, Japanese, and Chinese (see the introduction for further details). But the difficulty of obtaining access to primary sources is the root cause of the various problems that plague the field and the main obstacle on research that transcends both national boundaries and the limitations of historical periodization. The difficulty is also compounded by linguistic problems since only few, if any, scholars are competent in all the diverse languages of Asia that are required to engage in a comparative study of Pan-Asianism. To remedy these difficulties, the editors decided it would be a good idea to publish a collection of important primary sources in English. But when we started putting together documents along these lines, we ended up with more "seminal documents" than could fit in a single volume. As we kept working on it over a period of three years, our collection expanded into two hefty volumes of more than 100,000 words each. Yet, in spite of the size of this work, it was unfortunately impossible to include some very important documents. Some of the texts included in the work in their original languages can be accessed online on the following home page (see http://asianism.japanesehistory.de). The home page, which also includes additional sources of relevance as well as photographic material, will be expanded in the future as new sources come to our attention. Needless to say, the editors would have been unable to complete such a huge enterprise on their own. In this connection, we owe a great debt of gratitude to a number of institutions and individuals without whose cooperation, assistance, and support this publication would not have seen the light of day.

The editors, speaking also on behalf of the contributors to this volume, would like to express their gratitude, first of all, to the Toshiba International Foundation for providing funds vital for the completion of this project. We are also enormously grateful to Mark Selden for his advice and assistance and for agreeing to contribute at a very late stage of the project. We also thank the authors of the primary sources or their families for allowing us to reprint the texts included in this collection. Every effort has been made to trace copyright holders, but in the event of any omissions, the editors would be glad to hear from the copyright holders.

We would also like to thank all the contributors for their patience and cooperation in responding to our questions and suggestions, Paul Sorrell and Elena Neufeld for editorial assistance, and Nicholas Warren and Izabela Grocholski for their thoughtful comments. At Rowman & Littlefield, we are enormously grateful to Susan McEachern and Carrie Broadwell-Tkach for their support and help in bringing the production of this volume to fruition. We would also like to thank Rowman & Littlefield for their willingness to publish this collection, which, because of its size, must be a major commitment in terms of publishing policy. Finally, a word of appreciation for Skype and Dropbox, the providers of twenty-first-century communication technology. If they had not existed, the editors, who live 1000 miles apart, would have found it very difficult to overcome the vast distances between themselves and the contributors who live all over the globe.

Note on Transliteration and Translation

Transliteration was understandably a major challenge in a collection that includes primary sources from close to a dozen Asian countries and regions. We are in great debt to a number of contributors for the advice on how to transliterate personal names and place-names in English.

We have rendered East Asian names in the original order, surname first (however, the order in the English-language sources has been left unchanged), and have Romanized East Asian languages according to the Hepburn system for Japanese, the Revised Romanization of Korean from 2000 for Korean, and Pinyin for Chinese. When Japanese place names are established in English, macrons are omitted (e.g., Tokyo, not Tōkyō; Osaka, not Ōsaka; Ryukyu, not Ryūkyū; and so on). They were also not added when missing in the English-language original. In cases where the Wade-Giles Romanization for Chinese terms is commonly used in the West, it has been added in brackets on the first appearance of the term in each chapter. Cross references in brackets refer to volume and chapter number, i.e., II:10 refers to vol. 2, chapter 10 of this work. In the case of personal and place-names in Chinese and Korean that are long familiar in the West, such as Chiang Kai-shek or Sun Yat-sen, we have adhered to the common usage. In such cases, the Pinyin Romanization is given in brackets on the first mention.

Most texts included have been translated into English expressly for this collection. In such cases, the name of the translator (contributor) appears at the heading of the source. Some texts, however, were originally written and published in English. Such texts are reproduced faithfully with only obvious typographical errors being corrected. Any additions by the editors or contributors are placed in square brackets.

In order to ensure coherence and the uniformity of this work, the editors felt it necessary to make some editorial changes to the commentaries and translation. Generally, we gave priority to the readability over literalness and close philological adherence to the original. The editors assume the responsibility for any errors that may have resulted from this editorial policy.

Introduction

The Emergence of Pan-Asianism as an Ideal of Asian Identity and Solidarity, 1850–2008

Sven Saaler and Christopher W. A. Szpilman

> Asia is one. The Himalayas divide, only to accentuate, two mighty civilizations, the Chinese with its communism of Confucius, and the Indian with its individualism of the Vedas. But not even the snowy barriers can interrupt for one moment that broad expanse of love for the Ultimate and Universal, which is the common thought-inheritance of every Asiatic race, enabling them to produce all the great religions of the world. . . . (Okakura 1920: 1)

> Asia is not one. This is the reality, which the grave experience of the Sino-Japanese War [from 1937] has taught us. (Ozaki Hotsumi 1939, quoted in Yonetani 2006: 166)

The economic and political power of Asia, the world's largest continent, is increasing rapidly. According to the latest projections, the gross domestic products of China and India, the world's most populous nations, will each surpass that of the United States in the not-too-distant future. China's economy, like Japan's, is already larger than that of any single European country. With this new economic might comes diplomatic influence. On the world scene Asian countries pull more weight now than ever before. The twenty-first century, many pundits agree, will be an Asian century. This undisputed Asian success story, together with its accompanying tensions and discontents, has attracted much media and scholarly attention. Yet for all this talk of Asia, there is no consensus on what Asia actually stands for as a whole. Is the vast Asian landmass a single entity? As the previous quotations show, there has never been—and perhaps never will be—universal agreement on this question.

Attempts to define Asia are almost as old as the term itself. The word "Asia" originated in ancient Greece in the fifth century BC. It originally denoted the lands of the Persian Empire extending east of the Bosphorus Straits but subsequently developed into a general term used by Europeans to describe all the lands lying to the east of Europe. (The point where Europe ended and Asia began was, however, never clearly defined.) Often, this usage connoted a threat, real or perceived, by Asia to Europe—a region smaller in area, much less populous, poorer, and far less significant than Asia in terms of global history (see Arrighi, Hamashita, and Selden 2003: introduction).

The term "Asia" arrived in East Asia relatively late, being introduced by Jesuit missionaries in the sixteenth century. The term is found, written in Chinese characters (亜細亜), on Chinese maps of the world made around 1600 under the supervision of Matteo Ricci (1552–1610),[1] one of the founders of the Jesuit mission in China. However, it took two more centuries before the name gained wide currency in the region. For it was only with the resumption of European colonialist expansion in the nineteenth century that "Asia" ceased to be a technical term used by East Asian cartographers and, in reaction to the threat of Western colonialism, came to represent a specific geopolitical space bound together by such commonalities as a shared history, close cultural links, a long record of diplomatic relations, trade exchanges, and the notion of a "common destiny." Although the definitions of Asia were diverse and often contradictory, the real or perceived Western threat caused an increasing number of intellectuals, politicians, and activists throughout Asia to argue for a strengthening of "Asian" solidarity in relation to "the West."

These arguments about the definition and nature of Asia in reaction to the impending Western threat marked the beginnings of Pan-Asianism[2] as an ideology and a movement. Vague sentiments about strengthening Asian solidarity were gradually developed into concrete policy proposals for a united defense of Asia against the encroachments of Western imperialism. In many cases, such calls for Asian solidarity, integration, and unity were accompanied by endeavors to create an Asian identity by postulating commonalities and identifying traditions of interaction and interrelationship. Some thinkers took for granted the existence of an Asian identity. Others argued that such an identity must be deliberately forged as a necessary condition for realizing the ultimate objective of unifying Asia. Although individual writers in different places and at different times advocated a wide variety of strategies and views on the nature of Asian unity, we can nonetheless observe a certain degree of uniformity in the development of pan-Asian rhetoric from the nineteenth century down to the present—a pattern discussed further at the end of the introduction.

In this way, then, a pan-Asian worldview or "style of thought"[3] became established and diffused throughout the region. It can be identified in the writings of intellectuals, political statements, popular slogans, and even in songs and poems in a number of Asian states and nations. A representative selection of such texts, all of which are of great significance in the history of Pan-Asianism and Asian regionalism, is included in this collection. They were written or collected in various parts of Asia, from Japan, through Korea, China, Indonesia, and India to the Ottoman Empire, over the past 150 years. These texts, most of which have been translated into English from a number of Asian languages, are brought to the Western reader for the first time in an easily accessible form. Each source is accompanied by a commentary that provides essential information, such as a biographical sketch of the author and the historical context of the document under consideration.

A number of collections of pan-Asian texts have been published in Japanese.[4] The most important of these is Takeuchi Yoshimi's (1910–1977) volume *Asianism* (Takeuchi 1963a), which, in addition to providing a selection of sources, examines the significance of Pan-Asianism and attempts to place it in its historical context. Much less useful is the recently published three-volume anthology, *Ajiashugishatachi no Koe* (Pan-Asianist Voices; Tōyama et al. 2008; Miyazaki et al. 2008; Kita Ikki et al. 2008), which merely reproduces snippets of texts seemingly at random without any critical contextualization. Pan-Asianism, however, receives scant attention in widely available English-language source collections on Asia such as the volumes in the Introduction to Asian Civilizations series—*Sources of Japanese Tradition* (Tsunoda et al. 1958), *Sources of Chinese Tradition* (de Bary et al. 1960), *Sources of Korean Tradition* (Lee et al. 2000), and *Sources of Indian Tradition* (de Bary 1964).

The end of the Cold War in 1989 produced a surge of interest in issues of regionalism and transnational identity in contemporary East Asia (Katzenstein and Shiraishi 1997; Morishima 2000; Kang 2001; Wada 2003; Rozman 2004; Shindō and Hirakawa 2006; Hamanaka 2009). This new interest in contemporary regionalism was followed only a decade later by the recognition of the long-term historical developments underlying the geopolitical formation of the East Asian region and the idea of Asian solidarity (i.e., the ideology of Pan-Asianism) as important research subjects. Few works on Pan-Asianism were published before 2000 in any language (notable exceptions are Jansen 1954, Takeuchi 1963a, Hay 1970, Matsuzawa 1979, Hatsuse 1980, Hatano 1996, and the seven-volume series *Asian Perspectives* [Mizoguchi 1993–1994]). But since the beginning of the twenty-first century there has been an upsurge of interest in the historical development of Pan-Asianism, reflected in a stream of book-length publications on various aspects of Pan-Asianism (in English they include Saaler and Koschmann 2007, Hotta 2007, Aydin 2007b, Hamashita 2008, Tankha 2009, and Zachmann 2009; in Japanese, Yamamuro 2001, Miyadai 2004, Nakajima 2005, Inoue 2006,

Yonetani 2006, Matsuura 2007b, Li Cai-hua and Suzuki 2007, and Matsuura 2010; and, in Chinese, Wang 2004). In addition, a number of important articles have been published on the subject over the years.[5] Notwithstanding these publications, however, our knowledge of Pan-Asianism and its role in modern Asia remains fragmented, unsystematic, and unbalanced.[6]

This collection aims to remedy the situation by providing readers, first of all, with the seminal documents of Pan-Asianism and thus a comprehensive overview of the development of the ideals of Asian solidarity and regionalism in the hope of stimulating further research and providing the foundations for a synthesis of earlier work. The major difficulty with researching Pan-Asianism is a linguistic one, for it would be very difficult, if not impossible, for any one scholar to master all the languages necessary for a comprehensive study of the subject. So, while the community of scholars interested in issues of Asian regionalism continues to grow, linguistic difficulties and the barriers of specialization have prevented them from studying Pan-Asianism as an ideology that transcends linguistic boundaries and national narratives and examining the processes of regional integration in East Asia from the perspective of the *longue dureé*. We hope that this collection, with its comprehensive approach, will help scholars to look beyond the scope of their narrow specializations and open new possibilities for transnational cooperation in research on Asian regionalism.

The sources collected are arranged in chronological order, with some exceptions allowed for the presentation of a coherent sequence of texts. The book allows the reader to trace the development of Pan-Asianism and Asian regionalism from the mid-nineteenth century down to the present day and provides an insider's view of intra-Asian debates. The material discussed in each chapter falls roughly into three often overlapping and never mutually exclusive categories: 1) attempts to define Asia and assess the region's contribution to world civilization; 2) calls for Asian solidarity, integration, and unity; and 3) debates about Asia's role in world politics and, above all, about Asia's relations with Europe.

THE ORIGINS OF PAN-ASIANISM: MACRONATIONALISM AND TRANSNATIONALISM

The term "Asia" came into common use in East Asia only in the mid-nineteenth century in response to the increasing diplomatic, military, and economic presence of the Western powers, and their territorial expansion in East Asia. The Opium War of 1839–1842 was a watershed in the history of Asian–European encounters. The British victory led to the recognition, throughout East Asia, of Europe as a common threat, and it was at that time that intellectuals and politicians throughout the region began to consider the questions of "Asia" and Asian solidarity. With a view to giving the concept of solidarity some substance, they began exploring Asian cultural commonalities and the common historical heritage of the continent. It is of course true that, as Hamashita Takeshi (2008) and other scholars have pointed out, East Asian countries had a long history of interaction before the nineteenth century. This took the form of an interstate system, centered on China. It was this Sinocentric system (sometimes also known as the tributary system) to which the Western powers had to accommodate themselves when they first came into contact with East Asian states (see Fairbank et al. 1989: 195–96 and passim). But it was the acute sense of crisis brought about by the Chinese defeat in the Opium War that finally forced Asian writers and thinkers actively to pursue the agenda of a united Asia, an Asia with a common goal—the struggle against Western imperialism.

Ideas of Asian solidarity came in a large variety of forms, as did the geographical definitions underlying claims for regional solidarity (Arano 2007). Some forms of the concept were based on assumptions of racial unity, following, curiously enough, racial notions that had originated in the West (Hannaford 1996; Dikötter 1997). Others tended to emphasize commonalities in culture and language (more accurately written language). This was especially the case in East Asia, often referred to in the West as the "Orient" (Japanese: *Tōyō*; Korean: *Tong'yang*; Chinese: *Dongyang*), a region which for thousands of years had been under the powerful influence of Chinese civilization. (The term "East Asia" was used from the late nineteenth century on [Japanese: *Tōa*; Korean: *Dong-a*; Chinese: *Dong-ya*].) In this context, some thinkers saw the new quest for solidarity as a strengthening of the existing networks of economic and cultural exchange. Others were inspired by pan-movements emerging almost simultaneously in Europe and America. The various approaches to Pan-Asianism, however, all shared a common emphasis on transnationalism and Asian unity.

As some contributions in this collection show, Pan-Asianism was at times used to legitimize Japan's territorial aggrandizement and colonial expansion (see the next section for a discussion of this issue). One of the few detailed studies of pan-movements in general, Snyder's (1984) *Macro-Nationalisms*, characterizes pan-movements as "Nationalism Writ Large" or "extended nationalisms." However, as the present volume shows, advocacy of Pan-Asianism also reflected reservations about the concepts of nation and nationalism, which were also imported in their modern forms to Asia from the West in the nineteenth century. The popularity of a transnational Pan-Asianism and the transnational political activities of revolutionaries (see I:3, I:5, I:10, I:11, and so on) show that the nation was not, as is often believed, an absolute and unquestioned value in Asia. (The rise of pan-movements in other parts of the world, too, has been seen as an expression of skepticism over the absolute character of the "nation;" cf. Duara 1998.) To be sure, in a number of Asian countries protonationalism had already developed before the arrival of the European powers in the region (Mitani 1997; Hamashita 2008). Within the Sinocentric international order, the elites of tributary states in East Asia had developed their own sense of nationhood. However, in the nineteenth century new forms of nationalism developed in East Asia. In the same way as Pan-Asianism, they represented a reaction to Western colonialism and over time developed into national independence movements. Yet again, these nationalist aspirations and the independence movements they spawned were characterized by strong *trans*national links, alliances that were apparent in the activities of Asian revolutionaries described in this volume: Indians, Vietnamese, Indonesians, Filipinos, and activists from other Asian countries who went into exile in Japan, where they exchanged ideas, promoted pan-Asian solidarity, developed networks, and worked together to achieve national independence. Benedict Anderson has brilliantly traced the process by which the elites of colonized nations developed a sense of national identity and a desire for independence from their colonial masters during periods of residence in the metropole (Anderson 1983). It could be argued that a similar process was at work in the case of the revolutionary members of the Asian elites. When they found themselves in Japan, whether as students or exiles, they interacted with other Asians and in this way developed a common Asian consciousness.

In Japan they came also into contact with Japanese Pan-Asianists, many of whom supported independence movements throughout Asia (see I:11 for an example). The Japanese triumph in the war with Russia in 1904–1905 was an important turning point (Aydin 2007a), an event that accelerated the spread of pan-Asian ideas throughout the continent. Many Asians now believed that Japan would soon assume leadership in the struggle against the tyranny of the Western imperialist powers. Even in distant Egypt, a delighted Arab announced the news of the Russian defeat to the Chinese revolutionary leader Sun Yat-sen (Zhongshan; Japanese: Son Bun, 1866–1925), who was traveling by boat through the Suez Canal. "The joy of this Arab, as a member of the great Asiatic race," Sun recalled many years later, "seemed to know no bounds" (Jansen 1954: 117). However, as we describe here, disillusionment with Japan soon set in when it embarked on a program of carving out its own colonial empire at the expense of other Asian nations and justified these expansionist policies with pan-Asian rhetoric.

Pan-Asian cooperation was institutionalized in the form of numerous pan-Asian associations founded all over Asia and was also reflected in pan-Asian conferences that took place in Japan, China, and Afghanistan in the 1920s and 1930s (see II:8). These developments showed the diversity and interconnectedness of anti-Western movements throughout Asia. A few examples will suffice to illustrate this phenomenon. In 1907, socialists and anarchists from China, Japan, and India joined forces to found the Asiatic Humanitarian Brotherhood in Tokyo (I:16). In 1909 Japanese and Muslim pan-Asianists in Japan established the Ajia Gikai (Asian Congress; cf. Worringer 2006, which also includes a translation of the association's foundation manifesto) with the goal of promoting the cause of Asian solidarity and liberation. It was almost certainly this Ajia Gikai that a British intelligence report referred to when it mentioned "an Oriental Association in Tokyo attended by Japanese, Filipinos, Siamese, Indians, Koreans, and Chinese, where Count Okuma [Shigenobu, 1838–1922] once delivered an anti-American lecture" (Eliot to Curzon, 30 April 1921, 77B Foreign Office Documents pertaining to Japan, FO 371/6678, Public Record Office, Kew, Richmond). In 1921, the Pan-Turanian Association was founded in Tokyo to rally Japanese support for the unification of the Turks of Central Asia and their liberation from Russian rule. The association cooperated closely with the Greater Asia Association (Dai Ajia Kyōkai) and other Japanese pan-Asian organizations (cf. Dai Ajia Kyōkai/Dai Tsuran Kyōkai 1922).

The transnational character of Pan-Asianism was also apparent in its publishing activities. Indian pan-Asianists published material in Japan (Bose 1922; Das 1917a, 1944; see also I:24), China (Das 1917b), the United States (Das 1936), and Germany (e.g., Raja Mahendra Pratap in the *Zeitschrift für Geopolitik* [Journal of Geopolitics]; also Sarkar 1922); Japanese pan-Asianists published in China (Kodera Kenkichi; see I:26), India (Okakura Tenshin; see I:7 and I:8), and the United States (Kawakami 1919, 1921; Rōyama 1941). Koreans, too, such as the court noble An Kyongsu (1853–1900), published their works in Japan (An 1900). Journals with a clear pan-Asian message—the source of many of the documents in this collection—were published in Japan, China, and Southeast Asia (discussed here).

Although such writings might be dismissed as mere "propaganda" (on prewar Japanese propaganda activities, see O'Connor 2004–2005; Kushner 2006), there is no doubt that a significant number of Westerners were sympathetic to the ideals of Asian solidarity and Pan-Asianism. At the center of pan-Asian activities in Japan at the end of World War I stood the now obscure French mystic, Paul Richard (1874–1967; see I:29), whose works were published in Japan, India, and the United States and certainly widely read, at least in Japan. In the 1920s and 1930s, the famous editor of the *Zeitschrift für Geopolitik*, Karl Haushofer (1869–1946), paid tribute to the pan-Asian movement in his publications (e.g., Haushofer 1931), seeing it as proof of his theory that international relations would come to be dominated by regional blocs. Haushofer (1931: 14f) introduced to his readers the writings and activities of pan-Asianists such as Sun Yat-sen (see II:5), Rabindranath Tagore (1861–1941), and Benoy Kumar Sarkar (1887–1949; see I:21). The writings of these Asian activists and revolutionaries, Haushofer was convinced, reflected a trend toward a future world order that would be dominated by large, regional blocs, replacing the existing order characterized by the sovereign nation-state. Another proponent of pan-ideas, Richard Nikolaus Count von Coudenhove-Kalergi (1894–1972), the founder of the pan-European movement and the publisher of the journal *Pan-Europa*, also praised the pan-Asian movement; a Japanese translation of an enthusiastic article by him appeared in the journal *Dai Ajiashugi* (Greater Asianism; see II:13) (Coudenhove-Kalergi 1931, 1932).

As a final striking example of the appeal of Pan-Asianism to Westerners, in 1934 an anonymous Greek wrote a letter addressed "to the Eastern Asiatic people of the Mongolian race and colour," which he sent to the Japanese consulate at Surabaya in the Dutch East Indies (present-day Indonesia).[7] The letter called on Asians to

> cultivate the Pan-Mongolian consciousness, in feeling, in thought and above all in action; harmonize, cultivate and facilitate in every possible way the Inter-Mongolian race intercourse and understanding by adopting an official and compulsory taught and used Inter-Mongolian language composed of Words of Chinese, Japanese and Siamese languages; Eliminate from your mind and from your dictionaries the word FOREIGNER, and cultivate the Inter-Mongolian fellowship and community of interest; Harmonize your national, political, social, economic and religious life. . . . [F]orm and organize THE INTER-MONGOLIAN AND INTER-CONTINENTAL HARMONIZED AWAKENING, in every city, town, village and hamlet.

This bizarre letter was apparently inspired by the Japanese Foreign Ministry's so-called Amau Statement, which declared "special responsibilities for Japan in East Asia" and which was often interpreted as a declaration by Japan of an "Asian Monroe Doctrine,"[8] that is, a call for noninterference by Western powers in China (cf., e.g., Wang 1934). As far as one can tell, this eccentric appeal to an inter-Asian consciousness elicited no reaction either in Japan or elsewhere in Asia. Nevertheless, Pan-Asianism was stimulated, both positively and negatively, by Western influences. For example, the Japanese politician Kodera Kenkichi (1877–1949; see I:26), who had studied international relations in Europe and the United States for almost a decade, justified his advocacy of Pan-Asianism by constantly referring to the positive role of pan-movements in the West. In contrast to Kodera, Prince Konoe Fumimaro (1891–1945; see I:32) chose to stress the negative aspects of the West by rejecting the universalist pretensions of the League of Nations (founded 1919) when he proclaimed the need for Asian solidarity under Japanese leadership. Both Kanokogi Kazunobu (1884–1949; II:14) and Hirano Yoshitarō (1897–1980; see II:30) were strongly influenced by German ideas, as were the 1930s proponents of a regional bloc in East Asia such as the political scientist Professor Rōyama Masamichi (1895–1980; see II:18) and Kada Tetsuji (1895–1964; Kada 1939: 577ff).

While the West was important as a reference point, Pan-Asianism as an ideology also posed a significant challenge to the traditional Sinocentric order discussed previously—an order not limited to China proper but also appropriated by the nomadic conquerors of China and by states on the periphery such as Korea and Japan. In this context, the seemingly "more modern" ideology of Pan-Asianism served as an integrating force, helping to fulfill the requirement for the "de-centering of China" (Schmid 2002).

Arguably, in many cases the Sinocentric hierarchical view of the world influenced the thinking of some Japanese pan-Asianists who appropriated it faithfully with one significant change. For them it was Japan, not China, that was to be the new "Middle Kingdom" and the leader of Asia (Miwa 1973: 389–90). Although, as we show here, early forms of Pan-Asianism often envisioned cooperation on equal terms, insistence on Japanese leadership (*meishu*) in Asia increased in proportion to the growth and expansion of Japan's power in East Asia (on this "Meishuron" version of Pan-Asianism, see Hotta 2007: 44–49).

For advocates of this "Meishuron" Asianism, Japan's leadership was justified on moral grounds as well as by the realities of international relations. Japan qualified as the leader of Asia because it was morally superior to China, which was in political turmoil, and had always been as a result of its frequent dynastic changes. In contrast, Japan, many believed, was qualified to lead Asia because of its divine imperial dynasty that was "unbroken through ages immemorial." Japan, in this view, was a "chosen" country, the "Land of the Gods"—qualities that uniquely fitted it for a special "mission" to liberate Asia from Western oppression, become the leader of the region, and, as its more imaginative supporters asserted, unite the whole world under the benevolent rule of the Japanese emperor, following the ancient slogan *hakkō ichiu*, or "The Eight Corners of the World [United] under One Roof." Rather than drawing on the foundational myths, other pan-Asian writers justified Japan's leadership of Asia on the grounds of Japan's successful modernization program, an effort they contrasted with the failure of the rest of Asia in this regard. From this perspective, Japan's technological advances served as evidence of Japanese superiority. But whatever the grounds for such claims, the fact remains that many Japanese pan-Asianists, in various ways, consciously or unconsciously, provided justification for Japan's colonial rule and territorial expansion in Asia.

PAN-ASIANISM AND EMPIRE

One of the reasons why, for a long time after 1945, Pan-Asianism was largely ignored by researchers—not to mention politicians and diplomats—was its fateful connection to Japanese imperialism and the role it played as an ideology that legitimized Japan's empire-building project in the first half of the twentieth century. While some commentators insist that Japan never officially pursued a pan-Asian foreign policy (Aoki Kazuo, quoted in Yamamuro 2001: 573; see also I:12) before or even during the Asia-Pacific War (1931–1945), it is undeniable that the Japanese government frequently utilized pan-Asian rhetoric in the 1930s and 1940s in order to bolster claims to Japanese leadership in East Asia and legitimize its colonial rule over parts of Asia.

In *The Origins of Totalitarianism*, Hannah Arendt suggested a close link between nineteenth-century Pan-Germanism and Pan-Slavism and twentieth-century totalitarianism and expansionism. "Nazism and Bolshevism," she contended, "owe more to Pan-Germanism and Pan-Slavism (respectively) than to any other ideology or political movement. This is most evident in foreign policies, where the strategies of Nazi Germany and Soviet Russia have followed so closely the well-known programs of conquest outlined by the pan-movements before and during the First World War . . ." (Arendt 1985: 222). Although it would be an exaggeration to claim that Pan-Asianism formed an important component of any totalitarian developments in modern Asia, one cannot overlook the connection between Pan-Asianism and Japanese ultranationalism (which will be discussed in more detail here) and also the contribution of this ideology to the legitimization of Japanese colonial rule and Japanese empire building in Asia in the first half of the twentieth century (Oguma 1998: 225–30; 272; 321–44; 644–54).[9]

As early as 1910, pan-Asian rhetoric was used by the Japanese government to legitimize the annexation of Korea. The Annexation Treaty referred specifically to commonalities between Japanese and Koreans, such as racial origins, a common history and culture, and a shared destiny. This remained the orthodox way of justifying and legitimizing Japanese rule in Korea throughout the colonial period and was reiterated time and again in both public and private statements[10] (see I:4; Oguma 1995; I:5; Oguma 1998: 163–66). The same pan-Asian rhetoric was continuously reaffirmed and also applied to other colonial territories. For example, in 1939, in the semi-official journal *Contemporary Japan*, a writer insisted that

> contrary to the general assumption held abroad, and even entertained by some Japanese, Chosen [Korea], Taiwan, and even Manchukuo are not Japanese colonies according to the Western way of thinking. . . . "To make the world one household" is an expression used by the Japanese to indicate their moral principle of co-existence and co-prosperity. . . . Although their languages and customs are now different, Japan and Korea were especially close to each other until about thirteen centuries ago, there having been a large intermixture of both blood and culture before that time. . . . Japan's annexation of the peninsula might be taken as a reversion of the two countries to their ancient status of being one homogeneous whole. (Matsuzawa 1939: 455, 462f)

The assertion of racial and cultural commonalities presented here went hand in hand with the legitimization of Japanese superiority on the grounds that Japan was a country chosen by the gods (see the previous discussion). As early as the late 1910s, a number of writers, such as Kanokogi Kazunobu (II:14), Kita Ikki (I:27), and Ōkawa Shūmei (II:4), spoke of a divine Japanese "mission" to liberate Asia. This high-sounding objective was often difficult to distinguish from the substitution of one form of colonial oppression (by Europeans) for another (by fellow Asian Japanese). And a belief in Japan's divine mission was by no means limited to radical reformists. Even mainstream writers who eschewed ideologically driven rhetoric and sought to explain international relations in terms of Realpolitik, such as Tokutomi Iichirō (better known as Sohō, 1863–1957; see I:28), urged Japan to establish an "Asian Monroe Doctrine." In doing so, Tokutomi may have been applying an idea of Western provenance to international relations in East Asia, but he still believed, just like Kita and Kanokogi, that Japan had a special "mission" to accomplish in East Asia (Tokutomi 1917).

In the 1930s, claims that Japan's empire was an embodiment of pan-Asian ideals were voiced more frequently and much more openly than before. This was due to the impact of "regional bloc thinking" that was highly influential at the time. For example, the previously mentioned Rōyama Masamichi insisted in 1934 that "the Pan-Asiatic movement" was a "decisive influence responsible for the establishment of the Empire." Though he lamented that this movement lacked "any coherent programme under any prominent leader," he nevertheless regarded it as full of promise for the future. As evidence, he noted with satisfaction that "many small groups of so-called Pan-Asianists loosely affiliated through study organizations . . . have sprung up like mushrooms during the past two years in both Japan and Manchuria" (Rōyama 1934: 29f). Rōyama's notion of an "East Asian bloc," as introduced in II:18, gained wide prominence in Japan in the late 1930s, amplified by a fusion with the geopolitical ideas of Karl Haushofer and Carl Schmidt (1888–1985) and with earlier concepts of an "Asian Monroe Doctrine" (see

I:28 and Miwa 1990: 146–49). The notion of an "East Asian bloc" was also popular with Marxists and socialists, as can be seen in the writings of Takahashi Kamekichi (1894–1977; cf. Hoston 1984) and of some members of the Shōwa Kenkyūkai, the brain trust founded by Prince Konoe Fumimaro, prime minister in 1937–1939 and 1940–1941 (see II:20).

The intimate connection of Pan-Asianism with Japan's empire-building ambitions leads us to another central problem of Pan-Asianism—the inherent ambiguity of the concepts involved.[11] It is clear that, from the outset, pan-Asian thought was riddled with ambiguity and contradictions that made this ideology capable of being used to legitimize both the anticolonial struggle against the West and the domination of one Asian nation by another. This ambiguity is also inherent in the terminology used to describe the ideology, a question to which we shall turn next.

PROBLEMS OF TERMINOLOGY

As stated at the start of this introduction, Pan-Asianism poses a problem as a topic of scholarly inquiry even at the level of terminology. The object of inquiry is hard to define and is almost as elusive as a continuously shifting target. There is no scholarly consensus on the definition of "Asia," on pan-movements, or on ideologies with a transnational focus that have evolved over time. Likewise, the question of how Pan-Asianism is related to other pan-movements is far from settled.

As we have seen, the emergence of Pan-Asianism was inseparable from the rise of Japan as a major power and Japan's struggle with China for leadership in Asia. But Pan-Asianism also reflected attempts by East Asian elites to forge Asian unity by bringing Japan and China together. Thus, early manifestations of the movement were characterized by the close cooperation of ideologues, activists, and politicians from Japan, China, and Korea. But the need for cooperation and, thus, compromise resulted in pan-Asian ideas being characterized by a marked lack of specific content. The diffusion of the term over time is a case in point. Although this collection treats the subject from the mid-nineteenth century on, the term "Pan-Asianism" (or Asianism, Greater Asianism) was not in use in China, Korea, and Japan before the 1890s and occurs only infrequently prior to the 1910s.

Around the turn of the century, Western writers who were clamoring about the threat of the Yellow Peril (on the Yellow Peril, see Thompson 1978) occasionally used the terms "Pan-Asianism" or "pan-Asiatic league" in warning of the dangers a united Asia would pose for Western supremacy (for an early example, see Brandt 1903).[12] The Japanese government was quick to lay any Western suspicions on this score to rest, particularly after the start of the war with Russia, a Western power, in 1904 (cf. Matsumura 1987). It took this popular Western agitation so seriously that on many occasions it officially disclaimed any interest in promoting closer relations with its (weak) Asian neighbors (see, e.g., "No 'Yellow Peril.' Minister Kurino Denies That Japan Wants to Organize the Asiatics," *New York Times*, 18 February 1904). Japanese diplomats were dispatched to Europe and the United States expressly to dispel any Western suspicions as to Japan's pan-Asian ambitions. For example, in the United States, Harvard-educated Baron Kaneko Kentarō (1853–1942) dismissed rumors voiced in the "yellow" press that Japan was aiming to form an Asian federation, as did diplomat Suematsu Kenchō (1855–1920) in Europe (see I:12; for Suematsu's remarks, see *New York Times*, 21 February 1904 for Kaneko). As late as 1919, Takekoshi Yosaburō (1865–1950) ridiculed the idea of a Japanese-led Asian alliance against the West in a publication funded by the Japanese government:

> Among our own people, there are some who do not rightly interpret the history of their own country, and who do not take their national strength into proper consideration and who, being prompted by certain fanatical ideas, advocate the alliance of the yellow races against the white, an alliance of which Japan should be the leader, and with that object in view, they favour the partition of China. Those who argue in this strain have evidently lost their mental balance. (Takegoshi [*sic*] 1919: 83)

Just as the government went to great lengths to deny any association with Pan-Asianism, the opposition placed a strong emphasis on Pan-Asianism, calling for the unification of the "yellow race," that is, the Asian peoples. As early as 1874, Ueki Emori (1857–1892), a prominent member of the opposition freedom and People's Rights Movement (*jiyū minken undō*), had attacked what he considered the pro-Western policy of the government and, insisting that the West was Japan's enemy, called for the formation of an Asian League (*Ajia rengō*) (cf. Kuroki 2002: 19). Ueki held a version of Pan-Asianism that assumed equality among Asian nations. He even advocated independence for the Ryukyu archipelago (present-day Okinawa Prefecture), a previously independent kingdom that was annexed by Japan in the 1870s (Kuroki 2002: 24).[13] An anonymous writer in the journal *Ajia* (Asia) (see I:1) and the antigovernment activist and politician Tarui Tōkichi (1850–1922; see I:5) again made similar proposals in the 1880s. It was not until 1903 that the first acknowledgment of the potential of Pan-Asianism as a significant factor in international relations was made, when the art critic Okakura Tenshin (1862–1913), famous for coining the phrase "Asia is one," stated in his book *The Awakening of the East* that a "Pan-Asiatic Alliance" would "in itself constitute an immense force" (I:7). However, the impact of this statement may have been somewhat reduced in Japan by the fact that Okakura had written his book in English for an Indian and not a Japanese audience.

While the term "Pan-Asianism" entered the mainstream political vocabulary only in the 1910s, in the nineteenth century advocates of Asian unity could draw on a number of terms and slogans when propagating their ideals. In the 1880s, the term *Kōa*, or "Raising (or Developing) Asia," was the most widely used slogan, implying the need for Asia to modernize in order to catch up with the technologically advanced West. The term was not without its problems, however. For example, an organization called the Kōakai (Raising Asia Society) was founded in Tokyo in 1880 (see I:2 and Kuroki 2007). Its membership was predominantly Japanese—they had chosen the group's name—but it included some Koreans and Chinese who objected to the name on the grounds that it implied—in contrast to successful, modern Japan—that Asia was backward, oppressed, and downtrodden and could be saved only by "raising" it through Japanese leadership and advice. Following such criticism, the Kōakai was renamed Ajia Kyōkai (Asia Association) in 1883. But it was not only Japanese pan-Asianists who believed in Japanese superiority; many Asians also acknowledged their political and economic backwardness in relation to Japan. Many Chinese recognized the failure of modernization, at least implicitly, in their nation, accounting for the formation of political associations with names such as the Raise China Society (Xingzhonghui), founded by Sun Yat-sen in 1894, and the China Revival Society (Huaxinghui), founded in Hunan in 1904.

Another early term used to describe pan-Asian solidarity was the classical Chinese phrase *hosha shinshi* (Chinese: *fuche chunchi*; Korean: *poch'a sonch'i*), which means "mutual dependence" or, literally, "a relationship as close as that between the lips and the teeth or between the chassis and the wheels of a cart." This image implied a high degree of interdependence (Hashikawa 1980), but, in contrast to the potentially hierarchical Kōa, it presumed equal relations among Asian nations. Its origin also indicates the influence of Chinese classical scholarship on early Pan-Asianism. This phrase was used by early pan-Asianists particularly in the 1870s and 1880s, but it can be found in many of the texts presented in this collection well into the twentieth century.

A third influential slogan used to express pan-Asian sentiment and activism that was very popular at the turn of the century was "Same Culture, Same Race" (Japanese: *dōbun dōshu*; Chinese: *tongwen tongzhong*; Korean: *tongmun tongjong*), which likewise did not imply hierarchical relations between Asian nations or make claim to the superiority of any one country. In Japan, the term was used particularly often by Prince Konoe Atsumaro (1863–1904), who, uncharacteristically for an early pan-Asianist, was a member of Japan's ruling elite (I:6), and by the Tōa Dōbunkai (East Asian Common Culture Society; see I:9). The term also appears frequently in Japanese journals of the day and seems to have received some acceptance in other Asian countries. Closely related to the rise of racial thinking in Japan and East Asia, this slogan also has to be seen as an expression of the growing fear in Japan of a future "clash of races," that is, a war fought along racial lines in which Japan would have no choice but to side with the Asian, or "colored," peoples against the white powers of the West (cf. Saaler 2008a). Parallel with the development of this kind of racial thinking in Asia, the idea of the "White Peril" also gained ground (see Nagai 1913; Duus 1971; I:14). It was an inversion of the "Yellow Peril" hysteria that affected Europe at the time. The proponents of the "White Peril," including some Europeans (e.g., Gulick 1905), believed that the threat to civilization came not from the "yellow" peoples of Asia but from the predatory European powers (cf. Mori 1904; Kodera 1916).

It was only in the 1910s that the term "Pan-Asianism" made its debut in intellectual discourse. Japanese political scientist Ōyama Ikuo (1880–1955) used the term for the first time to describe Chinese political associations which were promoting "Greater Asianism" (*Da Yazhouzhuyi*) "in secretly published pamphlets" with the intention of spreading anti-Western sentiment in China.[14] Ōyama himself rejected Asianism because he saw the emergence of this ideology as a sign of increasing nationalistic and xenophobic tendencies in Japan (Ōyama 1916). While Ōyama criticized Asianism from his position as a liberal intellectual,[15] the Japanese government remained wary of pan-Asian proposals because it feared that such tendencies might undermine Japan's good relations with the Western powers. Between its signing in 1902 and 1921–1922, when it was superseded by the Washington treaty system, the Anglo-Japanese Alliance was always at the heart of Japan's foreign policy. The alliance, however, would be in jeopardy if it transpired that Japan was supporting an independence movement in India as part of a pan-Asian foreign policy. On several occasions, Britain showed suspicion over Indian–Japanese relations, particularly during World War I when members of the Indian independence movement were cooperating with Germany (see II:9). For example, the visit of the celebrated poet and first Asian Nobel laureate, Rabindranath Tagore, to Japan in 1916 caused "considerable uneasiness in London" over "a Japanese–Indian understanding that could eventually take a political and anti-British form" (Hay 1970: 80–81). The British intelligence service kept close tabs on Indian independence activists in Japan (and China) and their Japanese sympathizers.[16]

If only to avoid alienating its British ally and other Western powers, both the Japanese government and the press tended to be highly critical of pan-Asian schemes. The hostile tone adopted by Japanese newspapers during a short public debate on Pan-Asianism in 1913 well illustrates this point. In a debate with the British journalist and diplomat Sir Valentine Chirol (1852–1929), the celebrated American naval strategist Admiral Alfred Thayer Mahan (1840–1914) defended the 1913 California "Alien Land Bill" (cf. Daniels 1977), which would prevent Asian immigrants from owning land or property in the state on the grounds that America would not be able to "digest and assimilate the strong national and racial characteristics which distinguish the Japanese." Mahan seemed moreover to believe that in excluding the Japanese, Californians were acting in the interests not only of the United States but also of "the whole community of European civilization" (*The Times*, 23 June 1913). In the debate Chirol, who had retired from his position at *The Times* two years before and joined the Foreign Office, criticized the Land Bill. However, it appears that he was a voice in the wilderness. Even the editors of the *Times* seemed to support Mahan when they criticized Japan for what they regarded as contradictions in its foreign policy:

> On the one hand, she [Japan] demands recognition because her people are not as other Asiatics. On the other hand, . . . her publicists are now asserting that "to Japan is assigned the leadership in the claim of the 'coloured' races against the 'non-coloured.'" These two sets are mutually destructive. Japan cannot have it both ways. . . . She must make up her mind whether she wishes to present herself as aloof from other Asiatic races, or as the avowed champion of Pan-Asiatic ideals. (*The Times*, 23 June 1913)

Such criticisms clearly struck a sensitive chord in Japan. Throughout June and July 1913, these various statements were discussed at great length by Japan's leading newspapers, including the *Osaka Asahi Shinbun*, the *Osaka Mainichi Shinbun*, and the *Tokyo Nichinichi Shinbun*.[17] The *Asahi* unequivocally declared that it considered "Pan-Asianism an illusion (*kūsō*)," while the *Nichinichi* ridiculed the notion that Japan would "lead the Asian peoples to fight against the Euro-American white powers" as "useless and reckless." It was in these articles dismissing the accusations made by Mahan and the *Times* that the terms Han-Ajiashugi ("Pan-Asianism," *Mainichi* and *Nichinichi*) and Zen-Ajiashugi ("All-Asianism," *Asahi*) made their first appearance in the Japanese language. They were coined specifically to express the English term "Pan-Asianism," which previously had had no exact Japanese equivalent. At this stage, as indicated by the critical, derisory tone of the newspaper articles cited, these neologisms were used in a derogatory sense.

Yet, little by little, the negative connotations of the term "Asianism" were lost in the aftermath of World War I. The bloodbath in Europe made Japan the dominant power in East Asia and brought about an upsurge in Japan's self-confidence. At the same time, it stimulated international attempts to establish a new world order after the war, an order that would guarantee peace—if not permanent peace,[18] then at least peace for the foreseeable future. Within these developments, Japan's newly found self-confidence resulted in an outpouring of pan-Asian writings during the last two years of the war (see I:26). These writings should be seen as a Japanese contribution to the debate on how a new international order could guarantee peace. But Japanese writers were not alone in arguing for the necessity of regional integration. There were also notably some Chinese commentators who, while critical of Japanese Pan-Asianism, nonetheless advocated regional integration on the grounds that only a regional, pan-Asian order would result in the achievement of a permanent peace (see, e.g., I:22). When the idea of a League of Nations surfaced during World War I,[19] pan-Asian writers in Japan reacted by proposing an East Asian League (*Tōa renmei*) that would guarantee peace on a regional basis (e.g., Sugita 1916).[20]

By the war's end, pan-Asianist visions of regional integration had thus come to be accepted, at least by public opinion and some politicians, as a realistic scenario for future international relations in East Asia. Certainly, in contrast to the vague professions of pan-Asian unity that had been the norm up until the beginning of the twentieth century, the ideology of Pan-Asianism had by 1918 become concrete and well defined. It had gained recognition in public discourse and was no longer confined to the political fringes. Terms such as Pan-Asianism (*Han Ajiashugi*), Greater Asianism (*Dai Ajiashugi*), All-Asianism (*Zen Ajiashugi*), and the "Asian Monroe Doctrine" (*Ajia Monrōshugi*), largely absent from public discourse until then, now began to appear frequently in newspapers and journals. This proliferation of neologisms reflected a growth of diverse and sophisticated approaches to the issue of Asian solidarity in all its ramifications. The wide range of these responses can be gleaned from the flood of articles (e.g., Ōyama 1916; Sawayanagi 1917; Uchida 1917; Kita 1917a; Horiuchi 1918; Ukita 1918; Sawayanagi 1919b; Bose 1922) and books (Kodera 1916; Sawayanagi 1919a; Mitsukawa 1921; Ōkawa 1922; Tanaka 1924; Murobuse 1926) on Pan-Asianism that appeared during and after the war. While these works indicated the spread and acceptance of the term "Pan-Asianism" in Japanese discourse, perhaps more important they also defined Asianism in concrete terms and demanded that Japan act in accordance with pan-Asian principles in international relations.

The new popularity of Pan-Asianism in Japanese intellectual discourse and politics received a boost when news of a new immigration law that would bar Japanese from immigration to the United States (part of the 1924 Immigration or Johnson-Reed Act) reached Japan. Protests against the act were held through the length and breadth of Japan, events that in many cases turned into demonstrations of pan-Asian solidarity (see I:26 and Stalker 2006). In this climate of anti-American agitation, a number of new associations sprang up whose names—such as the Federation of East Asian Races (Ajia Minzoku Gikai, founded in 1923) or the Oriental Co-Existence Society (Tōyō Kyōzonkai)—proclaimed their pan-Asian orientation. The invigoration of popular interest in Pan-Asianism as a result of America's exclusionist policies was also attested to by a slew of articles on the subject in the Japanese press. For example, the influential journal *Nihon oyobi Nihonjin* (Japan and the Japanese) brought out a special issue on "Greater Asianism" (Dai Ajiashugi) in October 1924, and the Asian Newspaper Company published a call for the "Foundation of a Greater East Asian Federation" (Miyai 1925).

Not all pan-Asian slogans and catchphrases—like some of the new associations—survived for long. Many enjoyed a brief popularity and then quickly disappeared from public discourse. Some terms, however, resurfaced in later years, often in different contexts. The notion of an "East Asian League," for example, exemplified the entrenchment of the term "East Asia" in Japanese public discourse around the turn of the century. However, after the wave of anti-American protests subsided in 1924, "East Asia" receded from public discourse, only to return to the mainstream discussion in the late 1930s, in somewhat modified form, as the "East Asian Cooperative Community" (*tōa kyōdōtai* or *tōyō kyōdōtai*; see II:18 and II:20). The formation of a "Greater Asian League" (*Dai Ajia rengō*) was also proposed in the founding manifesto of the Dai Ajia Kyōkai (Greater Asia Association) in 1933. This manifesto, drafted a year after Japan had left the League of Nations, insisted that such a league was necessary given the global trend toward the formation of regional blocs (II:13).

"All-Asianism" (*Zen Ajiashugi*), another term for "Asianism" or "Pan-Asianism," was launched by Ōkawa Shūmei in the wake of the 1913 Chirol–Mahan debate in articles he contributed to *Tairiku* (The Continent) (Ōkawa 1916: 32). However, the term did not "catch on" and vanished from public discourse in the early 1920s. In any event, all these terms were used largely interchangeably. Even Ōkawa on occasion used *Han Ajiashugi* in the same context (Ōkawa 1916) as *Zen Ajiashugi*, and he appears to have made no distinction between the two.

The term "Kōa" perhaps enjoyed the most remarkable career of any pan-Asian term. Kōa first appeared in the 1880s (see I:2 and I:4), when it was used as the main slogan to express pan-Asian solidarity. However, as we have seen, it was quickly discarded because it implied Japanese leadership of the pan-Asian movement. But the term was not forgotten completely, as it reappeared in the 1930s at a time when Japan was adopting a form of Pan-Asianism in its foreign policy. By then, Japan had begun to abandon its policy of cooperation with the Anglo-American powers and was openly pursuing a strategy of destroying the political status quo in East Asia. The unity of Asia and, at the same time, the establishment of Japanese hegemony in East Asia had become Japan's ultimate objective. Although no government decrees contained the terms "Asianism" or "Pan-Asianism" even in the 1930s, the Japanese government demonstrated its commitment to the pan-Asian cause in 1938 by creating the Kōa-in, the Agency for the Development of Asia (sometimes also known in English as the East Asia Development Board). The Kōa-in was a cabinet-level agency with the primary task of coordinating political, economic, and cultural activities in regard to China. While it engaged in research on Chinese affairs and published its findings in the *Kōa-in Chōsa Geppō* (Kōa-in Monthly Research Bulletin), some scholars argue that it was also involved in the recruitment and management of forced labor and even in the opium trade in China. Such were the powers of this agency that only formal diplomatic relations with China remained within the jurisdiction of the Ministry of Foreign Affairs. The Kōa-in was integrated into the Ministry of Greater East Asia (Daitōa-shō) in 1942, which from that time on directed Japan's political and diplomatic relations with the members of the newly declared Greater East Asian Co-Prosperity Sphere (see II:24 and II:27).

This official endorsement of what is probably the oldest pan-Asian term caused a veritable boom in the use of Kōa. Newspapers used the term frequently; journals incorporating it in their title—such as *Kōa Kyōiku* (Education to Raise Asia) or simply *Kōa*—were founded, while politicians, diplomats, and intellectuals discussed the new Kōa policy (e.g., Ōtani 1939). These figures included a foreign minister (Matsuoka 1941b), and a prime minister who proclaimed the "Raising of Asia" a "holy task" (Tōjō 1943). Under the circumstances it is no surprise to learn that, in Japanese schools, children were taught from a "Colonial Kōa Textbook" (Hanzawa 1940). Newly founded political organizations and a number of political conferences held in the late 1930s and early 1940s also were characterized as contributing to the policy of "Raising Asia." In 1941, the Dai Nihon Kōa Dōmei (Greater Japanese League for Raising Asia) was founded.[21] Its members and advisers included venerable pan-Asianists such as Tōyama Mitsuru (1855–1944) and Kuzuu Yoshihisa (1874–1958), party politicians well known for their pan-Asian sympathies such as Nagai Ryūtarō (1881–1944; see I:14), as well as a large number of senior military figures, such as Araki Sadao (1877–1966), Yanagawa Heisuke (1879–1945), Koiso Kuniaki (1880–1950), Ōi Shigemoto (1863–1951), Hayashi Senjūrō (1876–1943), Honjō Shigeru (1876–1945), Matsui Iwane (1878–1948), and Abe Nobuyuki (1875–1943). This impressive lineup, which included two former (Hayashi and Abe) and one future prime minister (Koiso), reflected a growing interest in the potential of Pan-Asianism in military circles.

In the atmosphere of social mobilization that thickened as the war escalated, the League became a central organization, incorporating fifty-three associations and institutions of pan-Asian character under its umbrella. These included the Tōa Dōbunkai (I:9), the Dōjinkai (Comrades' Society), the Tōa Renmei Kyōkai (East Asian League Association; II:19 and II:22), the Tōa Kensetsu Kyōkai (Association for Constructing East Asia), the Tōa Kyōkai (East Asia Association), and the Tōyō Kyōkai (Oriental Association), in addition to think tanks engaged in research on East Asia, such as the Dōmei Tōa Kenkyūkai (Alliance East Asia Research Association), the Tōa Chōsakai (East Asia Investigation Association), the Tōa Kenkyūjo (East Asia Research Institute), and the Tōa Chitsujo Kenkyūkai (East Asian Order Research Association).

These wartime efforts to "raise Asia" had also an international dimension. A year before the founding of the League, a "Raising Asia Welfare Congress" (Kōa kōsei taikai) was held in Osaka in October 1940 that was attended by representatives of eleven countries, including Japan's Asian and also its two European allies, Germany and Italy (Tano 2009). Even today, the name of a Japanese insurance company, Nippon Kōa Sonpo, which was originally founded in 1944, reminds us of the former popularity of this pan-Asian term.

Another term pan-Asianists began to use in the late 1920s (see II:5 and II:12) was "Kingly Way" (Chinese: *wangdao*; Japanese: *ōdō*). In the 1930s it was used with increasing frequency as a way of emphasizing the region's legacy of Confucian values and the significance of Confucianism as a potential basis for the unification of Asians.[22] The "Kingly Way" implied benevolent rule and was used as a fundamental concept to help legitimize Japan's construction of the new state of Manchukuo after 1932 (cf. Duara 2003). Japanese "guidance" of this new, ostensibly independent state—in reality it was a puppet state—was seen in paternalistic, Confucian terms as the kindly direction and advice offered to a younger brother (Manchuria) by his elder brother (Japan) (see II:16). In fact, as is well known, under Japan's "benevolent" guidance Manchukuo became a cornerstone of the Japanese Empire. It was ruthlessly exploited to provide material for the Japanese war effort (see, e.g., Yamamuro 1993, who describes Manchukuo as a "concentration camp state"), and this economic exploitation, carried out under the cloak of paternalistic benevolence, contributed significantly to the discrediting of pan-Asian ideology—the subject to which we turn next.

PAN-ASIANISM AND THE ASIANS

As we have argued here, Pan-Asianism was particularly important in the framework of intellectual debate and policy formulation in Japan, but other

Asians also made an important contribution to the discussion—comment that was sometimes supportive, sometimes critical. While in China the term apparently made its debut in the 1910s, in Korea similar terms were used to express similar sets of ideas a decade or so earlier. At the turn of the century, the term "Easternism" (*Tong'yangjuyi*) was first found in Korean writings on the subject to describe the idea of close cooperation between Korea, China, and Japan (I:15). Although Koreans were on the whole suspicious of Pan-Asianism as a concept that served to cloak Japanese attempts to establish their leadership of East Asia, anxiety over a future "race war" with the West was just as widespread in Korea as in Japan. In fact, one of the first concrete pan-Asian policy proposals was penned by a Korean, An Chung-gŭn (Ahn Choong Kun, 1879–1910), a member of the anti-Japanese movement in Korea (I:20). In 1910, while imprisoned on death row for assassinating Prince Itō Hirobumi (1841–1909), Japan's minister-resident in Korea, he wrote a visionary essay in which he talked of a united Asia facing the reality of a coming war between the yellow and white races. In order to prepare for this conflict, An advocated a transnational military force and even a single currency for an East Asian political union. Although not very realistic in the climate of the time, An's vision testified to the increasing importance of Pan-Asianism in international relations in East Asia.

As official and public support for Pan-Asianism as a tool for establishing Japanese hegemony in East Asia grew stronger in Japan, the likelihood of the acceptance of pan-Asian ideals waned in other Asian countries. This tendency to distrust the ideology of Pan-Asianism was particularly pronounced in East Asia, where the Japanese threat was at its most palpable. In Korea, for example, Pan-Asianism became marginalized. Korea was a special case because of its geographical proximity to Japan. As Kim (2007) shows (see also I:15 and I:18), most Korean intellectuals and political activists had been fairly skeptical about the idea of Asian solidarity even in the nineteenth century, even if some pro-Japanese modernizers, such as Kim Ok-kyun (1851–1894), had promoted Pan-Asianism as a useful tool for cooperation with Japan against the threat posed by imperial Russia. In spite of Korean suspicions over Japanese ambitions for the Korean peninsula, many Korean intellectuals, strongly influenced by social Darwinism during the final years of the nineteenth century (cf. Shin 2005), were convinced that for historical reasons the Koreans—"a backward and thus inferior race"—had no choice but to form an alliance with China and Japan as a result of Korea's proximity to its two neighbors. Others, who feared the much-trumpeted Western peril much more than any alleged racial inferiority, reached the same conclusions (e.g., the series of articles on the prospects of a Sino-Japanese-Korean Alliance by reformer An Kyongsu published in a Japanese journal in 1900; see An 1900).

After Korea became a Japanese protectorate in 1905 and a Japanese colony in 1910, Korean writers naturally became highly suspicious of their powerful neighbor and advocated resistance and "self-strengthening" as a way of regaining their independence. Under Japanese rule, the appeal of Pan-Asianism to Koreans was greatly limited. But it was not extinguished completely. Some Korean pan-Asianists continued to advocate a more or less equal "union of the Korean and Japanese cultures within the context of a broader Asian alliance," or within "a pan-Asian community," until the end of Japanese colonial rule in 1945 (Caprio 2009: 173, 184–86, 200; cf. also Shin 2006: chap. 1). Some Koreans who continued to adhere to the ideal of pan-Asian solidarity even interpreted the outbreak of war with the United States in 1941 (or the "Greater East Asian War," as it was officially called in the Japanese Empire) as the beginning of "a real war of races—the Yellow against the White" (quoted in Caprio 2009: 184). For these Koreans it was clear that Korea, as an Asian nation, had to side (temporarily at least) with Japan in this war of the races, even though Koreans were unhappy with Japanese colonial rule.

Some Chinese intellectuals and activists also continued to adhere to Pan-Asianism in the first decades of the twentieth century, as is evident from the quotation by Sun Yat-sen discussed here. However, open criticism of Japanese Pan-Asianism as a tool of Japanese expansionism was voiced as early as 1907, when the scholar and revolutionary Zhang Taiyan (1868–1936; see I:16) described Japan as the "public enemy" (*kōteki*) of Asia (Yamamuro 2005). Zhang gave vent to his conviction that Japan was an imperialist predator rather than a victim of imperialist oppression to which calls for Asian solidarity could properly be directed (see I:11 for a similar criticism from within Japan). Zhang also questioned the validity of pan-Asian ideals in general. Rejecting the simplistic scheme of "oppressed yellow Asians" and "white oppressors," he stressed what he called the "double enslavement of the Chinese"—bondage by Western imperialism and by "foreign," that is, Manchu, rule. His argument led him to emphasize the urgent need to establish Chinese nationalism as a counterforce to Manchu rule (Kondō 1979: 17). However, these advanced views did not prevent him from forming the Asiatic Humanitarian Brotherhood to promote cooperation with other Asian peoples.

Another revolutionary leader of modern China, Li Dazhao (1888–1927), also rejected Pan-Asianism as advocated by its Japanese exponents. In 1919, he harshly criticized Japanese pan-Asian writings as an expression of Japanese expansionism. However, while rejecting Japanese forms of Asianism, Li nevertheless conceded that some kind of regional cooperation was necessary to counter the threat of Western imperialism and called for the formulation of a "New Asianism" that presumably would be untainted by Japanese distortions (I:22). The tense atmosphere of pan-Asian conferences organized by Japanese and Chinese groups in Nagasaki in 1926 and Shanghai in 1927, however, clearly demonstrated that Chinese hostility to Japanese versions of Pan-Asianism had undermined any realistic expectation of close Sino–Japanese cooperation in an atmosphere of true solidarity (II:8). Some Chinese, such as Sun Yat-sen (until his death in 1925) and his confidant Wang Ching-wei (1883–1944; see I:25, II:5, and II:23), remained hopeful that Pan-Asianism might yet play a constructive role in Asia's fight against Anglo-Saxon imperialism, and a group of Chinese Pan-Asianists published a journal, *Asiatic Asia*, in Shanghai from 1941. However, in the end Japanese efforts to legitimize its various forms of aggression, including the war against China (1937–1945), as a pan-Asian "holy war" (see II:15) completely discredited the idea of Asian solidarity in China for many years to come.

In India, by contrast, Pan-Asianism left few negative legacies, probably because, unlike Korea and China, that country had never come under Japanese rule. In India, attempts to secure Japanese support for the national independence movement had a long tradition and resulted in close connections with Japan (cf. Nakajima 2005, 2009; Hotta 2006; Matsuura 2007a). A number of Indian revolutionaries found asylum there, and some even used Japan as a base for their pan-Asian activities. Among them was Taraknath Das (1884–1958; see I:31), who frequently published in Japan under the pseudonym "An Asian." In works published in Japan and China, Das called on "Asian Youth" to resist the West: "Every Asian youth . . . who possesses even a tiny bit of the feeling of self-respect should strive to achieve the goal of assertion of Asia to the fullest sense of its meaning" (Das 1917a, 1917b). Clearly Japan's invasion of China did nothing to dampen Das's hopes for Japan as the liberator of Asia, for as late as 1941 he insisted that Japan was "the only Eastern Power which can challenge the mighty forces of the West. . . . People of the East . . . have set their eyes on [Japan] as their possible saviour."[23] Rash Behari Bose (1886–1945), who was naturalized as a Japanese subject in 1923, also used his Japanese contacts to campaign on behalf of Pan-Asianism and Indian independence. As his speech reproduced in I:24 shows, he was an influential advocate of a Japan-centered Pan-Asianism and remained so until his death in 1944. His compatriot Subhas Chandra Bose (no relation, 1897–1945), who met Hitler in his attempt to marshal support for Indian independence (cf. Hauner 1981), also entertained great hopes for Japan as Asia's savior. He held meetings with Japanese leaders to encourage their support for his nationalist cause and participated in the Assembly of the Greater East Asiatic Nations in 1943 (see II:27).

The celebrated writer and cultural nationalist Rabindranath Tagore also deserves mention in this context. Tagore, who is not given a separate chapter in this collection, was a longtime friend of Okakura Tenshin (I:7 and I:8; on the relationship between the two, see also Bharucha 2006) and visited

Japan several times in the 1910s and 1920s. During his first visit, Tagore condemned Japanese nationalism as an imitation of Western practices (cf. Hay 1970: 69f). However, in 1924, when demonstrations against the United States Asian Exclusion Act erupted in Japan, Tagore spoke out on a number of occasions in favor of pan-Asian unity to audiences of several thousand. Announced at these rallies as "The Pride of the Orient," Tagore called on his fellow Asians to "awake, arise, agitate, agitate and agitate against this monstrous and inhuman insult which America has heaped upon us" (cited in Stalker 2006: 166). He hoped that the discriminatory U.S. immigration law would "unite the Asiatic races who will awake from their long sleep and . . . prove invulnerable against the attacks of the White Races" and motivate them to erect an "Empire of Asia . . . [that would] spring roaring into the arena of the world's politics" (Stalker 2006: 166f).

South East Asians became suspicious of Japanese Pan-Asianism only in the late 1930s—much later than the Koreans and Chinese. The main reason for this was, unlike in Korea and China, the Japanese were not perceived as a threat to a region dominated by the Western powers. Consequently, Japanese-directed Pan-Asianism enjoyed great appeal throughout Southeast Asia. In the Philippines, Japanese pan-Asianists had already supported the independence movement under Emilio Aguinaldo (1869–1964) as early as 1898 (Jansen 1954: 68–74). In 1915, a Pan-Oriental Society was formed in Manila. The society was headed by General Jose Alejandrino (1870–1951), who had gained his rank in the struggle against the United States and, after surrendering in 1901, went on to enjoy a career as a senator. British intelligence reported that "he speaks and writes Japanese and speaks with the authority of the Japanese Foreign Office." To the British, the anti-Western position of the Pan-Oriental Society was clear. At its meetings "speeches are made favoring an 'Oriental Monroeism' headed by Japan." But it would be wrong to dismiss the society as nothing more than a front for Japanese propaganda. Alejandrino took a wider interest in Asian affairs and wrote newspaper articles in which he mentioned the Indian Independence Party and even discussed the possibility of a free India. And there was some evidence of contacts with other Asian proindependence movements. According to the British intelligence report, "an intercepted letter, written by a Filipino student returned from Tokyo, shows that there might be a danger of a connection between these Filipino students and disaffected Indians in Japan" (Eliot to Curzon 30 April 1921, 77B Foreign Office Documents Pertaining to Japan, FO 371/6678, Public Record Office, Kew, Richmond).

In Malaya, too, some looked to Japan as a liberating force. For example, the nationalist journalist Ibrahim bin Haji Yaacob (1911–1979) founded, with Japanese support, the pro-Japanese and pan-Malay (if not pan-Asian)

Kesatuan Melayu Muda (League of Malay Youth). Its members cooperated with the Japanese forces during the invasion of the Malay Peninsula against the British and continued to do so throughout the Japanese occupation (Bayly and Harper 2007: 17–18).

The Japanese occupation of Southeast Asia in the wake of Pearl Harbor and the economic exploitation of the region that followed called into question the sincerity of pan-Asian rhetoric. However, even under the Japanese occupation, Pan-Asianism remained an important factor in Japan's relations with Southeast Asia. The Japanese certainly milked pan-Asian sentiment to help mobilize the region's resources for the war effort. At the same time some Southeast Asians, such as the contributors to the *Greater Asia* newspaper in Indonesia (II:26) and to the eponymous newspaper in Burma (cf. Sareen 2004), embraced the anti-Western component of pan-Asian rhetoric.

However, relations between Japan and the leaders of independence movements in Southeast Asia remain a controversial subject in Asian historiography. The position of those Southeast Asians who supported the Japanese war effort was much more ambivalent than is generally believed. The Indonesian independence activist Mohammed Hatta (1902–1980) is a case in point. Hatta is known for his collaboration with the Japanese occupation authorities during the war, but even at that time he was no Japanese puppet. And even before the war, in the 1930s, he was capable of a sober critique of the problems inherent in the Japanese version of Pan-Asianism. This is made clear by an article that he published in 1934, shortly after returning from a visit to Japan, where he was wined and dined by members of the Dai Ajia Kyōkai (see II:13). In the article, pointedly titled "Does Japan Desire to Return to Asia?" Hatta predicted the failure of Japanese Pan-Asianism because, in his view, the two conditions necessary to ensure its success—a permanent peace between Japan and China and the achievement of perfect equality between the Asian nations—could not be realized in the foreseeable future. Indeed, notwithstanding his enthusiastic reception in Japan, Hatta regarded Asianism as tainted by fascist tendencies, among which he included Japan's ambition to become the leader of Asia (Gotō 2008: 5f).

In western Asia, hopes for Japanese leadership in the struggle against Western imperialism were growing, but in the end no significant cooperation between Japan and any western Asian nation materialized. Japanese contacts with the Ottoman Empire, official and unofficial, went back to the late nineteenth century. In the first decades of the twentieth century, pan-Islamic activists came to Japan, where (among other things) they cooperated with Japanese pan-Asianists in founding the Ajia Gikai discussed above (cf. Esenbel 2004). During World War II, hopes for Japanese support were strongly expressed throughout the Arab world (cf. Esenbel 2004); they were fueled by the founding of the Greater

Japan Islamic League (Dai Nippon Kaikyō Kyōkai) in Japan in 1938. However, although a number of influential individuals, including Ōkawa Shūmei (II:4) and General Hayashi Senjūrō (cf. Matsuura 2010: 365–75), were sympathetic to the Arab cause, the failure of the Japanese to advance west of India during the course of the war precluded any effective cooperation.

THE "GREATER EAST ASIAN WAR" AND PAN-ASIANISM

The use of pan-Asian ideology to legitimize war and Japanese colonial rule discredited the movement. As a result, Pan-Asianism came to be widely identified as an ideology of colonial rule—specifically, Japan's colonial rule over Asian countries and peoples, which, the Japanese rulers insisted, was more "benevolent" than Western colonial rule because Japanese were fellow Asians. Yet, as much recent research has shown, Japanese colonial rule was equally as oppressive as that of any European power. Just like the European imperialists, the Japanese ruthlessly exploited the territories they ruled. They mobilized their subject populations for the Japanese war effort, and, unlike most Western powers, they made efforts to assimilate the populations of at least some of the colonial territories they controlled (cf. Caprio 2009 for the Korean case). For the populations of Japanese-controlled territories, Japanese colonial rule was not substantially different from Western colonial rule, even if the Japanese proclaimed pan-Asian "brotherhood" and professed to save them from the evils of colonial rule by non-Asians.

Many prominent Asians, however—politicians, diplomats, intellectuals, and writers alike—were forced to choose sides, particularly after the outbreak of the "Greater East Asian War." China, where people were also forced to choose sides, was a special case. For the overwhelming number of Chinese "the war" meant not an "Asian" war of liberation against "the West" but a war against Japanese aggression in which the West was an ally. The war in China had started much earlier than in the rest of Asia: it had broken out in 1931 in northeastern China (Manchuria), spreading to the rest of China by 1937. The different terms to name the conflict that were used by the opposing sides are instructive. While the Japanese term "Greater East Asian War," used for the war against the United States and Britain from December 1941, implied some pan-Asian notion of liberation of the whole region, the Chinese term for the war against Japan rejected the notion that this was a racial war and had anything to do with pan-Asian ideals. It was—and still is—simply the "War of Resistance against Japanese Aggression" (*kangri zhanzheng*).

The Japanese government made concerted efforts to stress the pan-Asian character of the war. Its naming as the "Greater East Asian War" was only a beginning. Numerous government statements during the war emphasized the pan-Asian character of the conflict. However, it should be noted that it was only several months after the outbreak of hostilities that the Japanese government officially included the "liberation of Asia from Western imperialism" in its list of war objectives (Hatano 1996). Pan-Asian propaganda intensified as the war continued. In 1942, the Ministry of Greater East Asia was founded in order to coordinate and strengthen intra-Asian cooperation. As II:27 shows, this move was intended primarily to underline the rhetoric of pan-Asian liberation—but, at this point in the war, "strengthened cooperation" meant, above all, the mobilization of resources for Japan's war effort. The worse the military situation became for Japan, the more the Japanese government tended to draw on pan-Asian rhetoric. In this context, the declaration of the "Assembly of the Greater East Asiatic Nations" issued in 1943 sounds like a last, desperate appeal for pan-Asian unity.[24]

At that time even liberal intellectuals like Hasegawa Nyozekan (1875–1969), seemingly oblivious to the looming disaster ahead, was still insisting that the "Greater East Asian War" must be the starting point for the establishment of "a united cultural sphere [by] the races of East Asia" (quoted in Shillony 1981: 143). In similar vein, Nishida Kitarō (1870–1945), one of Japan's leading philosophers, in 1943 characterized the war as a holy, pan-Asian struggle to liberate and unify Asia:

> The Great East Asian War is a sacred war, because it is the culmination of the historical progress of Asia. . . . The task of the liberated peoples is now to win the war and establish the Great East Asia Co-Prosperity Sphere, in co-operation with the Germans, Italians, and other peoples in Europe, who are engaged in a heroic struggle to create a new order in Europe. . . . Japan will win this war because her people are determined to sacrifice their lives for it. . . . Japan's victory will save Asia and will offer a new hope for mankind. (quoted in Shillony 1981: 112)

So, even though schemes for pan-Asian unity became more and more unrealistic as the fortunes of war turned against Japan, the official espousal of Pan-Asianism by the Japanese government and military resulted in a further wave of publications on Asian solidarity and brotherhood (see II:29 and II:30).[25]

PAN-ASIAN SOLIDARITY AND THE LEGACIES OF PAN-ASIANISM IN THE POSTWAR PERIOD

Japan's surrender and the advent of the Cold War resulted in the disappearance of pan-Asian discourse from the international relations arena. Japanese proponents of Pan-Asianism were purged from office, and pan-Asian associations were disbanded by the occupation authorities. Pan-Asianism was no longer a subject that figured in debates on foreign relations, in Japan or elsewhere. Clearly, there was no room for pan-Asian schemes in the new bipolar world order. This situation did not change even after the estrangement between China and the Soviet Union in the 1950s (culminating in a formal Chinese declaration in 1961 denouncing the Soviet leadership as a "revisionist traitor group") because Japan, once again an important Asian nation, was now closely allied to the United States and thus in effect part of "the West." In the 1960s, however, the emergence of the nonaligned movement (NAM) led to the resurgence of pan-Asian ideals. The NAM was founded in 1961 under the leadership of India's Prime Minister Jawaharlal Nehru (1889–1964), President Gamal Abdul Nasser (1918–1970) of Egypt, and Yugoslav President Josip Tito (1892–1980). However, it was primarily Asian and African countries that played the central role in the activities of the movement, which had its roots in the 1955 Bandung Conference (see II:33). The Bandung Conference and the NAM assumed a firmly anti-imperialist stance and objected strongly to the domination of international relations by the United States, just as the pan-Asian movement before 1945 had opposed (and even fought) Anglo-American world hegemony (cf. Dennehy 2007).

Although Japan did not play a leading role in these developments, in Japan the sense of a pan-Asian "mission" was preserved in other forms. After the devastation wrought by the war had nullified the achievements of the prewar era and, as some suggested, turned Japan into an agricultural economy, intellectuals like Shimizu Ikutarō (1907–1988) felt impelled to proclaim that "now, once again, the Japanese are Asians" (cited in Oguma 2007: 200). Pan-Asian themes also survived in leftist critiques of Western modernity (see II:35) and in the related claims that Japan must side with the oppressed nations of Asia in their resistance to the continuing Western imperialist domination of the non-European world (II:32). Variations on the pan-Asian theme have continued to inform ideas of solidarity, both in left-wing circles and among those who became ultranationalists after giving up hope in the possibilities of socialism, such as the writer Hayashi Fusao (1903–1975; see II:34).

However, postwar Pan-Asianism was tainted by its association with Japanese imperialism and aggression. Indeed it became synonymous with it. For the most prominent political scientist of the postwar period, Maruyama Masao (1914–1996), Pan-Asianism, together with "familism" (*kazokushugi*) and "agrarianism" (*nōhonshugi*), was one of the three fundamental components of Japanese ultranationalism (Maruyama 1964: 40–57). Perhaps because of this association, there was no serious scholarly attempt to deal with Pan-Asianism as a subject of historical inquiry in the 1950s and the 1960s. One scarcely need mention that in Korea and China Pan-Asianism was completely discredited as an ideology of collaboration with the enemy and the colonizers. This was the direct consequence of the use of pan-Asian rhetoric to justify Japanese colonial rule in Korea, and (in wartime China) to justify Japanese aggression and legitimize the Nanjing puppet government (II:23). There are signs, however, that this situation is changing, as indicated by recent efforts by high-level Chinese diplomats to present Pan-Asianism in a more positive light (II:41; Wang 2004).

In Japan, the first serious attempt to grapple with the thorny question of the legacy of Asianism was made by the Sinologist and literary critic Takeuchi Yoshimi (1963a; see also II:35). Takeuchi, who in his youth had enthusiastically embraced pan-Asian ideals, had his beliefs shaken by Japan's defeat. Yet although some aspects of Takeuchi's faith were undermined, he had no doubt that there were positive features that were worth preserving. Pan-Asianism, he never ceased to believe, was much more than mere window dressing for Japan's Greater Asian Co-Prosperity Sphere. In Takeuchi's view, there was a core of pan-Asian ideals that retained validity and therefore needed to be remembered and even cherished. Interestingly, Takeuchi regarded Japan's aggression in China not as a consequence of Pan-Asianism but rather as Japan's "shedding" of Asia (*datsu-A*), a concept that emerged in the 1880s (see I:2) and became highly influential as the antithesis to Pan-Asianism throughout the course of modern Japanese history. From this perspective, Japan's aggression was in effect an application of inauthentic (and therefore culpable) Western methods to Asia and thus had nothing to do with the "Eastern spirit" or Eastern cultural practices or political norms. It was a natural, if deplorable, consequence of the westernization of Japan. This misguided attempt by Japan to depart from pan-Asian principles was corrected, to some extent at least, by the war Japan waged from December 1941 on the colonial powers of the United States, Britain, and the Netherlands. It was little wonder that Takeuchi welcomed this war enthusiastically (see II:35). Takeuchi is difficult to locate on the ideological spectrum. Although he would not classify himself as a rightist, his attempts to restore legitimacy to the discredited term Pan-Asianism were unusual. Those on the left preferred to talk of Asian solidarity, brotherhood, or cooperation, which often overlapped with socialist or communist forms of international solidarity, or the solidarity of the nonaligned movement (see II:33). For the Japanese left, the term "Pan-Asianism" was (and perhaps still is) practically synonymous with Japanese colonialism and aggression.

Yet, whether or not they eschewed the term itself, in postwar Japan the left incorporated pan-Asian elements into its own views. And the continuity between prewar pan-Asian rightists and postwar left-wing circles should not be overlooked in this context. This (at first sight) surprising continuity has only rarely been discussed in previous research.[26] The prewar flirtation with national socialism and Japanism by socialists like Asanuma Inejirō (1898–1960) is well known. It is less widely known, however, that Marquis Tokugawa Yoshichika (1886–1976), one of the major sponsors of the rightist movement in the prewar period and a close friend of pan-Asianists such as Ōkawa Shūmei (II:4), became a benefactor of the newly founded Socialist Party of Japan after the war. It appears that Tokugawa's support for the Socialist Party was motivated to some extent, at least, by pan-Asian motives (for the bizarre details of his support, see Tokugawa 1973: 214). These motives were also apparent in an extraordinary statement by Tokugawa's erstwhile comrade in the rightist movement, Ōkawa, who in 1949 detected a "close resemblance between today's communists and the early Muslims" and wished for "a second battle of Tours-Poitiers" to be fought between the communists and the West, which this time would result in victory for the communists (i.e., Asia) (Szpilman 1998b: 61).

Another right-wing pan-Asianist, Tsukui Tatsuo (1901–1989), well known in the postwar period as an "ultranationalist historian," is known to have lavished praise on communist China (Tsukui 1956). In the mid-1950s, a U.S. counterintelligence report accused Tsukui of bringing a large sum of money from mainland China, funds that were eventually given to the National Diet member and former army colonel, Tsuji Masanobu (1902–1961?), "for safe keeping" ("Rightist Groups in Japan Receive Funds from Communist China," extract from OSI "Counterintelligence Digest," 10 October 1956, 201, File #631 Tsuji Masanobu).

It should be noted that, like Tsukui, the recipient of this unspecified largesse, Colonel Tsuji, who had achieved notoriety during the war, made no secret of his pan-Asian sympathies in the postwar period (for an example of his views, see Tsuji 1950). According to Tsuji, on matters of regional solidarity ideological differences were less important than blood ties. At a gathering of former generals on 20 November 1954, Tsuji is reported as arguing that Japan should work with India to achieve neutrality and with communist China to maintain peace. Noting his friendship with Chinese Communist Party officials such as Zhou Enlai (also Chou En-lai, 1898–1976), he explained that, communist or not, "[a]fter all, they're Asians" (GB-S/C@A, 16 August 1955, Form Nr 137, File #631 Tsuji Masanobu). An American intelligence analyst concluded, "Tsuji, head of the neutralist Self-Defense League (Jiei Dōmei), has long been a vigorous exponent of 'the Asia for Asiatics,' doctrine of the late Ishihara Kanji [II:22]. Like right wing critic Tsukui Tatsuo (INTSUM 4497), who also returned from Communist China, Tsuji considers the ties that bind Asians together stronger than those between Communist China and the

USSR" (File #631 Tsuji Masanobu). A Japanese biographer of Tsuji agreed with this assessment, noting that the former colonel was "harsh on the Soviet Union and soft on communist China" (Sugimori 1963: 216). For members of the Japanese left, Tsuji, as an army colonel blamed for a number of wartime atrocities, was beyond the pale. However, they would no doubt agree with his support for the downtrodden peoples of Asia.[27]

Leftists might find the case of the politician and parliamentarian Utsunomiya Tokuma (1906–2000) even more ambiguous. The son of General Utsunomiya Tarō (1861–1922), commander of the Japanese army in Korea (on General Utsunomiya's pan-Asian views, see Matsuura 2010: 149–52 and note 10 of this introduction), Utsunomiya was one of the founding members of the Liberal Democratic Party in 1955 but cannot be categorized simply as a conservative politician. In the 1980s Utsunomiya emerged as a stern critic of the party he had helped to found but no longer supported, and, on a number of occasions, he appeared to be closely allied with the Socialist Party. He was a fervent proponent of disarmament and ran successfully in elections against the retired Self-Defense Forces general, Kurisu Hiroomi (1920–2004), an advocate of rearmament. In the 1960s Utsunomiya had been a prominent supporter of Algeria's struggle for independence. He went out of his way to support all expressions of "Asian and African nationalism" and never hid his pan-Asianist sympathies (Hayashi 1974: 685–728: see also Matsuura 2010: 847). It could be argued that Utsunomiya's pro-Asian attitudes were inseparable from his anti-Western and, more specifically, anti-American, sentiments.

This same set of attitudes has characterized many on the left, one of whose major criticisms of the Japanese government is its pro-American, pro-Western stance. Most left-wing commentators would never admit to entertaining pan-Asian sentiments, for, as we have seen, in their view Pan-Asianism was irredeemably besmirched by Japan's wartime aggression. But whether they recognize it or not, the political left in Japan is heir to the pan-Asian tradition. This is abundantly clear both from the activities of the Japanese pacifist movement in general and the movement against the Vietnam War (organized by the Citizens' League for Peace in Vietnam; Japanese: Betonamu ni Heiwa o! Shimin Rengō, abbreviated as Beheiren; cf. Hirai 2005) in particular. Numerous statements by members of these movements condemning American imperialism and American aggression have been issued over the years and continue today. The pan-Asian undertones of these criticisms are generally revealed in their appeals to Asian brotherhood and Asian solidarity. This tendency is also seen in gestures made by prominent left-wing politicians such as Doi Takako (1928–), the one-time leader of the Japan Socialist Party, who in 1990 traveled to Baghdad to shake hands with Saddam Hussein (1937–2006);

in statements by activists such as Dr. Nakamura Tetsu (1946–), who has devoted his life to the cause of helping the needy and sick in Afghanistan (II:40); and in lawsuits challenging Japanese logistical assistance to U.S. military activities in Afghanistan, Iraq, and elsewhere. Most recently, in a remarkable example of this tendency to pan-Asian solidarity, in late 2009 the Japanese cabinet, led by Hatoyama Yukio (1947–), the leader of the Democratic Party of Japan in coalition with the Social Democratic Party, halted Japanese military support for American-led operations in Afghanistan and recalled the Maritime Self-Defense Forces from the Indian Ocean.

RECENT DEVELOPMENTS

As stated at the outset, issues of regionalism and regional integration in East Asia have received considerable attention since the 1990s. In Korea, for example, pan-Asian unity is identified as a promising path to avoid domination not only by Japan but also by China. In 2002, for example, former South Korean President Roh Moo-hyun (1946–2009) declared that "the age of Northeast Asia is arriving" (quoted in Suh 2005: 611). At the same time, regional approaches in East Asia, especially since the beginning of the present century, have been an expression of increasing discontent with American-led globalization and a developing unilateral world system. In South Korea, pan-Asianist regionalism is thus "seen as an attractive alternative to Korea's dependence on America" (Shin 2005: 625). South Korean and Japanese interests seem to have converged in these respects. In Japan, from as early as the 1980s, a "New Asianism" (Duus 2001; see also II:36 and Nakagawa 2006 for examples) has begun to resurface, partly as an offshoot of the so-called Asian values debate of the 1980s, a discussion initiated by Malaysia's Prime Minister Mahathir Mohamad (1925–) and the prime minister of Singapore, Lee Kuan-Yew (1923–), supported by the xenophobic populist politician and writer Ishihara Shintarō (1932–), in 2010 governor of Tokyo (see II:37). Despite his frequent "Asian-bashing" outbursts, Ishihara is also known for his advocacy of pan-Asian views—which, essentially, are an expression of his strong anti-Americanism.

In the 1980s these politicians—and others like them—advocated a set of common "Asian values" (always vaguely defined), based on Confucian virtues, as a counter to the universalist claims of liberalism, democracy, and human rights, values that were dismissed as alien to the region and inauthentic for Asians on account of their allegedly Western provenance. However, many Asian politicians and writers, such as the future president of South Korea, Kim Dae-jung (1925–2009) (Kim 1994), strongly rejected the idea of a common set of "Asian" values, and the debate has made little headway since. However, recent work by Chinese scholars suggests an attempt to find some kernel of truth in the legacy of Pan-Asianism with the objective of criticizing "Western" (i.e., United States) policies or the West's claim to the universality of democratic values (see, e.g., Sun 2003). The new trend in Chinese academia to deal more openly with the once completely discredited ideology of Pan-Asianism (see also Wang 2004), in combination with statements by high-ranking diplomats acknowledging the potential of the region's pan-Asian legacy (Wang 2006a and 2006b),[28] arguably reflects a change in attitudes in China.

In Japan, the rise of a "New Asianism" has reflected concrete diplomatic and economic efforts to stimulate regionalist approaches. These efforts were, however, always placed under strain by the strong priority given by the Japanese government to the United States-Japan Security Treaty. Nonetheless, Japan, as a recent study notes, "has been a driving force of Asian regionalism throughout the post-war period," particularly in the economic sphere (Hamanaka 2009: 7). Particularly important in this regard was Japan's involvement in the founding of the Asian Development Fund in 1957 and the proposal for an Asian Monetary Fund in 1997. In addition, Japan has also been relatively active in the ASEAN+3 cooperative network, involving the ASEAN nations plus China, Japan, and South Korea (Hamanaka 2009: 7; see also II:39). But as the acronym indicates, the driving force of this new body is ASEAN—the only effective organization working for regional integration in Asia, which has brought a considerable degree of stability and economic growth to Southeast Asia. Japan also has been rather passive and reactive with regard to the development of a Free Trade Agreement network in East Asia, and, given its continuing dependence on the security treaty with the United States, it remains questionable whether Japan can play a leading role in the integration of the region in the immediate future—notwithstanding the outspoken advocacy of Pan-Asianism by some leading politicians (e.g., Nakagawa 2006).[29]

Nor should one forget the historical legacies of World War II and of Pan-Asianism as an ideology. As late as the 1990s, partly because of the difficulties Japan experienced in coming to terms with its past, writers in Asia as well as in the West warned that Japanese regionalist initiatives could be interpreted as a resurgence of claims for Japan's leadership in East Asia, with the objective of creating "a new version of the Greater East-Asia Co-Prosperity Sphere of World War II" (Johnson 1993: 216). In recent years, the issue of historical memory has become less contentious in Japan, but persistent elements of "retrospective Pan-Asianism"—the rehabilitation of wartime pan-Asian rhetoric to whitewash Japan's wars of aggression and colonial rule in

Asia—continue to hinder attempts to promote regional integration (Kingston 2004: 232–42; Saaler 2005).

On the academic level, however, considerable progress has been made over the past two decades, as witnessed by drafts for an "Asian Constitution,"[30] proposals for an East Asian Common House (II:42) and a myriad of academic conferences dealing with (and not infrequently advocating) regional integration. It is yet to be determined where all this activity will lead in the future. What surely can be said, however, is that attention to the historical legacies of Pan-Asianism and the identification of positive examples of pan-Asian solidarity and regional integration in the past will play an increasingly significant role in the years to come.

RECURRENT PAN-ASIAN THEMES

Pan-Asian styles of thought have always come most to the fore in debates on foreign policy and on Asian identity. If the many varieties of Pan-Asianism had anything in common, it was their opposition to the West: opposition to the West's presence in Asia (i.e., Western imperialism), opposition to Western culture and values, and, conversely, an emphasis on the importance (and in many cases, the superiority) of Asian culture and Asian values. In fact, it could be argued that anti-Westernism was central to Pan-Asianism. In opposition to the "West"—which was, to a large degree, an invented concept—pan-Asian writers constructed their own "Asia." Images of this constructed Asia varied greatly. They changed over time and took particular forms in different places and in the works of different authors. But all pan-Asianists assumed the existence of "one Asia" and based this assumption on one or more of the following categories:

- Geography (Asia, East Asia, the Orient)
- Cultural unity (influence of Indian and Chinese civilization, religions)
- Historical interconnectedness (Sinocentric system, tribute relations, trade networks)
- Racial kinship (the yellow race, races of color)
- The unity of Asian civilization in terms of its values and spiritual character (Confucianism, justice, and benevolence vs. Western materialism and rationalism)
- A common destiny (the fight against Western imperialism and colonial rule)

These are the major themes that the reader will encounter time and again throughout this collection. The idea that geographically Asia forms a unified entity, notwithstanding the relatively recent introduction of the term in the region, was discussed in some detail at the beginning of this introduction. It has to be emphasized again, however, that there was never a consensus on the geographical definition of Asia and that pan-Asian writers constantly revised their definitions of "Asia," blurring geographical exactitude with interpretations that allowed them to extend their definition of Asia even to some European and African nations (see I:25).

The perception and creation of cultural unity, brought to an extreme of simplification in the slogan "Asia is one" (I:7 and I:8), also remains an important theme of pan-Asian writers over the past one and a half centuries—and down to the present day. In 2010, an Internet search (google.com) of the term generates a large number of hits. Although it is clear that any particular assertion of what constitutes cultural commonalities (or differences) is highly arbitrary and subjective, it is important to acknowledge that such a particularized insistence on the existence of commonalities has played an important role in the construction of Pan-Asianism, as the texts reproduced in this collection show.

Recent research has stressed the importance of historical interconnectedness as an authentic foundation for forces encouraging the development of regional integration (cf. Arrighi, Hamashita, and Selden 2003: introduction). The notion of a world system that connected the various states of East and Southeast Asia for centuries, before the imposition of Western-based international law, had sufficient coherence to bind indigenous forces against the threat of external domination. In recent years, these approaches have once again been attracting attention as a reaction to the emergence of a unipolar world order.

Enough has already been said about the incorporation of the Western ideas of race into pan-Asianist rhetoric. References to "racial kinship" were frequent, as the documents in this collection make clear. However, the Western provenance of the concept of race made it highly questionable that such an ideology could serve as the basis for a regional identity—not least since a Pan-Asianism based on racial motives limited "Asia" to East Asia and tended to exclude India, western Asia, and other areas. Further, the ideal of racial equality and the reality of racial discrimination within Asia eventually thoroughly discredited the racial component within Pan-Asianism, particularly in Korea (after 1910) and other territories under Japanese colonial rule.

The complex notion of Asian values—Asian "spirituality" versus the "materialism" of Western civilization—is also highly contested and riddled with contradictions. As we have already noted in the discussion of geographical definitions, the "Asia" of the pan-Asianists sometimes included territories that are generally classified as "Western" countries, such as Germany, Italy, or even Ireland. The 1920s saw a wave of sympathy for the cause of Irish independence in Asian publications, and in the 1930s, Japan allied itself with Germany and Italy—ostensibly since Germany and Italy had chosen to join the fight against "Western" materialism, now limited to Anglo-Saxon civilization.

Notwithstanding the various contradictions generated by any definition of Asia or the West, pan-Asianists have generally regarded "the West" as the alien Other. Time and again, as this collection shows, for pan-Asianists Asia represents the *antithesis* of the West. Indeed, these writers regularly define Asia in terms of the West. This is true of such diverse figures as Okakura Tenshin, Ōkawa Shūmei (see I:7, I:8, and II:4) and, in the postwar period, Takeuchi Yoshimi, Ishihara Shintarō, and Nakamura Tetsu (see II:35, II:37, and II:40). The corollary to this vision of the West as the Other is the assumption that there exists a coherent set of Asian values and that these values, *ex definitione* shared by all Asians, are superior to Western values. This idea is often linked to an emphasis on the antiquity of Asian culture, which is often presented by pan-Asianists as the cradle of civilization, including European civilization. In this connection, much has been made of the fact that all of the major religions of the world, including Christianity, originated in what is geographically considered Asia. On these grounds, it is often argued that only "Asian" civilization has the potential to ultimately save mankind, including the West. In the words of Tagore, "If Asian civilization constituted a great reservoir of spiritual power, and if modern civilization was about to destroy humanity itself, then it must be from a regenerated Asia that man's salvation would come" (quoted in Hay 1970: 64–65). Tagore was an outspoken critic of nationalism in at least some of his writings. There is no doubt that the kind of Pan-Asianism to which he subscribed was "a vision of community that sought to transcend the territorial nation-state and redeem and regenerate the world through Eastern spiritual morality" (Duara 1998: 655).

Nonetheless, others have argued that an affirmation of Asian values is fundamentally misguided, that no single set of moral values is shared by all Asians (e.g., Kim 1994). It can moreover be argued that the East–West opposition is in fact based on an illusion. For, in essence, it is not Asian and Western values that are antithetical to each other, nor is it Asia and the West (comprising Europe and North America) that are in opposition, but rather the forms of society contained in them—modern and premodern. The geographical opposition is not exact: one could no doubt find modern forms of society in Asia and premodern societies in Europe and North America, and all have developed in diverse ways over the last two centuries. We have here a classical conflict between the modern and the premodern masquerading as a conflict between East and West. For a number of reasons, modernity in all its ramifications—secularism, individualism, liberalism, democracy, the decline of traditional morality, the advent of the money nexus and the contract society, and so on—has often been perceived as a specifically Western phenomenon. Likewise, pan-Asianists have tended to see Asian *Gemeinschaft* in conflict with Western *Gesellschaft*. Expanding on these German terms borrowed from the social sciences, some pan-Asianists have regarded the former as a positive collective entity, based on custom, moral, humane, all-embracing, with its members identifying strongly with their community (see, e.g., II:30); the latter they saw as inhumane, soulless, characterized by alienation, individualistic, and atomized, where all transactions are based on money and the contract system (the cash nexus). However, tensions between *Gemeinschaft* and *Gesellschaft* are not specific to the opposition between Asia and the West; rather, they represent the friction or conflict that operates between modern *Gesellschaft* and premodern *Gemeinschaft*. These conflicting impulses, that had riven Western societies (and arguably continue to divide them), were introduced into East Asia in the nineteenth century when the major Western powers extended their influence in the region.

Yet, for all this cultural tension, the material advantages of the West and of modernity in general became obvious to most Asians, except for a very small number of reactionary obscurantists. Western-style modernity was an indispensible condition for success in the nineteenth-century world. For that reason, along with the majority of Asians, most pan-Asianists never rejected modernity as such.[31] Many ancient Asian customs and practices were patently useless in the modern world, and, under the circumstances, the chief problem that had to be overcome was the antiquated structure of state and society. But was everything distinctive about the East to be denied? Initially there was a tendency to discard the whole culture, lock, stock, and barrel. In an excess of modernizing enthusiasm, some Japanese even wanted to give up their native tongue in favor of English. Needless to say, such proposals were at best impractical. But were there aspects of Eastern tradition still of relevance in this Western-dominated world? Was there nothing that could or should be salvaged? With regard to technology, the answer was clearly no. But in the realm of ethics, morals, and philosophical and religious thought, convincing arguments could be made for the relevance, if not the superiority, of Eastern traditions—arguments that the reader will encounter time and again throughout this collection.

While the meaning—and even the existence—of "Asian values" remains debatable, the notion of commonly held Asian values and a common culture and racial identity, which together constitute the basis of Pan-Asianism, is closely related to the sentiment of a "common destiny" for Asian peoples. This latter notion represents another recurrent theme in Pan-Asianism—one that perhaps retains much of its appeal even today, if recent statements by

Asian governments (e.g., the initiative of former Japanese Prime Minister Hatoyama Yukio; cf. Mulgan 2009) or declarations by transnational organizations such as ASEAN (cf. Association of South East Asian Nations 2009) are anything to go by. It is impossible to gauge whether such sentiments will contribute to the realization of closer transnational cooperation or even regional integration in the future. To be sure, obstacles to regional cooperation in East Asia remain in plenty. They include not only strong expressions of nationalism and the negative legacies of World War II but also the geography and demographics of Asia. Unlike in the case of European countries, the "Other," or the "enemy," for many smaller Asian nations is to be found within Asia, not somewhere outside. While Asia will certainly never be "one," progress will continue to be made in the areas of regional cooperation and integration, and there is no doubt that such developments will contribute to the stability and the prosperity of the region.

NOTES

1. Accessible online at http://www.riccicenter.com/maps/map_world01.JPG. Useful resources (original sources, links to sources, photographs, and so on) can be accessed at http://asianism.japanesehistory.de.

2. Unless indicated otherwise, we follow Takeuchi Yoshimi who regards the terms "Pan-Asianism," "Asianism," and "Greater Asianism" as essentially synonymous. In other words, the variations of "Pan-Asianism" do not necessarily imply any difference of content. It should be noted however that the term "Pan-Asianism" (or any of its numerous synonyms) can stand for a variety of meanings including contradictory ideas, as we show in this introduction.

3. For the concept of "the style of thought," see Mannheim (1953: 74–77).

4. At the time of writing, we have not come across comparable collections in other languages.

5. Notable articles on Pan-Asianism include Norman (1944), Jansen (1980), Hashikawa (1980), Reynolds (1986), Beasley (1987), Nakamura (1991), Hiraishi (1994), Koschmann (1997), Iida (1997), Sun (2000), Hazama (2001), Duara (2001), Duus (2001), Mutō (2003), Kuroki (2005), Shin (2005), and Mark (2006). Further, in 2000, the classic article "Japan's Asianism" (see II:35) by Takeuchi Yoshimi (1963b) was reprinted in book form with a commentary by Matsumoto Ken'ichi (Matsumoto 2000). The bibliography should be consulted for further articles on Pan-Asianism, including those written by the editors and contributors to this volume. A number of important studies that, although not specifically focused on Pan-Asianism, address some important related issues, should not be overlooked. In English they include Goodman (1991), Goto (1997), Shimazu (1998), Karl (2002), Oguma (2002), Esenbel and Inaba (2003), and Duara (2003); in Japanese, Eizawa (1995), Oguma (1995), Furuya (1996), and Yamamoto (2001).

6. In China and Korea, research on Pan-Asianism was discouraged for many years. It was seen as an ideology that was inseparable from Japanese expansionism and imperialism, while its Chinese and Korean advocates were dismissed as traitors who collaborated with the Japanese invader.

7. The acting consul Mizuta Shin regarded this letter, posted in Nice, France, as a case of "extreme anti-Western activism." He thought it important enough to forward to Japanese Foreign Minister Hirota Kōki. Miscellaneous documents relating to problems of ethnic groups: Vol. 2. Gaimushō Kiroku (Diplomatic Records), I.4.6.0.1, Gaimushō Gaikō Shiryōkan (Diplomatic Record Office of the Ministry of Foreign Affairs of Japan).

8. The "Amau Statement" stated that "Japan . . . opposes any joint action on the part of foreign Powers that tends to militate against the maintenance of peace and order in Eastern Asia. . . . Owing to the special position of Japan in her relations with China, . . . it must be realized that Japan is called upon to exert the utmost effort in carrying out her mission and in fulfilling her special responsibilities in East Asia." Cited in United States Department of State: *Papers Relating to the Foreign Relations of the United States, Japan: 1931–1941*, vol. I, pp. 224–29. Washington, DC: U.S. Government Printing Office, 1931–1941. Accessible online at http://digital.library.wisc.edu/1711.dl/FRUS.FRUS193141v01.

9. For a more detailed analysis of the relationship of Pan-Asianism to ultranationalism and the growth of fascism in 1930s Japan, see below; see also Maruyama (1964: 40–57).

10. In a recently published diary, General Utsunomiya Tarō, commander of the Japanese army in Korea from 1918 to 1920, frequently expresses his fervent desire for a "true union of spirits" between Japanese and Koreans. For example, he made a case for such a union in an unpublished document entitled *Daihongan* (My Great Desire), which he distributed to visitors. See Utsunomiya Tarō Kankei Shiryō Kenkyūkai (2007: 225f; see also 255, 296f, 312, 371, and so on).

11. The inherent ambiguity of Pan-Asianism relates to another problem that needs to be addressed, namely, that not all pan-Asianists expressed their ideas in writing. In compiling this collection, we had no choice but to concentrate on written sources. Consequently, the collection includes only texts that contain clear statements of pan-Asian solidarity or Asian unity (even if they do not specifically use such key words as "Asianism," "Pan-Asianism," or "Asian regionalism"). But the problem is that Pan-Asianism was not only an ideology; it was also a movement. Many activists who played central roles in the pan-Asian movement and who regarded themselves as pan-Asianists have left no written record of their views on the subject. Tōyama Mitsuru, introduced in this volume in connection with the Genyōsha, is a case in point, as is Inukai Tsuyoshi. Although his life was dedicated to the pan-Asian cause (see I:25), Inukai, a journalist turned politician with a prolific literary output, has left (to our knowledge) no explicitly pan-Asianist text. Since this is not a collection of general writings by pan-Asianists, Inukai is not included.

12. Max von Brandt (1835–1920), a longtime German diplomat in Japan and China, was well known for the anti-Japanese tone of his writings throughout the late imperial period.

13. As Kuroki (2002: 25) points out, however, at times Ueki also discussed Japanese leadership in Asia—leadership seen primarily in terms of modernization and reform.

14. The editors have been unable to identify the "pamphlets" that Ōyama refers to in his 1916 essay.

15. Liberalism did not necessarily imply hostility to Pan-Asianism. For an example of an early Japanese liberal pan-Asianist, see Ueki Emori above. In the twentieth century, too, some liberals, including Yoshino Sakuzō (1878–1933) and Ishibashi Tanzan (1884–1973), advocated Pan-Asianism; cf. Matsuura (2010: chap. 2).

16. See file FO 371 5350 1-E (1920), Public Record Office, Kew, Richmond, London, for an example of intelligence reports on the movements of anti-British Indians and Japanese pan-Asianists.

17. "Nihonjin to Hoka no Ajiajin" (The Japanese and the Other Asians), *Tokyo Nichinichi Shinbun*, 26 June 1913; "Nihon Minzoku no Dōkasei (Shasetsu)" (The Assimilation of the Japanese Race [An Editorial]), *Ōsaka Asahi Shinbun*, 27 June 1913 (part 1); 28 June 1913 (part 2); "Nihon no Chii" (Japan's Position [in the World]), *Ōsaka Mainichi Shinbun*, 22 July 1913.

18. The idea of "permanent peace," of course, goes back to Immanuel Kant's famous essay *Perpetual Peace*, 1795.

19. The idea pre-dated Woodrow Wilson's "Fourteen Points;" see Archer (2001) and Northedge (1986).

20. The author, Sugita Teiichi, an advocate of Pan-Asianism, had been active in the freedom and People's Rights Movement since the 1870s (see I:26).

21. In a special issue (Kōa Dōmei Kessei Tokugō [The Special Issue on the Founding of the Greater Japanese League for Raising Asia]), the journal *Kōa*, which was destined to become the League's official organ, gave extensive coverage to the proceedings that resulted in the founding of the League and reported the apparently enthusiastic reaction both among political circles and the general public. The issue is accessible online at http://asianism.japanesehistory.de.

22. In Japan, the Confucian Society Shibunkai was founded in 1918. Although Confucianism has been used by pan-Asianists in the service of a revival of Asian values, the Shibunkai advocated Confucianism within a nationalist framework, insisting that it was an expression of "the good ways and beautiful customs of our nation since its founding," traditions that "still exist in our villages" but that had been forgotten in the cities because of modernization, Westernization, and the growth of materialistic attitudes. See Smith (1959: chap. 3).

23. Compilation of miscellaneous documents relating to [the] domestic politics of Britain/Territories and Possessions/India/Anti-Britain Movement, 30 May 1940 to 17 March 1941, Gaimushō Kiroku (Diplomatic Records), A.6.6: Gaimushō Gaikō Shiryōkan (Diplomatic Record Office of the Ministry of Foreign Affairs of Japan).

24. Ironically, the Greater East Asia Conference of 1943 was conducted in English (Shillony 1981: 150). After the expansion of Pan-Asianism's "Asia" into South and Southeast Asia, written Chinese could no longer play the role of a lingua franca and was increasingly replaced with English. This trend away from a narrow focus on East Asia is also apparent in publications produced by the pan-Asian movement. The

turning point came at some time during World War I. For example, the Kokuryūkai (I:10), which until 1908 had published the journal *Tōa Geppō* (East Asian Monthly) in classical Chinese, went to considerable expense in February 1920 to launch the English-language *Asian Review*, intended as a companion journal to the Japanese-language *Ajia Jiron* (Asian Review), published from 1917 to 1921. The Kokuryūkai now saw itself as addressing the entire world, not merely a narrow audience made up of the Japanese and the East Asian elites. In the pages of this glossy monthly the society proclaimed its Japanese-centered pan-Asian program as a regional alternative to Wilsonian universalism. Support for its program came from mainstream figures: Prime Minister Hara Takashi allowed an address of his to be reprinted; Hamaguchi Osachi and a number of other prominent politicians and bureaucrats provided their endorsement. The Japanese government apparently appreciated the "public relations" efforts being made by the Kokuryūkai—several articles from *The Asian Review*, including Hara's contribution, were reprinted in a volume edited by Karl Kiyoshi Kawakami (1873–1949), a publicist in government pay (Kawakami 1921).

25. See also the tables, "Occurrence of terms related to Pan-Asianism in Japanese intellectual discourse," at http://asianism.japanesehistory.de.

26. Research has tended to focus on left-wing defectors to the right, a phenomenon known in Japan as *tenkō* (apostasy); cf. Ishidō (1985) and Steinhoff (1991). Koschmann's article, "Asianism's Ambivalent Legacy," which notes that postwar "left-wing Asianism revived familiar, prewar conceptions of Asian identity" (Koschmann 1997: 104), is a notable exception.

27. Tsuji vanished in mysterious circumstances during a trip to Laos in 1961. His body was never found, and he was presumed deceased by the Tokyo Family Court in 1969.

28. See also a number of Chinese contributions to the booklet *Japanese-Chinese Dialogue* published by Genron NPO in 2006 (e.g., Shi 2006).

29. It is perhaps significant that the article quoted here as Nakagawa (2006) has a different title from Nakagawa's talk reproduced on the Genron NPO website, which does not use the term "Asianism." See http://www.genron-npo.net/world/type/cat159.

30. See "The Draft Charter for an East Asian Community" in *Social Science Japan* 38 (March 2008), also accessible online at http://newslet.iss.u-tokyo.ac.jp/ssj38/index.html.

31. It should be noted that there were considerable regional differences in Asian reactions to Western aggression and to the Asian enthusiasm for Western technology.

Part I

THE RADICALIZATION OF JAPANESE PAN-ASIANISM AND INTRA-ASIAN DISPUTES, 1920–1930

This section focuses on two leading themes: the radicalization of Japanese Asianism and intra-Asian disputes in the 1920s. During these years pan-Asianists in Japan expressed their views in more direct and provocative ways than ever before. Pan-Asianism was increasingly promoted as part of Japan's "national mission." The line between pan-Asianist objectives and the agenda of Japanese ultranationalists became increasingly blurred. At the same time, pan-Asianists expanded their definitions of Asia. They now included, as a matter of routine, West Asia as an integral part of their Asia. This reflected both Japan's growing power and self-confidence but also the revolutionary changes occurring in West Asia—such as the founding of the Turkish Republic following the collapse of the Ottoman Empire, a significant Turkish military victory over Western forces in 1923, and the emergence of Saudi Arabia as an independent state.

Pan-Asianism received another powerful boost in 1924 as a result of new immigration laws in the United States that discriminated heavily against Asians in general and Japanese in particular.

Asians outside Japan continued to actively participate in pan-Asian discussions. Under the auspices of Pan-Asianism, Chinese revolutionaries continued their struggle against Western imperialism with the aim of establishing complete independence for China, while Indians continued to place hope in the movement as a source of support for their national independence struggle. Transnational cooperation reached a peak in 1926 and 1927 when pan-Asian conferences were held in Nagasaki and Shanghai. However, these conferences also exposed the limitations of the ideology by making it clear that most Asians would not accept Japanese claims to leadership in Asia.

Chapter One

Nakano Seigō: Populist, Fascist, Pan-Asianist, 1917/1942

Stefano von Loë

Born in 1886, Nakano Seigō grew up in the city of Fukuoka in Kyushu. His father, a former samurai of the Kuroda feudal domain, had lost his stipend in the course of the Meiji reforms and began operating a pawnshop. Profitable at first, the business went through a difficult period and eventually went bankrupt while Nakano was still at university. Throughout his life, he would downplay his father's real occupation and instead stress his more prestigious samurai origins (on Nakano's life and career, see Muro 1999; Oates 1985; Nakano 1988; Najita 1971).

In middle school Nakano's gift for Chinese studies was recognized by his teacher, who introduced him to the teachings of Wang Yang-ming (1472–1528), a Confucian philosopher often embraced by dissenters as his stress on the unity of knowledge and action implied the right—and even duty—to act against perceived injustices. This ideal was to form the philosophical foundations of Nakano's political thinking. From middle school, Nakano proceeded to the Shūyūkan High School—the former feudal domain school (*hankō*) and to this day the most prestigious high school in Fukuoka Prefecture. There, Nakano excelled not only in the humanities but also in kendo and especially judo, which he would practice successfully throughout his life—even after failed surgery had necessitated the amputation of his leg.

Nakano's youth in Fukuoka also defined his basic political views. In the turbulent years of the Meiji Restoration, the Kuroda feudal domain had sided with the Tokugawa forces, and, as a result, Fukuoka-born men with political ambitions found access to positions in the newly founded Meiji government difficult. Frustration over this reality found expression in political protest. Many former samurai from Fukuoka joined the samurai uprisings of the early Meiji years (most notably the Satsuma Rebellion under Saigō Takamori, 1877) and became active in the People's Rights Movement, most notably the Genyōsha (see I:3). While Nakano never formally joined the Genyōsha, throughout his life he idolized Saigō Takamori and other rebels and never lost contact with Tōyama Mitsuru and other Genyōsha leaders. Raised in this atmosphere, Nakano absorbed a strong antiestablishment attitude that in his younger years had been directed mainly against the *genrō* (elder statesmen) from the former Satsuma and Chōshū domains and their *hanbatsu* (clique) politics but was later directed against military and bureaucratic cliques at home and the Anglo-Saxon imperialist powers internationally. The romantic vision of revolution that Nakano adopted in his youth was to remain an integral part of his intellectual makeup—and whenever there was an uprising, rebellion, or revolution, his heart would side with the rebels.

Nakano's original intention had been to pursue a military career, but a leg injury made this impossible. Instead, he enrolled at Waseda University, where he read political science. As a student, Nakano made his first contacts with Chinese revolutionaries in exile in Tokyo. While interest in Chinese affairs and a desire to learn Chinese were part of Nakano's motivation, his primary motive was financial. Following the failure of his father's business, the entire Nakano family had moved to Tokyo, and, in order to support them, Nakano opened a boarding house for wealthy Chinese students. The income from this venture enabled Nakano to complete his studies, support his parents and three siblings, and even to travel to Manchuria during his vacations in 1908. He graduated in 1909 with a senior thesis on China.

Following graduation, Nakano became a journalist, first briefly at the *Nichi Nichi Shinbun* and later at the more prestigious *Asahi Shinbun*, where he soon made a name for himself with his outspoken political commentaries. Many of the articles that Nakano published during his writing career were so popular that they were subsequently republished as books, earning him both fame and money. This success, however, bred arrogance in Nakano and envy among his colleagues, leading to Nakano's isolation at the newspaper.

In 1911, together with Inukai Tsuyoshi (1855–1932) and Tōyama, Nakano traveled to China to cover the Chinese revolution for the *Asahi*. Unlike many of his contemporaries, he supported the Chinese Revolution in his dispatches on the grounds that it was a popular rising against a corrupt regime.

The Japanese government's failure to support the Chinese Revolution and the outcome of events there greatly disappointed Nakano. Back in Japan, perhaps because he was affected by the death of the Meiji Emperor, Nakano returned to a project that he had started before leaving for China—a study of the People's Rights Movement in the Meiji period. In a series of articles under this title, Nakano argued that the Meiji Restoration was still unfinished and that the task of its completion had been left to future generations. He had just finished the series in 1912 when Japan's political world was shaken by the Taishō political crisis, when an upsurge of popular protest known as the "Movement to Protect the Constitution" forced the resignation of the third Katsura Tarō cabinet.

From the beginning Nakano had seen journalism, or writing in general, as a way of expressing his political views. This politicization of his position at the *Asahi* reached a climax during the Taishō political crisis, as Nakano virtually monopolized the political pages of the newspaper to attack the government. Already isolated within the *Asahi*, his arrogance cost him all his remaining support, and soon afterward the management dispatched him to Seoul, Korea (1913), to be followed by a year of study in Britain. Before his departure, Nakano married the daughter of Miyake Setsurei (1860–1945), editor in chief of the influential nationalistic monthly *Nihon oyobi Nihonjin* (Japan and the Japanese).

Nakano remained in Korea for nineteen months, writing articles critical of Japan's heavy-handed colonial policy. He also traveled extensively throughout Korea and Manchuria. While in Korea he met Tokutomi Sohō (1863–1957; see I:28), with whom he formed a lifelong friendship. In 1915, Nakano traveled to Britain. It was during this trip that his pan-Asianist views acquired a strong anti-Western dimension (see Nakano's description of the trip quoted here). Nakano's stay in England disappointed him so much that he cut it short, retuning to Japan in 1916.

Back home, Nakano quit the *Asahi* and took up a post with the monthly *Tōhō Jiron* (Eastern Review), where in his editorials he supported the violent Rice Riots of 1918, the Russian October Revolution, and Chinese unification while opposing the Twenty-One Demands (1915) and the Siberian Intervention (1918). Among his most popular pieces was his highly critical coverage of the Paris Peace Conference of 1919, which helped increase the circulation of the magazine threefold.

It was at this time that Nakano joined various study groups and think tanks, such as the Tōhōkai (Eastern Society), the Rōsōkai (Old and Young Society), and the Kaizō Dōmei (Reconstruction League), an organization dedicated to liberal-style reform within the existing constitutional structure (e.g., universal suffrage and recognition of trade unions). He also made his first attempt at entering politics by running for a seat in the Diet in the general election of 1917. Though he failed on this occasion, Nakano would be successful in the following election of 1920—and thereafter was reelected continuously until his death in 1943.

With his election to the Diet, Nakano became financially secure. From 1920 onwards, he pursued the dual and mutually supportive career of journalist and Diet politician. He acted as editor in chief of several magazines and one newspaper, frequently contributing articles to other periodicals and newspapers. As in the past, he would travel frequently to Asia (mostly East Asia) and also to Europe, where in 1937 he met Mussolini and Hitler.

Counted among the younger generation of politicians advocating reform and national reconstruction, Nakano initially remained independent from the three established parties, joining instead the Independents' Club (Mushozoku Kurabu) in 1921, which combined the following year with the Kokumintō (led by Inukai) to form the Kakushin Kurabu (Renovation Club). Realizing that in order to gain any position of power he would have to affiliate himself with one of the major parties, in 1924 he joined the Kenseikai (Association of Constitutional Politics) and specifically the faction headed by Adachi Kenzō (1864–1948), which was known for its interest in Chinese affairs and the fact that it did not include any imperial university graduates.

Entering the Kenseikai was a move closer to power, but it was also a move closer to the establishment and demanded some degree of conformity as a price. Still, more often than not, Nakano would take radical positions on issues such as universal manhood suffrage, relations with the Soviet Union (traveling there in late 1925), and especially the Peace Preservation Law (1925), which he strongly opposed. These radical views were sufficient to maintain Nakano's rugged rebel image and made him the target of various right-wing thugs. Luckily, this was offset by Nakano's dexterity with words and his powerful skills as an orator. These skills soon led to his appointment as head of the party's propaganda section. When the Kenseikai transformed itself into the Rikken Minseitō in 1927, Nakano was responsible for drafting the party program.

Nakano gained his greatest fame, however, for taking on General Tanaka Giichi (1864–1929), head of the Seiyūkai and later prime minister. When, after the resignation of the Tanaka cabinet in 1929, the Minseitō's Hamaguchi Osachi (1870–1930) formed a successor cabinet, Nakano had good grounds to hope that he would be rewarded with an important ministerial position. Instead he was offered only the position of parliamentary vice minister in the Ministry of Communications. Swallowing his disappointment, he accepted this post and over the next eighteen months spent long hours at the Ministry formulating plans for the privatization of the expanding telephone industry. By the time the plan was ready for submission to the cabinet in late 1930, Premier Hamaguchi had been shot and was replaced by Foreign Minister Shidehara Kijūrō (1872–1951), who shelved it. In protest, Nakano resigned.

This event marked the end of his attempts to gain political influence within the established political structure and the beginnings of a transformation that was to last until roughly 1935, when Nakano would take a position closely resembling European-style fascism. During this period, Nakano moved closer to the army (particularly to Ishiwara Kanji, one of the architects of the Manchurian Incident; see II:22) and experimented with new methods of mass-based political mobilization.

The first step in this process was Nakano's breakaway from the Minseitō at the end of 1931. The deeper motivation for this move was a disagreement over matters of policy. While the Minseitō leaders still upheld the principles of laissez-faire economics, Nakano was convinced of the futility of these policies in dealing with the consequences of the Great Depression and demanded a strong interventionist policy by the state. He similarly argued for a hard line in foreign affairs, lavishing high praise on the architects of the Manchurian Incident. To these ends he demanded the creation of a strong government. It was when the attempt to create such a government by forming a coalition between the Seiyūkai and the Minseitō failed that Nakano and other members of the Adachi faction left the Minseitō in protest.

During 1932 this group set out to form an independent political party named the Kokumin Dōmei (National League). Although officially headed by Adachi Kenzō, Nakano drafted the party's program (emphasizing international justice and economic controls) and decided that party members should wear uniforms and armbands similar to those worn by European fascists. From the beginning, other party members' enthusiasm for mass mobilization was lukewarm (Adachi refused to wear a uniform on the grounds that it looked silly), and when the sense of crisis in Japan eased in early 1933, the Kokumin Dōmei soon ran out of steam. Nakano remained a member for another two years, resigning in 1935 in protest over Adachi's decision to support the Okada Keisuke cabinet.

After leaving the Kokumin Dōmei, Nakano set out to form a mass-based protofascist party on his own. To this end he transformed the Tōhōkai think tank (the members of which included Waseda University's Professor Sugimori Kōjirō (1881–1968), China expert and former Japanese ambassador to Germany Honda Kumatarō (1874–1948), and General Ishiwara Kanji (1889–1949; see II:22) into a political party and turned the monthly magazine *Gakan* (Our Views) into the party's organ under the name *Tōtairiku* (Eastern Continent). After Nakano's meetings with Mussolini and Hitler in 1937–1938, the Tōhōkai's fascist tendencies received even more emphasis—members wore uniforms, a youth organization was founded, and mass rallies were organized, eventually attracting over 100,000 people. Party membership increased dramatically, partly through organic growth but also by absorbing labor and farmer unions; the process came to a halt only when the party was dissolved in 1940 and incorporated into the Imperial Rule Assistance Association (IRAA).

Ideologically, Nakano's position also underwent an important shift. If previously he had advocated domestic reform as a precondition for dealing with international problems, in the second half of the 1930s this order was reversed. Now he saw the reconstruction of the international order—if necessary, by military force—as a means by which Japan's domestic structure could be reformed. War and the mobilization of the masses that this necessitated was the process by which the Japanese people, together with their continental Asian brethren, were to be emancipated. This fundamental shift was reflected in Nakano's advocacy of an economic bloc—initially including only Japan, Manchuria, and China but eventually all of East Asia—but also in his pressing for a rapprochement with Nazi Germany and fascist Italy, with the goal of forming an anti–status quo camp consisting of the "have-nots" in opposition to the "haves"—the Anglo-Saxon powers.

It was against this background that Nakano tried to promote the Tōhōkai as the nucleus of a national party that Prince Konoe Fumimaro (see I:32) sought to create to mobilize Japan for the war effort in 1939–1940 and that eventually led to the creation of the IRAA in 1940. Despite some spectacular successes (party membership topped 22,000 in 1941, and many of the policies that Nakano had advocated, such as the southern advance or the forming of an alliance with Germany and Italy, were implemented), Nakano's hopes that Konoe would use the Tōhōkai as a means of mobilizing and transforming Japan from below remained unrealized. Konoe did not bring Nakano into his cabinet, offering him instead a position in the IRAA. Aware that the IRAA lacked the political character that he had hoped for, serving only as a channel to communicate the will of the government to the people, Nakano resigned from the IRAA board of directors and revived the Tōhōkai as a cultural society in March 1941.

This marked the beginning of the final phase of his life, characterized by opposition to General Tōjō Hideki (1884–1948), prime minister from 1941 to 1944. If Nakano had previously advocated economic controls, he opposed them now that they were being implemented by the bureaucracy. Likewise Nakano also came to oppose Tōjō's conduct of the war. He had advocated the advance of Japan into Southeast Asia, arguing that while the European colonial powers were busy fighting Germany, their Asian colonies were ripe for the picking. Nakano's argument, however, had been premised on the assumption that the United States could be kept out of the conflict, an assumption rendered meaningless by the attack on Pearl Harbor in December 1941.

Following the Japanese defeats at Midway and Guadalcanal in 1942 and 1943, Nakano concluded that Japan had lost the war and should sue for peace. This brought him into head-on conflict with Premier Tōjō, who was determined to fight to the end. In the ensuing power struggle, Nakano was first prohibited from publishing, then from speaking in public, and was eventually arrested in October 1943, along with many Tōhōkai members. The night after his release, Nakano committed ritual suicide, *seppuku*, at his house. Despite efforts by the Tōjō government to limit numbers at his funeral, over 20,000 people turned out to pay their last respects.

Nakano's Pan-Asianism was of a piece with his general views on society, characterized by a strong antiestablishment, at times even revolutionary element. In that sense Nakano was as much pan-Asian as he was anticolonial, with the notable exception of Japanese colonialism. The notion that when waging war in Asia, Japan was fighting not Asians but the Western colonial powers (especially Britain) formed an integral part of Nakano's thinking from the Paris Peace Conference onwards. That being said, his position stands out in two important respects when compared to other Japanese pan-Asian thinkers.

First, Nakano's pan-Asian views were based on a universal humanism and hence were free of explicit racism. Thus, he opposed "Anglo-Saxon" interference in Asian affairs because he saw it as the root of political and economic injustice, not because the "white race" was inferior to Asians. Likewise, he never embraced the notion that the superiority of the Yamato race could legitimize Japanese domination over other Asians. If Japan shouldered the mission to liberate Asia, this was because continental Asians were the equals of the Japanese, not because they were inferior. On various occasions Nakano criticized older pan-Asianists for their racism and hatred for all "white" nations. He contrasted these views with those of Sun Yat-sen (see II:5), who was free of racism and ready to make common cause with ostracized European nations against the imperial powers. This attitude exposed him to criticism from the Japanist rightists.

Second, the concept of the sacredness of the emperor and the imperial household, or the idea that sovereignty lay with the emperor—political notions fundamental to prewar Japan—were largely absent from Nakano's thinking. Deprived of that foundation, related concepts, such as the belief in the invincibility of the Yamato spirit and the ideology of *kokutai* (national polity), never gained a foothold in his writings.

The first of the two texts translated here describes Nakano's reactions to the impressions gained during his first trip to Europe (1915). It is typical of Nakano's writings in its strong appeal to emotion and empathy with the oppressed peoples of Asia and the indignation born out of it. It is also typical in that, for all the pathos of his prose, Nakano remains sober and aloof from any notion of Japanese superiority. The second text is based on a speech delivered in the immediate aftermath of the attack on Pearl Harbor and published by the Tōhōkai. While explaining the pan-Asian ideas of the association, it shows the reverse side of Nakano's indignation and resentment against the Western colonial powers—the exhilaration produced by Japan's bold attack on them and the formidable prospects this seemed to open up.

Source 1 (translations from the Japanese original by Stefano von Loë)
Nakano Seigō, "Bōkoku no Sanga" (The Mountains and Rivers of a Fallen State), *Sekai Seisaku to Kyokutō Seisaku* (Global and Far Eastern Policy). Shiseidō Shoten, 1917, 326–328, 396–398.

Between our departure from Kobe and our arrival in Marseilles, all the countries we visited had been either destroyed or half destroyed. Moreover, the people of all those devastated countries all subscribe to the intellectual, emotional and cultural traditions of the colored races, while their masters, who have conquered and are now exploiting them, all belong to the white races, which are different from us and our forefathers and hold different religious beliefs. We hold no grudge against the white people and we openly accept their teachings without reluctance. However, just as they have a word called humanity, we too have a concept of humanism. If they really wanted to realize their lofty rhetoric, they would not permit any injustice based on race. Thus the account of my voyage to Europe has unexpectedly turned into a lyric poem condemning racial prejudice. . . .

I have traveled thousands of miles since leaving my own country. From onboard ship in the middle of the ocean I look up at the clear moon, but whenever I go on land I see the traces of the rise and fall [of nations]. At times this is unbearably sad, at times unbearably delightful. When I see a people that shares my customs and beliefs, unable to walk on this earth in freedom, I cannot suppress secret tears of sympathy welling up inside me. However, when these, our cursed, colored relatives rise up, yearning for leadership from our quarter and hoping for our tide to rise, I cannot suppress a secret smile of satisfaction. What did I really see in Shanghai, Hong Kong, Singapore, Malaya, and further south in Colombo? What is the fate of the country that once produced someone like Confucius? What is the present state of affairs of the Malay people who once used to sleep peacefully in the shade of the trees? What has happened to the descendants of the people who brought Buddha into this world? They are the wheels on the road, while the passengers all have fair skin and blue eyes. Those in front of the car being whipped, and those covered with dust from its wheels, are all colored people like ourselves. I do not mean to criticize the white people, I simply wish to describe the situation of the weak. . . . What sins have the people of India—who won't even eat meat—and the people of Malaya (who, enjoying the shade of the trees, have never known war) committed to deserve being reduced to their present condition? Alas, they are free of sin. Their only sin lies in the fact that they are weak. Representing the Powers, Bernhardi [German General Friedrich von Bernhardi (1849–1930), who wrote on geopolitical and military affairs prior to World War I and was notorious for his bellicose attitudes and writing style] once said that of all the sins in this world, the worst sin for a nation lies in being weak. They [i.e., the people of Asia] have truly come to this pass on account of their being weak. To whom can they appeal today? Only to that youthful empire in the East [i.e., Japan]. However, all it can do is take pity on them. When, taking pity, we walk amongst them, you feel as if even the people on the roadside are demanding that we provide them with comfort. If you stop to talk to the more ambitious amongst them, you will realize that they look up to us, that they want to learn from us and then rise up. . . . No need to worry! Being bullied by a strong person is a shame, but being idolized by a weak person is an honor. . . .

In centuries to come, the people of Buddha and the people of Confucius will either recover their former drive or—after having risen up and been defeated, having gone forward and then backward—they will be destroyed by oppression at the hands of the white people. . . .

In order to create a new paradise in the economic sphere and to do away with oppression by other races, we must bring the races of the East and the West to the same level. That mission rests upon our shoulders.

Source 2 (translations from the Japanese original by Stefano von Loë)
Nakano Seigō, "Kono Issen: Kokumin wa ika ni Tatakaubeki ka!" (This One War—How the People Should Fight!), Tōhōkai, Tokyo, January 1942, 13–16.

Now that we have entered a long-term war, how should Japan strengthen the Greater East Asian Co-Prosperity Sphere and oppose the roundabout encroachment of Britain and America, while at the same time establishing a Greater Asia together with the other Asian peoples? (applause) Yes, gentlemen, through this single blow, the feelings of the East Asian people have changed. Although the Tōhōkai has previously held conferences bringing together the leaders of the East Asian people, as long as Japan was fighting solely against China the emotions of the East Asian people were disengaged. However, when the war we were fighting ceased being seen as a war against China and came to be seen as a war against Britain and America, its popularity among the East Asian peoples increased dramatically. The representative of Turkey, 93-year old Mr. Ibrahim [see I:19], Mr. Pratap from India [see II:9], Mr. Bose from India [see I:24], and the youth representatives from Indonesia, present here today—all these people experienced a surge of emotion which they would not have felt possible during our last conference. (applause) Their respect, trust and affection towards Japan has moved them in unexpected ways. (applause) . . . Through this single blow, Japan has already secured a victory in East Asia's ideological war. (applause) She has captured the hearts of the East Asian people. One hundred years after the Opium War, on this deplorable centennial of British rule over Hong Kong, the cannons of the [Japanese] Imperial Army are fixed on Hong Kong, and the people of China, the people of India, and all the peoples of Asia are rising up spontaneously to shout their *banzai*! (applause) . . . Not only India, but also Iran and Iraq share Japan's ambition and hope to escape the reactionary control exerted by Britain and America. (applause) Ideological warfare precedes military warfare. The ideological army is the advance guard of the Imperial Army and it has already attacked America's foothold and lunged at Britain's throat. . . . If Japan can gain control of the resources of Greater East Asia, its tin, its rubber, its iron, its manganese, its endless supply of foodstuffs, and—with a little patience—its petroleum wells also, then we can wage a long-term war for as long as we want. (applause) Then America will suffer an economic embargo at Japan's hands. (applause) Then Britain will be deprived of her military supplies by Japan. (applause) If the Imperial Army can occupy the most strategic sites in Greater East Asia and defend them, then the mobilization of Asia's resources comes within sight, does it not? (applause) . . . We are delighted. Once in ten years we can rejoice from the bottom of our hearts without a second thought. (applause and shouts) We can laugh out loud, can we not? (applause and shouts) Gentlemen, a man who cannot show anger when he is angry can only put on a bitter smile when he should be laughing out loud. Let us laugh happily (applause and shouts), because we deserve to laugh.

Chapter Two

The Yūzonsha's "War Cry," 1920

Christopher W. A. Szpilman

A series of major upheavals both abroad (World War I, the Bolshevik Revolution, the republican revolutions in Germany and Austria-Hungary, and the emergence of the United States as the world's dominant power) and at home (the Rice Riots of August 1918 and the formation of the Seiyūkai party cabinet led by Hara Takashi) provided a dramatic setting for the founding in August 1919 of a radical pan-Asianist organization known as the Yūzonsha (The Society of Those Who Yet Remain).

The Yūzonsha's antecedents go back to 1915, when Mitsukawa Kametarō (1886–1936; see Szpilman 2007), the editor in chief of the monthly *Dai Nihon* (Greater Japan), formed a discussion group on current affairs. Under the impact of the worldwide turmoil unleashed by World War I, this group was reorganized and renamed itself the Rōsōkai (Old and Young Society) in October 1918.

The Rōsōkai was a debating society, not an association that could engage in political activism. Though it is sometimes described as a pan-Asianist body, Pan-Asianism was not its ideology but merely one of many subjects discussed at its meetings. In fact, the Rōsōkai had neither a political program nor an ideological focus. No publications appeared under its imprint, and it eschewed political action. Its only discernible activity was regular, monthly lectures followed by discussion. Its members were drawn together not by ideological affinities but by their interest in current affairs, especially the rapidly changing international situation. They included rightists (e.g., Ōkawa Shūmei; see II:4; see also Szpilman 1998b) and leftists (e.g., Sakai Toshihiko) and military men both on active duty (who preferred to keep a low profile and so do not appear in the published members' lists, because soldiers and sailors on active duty were legally forbidden to join political associations) and in retirement (General Satō Kōjirō, 1862–1927, and Admiral Kamiizumi Tokuya, 1865–1946).

Though the Rōsōkai lacked an ideological focus, a high proportion of its leading members espoused pan-Asian views and went on to distinguish themselves in the pan-Asian movement in the 1920s and 1930s. Both Ōkawa, who having joined the body quickly became its leading light, and Mitsukawa were dissatisfied with the indefinite character of the Rōsōkai and on 8 August 1919 founded the Yūzonsha, an organization with a clear pan-Asianist and reformist agenda.

In addition to Mitsukawa and Ōkawa, the core members of the Yūzonsha included Kanokogi Kazunobu (1884–1949; see II:14), Nunami Takeo (1877–1927), Kasagi Yoshiaki (1892–1955), Shimonaka Yasaburō (1878–1961), Kanauchi Ryōsuke (1895–1966), Ayakawa Takeji (1891–1966), Yasuoka Masahiro (1898–1983; see II:29), Shimizu Kōnosuke (1895–1981), Iwata Fumio (1891–1943), and Nishida Mitsugi (1901–1937). Most of these men had also been associated with the Rōsōkai. The new organization complemented rather than superseded the Rōsōkai. The manifesto reproduced here stated clearly that the Yūzonsha would engage in political action.

Mitsukawa and Ōkawa asked pan-Asianist radical Kita Ikki (1883–1937; see I:27) to provide ideological leadership for the new organization. Kita, who, having accepted the invitation, arrived in Tokyo from his self-imposed exile in Shanghai in January 1920, moved into the Yūzonsha headquarters but on the whole kept aloof from its day-to-day activities—even if his quasi-totalitarian *Kokka Kaizō Hōan Daikō* (A Plan for National Reconstruction, 1919) did provide the society with some ideological guidance. The Yūzonsha illicitly circulated stenciled copies of this banned work, and its radicalizing influence apparently inspired right-wing activist Asahi Heigo (1890–1921) to assassinate the financier Yasuda Zenjirō (1838–1921). Copies of Kita's plan were also given to a number of young army officers, some of whom were involved in the military coups and terrorist acts that shook Japan in the 1930s.

The Yūzonsha had ambitious plans to spread its radical pan-Asianist and nationalist message to university students as an alternative to the liberal and democratic views propagated by Dr. Yoshino Sakuzō's Shinjinkai (New Men's Association), but this attempt to recruit Japan's future elite was not successful. Several branches were set up at universities, but they attracted only a small fraction of the student body.

The Yūzonsha also made efforts to spread its message to a wider audience by launching, in August 1920, a monthly journal, *Otakebi* (War Cry). The funds for the journal were provided by the financier Inoue Junnosuke (1869–1932), who, in an ironic twist of fate, was assassinated in 1932 by a right-wing terrorist partly inspired by Yūzonsha ideology. But even with Inoue's support, the journal turned out to be ephemeral: only three issues were printed, in small runs and at irregular intervals, before it folded up. Equally ineffectual were the Yūzonsha's efforts to publish books. Only a few pamphlets were published under its imprint, notably Ōkawa Shūmei's *Kakumei Yōroppa to Fukkō Ajia* (Revolutionary Europe and Asia in Revival, October 1922; see Ōkawa, 1993).

As mentioned, Ōkawa and Mitsukawa had founded the Yūzonsha to engage in political action, not to deal in words. Some action indeed ensued. In 1920 the Yūzonsha, alongside the Kokuryūkai (see I:10), was involved both in a successful campaign to prevent the annulment of the crown prince Hirohito's engagement to Princess Kuni Nagako (1903–2000) and in an unsuccessful campaign to prevent the crown prince's forthcoming European tour. Some Yūzonsha members engaged in violence (e.g., an attack on Saionji Hachirō [1881–1946], a court official who was Prince Saionji Kinmochi's son). However, this was about the sum of the group's activities, and one is forced to conclude that, in spite of all the talk, the Yūzonsha achieved little more than the Rōsōkai. This dearth of achievements may have been caused by a rift between Kita and Ōkawa, who, after a brief period of friendship, decided they could not stand each other. Ōkawa's enmity toward Kita may have been grounded in self-interest, for Ōkawa had by then realized that his own career was suffering because of his association with Kita, who had acquired a reputation for blackmail and extortion. But Ōkawa was also vexed by Kita's ad hominem attacks on Viscount Gotō Shinpei (1857–1929), Ōkawa's mentor, over his efforts to normalize Japan–Soviet relations (Szpilman 2002: 472).

Whatever the reason, the conflict between Kita and Ōkawa caused the dissolution of the Yūzonsha in March 1923, even if, for the sake of appearances, Kanokogi Kazunobu's departure for Germany provided a convenient pretext. The Rōsōkai too petered out more or less at the same time, though no official dissolution was announced.

Since the Yūzonsha was a body consisting of individuals, each with a mind of his own, it would be simplistic to assume that the society had a monolithic pan-Asian policy or that its members espoused a uniform set of pan-Asian ideas. That clearly was not the case. The leading members differed over the details and even over the scope of their Pan-Asianism. For instance, Kita limited his pan-Asian disquisitions largely to China, Manchuria, and Mongolia, even if on occasion he talked of the conquest of Australia. Ōkawa, by contrast, stretched his conception of Asia to areas that are conventionally included in Africa (Egypt) and Europe (the Balkans).

But if it is possible to generalize about the group of diverse individuals who formed the membership of the Yūzonsha, it can be safely asserted that, first of all, they agreed on what they hated. They despised Western (or as they would have put it, "Anglo-Saxon") civilization, which they regarded as the incarnation of materialism, egoism, hedonism, individualism, and such like; they despised ideals such as pacifism, liberalism, and democracy, which President Wilson propagated; they hated the idea of armament reductions; they despised the Japanese advocates of liberalism and democracy; they despised the established political parties, which reminded them too much of the Anglo-American system of governance; and, above all, they hated Western imperialism. From this perspective, they denounced the Treaty of Versailles (1919) and the League of Nations (1920) and condemned the Washington Treaties (1922). The Versailles–Washington treaty system, as they saw it, was designed to preserve the teetering imperialist status quo, perpetuated racial discrimination, and hypocritically prevented Japan from expansion on the Asian continent in pursuit of its pan-Asian mission to liberate Asia from the Western yoke.

Emphasis on domestic reform went hand in hand with the society's stress on Japan's pan-Asian mission. These two aspects of the Yūzonsha's program were inseparable (as the text reproduced here shows). Though the Yūzonsha's leading figures stressed the primacy of domestic reform, they all regarded domestic reforms as a precondition for the realization of a higher purpose: the liberation of Asia.

Second, all the members of the Yūzonsha without exception were ardent nationalists. This nationalism informed their sense of history, which they interpreted as an ongoing racial struggle between the peoples of color (representing Asia) and the whites (Ōkawa, Mitsukawa, and Ayakawa) or as a contest between the Western "have" states and "have-not," proletarian Japan (Kita and Kanokogi). Sometimes both views were held concurrently.

This nationalism also colored their Pan-Asianism, as is clear both from their axiomatic assumption that Japan would play a commanding role in the mission to liberate Asia that they envisaged and in their subsequent (post-Yūzonsha) writings (Ōkawa, Kanokogi, Mitsukawa, and so on) that justified Japanese expansion in China in terms of a pan-Asian mission.

Yet it would be wrong to regard the Yūzonsha's Pan-Asianism as mere window dressing for Japanese expansionism and racial supremacism. That this was not the case is apparent both in Mitsukawa's criticisms of Japanese colonial policy and in the Yūzonsha's quixotic commitment to propagate Esperanto as a lingua franca that would, the leaders of the organization somewhat naively hoped, facilitate the advent of Asian unity. Kita favored Esperanto because he thought the Japanese language was so difficult for foreigners to learn that it constituted a significant obstacle to the realization of Japan's pan-Asian mission (Wilson 1969). But Kita was not the only Yūzonsha member to promote this artificial language. Ga Minezō, too, was a well-known Esperanto enthusiast, and as early as October 1919 (i.e., several months before Kita's return to Japan), Fujisawa Chikao (1893–1962), who during the Pacific War was to gain notoriety for his rabid and narrow-minded nationalism, gave a talk at the Rōsōkai titled "The Origins of Esperanto."

This internationalist emphasis on Esperanto combined with the Yūzonsha's inherent nationalism formed an incongruous mix, but it was not the only paradox presented by the society.

Yūzonsha members' outlook on Japan's pan-Asian mission fluctuated between optimism and pessimism. Its leading members allowed themselves a degree of optimism because they had become convinced, possibly even before they read Oswald Spengler's *Der Untergang des Abendlandes* (The Decline of the West, 1917) and Lothrop Stoddard's *The Rising Tide of Color against White World-Supremacy* (1919), that World War I marked the beginning of the collapse of Western civilization, and consequently that Western imperialism and the Western domination of Asia was about to crumble. But, at the same time, they feared that Japan's party government would, by failing to reform the country rapidly enough, miss a golden opportunity to implement a pan-Asian mission of liberation that had presented itself as a result of the decline of Western power in the aftermath of World War I.

The Yūzonsha's concrete achievements may have been meager, but its influence was considerable. After its dissolution, most members (minus Kita) joined the Kōchisha (Society for Action on Earth), which was headed by Ōkawa. Officially the Kōchisha was founded in April 1925 with the appearance of the monthly *Nihon*, though meetings of a Kōchikai were held as early as January 1924. In 1926 several members, including Mitsukawa, Nakatani, and Ayakawa, resigned, mainly because of personal differences with Ōkawa Shūmei, but the Kōchisha managed to survive this schism. Under Ōkawa's leadership the Kōchisha expanded its membership and carried on the publication of *Nihon* until 1932. It collapsed only when Ōkawa was arrested for his involvement in the 1932 conspiracy to assassinate Prime Minister Inukai Tsuyoshi (May 15 Incident).

The enduring legacy of the Yūzonsha's Pan-Asianism was due to a number of factors. First, Ōkawa, Mitsukawa, Kanokogi, Nakatani, and Yasuoka were prolific writers who throughout the 1920s and 1930s published a veritable stream of popular pan-Asianist books and articles. Second, many of them pursued successful academic careers, which gave them a considerable advantage and provided them with a captive audience in propagating their pan-Asian views. Third, they were active in various pan-Asian organizations. Mitsukawa, for example, after he had quit the Kōchisha, was involved in the Kōa Gakujuku (Asian Revival Academy) and, after 1932, together with Kanokogi and Nakatani, played a important role in the pan-Asian Dai Ajia Kyōkai (see II:13). It was the activities of these members as much as the personal connections of Ōkawa Shūmei or Kita Ikki's political intrigues that ensured the relatively short-lived Yūzonsha's enduring influence as a pan-Asian organization—an influence that intensified in the 1930s.

Source (translation from the Japanese original by Christopher W. A. Szpilman; see also Wilson 1969: 98, for an alternative, somewhat abridged version of the same passage)
Foundation Principles of the Yūzonsha, *Otakebi*, October 1920.

The Eight Main Policy Planks of this Magazine:
The movement to build a great revolutionary empire
A creative revolution of the national spirit
Advocacy of a moral foreign policy
The formation of a great military state with the goal of liberating Asia
Coverage and critique of the reform situation in various countries
Propagating and popularizing Esperanto
[Serving] as a liaison organ for reformist movements
Spiritual training for comrades (*dōshi*) to turn them into pillars of the nation
Yūzonsha Associates

We publish "War Cry," determined to cast aside the pen.

Our decision to cast aside the pen is also a decision to take up the sword. The time has now come for Japan to fight a war to liberate slaves, both domestically and internationally. But this new history must be recorded in our own hot blood (*keiketsu*), not in ink. We, the Japanese people, must stand at the vortex of a tornado that is the war to free mankind from slavery. Accordingly, the Japanese state must serve as an absolute [standard] for forging our ideal of world revolution. [But] before we achieve this absolute goal, our God-given task is to realize the moral fulfillment of the Japanese state and prepare it for war. [For] the Japanese nation-state is about to realize the ideal of Martin Luther, who said that the state is an ethical institution.

The multiple dangers and difficulties that are staring us in the face do not afford us the luxury of shrinking from radical reform of the state organism and of shunning a creative revolution of the national spirit. Nor do we think it enough to limit reform and revolution to Japan alone. We want to liberate Japan first precisely because we in fact believe that the Japanese people are destined to become the great apostle of the war to liberate mankind. Our gods point toward China and India, and Vietnam, Burma and Siam which lie at the center of a circle formed by China, India and Australia. They point toward the plain through which the Tigris and Euphrates flow, and towards the area where the Nile empties into the sea—that is, to the areas where yellow and white races abut each other. The area where the most ancient human history was recorded will be where the Japanese people will write the latest human history. We must raise the Japanese people to turn it into a great Lincoln for the sake of 900 million Asian slaves.

The gods of the State of the Rising Sun will without fail take up the sword. Justice without the sword is after all an empty word. We will not add another empty argument to the many empty words that [already] fill the world. The present in particular is no time to govern a state by resorting to the written word.

Ōkawa Shūmei and Mitsukawa Kametarō

Chapter Three

Japan, Korea, and Pan-Asianism: The Dōkōkai, 1921

Sven Saaler

In 1919, an insurgency shook Japanese colonial rule in Korea (March 1 Movement) and undermined belief in the possibility of a union between Japanese and Korean "subjects of the emperor" (*shinmin*). Two years later, Uchida Ryōhei and other leaders of the Kokuryūkai (Amur Society; see I:10) founded a political association, the Dōkōkai (The Same Light Society), with the objective of improving the relationship between Japanese and Koreans and eventually bringing about equality of the two peoples.

When the Sinocentric system of international relations in East Asia began to disintegrate in the second half of the nineteenth century, the future position of Korea became one of the central questions for Japanese policymakers. While some pan-Asian thinkers, such as Katsu Kaishū (1823–1899) and Tarui Tōkichi (see I:5), argued for a more or less equal relationship—which, however, might also mean a union (*gappō*) with Korea—in most instances, Japanese policymakers used the Korea question (just as they had the Ryukyu question) as a lever with which to implement an anti-Chinese policy and destroy the close link between Korea and China. To that end, Japan continuously strove to increase its influence on the Korean peninsula, at times, also by resorting to force. After several military interventions, tensions between Japan and China over the Korean question resulted in the Sino-Japanese War of 1894–1895, which formally ended Chinese suzerainty over Korea and in practice put an end to the Sinocentric system.

Thus, at the beginning of the twentieth century Japan was in a position of strength in relation to Korea and China. Japan's military victories on the Asian continent had inspired a feeling of "national greatness" (Wilson 2005), implying the possibility of colonizing its weaker neighbors through a policy of Realpolitik within the framework of Western imperialism. In particular, the idea of annexing Korea acquired a new and increasing urgency at that time (Schmid 2002). This notion was based not so much on pan-Asian thought as on the political realism that had come to rule Japanese foreign policy. However, pan-Asian rhetoric was *instrumentalized* by constructing historical (and prehistorical) precedents of Korean–Japanese interrelatedness in order to legitimize the Japanese annexation of Korea. Although Japanese pan-Asianists were divided and did not unanimously favor the idea of annexation, only few eventually opposed the idea of a Japanese colonization of Korea, and even fewer openly raised their voices in protest. After all, the desirability of a close relationship between Korea and Japan was at the core of their thinking.

Most pan-Asianists, such as the members of the Kokuryūkai, believed that the annexation of Korea would lead to an equal union of the two nations that would be appreciated on both sides of the Tsushima Straits and would be advantageous for both Japanese and Koreans—or even for the security of East Asia as a whole. Kokuryūkai leader Uchida Ryōhei, who served as an adviser to the Japanese authorities in Korea, cooperated with Korean political activists to rally support for a Japanese annexation of Korea and served also as an adviser to the Korean Ilchinhoe (Japanese: Isshinkai, literally, Restoration Society; cf. Duus 1995).

Notwithstanding their efforts to secure annexation, members of the Kokuryūkai remained critical of the Japanese colonial administration in Korea after 1910, openly condemning Japanese colonial policies. Uchida criticized the policy of "enforcing the jurisdiction of the home country (*naichi*) in complete ignorance of [Korean] manners and customs (*fūzoku shūkan*)" (Yamanokuchi 1996: 158). The rejection of the government's Korea policies reached a new climax in 1919 after the beginning in Korea of the March 1 Movement (*san ichi undō*), an independence movement that was brutally suppressed by the military police (*kenpeitai*) and other units of the Japanese army. Uchida and other Kokuryūkai members believed that the obvious discontent of Koreans with their having to become "Japanese" (or, rather, subjects, *shinmin*, of the Japanese emperor) but not having the same constitutional rights as the population of the Japanese islands needed to be addressed. However, the changes in colonial policies made by the Government-General of Korea (Chōsen Sōtokufu) under its new governor Admiral Saitō Makoto (1858–1936), from "military rule" (*budan seiji*) to "cultural rule" (*bunka seiji*), failed to rectify the grave problems of Japanese colonial rule in Korea. In an attempt to address the situation, in 1921 Uchida and his associates Sugiyama Shigemaru, Tōyama Mitsuru, and Professor Terao Tōru, with the support of public figures not hitherto associated with the Kokuryūkai, such as former Prime Minister Ōkuma Shigenobu, founded the Dōkōkai. The proclaimed objective of this organization was to bring Japanese and Koreans closer together and establish "real" equality between the Korean (Choson) and Japanese subjects of the emperor.

The Dōkōkai directed harsh criticism at the government's colonial policies, but it nevertheless remained committed to strengthening Japanese colonial rule in Korea and did not consider Korean independence an option. Although Uchida at times went as far as claiming the necessity of "domestic self-governance" (*jichi*) by Koreans, the society never won much support in Korea. In Japan also, although it earned some reputation as a critic of government policy, the Dōkōkai remained virtually without influence. The story of the formation of the society and the statements made on the occasion of its founding reprinted here are, however, proof of the intense debate within Japan over the direction of Japanese colonial policy in Korea and testify to the grave problems faced by the Japanese colonial government, which had failed to address even the most basic needs of its colonial subjects. The pan-Asian rhetoric of "Asian brotherhood" and "one harmonious (Asian) family" held together by "racial bonds," which stood at the center of the Dōkōkai's policies, could not gain traction while concrete, practical manifestations of pan-Asian "solidarity" were entirely lacking.

The source reproduced here is an article documenting the founding of the Dōkōkai that appeared in the Kokuryūkai's English-language journal *The Asian Review* in 1921, while a Japanese version of this article was published in *Ajia Jiron* (Asian Review), the Japanese-language journal of the Kokuryūkai (for the journals published by the Kokuryūkai, see Saaler 2008b). It describes the Dōkōkai as an association whose purpose was "to bring about equality between Koreans and Japanese" and outlines the association's main goals.

Source (English in the original)
The Dokokai. An Association for Bringing about Equality between Koreans and Japanese. *The Asian Review* 2:3 (March–April 1921), 277–79.

An important association has recently come into being in this country, which aims at the abolition of all discrimination between Japanese and Koreans. It has been organized under the auspices of Marquis Okuma; Messrs. Kunisuke Okazaki, and Heikichi Ogawa, leaders of the Seiyukai; Messrs. Hironaka Kono, and Katsuundo [Katsundo] Minoura, leaders of the Kenseikai; Mr. Naohiko Seki, leader of the Kokuminto; Prince Fumimaro Konoe; Mr. Teiichi Sugita, member of the House of Peers; Messrs. Mitsuru Toyama, and Ryohei Uchida; Dr. Giichi Soyejima, and other influential men in various spheres of activity. Therefore, it is not too much to say that this new and important association is representative of national thought and has the support of the nation behind it. Furthermore, among the promoters of the association there are many influential Koreans, including Boku Jikei and other literati.

The prospectus of the Association reads in substance as follows:

"The basic principle of the annexation of Korea, on the part of Japan, was to establish equality between the two nations, it being quite foreign to Japan's intention to discriminate against Korea; while on the part of Korea, it was the desire of her people to share equally in the honours as well as the blessings and welfare of Japan, with the Japanese nation. The supreme aims and aspirations held in common by the two peoples were to have been realised through mutual understanding and trust in pursuance of the dictates of geographical and historical relations, so as to establish an example of cooperation between Asiatic nations, on the one hand; and on the other, to safeguard peace in the Far East as well as civilization in the world. This is shown in unequivocal terms in the records of the annexation of Korea.

"Unfortunately, however, the Japanese and Koreans, who should be one family, do not yet enjoy harmony and unity, the trend of events threatening to go counter to the spirit in which the annexation was accomplished, and its aims and aspirations. The urgent task, therefore, for Japan and Korea is to bring themselves into a harmonious whole and act in perfect brotherhood, so as to give effect to the spirit of the annexation. This is the reason why we have undertaken to organise the Dokokai, an association for bringing about equality between Japanese and Koreans. It is our sincere desire that both Japanese and Koreans who have the promotion of the welfare of the two peoples at heart, shall lend their valued assistance to us and make the Japanese and Koreans into one harmonious family, by doing away with maladministration and dispelling misunderstandings, in accordance with the dictates of justice and humanity. . . ."

The Dokokai has its headquarters in Tokyo with branches in Seoul and other important centers of Korea and Japan. It is intended to bring about the thorough unification and harmony of the Japanese and the Koreans by means of racial bonds. It proposes to undertake the following enterprises:

1. The investigation of the current administration in Korea and the submission of proposals for its improvement and reform.
2. The safeguarding of human rights equally for the Koreans as for the Japanese.
3. The encouragement and dissemination of education in Korea.
4. The purification of religious circles.
5. The study of the ancient history bearing upon the old relations between Korea and Japan.

6. The establishment of organs for giving relief and employment to Koreans who are in need of them, as well as for social reunion between the Koreans and the Japanese.
7. The taking of adequate measures for appreciating the Koreans who have rendered meritorious services; and for redressing the Korean wrongs.
8. The encouragement of moral culture among the Koreans by giving due honor to those Koreans who have distinguished themselves in filial piety, or other virtues.
9. The encouragement and protection of the Korean students in Japan.
10. The publication of the transactions of the Association.

The inaugural meeting of the Association was held on February 3 at the Tsukiji Seiyoken Hotel, Tokyo. It was attended by about three hundred persons, including Koreans. . . .

Chapter Four

Ōkawa Shūmei: "Various Problems of Asia in Revival," 1922

Christopher W. A. Szpilman

Ōkawa Shūmei (on Ōkawa in general, see Ōtsuka 1995; Szpilman 1998b; Takeuchi 1969) was born in 1886 in Sakata, Yamagata Prefecture, the son of a physician. He attended the Fifth Higher School in Kumamoto, after which he went on to study Indian philosophy with the famous scholar of Buddhism, Anesaki Masaharu (1873–1949), at the Faculty of Literature, Tokyo Imperial University. There he also attended lectures by the art historian and pan-Asianist thinker, Okakura Tenshin (see I:7 and I:8). Although Okakura's Pan-Asianism must have influenced him, both in *Fukkō Ajia no Shomondai* and in his postwar autobiography, Ōkawa traces the awakening of his Pan-Asianism to his chance discovery of Sir Henry Cotton's (1845–1915) *New India* (originally published in 1889): the book transformed him "from a complete cosmopolitan into an Asianist" (Ōkawa 1961: 804). By 1915 Ōkawa was involved in assisting Indian independence fighters taking refuge in Japan. One of them was Rash Behari Bose (see I:24), who introduced him to Mitsukawa Kametarō (1888–1936), the founder of the Rōsōkai (Old and Young Association), a study group with a vaguely renovationist orientation. In 1919 Ōkawa and Mitsukawa, dissatisfied with the unfocused nature of the Rōsōkai, founded the explicitly pan-Asian Yūzonsha (Society of Those Who Yet Remain; see II:2).

After the Yūzonsha disintegrated in 1923 as the result of a personality clash between Ōkawa and Kita, in 1925 Ōkawa founded the relatively long-lived Kōchisha (Society for Action on Earth) and wrote regular contributions for that body's monthly publication, *Nihon* (Japan). *Nihon* continued to be published until 1932.

Ōkawa's activities in the right-wing (reformist) movement were helped by the fact that, in 1919, he obtained a well-paid job at the prestigious Research Institute (Chōsabu) of the South Manchurian Railway Company (Minami

Manshū Tetsudō Kabushiki Kaisha), which gathered and analyzed political and economic information on Asia (Kobayashi 2005). He was so good at his job that by 1927 he had been promoted to the head of the by now independent institute. In addition to doing research, Ōkawa was also a teacher. In 1921 he became a professor at Takushoku University (Colonial University—briefly known at that time as Tōyō Kyōkai Daigaku, or Oriental Association University)—and also taught concurrently at the Shakai Kyōiku Kenkyūjo (Institute of Social Education, known subsequently as the Daigakuryō, or Great Learning Dormitory), located within the grounds of the Imperial Palace and patronized by notables such as Viscount Makino Nobuaki (1861–1949), Admiral Baron Yashiro Rokurō (1860–1930), and Colonel (later General Baron) Araki Sadao (1877–1966).

In 1926, Ōkawa's academic career received official recognition when he was granted the degree of doctor of philosophy by the faculty of law at his alma mater for a dissertation on the history of European chartered colonial companies. In addition to scholarly monographs, he also wrote prolifically for a popular audience, publishing throughout the 1920s an impressive number of relatively high-selling volumes such as *Shūkyō Genri Kōwa* (Lectures on the Principles of Religion, 1921), *Nihon Bunmeishi* (A History of Japanese Civilization, 1921), *Nihon oyobi Nihonjin no Michi* (The Way of Japan and the Japanese, 1926), and *Kokushi Gairon* (An Outline of the National History, 1929).

Neither his academic career nor his writing prevented Ōkawa from taking part in various political conspiracies and terrorist acts against the government. In 1932 he was arrested on charges of aiding and abetting the assassination of Prime Minister Inukai Tsuyoshi and sentenced to fifteen years in prison. After various amnesties, Ōkawa spent only sixteen months behind bars, and his criminal record caused no damage to his social standing. When he was released from prison in 1937, he was appointed dean of the newly established Faculty of Colonial Studies at Hōsei University. His books were now more popular than ever, and *Nihon 2600 Nenshi* (A History of Japan over 2600 Years, 1939) became a runaway best-seller. He continued to write and publish throughout the Pacific War, extolling the traditional virtues of Japan and lambasting the evils of Western civilization, Britain, and America.

After Japan's defeat in 1945, Ōkawa was arrested as a class A war criminal but was not tried by the Tōkyō War Crimes Tribunal. Because of his erratic behavior, he was placed under medical observation and eventually released on grounds of mental incompetence. He spent the rest of his life in relative seclusion, passing the time by translating the Koran into Japanese (1949) and working on his autobiography, *Anraku no Mon* (The Gate to Serenity). He died in 1957.

Though Ōkawa published on a wide range of topics that included Japanese and world history, philosophy, and religion, Pan-Asianism was a constant interest throughout his entire adult life. Although *Fukkō Ajia no Shomondai*, which appeared in 1922, was the first book inspired by his Pan-Asianism, Ōkawa went on to publish several other books and articles on the subject.

Fukkō Ajia no Shomondai must be read in the context of World War I and the revolutionary upheavals that followed in its wake. While in Europe Oswald Spengler and other pessimists may have despaired over the collapse of Western civilization in the aftermath of the war, Ōkawa and his associates in the Yūzonsha welcomed the West's decline. Like his comrade, Mitsukawa Kametarō in his *Ubawaretaru Ajia* (Stolen Asia, 1921), Ōkawa saw Europe's fall as a golden opportunity for Japan to pursue its "divine mission" to liberate Asia. The success of such a mission would, he insisted, be contingent on Japan's ability to reform its political structures. This insistence on the primacy of domestic reform was a salient characteristic of radical Pan-Asianism in Japan as advocated by Ōkawa, Mitsukawa Kametarō, and Kita Ikki (see I:27). For, without comprehensive reforms at home, Ōkawa and other pan-Asian radicals reasoned, Japan's challenge to the Western powers and the liberation of Asia were doomed to failure. Given the urgent necessity of such reform, *Fukkō Ajia*'s aim was to inform the Japanese public of the movements stirring throughout the length and breadth of Asia—India, Turkey, Central Asia, and so on—against white oppression and to demonstrate, first, that a golden opportunity for Japan on the Asian continent might be lost unless decisive reforms were introduced at home and, second, that the policy of the Japanese government in cooperating with the Anglo-Saxon powers at Versailles and Washington was mistaken.

Ōkawa, like other radicals, rejected Wilsonianism and despised the Versailles–Washington treaty system. He dismissed Wilson's "human way," "freedom," and "national self-determination" as hypocritical "slogans" made up by Anglo-Saxon imperialists to gain Asian support during the war (Ōkawa 1993: 164), and he condemned the League of Nations as a tool that the United States, Britain, and France had conjured up as a device to preserve the status quo (Ōkawa 1993: 40).

While deploring what he (and other radicals) regarded as the dilatoriness of the Japanese government in implementing the necessary reforms and assisting the various Asian independence movements, Ōkawa cast an admiring look at Bolshevik Russia, where Bolshevism provided the "greatest external stimulus to Asian revival" (Ōkawa 1993: 164). Ōkawa viewed the Bolsheviks as Japan's allies, a sympathy that had its origins in his own brand of Pan-Asianism. It was in Japan's interests to destroy the status quo—and the Bolsheviks, ever since they came to power, had been doing just that.

The Bolsheviks had been doing what the Japanese government should have been doing but had signally failed to do: assisting independence movements throughout Asia. In some quarters in Japan, the rise of Bolshevism had inspired fears that the revolution would spread to Japan. Ōkawa dismissed this fear. There was, as he saw it, no communist threat to Japan because Bolshevism—a phenomenon that had arisen in the West to address uniquely Western problems—was of no relevance to Japan or the rest of Asia, regions that were (in his view) historically completely different from the West. The Bolsheviks were the product of the West's own pathology, a specifically Western disease to which Japan, because of its own unique political and social structure, was impervious.

Ōkawa's positive assessment of the Bolsheviks was related to the remarkable breadth of his pan-Asian vision. In contrast to most earlier well-known Japanese advocates of Pan-Asianism, Ōkawa included in "his" Asia *western* Asia and even Islamic areas outside Asia, such as Egypt and parts of the Balkan Peninsula. This inclusion of western Asia forms a defining feature of Ōkawa's Pan-Asianism. In this Ōkawa was probably inspired by Mitsukawa's *Ubawaretaru Ajia*, which he praised enthusiastically in the introduction to *Fukkō Ajia* (Ōkawa 1993: 20) and which largely covers the same geographical areas as Ōkawa's book. But Ōkawa's brilliant style ensured that *Fukkō Ajia no Shomondai*, unlike Mitsukawa's book, was widely read. Ōkawa, whose pan-Asian ideas were influenced by Okakura Tenshin, Indian exile Rash Behari Bose, Paul Richard, Kita, and Mitsukawa, not only influenced in turn a number of Japanese pan-Asianists whom he took under his wing (e.g., Kasagi Yoshiaki) but also, thanks to his outstanding writing talents (where his real importance as a pan-Asianist lies), exerted a powerful influence on the Japanese public whose perceptions of Asia and Japan's mission in Asia were formed largely under the impact of his best-selling books.

Source (translation from the Japanese original by Christopher W. A. Szpilman)
Ōkawa Shūmei, *Fukkō Ajia no Shomondai*. Chūō Kōronsha, 1993 (originally published in 1922 by Daitōkaku), 23–26.

The Asian peoples (*minzoku*) must first of all obtain freedom. The Asia that obtains freedom must be completely and strongly unified. For some time to come, the most important problem that Asia will in fact confront is how to obtain its freedom and how to realize its unification. Today's Asia is Europe's slave. What problems can a slave have? What ideals can a slave hold? A slave is nothing but a machine made of flesh that obeys his or her master's wishes and works for his master's profit. That is why, in their true sense, the problems of Asia will only begin when Asia obtains its freedom.

Asia must rise as one and, first of all, throw off its enslavement. Asia has not always lain prostrate before Europe. Some Asian peoples possessed splendid cultures at a time when the English and the Germans were barbarians, eking out a living as hunters on the [European] plains. Some Asians were sailing the treacherous routes between the islands of the southern seas at a time when the Europeans were still hemmed within the narrow confines of Western Europe. Other Asian peoples trekked through the northern wastes to create a wonderful state in a land of extreme cold that had been considered unfit for human habitation. Heroes rising from amidst their ranks advanced out of Central Asia into Europe. They founded a state on the coast of the Black Sea and frequently crossed the Danube to threaten Eastern Europe.

Some Asians, moving with lightning speed, invaded Italy where, as a scourge of God, they made Western Europeans tremble in fear.

They demonstrated not only extraordinary powers of external expansion; internally, they also administered their home states through their unique political structures. They erected great walls and constructed vast canals that are without parallel anywhere in the world. They used the magnet earlier than the Europeans, invented the art of printing, and invented gunpowder and the gun. They created lofty literature, profound philosophy, and noble morality. Moreover, the great religions that exercise power over the minds of the peoples of the world all arose in Asia. That is why the Asians, whether seen from the point of view of their character as it manifests itself in history or from the perspective of their contributions to world culture, are in no way inferior to the Europeans.

But 300 years of military victories have given the Europeans self-confidence and pride, while 300 years of defeats have made the Yellow Men desperate and subservient.

The Russo-Japanese War, however, was a tocsin that sounded the self-awareness of Asia. Japan's victory in the Russo-Japanese War, moreover, marked the beginning of a new stage in world history. Our victory delivered the first blow to the people of the West who, for the previous 400 years, had never been defeated by a people of color. This was in fact the first stumble in their long victory march. At the same time the Asian peoples, who racially are the same as us, suddenly began to become self-aware. And not only the Asian peoples, but among every people suffering under the yoke of the Western powers resistance to them increased. For all the other Asian countries, it surpassed their wildest dreams that a small country of yellow people in the Far East (*kyokutō*) had stood up to and decisively defeated a state 60 times as large in area and three times as large in population, whose military power was feared by the entire world. Moreover, we made it possible for everyone to see what everyone had considered impossible. And this gave them the hope that "we too can do it."

Inevitably, this hope has manifested itself as an independence movement among the enslaved nations of Asia and as a state reform movement among those nations that nominally maintain their independence. It is not at all strange that Europe wants to suppress the independence of the nations that it has enslaved. The rise of the Asian peoples is the last thing Europe wanted. The history of the first twenty years of the twentieth century makes it abundantly clear that the European powers do not want a revival of Asia; that they do not want the introduction of a parliamentary system or the establishment of accountable governments in Asia. And why not? No sooner had the [Young] Turkish revolution [1908] succeeded and the old, exhausted state was replaced by a new, vibrant one than they did all they could to prevent [the Ottoman's Empire] development and, by means of the Italian-Turkish [1911–1912] and the Balkan wars [1912–1913], weakened its national power. Again, as the constitutional politics of Persia stood in the way of the ambitions of Russia and Britain, who wanted to partition the country into two, Persia's parliament was overthrown by foreign troops in an extremely brutal fashion.

When the Chinese revolutionaries, having adopted a new five-colored national flag [in 1912] to symbolize the fusion of the five races (*gozoku tōitsu*) of China [Chinese, Manchurians, Mongolians, Tibetans, and the Muslim Hui people], took steps to realize this ideal, Britain and Russia, which had occupied Inner Mongolia and wanted to gain control over China, were naturally unhappy about the Chinese revolutionaries' successes. Most sadly and shamefully, however, Japan, which should be acting as the leader of an Asian revival, became an instrument of British diplomacy. It helped ensure the success of Britain's divide-and-rule policy and spread the seeds of factional strife throughout China, causing an estrangement between Japan and China.

Thus even in recent times, the future of Asia has remained dark. Although there were faint stirrings of the Asian spirit demanding freedom and unity, aptly summed up in the phrase "Asia for the Asians," and desiring that they become the new ideals for Asia, developments on the international stage cast doubts on when these ideals would be realized.

Europe was still confident of its "holy mission" as ruler of the world and maintained its domination over Asia. Thus, the so-called "Asian question" in international relations boiled down to the question of exactly how the European powers would place Asia on the chopping board of their selfish interests, how they would cook it and how they would divide it up among themselves.

At this stage in the world-historical process the larger significance of the Russo-Japanese War [1904–1905] had not yet become clear. This was in fact clarified by the World War [that followed].

Chapter Five

Sun Yat-sen: "Pan-Asianism," 1924

Roger H. Brown

Born to commoner parents in Canton (Guangzhou or Guangdong) near Macau, Sun Yat-sen (Sun Zhongshan, in Japan referred to as Son Bun, 1866–1925) received a Christian education in Hawaii and studied medicine in Hong Kong. In 1894, Sun established his first revolutionary organization in Hawaii and succeeded in attracting enough overseas support that agents of the Qing (Ch'ing) court considered him worthy of their attention and seized him in London in 1896. Saved from deportation and likely execution by British intervention, he emerged with his revolutionary credentials bolstered and became the most well-known expatriate opponent of Manchu rule. By 1905, Sun had taken up residence in Japan, and when the Qing dynasty collapsed in 1912, it appeared he might soon lead a new republican China based on his Three Principles of the People: nationalism, democracy, and the people's livelihood. However, although briefly proclaimed president in 1911, Sun was forced to give way to the powerful military leader Yuan Shikai (Yuan Shih-k'ai, 1859–1916) and, by 1913, was once again exiled in Japan.

Yuan's death in 1916 made possible Sun's return to China, where he began working to strengthen his Nationalist Party (Guomindang [GMD], or Kuomintang). In 1923, frustrated by his inability to complete the revolution in a country fractured by petty military rulers and disillusioned with the lack of progress in improving China's standing with the imperialist powers, Sun turned to the newly established Soviet Union for material assistance. While not a Marxist, he sought to take advantage of Soviet support in order to address the organizational weaknesses of the GMD. Moreover, the rejection by Soviet leaders of tsarist claims on China resonated with Sun's increasingly anti-imperialist nationalism. Sun thus in 1923 arranged a marriage of convenience between the GMD and the Chinese Communist Party (CCP) that would last until his successor, Chiang Kai-shek, broke violently with the CCP on the cusp of establishing the Nationalist regime in 1927. Despite this fracturing of the alliance and the onset of endemic civil war between the GMD and CCP, both parties, as well as the Japanese-backed regime of Wang Jingwei (Wang Ching-wei, 1883–1944; see II:23), shared in using the memory of Sun to legitimize their respective claims to govern China.

Some Japanese also utilized Sun's memory and his ideas to articulate pan-Asian objectives, an endeavor facilitated by Sun's own Pan-Asianism and by his long-standing ties in Japan. Throughout the first two decades of the twentieth century, Sun received support from Japanese of divergent political ideologies, including the progressive Miyazaki Torazō (Tōten, 1877–1922; see I:11), the Genyōsha leader Tōyama Mitsuru (1855–1944; see I:3), and the party politician Inukai Tsuyoshi (1855–1932)—men who, despite their differences, incorporated pan-Asian elements into their respective agendas for Japan and its role in Asia (see Jansen 1954). Sun's enduring relations with these men were facilitated by the larger context of Western imperialism, resentment of white racism, and mutual belief in a revival of Asian civilization. However, any possibility of Sino–Japanese cooperation faded before Japan's own imperialist ambitions. Indeed, just as Sun defined Asian civilization and any renaissance thereof in Sinocentric terms and in line with his understanding of Chinese national interests, many Japanese took for granted the fundamental justness of their own empire and manifest destiny to lead Asia. The ultimate expression of this conceit came in the 1930s when Japanese used Pan-Asianism, including some of the same ideals articulated by Sun, in an effort to convince Chinese and other Asians to assume their proper position beneath the roof of an expanded Japanese Empire.

Nevertheless, in 1924 a mix of idealism and strategic considerations compelled Sun to continue to hope for accommodation between China and Japan in order to resist what he viewed as the larger threat of Western imperialism. Having recently brokered the GMD–CCP alliance and increasingly resentful of Western, particularly British, imperialism, he sought to convince Japanese to turn away from their imperialist ways and pave a path toward Sino–Japanese amity.

Leaving in his wake the intense hostility of the foreign community in Canton and Shanghai, Sun received the welcome of an honored guest in Japan and, on 28 November 1924, appeared before an audience at Kobe Prefectural Girls School to give one of his most famous addresses. Speaking in Chinese with a Japanese translation, Sun took as his subject Pan-Asianism (*Da Yaxiyazhuyi*, literally Greater Asianism) and restated his fundamental belief in the superiority of Asian culture and civilization, which he defined in Sinocentric terms based on the Confucian dualism of the Kingly Way (Chinese: *wangdao*; Japanese: *ōdō*), or rule through benevolence, and the Despotic Way (Chinese:

badao; Japanese: *hadō*), or rule through force. Determining the relative virtue of Western nations based on their attitude toward China, he characterized these states as products of a derivative, materialistic civilization epitomizing rule through force. In a manner clearly reflecting Sun's understanding of China's national interest, he thereby designated British imperialism in Asia as exemplifying Western despotism and portrayed the Soviet Union's renunciation of imperialist treaty rights as evidence of governance reminiscent of Asian benevolence. Turning to Japan, Sun praised his hosts for having mastered Western material power while continuing to bear the virtues of Asian civilization and for having thrilled Asians with their 1905 victory over tsarist Russia and thereby demonstrated the possibilities of Asian revival; however, in his famous closing line, Sun challenged Japanese to resist the temptation of the West's Despotic Way and to embrace the East's Kingly Way.

Indeed, Sun's idealization of the Kingly Way was so central to his discourse on Pan-Asianism that a contemporary English translation of his lecture by Sun's secretary and interpreter Tai T'ien-ch'ou took as its title "The Kingly Way" rather than "Pan-Asianism." The speech exemplifies the blend of idealism and opportunism often found in commendation of the Kingly Way in particular and of pan-Asian ideals in general. For while the sincerity of Sun's Pan-Asianism is generally accepted, his casting of the Bolsheviks as converts to Confucian benevolence and of Japanese as bulwarks against white imperialism—not to mention his omission of Japanese imperialism in China—dovetailed obviously with his geopolitical conception of the Chinese national interest as it stood in 1924.

The later irony of Sun's reliance on such terminology is likewise clear: within a decade of his death Japanese ideologues were presenting the Kingly Way as exemplifying the Asian political values that might serve as the philosophical foundation of the new state of Manchukuo (Duara 2003; Komagome 1994) and, moreover, as the principles by which to guide a larger reordering of international relations in East Asia. As the 1930s progressed, Japanese officials and intellectuals used pan-Asian rhetoric to legitimize an "Asian Monroe Doctrine," a "holy war" against the GMD and CCP, and a "New Order" for East Asia. In short, rather than an Asian revival in line with Sun's Sinocentrism, Japanese offered a Japan-centered Asia liberated from Western imperialism and placed under the "benevolent rule" of the Imperial Way. This history, remembered with stark emphasis on Japanese opportunism, has deflected sustained attention from Sun's Pan-Asianism and from the appeal of pan-Asian ideas among Chinese in the years prior to the 1930s.

The following translation of Sun's Kobe address appears in a compilation of his speeches and statements published in Shanghai in 1941. The book in question, titled *China and Japan: Natural Friends—Unnatural Enemies*, also includes a foreword and epilogue by Wang Jingwei and an appended pamphlet by General Itagaki Seishirō (1885–1948). Apparently translated by T'ang Leang-Li (1901–1970), an associate of Wang and compiler of the volume, the document largely accords with the postwar Japanese translation by historian Itō Teruo of a Chinese version found in Sun's collected writings (Son Bun 1974). The speech received wide coverage in Japan at the time, with reactions ranging from affirmation of Sun's indictment of white imperialism to criticism of his simplistic characterization of the materialistic West and spiritual East (see Chen and Yasui 1989). Although some newspaper articles covering the speech famously redacted Sun's closing challenge to Japan, the passage appears in the following version.

Source (English in the original)
Sun Yat-sen (1941), "Pan-Asianism." *China and Japan: Natural Friends—Unnatural Enemies*, Shanghai: China United Press, 141–51.

GENTLEMEN:—I highly appreciate this cordial reception with which you are honouring me to-day. The topic of the day is "Pan-Asianism" (*Dai Ajiashugi*), but before we touch upon the subject, we must first have a clear conception of Asia's place in the world. Asia, in my opinion, is the cradle of the world's oldest civilization. Several thousand years ago, its peoples had already attained an advanced civilization; even the ancient civilizations of the West, of Greece and Rome, had their origins on Asiatic soil. In Ancient Asia we had a philosophic, religious, logical and industrial civilization. The origins of the various civilizations of the modern world can be traced back to Asia's ancient civilization. It is only during the last few centuries that the countries and races of Asia have gradually degenerated and become weak, while the European countries have gradually developed their resources and become powerful. After the latter had fully developed their strength, they turned their attention to, and penetrated into, East Asia, where they either destroyed or pressed hard upon each and every one of the Asiatic nations, so that thirty years ago there existed, so to speak, no independent country in the whole of Asia. With this, we may say, the low water mark had been reached.

When Asia reached this point, the tide started to turn, and the turn meant the regeneration of Asia. It started thirty years ago when Japan abolished all the Unequal Treaties that she had entered into with the foreign countries. The day when the Unequal Treaties were abolished by Japan was a day of regeneration for all Asiatic peoples. After the abolition of her Unequal Treaties, Japan became the first independent country in Asia. The remaining countries, such as China, India, Persia, Afghanistan, Arabia, and Turkey were not independent, that is to say, they were still dominated, and treated as colonies, by Europe. Thirty years ago, Japan was also a colony of the European countries. But the Japanese were far-sighted. They realized that the only way to power was to struggle with the Europeans and to abolish all Unequal Treaties, which they did, thus turning Japan into an independent country. Since Japan has become an independent country in East Asia, the various nations in this part of the world have been buoyed up with a new hope. They realized that since Japan has been able to achieve her independence through the abolition of the Unequal Treaties, they could do the same. So once again they have mustered courage to conduct their various independent activities with the hope of shaking off the yoke of European restriction and domination and regaining their own rightful position in Asia. This has been the prevailing thought in Asia during the past thirty years, which indeed gives ground for optimism.

Thirty years ago the idea was different. Men thought and believed that European civilization was a progressive one—in science, industry, manufacture, and armament—and that Asia had nothing to compare with it. Consequently, they assumed that Asia could never resist Europe, that European oppression could never be shaken off. Such was the idea prevailing thirty years ago. It was a pessimistic idea. Even after Japan abolished the Unequal Treaties and attained the status of an independent country, Asia, with the exception of a few countries situated near Japan, was little influenced. Ten years later, however, the Russo-Japanese war broke out and Russia was defeated by Japan. For the first time in the history of the last several hundred years, an Asiatic country has defeated a European Power. The effect of this victory immediately spread over the whole of Asia, and gave a new hope to all Asiatic peoples. In the year of the outbreak of the Russo-Japanese war I was in Europe. One day news came that Admiral Togo had defeated the Russian navy, annihilating in the Japan Sea the fleet newly dispatched from Europe to Vladivostok. The population of the whole continent was taken aback. Britain was Japan's Ally, yet most of the British people were painfully surprised, for in their eyes Japan's victory over Russia was certainly not a blessing for the White peoples. "Blood," after all, "is thicker than water." Later on I sailed for Asia. When the steamer passed the Suez Canal a number of natives came to see me. All of them wore smiling faces, and asked me whether I was a Japanese. I replied that I was a Chinese, and inquired what was in their minds, and why they were so happy. They said they had just heard the news that Japan had completely destroyed the Russian fleet recently dispatched from Europe, and were wondering how true the story was. Some of them, living on both banks of the Canal had witnessed Russian hospital ships, with wounded on board, passing through the Canal from time to time. That was surely a proof of the Russian defeat, they added.

In former days, the coloured races in Asia, suffering from the oppression of the Western peoples, thought that emancipation was impossible. We regarded that Russian defeat by Japan as the defeat of the West by the East. We regarded the Japanese victory as our own victory. It was indeed a happy event. Did not therefore this news of Russia's defeat by Japan affect the peoples of the whole of Asia? Was not its effect tremendous? While it may not have seemed so important and consequently have had only a slight effect on the peoples living in East Asia, it had a great effect on the peoples living in West Asia and in the neighborhood of Europe who were in constant touch with Europeans and subject to their oppression daily. The suffering of these Asiatic peoples was naturally greater than that of those living in the further East, and they were therefore more quick to respond to the news of this great victory.

Since the day of Japan's victory over Russia, the peoples of Asia have cherished the hope of shaking off the yoke of European oppression, a hope which has given rise to a series or independence movements—in Egypt, Persia, Turkey, Afghanistan, and finally in India. Therefore, Japan's defeat of Russia gave rise to a great hope for the independence of Asia. From the inception of this hope to the present day only 20 years have elapsed. The Egyptian, Turkish, Persian, Afghan, and Arabian independence movements have already materialized, and even the independence movement in India has, with the passage of time, been gaining ground. Such facts are concrete proofs of the progress of the nationalist idea in Asia. Until this idea reaches its full maturity, no unification or independence movement of the Asiatic peoples as a whole is possible. In East Asia, China and Japan are the two greatest peoples. China and Japan are the driving force of this nationalist movement. What will be the consequences of this driving force still remains to be seen. The present tide of events seems to indicate that not only China and Japan but all the peoples in East Asia will unite together to restore the former status of Asia.

Such a tendency is clearly evident to the eyes of Europe and America. One American scholar has written a book to discuss the rise of the coloured peoples [reference to Lothrop Stoddard's *The Rising Tide of Color against White World Supremacy*, 1920], where he maintains that Japan's defeat of Russia amounts to a victory of the Yellow race over the White race, and that such a tendency, if unchecked, will result in the unification of the entire Yellow race, which will be a calamity for the White peoples, and ways and means should therefore be devised to prevent it. Subsequently, he wrote another book in which he described all emancipation movements as Revolts against Civilization. In his view, emancipation movements in Europe should be regarded as revolts against civilization; even more so should such emancipation movements in Asia be regarded. Such views are common among the privileged classes of people in both Europe and America. A minority, they oppress the majority in their own continent or country. Now they wish to extend their evil practice to Asia, with a view to suppressing the nine hundred million people of Asia, and treating them as their slaves. This American scholar considers the awakening of the Asiatic peoples as a revolt against civilization. Thus, the Westerners consider themselves as the only ones possessed and worthy of true culture and civilization; other peoples with any culture or independent ideas are considered as Barbarians in revolt against Civilization. When comparing Occidental with Oriental civilization they only consider their own civilization logical and humanitarian.

From the aspect of cultural development during the last several hundred years, the material civilization of Europe has reached its height while Oriental civilization has remained stagnant. Outwardly, Europe is superior to Asia. Fundamentally, European civilization during the last several hundred years is one of scientific materialism. Such a civilization, when applied to society, will mean the cult of force, with aeroplanes, bombs, and cannons as its outstanding features. Recently, this cult of force has been repeatedly employed by the Western peoples to oppress Asia, and as a consequence, there is no progress in Asia. To oppress others with the cult of force, in the language of the Ancients, is the rule of Might. Therefore, European civilization is nothing but the rule of Might. The rule of Might has always been looked down upon by the Orient. There is another kind of civilization superior to the rule of Might. The fundamental characteristics of this civilization are benevolence, justice and morality. This civilization makes people respect, not fear, it. Such a civilization is, in the language of the Ancients, the rule of Right or the Kingly Way. One may say, therefore, that Oriental civilization is one of the rule of Right. Since the development of European materialistic civilization and the cult of Might, the morality of the world has been on the decline. Even in Asia, morality in several countries has degenerated. Of late, a number of European and American scholars have begun to study Oriental civilization and to realize that, while materially the Orient is far behind the Occident, morally the Orient is superior to the Occident.

Which civilization, the rule of Might or the rule of Right, will prove to be beneficial to justice and humanity, to nations and countries? You can give your own answer to this question. I may cite an example here to illustrate the point. For instance, between 500 and 2000 years ago, there was a period of a thousand years when China was supreme in the world. Her status in the world then was similar to that of Great Britain and America to-day. What was the situation of the weaker nations toward China then? They respected China as their superior and sent annual tribute to China by their own will, regarding it as an honour to be allowed to do so. They wanted, of their own free will, to be dependencies of China. Those countries which sent tribute to China were not only situated in Asia but in distant Europe as well. But in what way did China maintain her prestige among so many small and weaker nations? Did she send her army or navy, i.e. use Might, to compel them to send their contributions? Not at all. It was not her rule of Might that forced the weaker nations to send tribute to China. It was the influence of her rule of Right. Once they were influenced by the "Kingly Way" of China they continued to send tribute, not merely once or twice, but the practice was carried on from generation to generation. This influence is felt even at the present moment; there are still traces and evidences of it.

There are two small countries situated to the north of India, namely, Bhutan and Nepal. These countries are small in size, but are inhabited by a brave, strong, and warlike people. During the present British rule of India, Britain often went to Nepal in search of soldiers in order to rule the Indians. A great deal of money by way of subsidies had to be spent before Britain was allowed to dispatch a political observer to Nepal. Even a great Power such as Great Britain had to respect her; Nepal was, in fact, a great Power in Asia. But what is the attitude of Nepal toward Great Britain during the past hundred years? Over [a] hundred years ago India was conquered by Great Britain, and during this period Nepal was able to live peacefully on the border of the British colony. Although [a] hundred years have passed, Nepal has never sent tribute to Great Britain. Great Britain, on the other hand, has to spend a large sum by way of subsidies to Nepal. But what is the attitude of Nepal toward China? The status of China has deteriorated to such an extent that it is now inferior even to that of a British colony. Though far away from China Proper and separated from her by Tibet, Nepal considered China as her suzerain State and up to 1911 Nepal sent annual tribute to China via Tibet. In that year, however, when the Nepal commissioners reached Szechuan and found communications interrupted, they returned to their country. The differential attitude of Nepal toward Great Britain and toward China is due to the difference between the Oriental and Occidental civilization. China has degenerated during the last several hundred years, yet Nepal still respects her as a superior State. Great Britain, on the other hand, is a powerful country, but Nepal has been influenced by Chinese civilization, which, in her eyes, is the true civilization, while that of Britain is nothing but the rule of Might.

Now, what is the problem that underlies Pan-Asianism, the Principle of Greater Asia, which we are discussing here to-day? Briefly, it is a cultural problem, a problem of comparison and conflict between the Oriental and Occidental culture and civilization. Oriental civilization is the rule of Right; Occidental civilization is the rule of Might. The rule of Right respects benevolence and virtue, while the rule of Might only respects force and utilitarianism. The rule of Right always influences people with justice and reason, while the rule of Might always oppresses people with brute force and military measures. People who are influenced by justice and virtue will never forget their superior State, even if that country has become weak. So Nepal even now willingly respects China as a superior State. People who are oppressed by force never submit entirely to the oppressor State. The relations of Great Britain with Egypt and India form a typical example. Although under British rule, Egypt and India have always entertained the thought of independence and separation from Great Britain. If Great Britain becomes weaker some day, Egypt and India will overthrow British rule and regain their independence within five years. You should now realize which is the superior civilization, the Oriental or the Occidental?

If we want to realize Pan-Asianism in this new world, what should be its foundation if not our ancient civilization and culture? Benevolence and virtue must be the foundations of Pan-Asianism. With this as a sound foundation we must then learn science from Europe for our industrial development and the improvement of our armaments, not, however, with a view to oppressing or destroying other countries and peoples as the Europeans have done, but purely for our self-defense.

Japan is the first nation in Asia to completely master the military civilization of Europe. Japan's military and naval forces are her own creation, independent of European aid or assistance. Therefore, Japan is the only completely independent country in East Asia. There is another country in Asia who joined with Central Powers during the European War and was partitioned after her final defeat. After the war, however, she was not only able to regain her territory, but to expel all Europeans from that territory. Thus she attained her status of complete independence. This is Turkey. At present Asia has only two independent countries, Japan in the East and Turkey in the West. In other words, Japan and Turkey are the Eastern and Western barricades of Asia. Now Persia, Afghanistan, and Arabia are also following the European example in arming themselves, with the result that the Western peoples dare not look down on them. China at present also possesses considerable armaments, and when her unification is accomplished she too will become a great Power. We advocate Pan-Asianism in order to restore the status of Asia. Only by the unification of all the peoples in Asia on the foundation of benevolence and virtue can they become strong and powerful.

But to rely on benevolence alone to influence the Europeans in Asia to relinquish the privileges they have acquired in China would be an impossible dream. If we want to regain our rights we must resort to force. In the matter of armaments, Japan has already accomplished her aims, while Turkey has recently also completely armed herself. The other Asiatic races, such as the peoples of Persia, Afghanistan, and Arabia are all war-like peoples. China has a population of four hundred millions, and although she needs to modernize her armament and other equipment, and her people are a peace-loving people, yet when the destiny of their country is at stake the Chinese people will also fight with courage and determination. Should all Asiatic peoples thus unite together and present a united front against the Occidentals, they will win the final victory. Compare the populations of Europe and Asia: China has a population of four hundred millions, India three hundred and fifty millions, Japan several scores of millions, totaling, together with other peoples, no less than nine hundred millions. The population in Europe is somewhere around four hundred millions. For the four hundred millions to oppress the nine hundred millions is an intolerable injustice, and in the long run the latter will be defeated. What is more, among the four hundred millions some of them have already been influenced by us. Judging from the present tendency of civilization, even in Great Britain and America, there are people who advocate the principles of benevolence and justice. Such an advocacy also exists in some of the barbarian countries. Thus, we realize that the Western civilization of utilitarianism is submitting to the influence of Oriental civilization of benevolence and justice. That is to say the rule of Might gives way to the rule of Right, presaging a bright future for world civilization.

At present there is a new country in Europe which has been looked down upon and expelled from the Family of Nations by the White races of the whole of Europe. Europeans consider it as a poisonous snake or some brutal animal, and dare not approach it. Such a view is also shared by some countries in Asia. This country is Russia. At present, Russia is attempting to separate from the White peoples in Europe. Why? Because she insists on the rule of Right and denounces the rule of Might. She advocates the principle of benevolence and justice, and refuses to accept the principles of utilitarianism and force. She maintains Right and opposes the oppression of the majority by the minority. From this point of view, recent Russian civilization is similar to that of our ancient civilization. Therefore, she joins with the Orient and separates from the West. The new principles of Russia were considered as intolerable by Europeans. They are afraid that these principles, when put into effect, would overthrow their rule of Might. Therefore they do not accept the Russian way, which is in accord with the principles of benevolence and justice, but denounce it as contrary to world principles.

What problem does Pan-Asianism attempt to solve? The problem is how to terminate the sufferings of the Asiatic peoples and how to resist the aggression of the powerful European countries. In a word, Pan-Asianism represents the cause of the oppressed Asiatic peoples. Oppressed peoples are found not only in Asia, but in Europe as well. Those countries that practice the rule of

Might do not only oppress the weaker peoples outside their continent, but also those within their own continent. Pan-Asianism is based on the principle of the rule of Right, and justifies the avenging of the wrongs done to others. An American scholar considers all emancipation movements as revolts against civilization. Therefore now we advocate the avenging of the wrong done to those in revolt against the civilization of the rule of Might, with the aim of seeking a civilization of peace and equality and the emancipation of all races. Japan to-day has become acquainted with the Western civilization of the rule of Might, but retains the characteristics of the Oriental civilization of the rule of Right. Now the question remains whether Japan will be the hawk of the Western civilization of the rule of Might, or the tower of strength of the Orient. This is the choice which lies before the people of Japan.

Chapter Six

Tanaka Ippei: "Islam and Pan-Asianism," 1924

Eddy Dufourmont

Tanaka Ippei was born in Tokyo in 1882. After graduating in 1902 from Taiwan Kyōkai Senmon Gakkō (Taiwan Association College, subsequently Takushoku University), where he majored in Chinese thought, he accompanied his mentor, the Sinologist Hattori Unokichi (1867–1939), during his research trip to Beijing, where Tanaka started his research on Confucianism. During the Russo-Japanese War of 1904–1905 Tanaka served as an army interpreter. After the war, he continued his research on Confucianism in Manchuria and Shandong (Shantung). When the Japanese attacked the German-leased territory of Qingdao (Tsingtao) after the outbreak of World War I, Tanaka again served as an interpreter for the army and, after the hostilities in China, obtained a job with the Chinese daily newspaper *Jinan Benpao* (The Jinan Daily). There he came into contact with Wakabayashi Nakaba (also Han, died in 1936), one of the pioneers of Islam in Japan and an associate of Tōyama Mitsuru and Uchida Ryōhei (see I:3 and I:10).

It was under Wakabayashi's influence that Tanaka developed an interest in Islam, leading to his conversion to that religion in 1924. A year later Tanaka went on the *hajj*, the pilgrimage to Makkah (Mecca) that every Muslim is required to make once in his lifetime. Tanaka was one of the first Japanese to complete this pilgrimage. A record of his journey, *Haku'un Yūki: Isuramu Junrei* (White Cloud Chronicles: An Islamic Pilgrimage, 1925) played an important role in introducing Islam to Japan (Tanaka's writings have been republished by Takushoku Daigaku Sōritsu Hyakunenshi Hensanshitsu, 2002–2005). Back in Japan, Tanaka taught at Daitō Bunka Gakuin (Greater East Culture Academy) in Tōkyō and opened a private academy, the Reisaisha (Society of the Great Rhinoceros), where he gave seminars on Islam. He also lectured throughout Japan, published in journals such as *Nihon oyobi Nihonjin* (Japan and the Japanese). It was at that time that he got to know pan-Asianists such as Ōkawa Shūmei (see II:4), Mitsukawa Kametarō, and Yasuoka Masahiro (see II:29). In 1931, Tanaka founded the Gōitsukai (Society for Unity), an organization dedicated to demonstrating the fundamental identity of the five "world religions" (Islam, Shintō, Christianity, Buddhism, and Confucianism). His work came to a halt, however, when he was diagnosed with stomach cancer in 1933. Facing imminent death, he decided to make one last pilgrimage to Makkah, where he was granted an audience with Saudi Arabia's King Ibn Saud. Tanaka died shortly after his return to Japan in 1934.

Tanaka's Pan-Asianism was based on his conviction of the spirituality of Asia, which he juxtaposed to the hedonistic materialism of "the West." In Tanaka's view, the diffusion of "the Great Way" (Daidō)—an ideal based on humanitarianism—was the fundamental divine message included in Shintō, traditional Chinese thought, Buddhism, Judaism, Christianity, and Islam. For Tanaka, the Great Way was not only the ultimate religious "truth"; he regarded it also as a political tool to unite all Asians against "the West." His views were not unique in Japan at that time. For example, Matsumura Kaiseki (1859–1939), who in 1912 founded a new religious sect, the Society of the Way (Dōkai), of which Ōkawa Shūmei was also a member, also favored a synthesis of the same religions, while not under the banner of Pan-Asianism (Dufourmont 2008).

The distinctive aspects of Tanaka's thought were his belief in the similarities between Japan's indigenous religion, Shintō, and Islam and his linking of religion with Pan-Asianism as well as Japanism (*Nihonshugi*). Tanaka was convinced that all Muslims fighting for independence from Western colonialism as well as the Turks, who were struggling to preserve their independence, looked to Japan for leadership. However, he rejected the notion that Asia could be liberated from Western domination by military force. He believed that liberation could be achieved only by ideological means: Asians had to draw on their own authentic traditions to fight "Western materialism." Despite their radical differences in dogma and practice, Tanaka came to regard Shintō and Islam as identical systems of thought, at least in this respect. Tanaka was not concerned with scholarly distinctions between the two religions, but rather his primary goal was to introduce Islam to Japan and develop a "Japanese Islam," an Islam nourished by the Japanese spirit. This explains why he downplayed differences that might deter the Japanese from embracing Islam. Before his conversion to Islam, Tanaka Ippei had sought to discover values that would allow him to combat "Western materialism" in the Confucian concept of the "Kingly Way" (Chinese: *wangdao*; Japanese: *ōdō*), that is, the idea of benevolent rule. However, after he had studied Confucianism in China, he concluded that the Kingly Way involved much more than what Confucius and Mencius and subsequent Confucian scholars had envisaged. For Tanaka, the Kingly Way was less a counterideology to the "Despotic way" (Chinese: *badao*; Japanese: *hadō*), as some contemporaries of Tanaka had interpreted it, than proof of a *union* between Heaven and Man. Tanaka became convinced that the Kingly Way was much older and more original than Confucianism. The fact that, in China, Islam had become intertwined with Confucianism was proof for Tanaka that Islam had fundamental commonalities with all the "Oriental" systems of thought despite what he considered as its superficially striking differences (such as monotheism). This notion was an important one for his Pan-Asianism because it provided rhetorical weapons for representing Asia as a single cultural sphere—a large part of Asia was inhabited by Muslims—and on the other hand it provided reasons for solidarity with the colonized peoples elsewhere.

In the quest for "the Way," Tanaka sought a teaching that could be applied to all aspects of daily life, and he believed Islam could offer this. He was strongly influenced by his encounters with Chinese Muslims and was, for example, drawn to the thought of Liu Jielian (1670–1724), a Muslim scholar who attempted a synthesis of Confucianism, Taoism, and Buddhism within Islam. This was exactly the kind of syncretism that Tanaka aimed at, and he translated some of Liu's writings into Japanese. Tanaka's ideas may have influenced Ōkawa, who made active efforts to expand Islamic studies in Japan during the war. Like Tanaka, Ōkawa also believed that Islam could potentially play an important role in uniting Asians under Japanese leadership (see II:4).

Despite his influence, Tanaka's perception of Islam was flawed. For example, in the text reproduced in translation here, Tanaka made no attempt to critique the crude statements about Islam and Christianity propounded by European scholars such as Ernest Renan (1823–1892), who claimed that Christianity was spread by love and Islam by the sword. On the contrary, the image of Islam as a violent religion was useful to Tanaka in the propagation of his ideal of a strong Asia. Tanaka's understanding of the international environment was also dubious. In the text, Tanaka is correct when he writes that Hindus and Muslims in India had become closer. Indeed, at this time Muslim leaders like Abul Kalam Azad (1888–1958), Mukhtar Ahmad Ansari (1880–1936), and Hakim Ajmal Khan (1863–1927) were making common cause with Gandhi, whose influence was growing within the National Congress. But Tanaka overestimated the level of independence enjoyed by the new Arab kingdoms created after World War I, as, contrary to what he suggested, these kingdoms were closely controlled by Britain and France, even if incipient nationalist movements existed there.

In sum, despite his early death Tanaka Ippei played a key role in the establishment of connections between Japan and the Muslim world—connections that were utilized by Japan during World War II when Japan's military expansionism embraced China and Southeast Asia, areas inhabited by Muslims (cf. Esenbel 2004).

Source (translation from the Japanese original by Eddy Dufourmont)
Tanaka Ippei, *Isureamu to Dai-Ajiashugi* (Islam and Pan-Asianism). Self-published, 1924, 14–16.

Islam as a religion is neither superior nor inferior to Christianity. Is it wise for our empire, which is part of Asia, to have ignored Islam on the scientific and international levels, and for our compatriots to imitate the Whites in dismissing Islam as a primitive religion for inferior Asian nations? Britain, a Christian country, which rules over more than 100 million Muslims, has tried to convert them to Christianity but without success, despite years of effort. Britain must even now come to terms with the imminent independence of Egypt, the resurgence of Turkey and the formations of new kingdoms such as Hedjaz, Iraq and Kerek [Jordania]. In India also, the main problem for Britain were the troubles between Hindus and Muslims, but recently the two communities have drawn closer together and Britain has been forced to recognize the possibility of an independence movement there. That is the reason why Britain's policies have become more conciliatory—there are already some British aristocrats who have converted to Islam, and a mosque has been built in London [actually Liverpool, in 1889]. Moreover, imperial policy toward Muslims in the colonies is now less harsh than in the past.

Yet it is impossible to assume that relations between Islam and Christianity will remain peaceful when one considers the historical circumstances and modern lifestyle of the Whites. But in the case of Japanese and Muslims, the distance is not unbridgeable. Some years ago I wrote a book entitled *The Future of Chinese Muslims and the Japanese Shintō*, in which I showed that the Japanese spirit and the Muslim spirit had many points in common and that this fact would be of great advantage for the future politics of Asia.

The Meiji Restoration of direct imperial rule was clearly a Shintoist revolution which proclaimed the union of politics and religion, but separated Shintō from Buddhism and defined relations between the ancient Shintō and the national character. We even saw the rejection of Buddhism. However, following various developments freedom of belief was recognized and became a tool to protect The Way and promote it. First comes The Way, and then individual beliefs. That is to say, the Japanese must follow our Way first, and only then will they embrace our religion. Religions such as Buddhism, Confucianism, Taoism, and Christianity all originated outside Japan but were assimilated there.

Islam is the only one of the five great religions that has yet to enter Japan. This is because its teachings are transmitted from individual to individual, and because they are written in the original language [Arabic] and have never been translated. The five great religions of the world uphold our Way and support our national character; they are useful in shaping people's minds and in managing political affairs. With the help of Islam, our country and the nations of Asia will prosper.

I have already explained the circumstances in which Muhammad proclaimed Islam and started a holy war. He can be compared to Nichiren [1222–1282, founder of a Japanese Buddhist sect] who started a kind of holy war in the name of Buddhism. Although such a comparison is preposterous, Nichiren banished feminine mercy from the path of Buddhist enlightenment and introduced a spirit of initiative and a temperament of rigor and vigor to the spiritually confused and muddled Japan of his time. Nowadays, it is clear that one of the problems that our country will face in the future is the exclusive emphasis which modern thought places on Love. This emphasis, offered without any explanation, gives birth to false new ideas, spreads the spirit of opposition to the state and the abandonment of old ways, promotes contempt for the national virtues of diligence and courage, and harbors the seeds of danger for the empire if it were ever to interfere in international relations.

Thus, in a period of decadence such as the present, we urgently need the temper of rigor and vitality found in the moral discipline of our Japanese spirit. And if we want to find it elsewhere—since "Jesus preached with love, Muhammad with severity," as the Westerners say—I have no hesitation in affirming that the austere message of Islam will not only be very useful in the restoration of our country but will also prove indispensable both to the establishment of Pan-Asianism and to the completion of Japan's imperial mission.

Chapter Seven

The Greater India Society: Indian Culture and an Asian Federation

Brij Tankha

In the first decades of the twentieth century, reclaiming the glories of the Indian past to assert equality, if not superiority, to the West was an important part of the struggle against British colonialism. As part of this quest some intellectuals turned to exploring Indian influence beyond its territorial borders as a way of defining Indian civilization. From this perspective, the spread of Indian influence became a source of pride because, these intellectuals argued, it was based on ideas and cultural forms unlike those of the West, which were seen as the products of looting, plunder, and military domination. It was at this time that Indian nationalists began to talk of bringing the oppressed nations of Asia together through an Asiatic federation.

These ideas assumed concrete form in the Greater India Society, which was founded in 1926 by Bengali cultural nationalists. The noted historian Sir Jadunath Sarkar (1870–1958) was elected president. Members of the society were strongly influenced by the writings of European Orientalists, particularly the French Indologist Sylvain Lévi (1867–1935) and by the ongoing excavations at Angkor, Cambodia.

The Greater India Society and the views it represented was not just the product of European Orientalism but arose from and was shaped by the cultural milieu of Bengal; it was part of a movement that desired to strengthen society and build the basis for a new nationalism. Old networks of trade and culture that linked this region with Southeast and East Asia formed the basis of these new aspirations, which were embraced at one time by the poet and Nobel Prize laureate Rabindranath Tagore (1861–1941) and other prominent intellectuals.

The prominent nationalist intellectual Chitranjan Das (1870–1925), a noted lawyer and editor of the influential literary publication *Forward* (later renamed *Liberty*), was among those who supported the idea of India as part of a greater Asiatic federation. Das was very critical of Tagore's nebulous conception of universal humanity, and, as president of the Indian National Congress in 1922, he stressed the need to create a federation to bring Asians together.

When Tagore declared that Asia must "find her voice," Das supported this statement in his magazine but wrote that, while Asians share cultural ties and India has supplied the religious teachers of the world, it was the "menace which threatens all alike"—that of Western domination and racism—that was more important and urgent than the ties of ancient culture.

Arguments were thus advanced for a broader unity based on the idea of confronting colonial oppression as opposed to a regionally based unity, but, partly under the influence of European Orientalists, Indian scholars began investigating India's historical relations with Southeast Asia. This led them to argue that India, too, had established colonies, but, unlike Western colonialism, India's was a benign cultural imperialism that benefited the primitive peoples of the areas concerned. This assertion of superiority—of having given birth to philosophies that spread all over Asia, coupled with the notion that India was a crucial link in the British Empire—served to justify in the minds of many nationalists the notion that India needed to play a leadership role in Asian unity and that this unity could only be reestablished on the basis of Indian cultural superiority.

Most representative of the ideas of the Greater India Society are the writings of the historian Ramesh Chandra Mazumdar (also Majumdar, 1888–1980). Mazumdar wrote his study of the kingdom of Champa as part of a series on ancient India. In his introduction, he argues for the thoroughgoing nature of the Indian influence on the whole of Asia, from religion and government to geographical names and measurement systems and even the fusion of races.

Jadunath Sarkar, the president of the Greater India Society, advocated modernization and argued that Indians must lay less emphasis on the peculiar heritage of an Aryan India of the past and embrace the spirit of progress. The study of Indian influence and its revival in Southeast Asia as testament to the strength of such ideas was initiated largely by Sarkar, and the foundation of the Greater India Society was built on this ideal. The cultural nationalists, as represented by groups such as the Greater India Society, were part of the Indian nationalist project, where a broad and inclusive nationalism contended with a narrow religious nationalism. These two tendencies need to be unraveled when examining the texts produced by the cultural nationalists. Their writings influenced a generation of nationalist leaders and shaped the thinking of the postindependence intelligentsia; Jawaharlal Nehru (1889–1964), India's first prime minister, wrote approvingly of the dissemination of Indian cultural influence while remaining critical of the idea of a Greater India.

Contemporary historians have moved away from the idea of a one-way influence, arguing for a greater independent development. In the struggle for independence these ideas were important, as they rejected the colonial view of isolation and detachment as the defining features of Indian civilization—a country physically cut off by the mountains and the sea—to argue that, just as ancient Greece and Rome played a role in the developing civilization of the West, India too had played an important role in the development of the civilization in the East. In the early twentieth century, this was an important way for Indian intellectuals of asserting equality with the West and engaging the wider Asian region in order to create a shared past and, based on this past, the hope for a bright future.

Source (English in the original)
R. C. Mazumdar, "Introduction." *Ancient Indian Colonies in the Far East* Vol. I. Champa: The Punjab Sanskrit Book Depot and Lahore, 1927, i–xxiv.

The story of Greater India is bound to be of absorbing interest, not only to every student of history, but also to all educated people of this country. The Indian colonies in the Far East must ever remain as the high-water mark of maritime and colonial enterprise of the ancient Indians. But although an extensive literature in French has grown up on this subject, hardly anything has yet been written in English. This alone accounts for the comparative apathy and ignorance in this matter which is generally noticed in this country.

. . . Champa has been selected as the subject of the first volume, partly because it is the remotest colony in the East, and partly because it is less well known than Cambodia and Java on which general attention has been focused on account of the famous monuments of Angkor and Boro-budur.

All these evidences agree in referring the beginnings of Indian colonial kingdoms to a period not later than the second century A.D. . . .

About the time when Indians gradually penetrated into Burma and countries further east these were settled by savage tribes. Those in Burma were Mongoloid in character, and akin to the present tribes of Abors and Mishmis. The people of Indo-China and the islands of Sumatra, Java and Borneo were Malayo-Polynesian or Austronesian in character. In native traditions the early inhabitants of the coast, specially near the mouth of the Salween river, are represented as savages, called in Burmese Bilu, the equivalent of Raksasu. They rejected all intercourse with civilised men and even Gautama himself who, it is fabled, came to the country was stoned and driven away by them. The Chinese also speak of the people of Annam in the same strain. "They are," we are told "so savage that they do not know cultivation and live by fishing and hunting alone. They are turbulent people who frequently rise in revolt, invade the Chinese official quarters, burn, pillage and massacre wherever they go, and take refuge in their impenetrable forests whenever they are attacked by a strong enemy."

It was the mission of Indian colonists to bring this heterogeneous mass of barbarians within the pale of civilisation, a task which the Chinese, their next-door neighbours, had hitherto failed to accomplish.

As a matter of fact the political conquest of Further India and the adjacent islands was rapidly followed by a complete cultural conquest. The local people readily assimilated the new civilisation and adopted the religion, art, social manners and customs, alphabet, literature, laws and administrative systems of the conquerors. This will be amply evident from the picture of civilisation in Champa contained in Book II of the present volume.

In short, Indian civilisation made a thorough conquest of these lands and a new India was established in that far-off region. The Indian colonists even tried to complete the transformation by importing celebrated place names of their motherland into their new home, and thus we find new towns and countries called Ayodhya, Kaushambi, Srikshetra, Dvaravati. . . .

Chapter Eight

The Pan-Asiatic Society and the "Conference of Asian Peoples" in Nagasaki, 1926

Sven Saaler

The renewed upsurge of pan-Asianist writings such as Tanaka Ippei's *Isureamu* [*sic*, Islam] *to Ajiashugi* (Islam and Asianism, 1924), the special number on "Asianism" in the journal *Nihon oyobi Nihonjin* (Japan and the Japanese) in the same year, and Murobuse Kōshin's (1892–1970) book *Ajiashugi* (Asianism, Murobuse 1926)—in tandem with the founding of several new political organizations with pan-Asian objectives—was a reaction to the curtailing of Japanese immigration to the United States in 1924, which led to an outburst of anti-American sentiment in Japan (see I:26 and Stalker 2006). The newly founded pan-Asian organizations followed in the footsteps of older bodies, such as the League for the Equality of Races, which, in 1919, had fervently urged the government to demand the insertion of a racial equality clause into the Charter of the League of Nations. One of the most important of the organizations founded in 1924 was the All Asia Society (Zen Ajia Kyōkai, official English designation Pan-Asiatic Society), which is remembered chiefly for organizing several pan-Asian conferences, such as the Conference of Asian Peoples in Nagasaki in 1926 and conferences in Shanghai in 1927 and Kabul in 1928 (on these conferences, cf. Mizuno 1996; Matsuura 2010: chap. 3). Further conferences were held under government auspices in 1934 in Dairen (cf. Pratap 1947: 269; Matsuura 2010: chap. 3) and in 1942 in Osaka (Ohsawa 1954: 39), by which time the All Asia Society had already been disbanded. The society between 1926 and 1928 also published the journal *Ajia* (Asia), which included contributions from sympathizers of the pan-Asian movement, both Japanese and non-Japanese, including Kurban Ali (see I:23) from Central Asia and Rash Behari Bose (see I:24) from India.

The driving forces behind the formation of the All Asia Society in 1924 were members of the Lower House, notably Iwasaki Isao (1878–1927) and Imazato (sometimes also rendered as Imasato) Juntarō (1886–1976).

Supporters included influential politicians such as Viscount Gotō Shinpei (1857–1929); members of the Imperial Diet Dr. Kodera Kenkichi (see I:26), Dr. Takebe Tongo (1871–1945) (both members of the Kenseikai), and Tokonami Takejirō (1866–1935, Seiyū Hontō); and law professors Uesugi Shinkichi (1878–1929) and Baba Ei'ichi (1879–1937), as well as a bevy of well-known pan-Asianists, such as Tanaka Morihei (1884–1928), Tanabe Yasunosuke (1863–1946), Ōkawa Shūmei (1886–1957), Mitsukawa Kametarō (1888–1936), and Nakatani Takeyo (1898–1990). After the arrest of Iwasaki on charges of bribery (the so-called Matsushima Red Light District incident) in 1926, Imazato became the de facto leader of the All Asia Society and the moving figure behind the pan-Asian conferences. Imazato traveled to China several times and in August 1925 was in Beijing, where he concluded an agreement with the Association for the Great Federation of Asiatic Races to organize an international conference at which delegates from Asian countries would discuss the problems of Asian nations, particularly the question of how to promote Asian solidarity in order to win independence from Western colonialism (Mizuno 1996: 511). Invitations were "sent to each country (through the [local] newspapers) or to public bodies representing the race, provided that in case such bodies are unknown, invitations may be sent to individuals for the sake of convenience." In effect, however, apart from the Chinese and Japanese delegates, the conference was attended mostly by Asian independence activists residing in Japan—which was one reason why the Japanese authorities regarded it with suspicion and refused to cooperate with the organizers.

A report by the Home Ministry questioned the legitimacy of the "so-called representatives," who "lack any qualification or designation that they would have received through a regular method such as an election. They have been nominated by small associations (*shō-dantai*) or self-proclaimed representatives (*jishō daihyō*) and therefore have no authority whatsoever" (Naimushō Keihokyoku Hoanka [NKH] 1926:1–2). Naturally, the government also viewed the conference with suspicion since this kind of private involvement in diplomacy (*kokumin gaikō*) threatened the government's foreign policy monopoly. The fact that the conference was held in Nagasaki—far from the political center in Tokyo—shows that the organizers were aware of the government's hostility to the group's activities. Furthermore, the promotion of pan-Asian solidarity was contrary to the government's official foreign policy, which was wary of antagonizing the West by any attempts to undermine Western colonial rule. The government therefore carefully monitored reactions to the conference in the Western press (cf. NKH 1926) and remained highly sensitive to fears in Europe and the United States of the formation of an anti-Western pan-Asian league.

The conference, known officially as "the Conference of Asian Peoples" (Zen Ajia Minzoku Kaigi, literally, the "All Asian Peoples' Conference"), was held between 1 and 3 August 1926 in the Nagasaki YMCA (for the program of the conference, see NKH 1926: 1819). It was attended by twelve Japanese delegates, eleven Chinese delegates, seven Indian representatives, two Koreans, one Vietnamese, and one delegate from the Philippines. A good deal of public attention was given to the case of the Afghan representative, Mahendra Pratap (on Pratap see II:9), who was refused entry to Japan on the grounds that he was traveling without a passport—which he had reported stolen en route from China to Japan (cf. Pratap 1947). Pratap already had a reputation as an (Indian) independence activist in Japan and his case was much publicized in the media—so much so that it was given a special place as an appendix in the Home Ministry's report on the conference (NKH 1926: 143–90). Several well-known Japanese pan-Asian societies sent representatives who addressed the assembly—figures such as Inoue Tomegorō from the Ōmotokyō (on the Ōmotokyō, see Li 2007; Stalker 2008) and Yoshida Masuzō (1895–1967) from the Kokuryūkai (on the Kokuryūkai, see I:10).

About a hundred attendees including journalists and foreign observers made up the audience. The conference passed nine major resolutions: 1) the founding of an All Asian League (*Zen Ajia Renmei*) and the formulation of statutes attached to it (reproduced in the English translation here), 2) the establishment of an Asian communication organization, 3) the establishment of an Asia Center (*Ajia kaikan*), 4) the establishment of a central financial institution, 5) the promotion of research into a common language for all Asia, 6) the promotion of a racial equality proposal with regard to the League of Nations, 7) the establishment of a research institution within the Asian League, 8) the establishment of an Asian University, and 9) the revocation of Japanese surveillance of Chinese merchants and workers (NKH 1926: 47–50). The conference also decided to send letters of commendation to individuals who had demonstrated their dedication to the cause of Asia. Addressees included the king of Afghanistan, the president of the Republic of Turkey, the Shah of Persia, Mahatma Gandhi and Jawaharlal Nehru, and the previously mentioned Pratap (NKH 1926: 52). Finally, the conference also chose an official anthem for the Asian League (GGS, MT I.4.6.0.1-1, Minzoku Mondai Kankei Zakken, vol. 2: Ajia minzoku mondai, 91).

Contrary to the organizers' claims, however, it was obvious that the conference had aims that went much further than those that were publicly announced and that the underlying consensus was to promote the unity of Asian nations against the menace of the West. In his opening speech, Imazato Juntarō emphasized that, given the failure of the League of Nations, Asian peoples had to unite to promote the welfare of Asia and Asians, with the ultimate objective of fostering the happiness of the whole of mankind (NKH 1926: 29f). Indian representative Rash Behari Bose (I:24) further stressed the importance of an Asian League as an expression of the Asian nations taking their destiny into their own hands (NKH 1926:43). Tanaka Morihei, who had authored a series of articles on the necessity for an Asian League as early as 1906, was even more outspoken, pointing out that the Asian League would be an instrument for promoting the solidarity of Asian nations against the imperialist "white race" and that the "great union of our ["yellow"] race" (*jinshu dai danketsu*) must be realized to prepare for a "coming world war along racial lines" (NKH 1926:42)—a common theme in pan-Asian writings from the turn of the century on (cf. Saaler 2008a).

However, the conference was characterized by unity only on the surface. There were many internal squabbles that demonstrated that "Asian unity" was a wish rather than a reality. Even before the conference, there was hot debate over the participation of Korean delegates. If the Koreans were allowed to attend, they might raise the question of *Japanese* colonialism—a problematic issue in a conference emphasizing Asian unity—as opposed to the threat of *Western* colonialism. The Japanese organizers eventually agreed to invite Korean representatives friendly to Japan but still worried that the question of Korean independence might be raised. However, even some Japanese at the conference acknowledged that "the Japanese (*waga kokumin*) still harbor contempt for China and Korea" (NKH 1926: 136). On the first day of the conference, the Chinese delegates demanded that the conference consider a remit for the revocation by Japan of the "21 Demands" of 1915, which were seen as a symbol of Japanese imperialist encroachment in China. But the Japanese delegates were unable to accept this proposal, simply because that would have made the Japanese government even more suspicious of the conference. The Chinese delegates were on the point of walking out of the conference in protest but eventually agreed on a compromise declaration demanding the abolition of *all* unequal treaties in East Asia (NKH 1926: 21–23; cf. also *The Times*, 4 August 1926, 11).

Japanese newspapers remained skeptical about the outcome of the conference, particularly about the feasibility of its ambitious agenda (*Ōsaka Asahi Shinbun*, 1 July, quoted in NKH 1926: 98). Some journalists and Japanese economic experts who attended the conference were also worried that the formation of an All Asian League, aimed at excluding the Western powers from Asia, might have repercussions for Japan's diplomatic and economic situation (*Japan Advertiser*, 5 August, quoted in NKH 1926: 99f; cf. also the assessment by the representative of the Nankai Railways, NKH 1926:136).

Although Western newspapers generally downplayed the importance of the conference, they noted its "frankly anti-Western" character. Some even warned of a rising "Pan-Asia Movement" (*The Morning Post*, 2 August 1926). "Anti-Westernism," the *New York Times* emphasized, "is the only bond holding the delegates together." However, the newspaper continued, "the conference is essentially a confab between comparatively uninfluential Japanese and Chinese professors, as the Indians present all lived long in Japan, the Filipinos are taking little part and the Koreans are not permitted to speak" (*New York Times*, 3 August 1926: 9). Some newspapers related the conference to the remarks of former German Emperor Wilhelm II, who had, in various interviews after World War I, reaffirmed his late nineteenth-century visions of the "Yellow Peril." For example, *The Morning Post* in London emphasized that the "ex-Kaiser" as well as the ex–crown prince "no doubt . . . will see in the first Pan-Asian Conference . . . in Nagasaki a partial realization of their fears" (*The Morning Post*, 2 August 1926).

Most critical of the conference were, hardly astonishing, Chinese newspapers, many of which dismissed it as an instrument of "the Greater Asianism of Japanese imperialism and expansionism" (NKH 1926: 114). Many Chinese concluded that, in Japan, pan-Asian solidarity had been developed into an ideology to legitimize Japanese expansion in China. While Li Da-zhao had raised this concern as early as 1919 (see I:22), during the Nagasaki conference, it was also expressed in Western newspapers influenced by the growing Chinese resentment of Japan. One of these was the *New York Times*, where the journalist Thomas F. Millard wrote,

> Japan's Pan-Asian doctrine has been about 90 per cent humbug, and usually it was injected into international affairs to serve an immediate convenience of Japanese diplomacy. But intimations can be observed that a doctrine which was advanced primarily as a pretext now begins to impress Japanese statesmen as having actual merit. (*New York Times*, 13 June 1926: 21)

In the end, although it was followed by conferences in Shanghai in 1927 and Kabul in 1928, the Nagasaki conference had little lasting impact, and the All Asian League failed to develop into a functioning organization. Even the suspicious Japanese authorities eventually concluded that "the conference had avoided as much as possible touching on diplomatic questions . . . and ended without turbulence" (NKH 1926: 143). Former newspaper publisher and founder of the *Japan Times*, Zumoto Yoshisada (1862–1943), who, as a Japanese representative, attended the Third Annual Congress of the International League of Nations Federation in Geneva in September, one month after the conference in Nagasaki, gave a speech in which he assured his Western counterparts that, while some "sensational press despatches appear to have been printed in Europe and America, . . . the Nagasaki conference . . . was an event of no consequence whatever, no person of any importance in any country taking part in it" (Zumoto 1927: 15).

Nevertheless, the Nagasaki conference demonstrates a growing desire among Japanese pan-Asian activists and politicians (the leaders of the All Asia Society, after all, were members of the Imperial Diet) to position Japan as the leader of an anti-Western pan-Asian alliance in preparation for a future world war along racial lines. Japanese pan-Asianists tended increasingly to consider it a matter of course that Japan, as the greatest economic and military power in the region, would be the center of any future pan-Asian alliance. As a consequence, although they called for "Asian solidarity," they tended to look down on Japan's "Asian brothers" as subordinate partners or even mere auxiliaries without a voice of their own. The rhetoric of Japanese leadership that was heard at the conferences of 1926–1927 should be seen as a precursor of the aggressive tone adopted by Japanese Pan-Asianism in demanding the subordination of Asian nations to Japanese war aims in the wake of the Manchurian Incident in 1931 and particularly after the outbreak of the Pacific War in December 1941. Even though the authorities were reluctant to recognize the conference as proof of the growing attraction of pan-Asian rhetoric in Japan, it paved the way for the emergence of an official Japanese pan-Asian foreign policy and in later years was also utilized to demonstrate the long history of Japan's pan-Asian commitment.

Source 1 (translation from the Japanese original by Sven Saaler)
Foundation Manifesto of the All Asia Society (Zen Ajia Kyōkai Setsuritsu Shushi). Gaimushō Gaikō Shiryōkan (Foreign Ministry Historical Archive, Tokyo), Gaimushō Kiroku (Diplomatic Records), MT I.4.6.0.1-1, Minzoku Mondai Kankei Zakken (Miscellaneous matters relating to the question of Asian nationalities), vol. 2: Ajia Minzoku Mondai (The question of Asian nationalities), 1925–1926, 9.

All races on earth are equal, should be free to pursue their own development and have a duty to contribute to the advancement of the world and the prosperity of mankind. However, at present, we perceive racial discrimination and obstacles [to racial equality], and it is obvious that incidents of racial strife have been increasing in number in recent years. If these developments are left without intervention, they will inevitably lead to severe and repeated racial disturbances. Today, we can hardly overlook such developments.

Future world peace, we should be aware, will be preserved only if each race promotes mutual understanding [with other races]. Asians must forge ahead and promote a union and harmony of races. This is our responsibility and our mission, and it is an extremely important and major one. Those who live on Asian soil must rise up! We gather here today to found the All Asia Society, to stimulate the revival of contemporary Asian peoples, offspring of the Asian race which had already reached a high level of civilization (*bunmei*) several thousand years ago and which is [also] a source of modern culture (*bunka*), to raise their potential for unity and solidarity; to prevent the advent of racial disaster; and, furthermore, to realize the unity of Eastern and Western civilization in an attempt to create a new world civilization, thus contributing to the stability and prosperity of the whole of mankind. We hope for the support of many distinguished figures.

10 July 1924

STATUTES

The society is to be called the All Asia Society.
The society will establish its General Headquarters in Tokyo and headquarters and branches in other parts of Asia.
The society's goal is to contribute to the development of all Asia and thereby to contribute to world peace and the prosperity of the whole of mankind.

To achieve the above-mentioned objectives, the society will engage in the following activities:

- Research on Asia
- The reconnaissance, investigation and exploration of the regions of Asia
- The foundation of schools with the objective of [fostering] Asian development
- Organizing lectures on Asia
- The exchange of Asian teachers and students with other Asian as well as European and American countries
- The organizing of lectures on Asian revival and the dispatch of a propaganda corps (*sendentai*)
- The exchange of permanent or extraordinary civilian delegates knowledgeable about Asian questions with Asian countries as well as with European and American countries
- Propaganda activities regarding Asian questions directed to international public opinion and the media
- Information policy on Asian revival in the countries concerned
- The promotion of trade and commerce in Asian countries

- The promotion of movements for enlightenment and development that have the objective of developing Asia
- The publication of newspapers, magazines and books on Asia
- The holding of an annual Conference of Asian Peoples in Tokyo or elsewhere.

Membership of the society is open to regular members and patrons (*sanjo*). The regular membership fee is six yen per year; those who contribute at least 100 yen a year will become patrons. . . .

Source 2 (English in the original)
(Provisional) Rules of the Conference. Gaimushō Gaikō Shiryōkan (Foreign Ministry Historical Archive, Tokyo), Gaimushō Kiroku (Diplomatic Records), MT I.4.6.0.1-1, Minzoku Mondai Kankei Zakken (Miscellaneous matters relating to the question of Asian nationalities), vol. 2: Ajia Minzoku Mondai (The question of Asian nationalities), 1925–1926, 11.

1 The Conference will be held under the auspices of the Pan-Asiatic Society of Tokyo and the Great Federation of Asiatic Races of Peking.
2 The place and date of the Conference follow:
A Place: Nagasaki, Japan
B Date: Executive Committee Meeting on and after July 15th 1926
Main conference on and after August 1st 1926
3 Delegates to the Conference shall be elected in the following way:
Japanese: by Pan-Asiatic Society
Chinese: By Great Federation of Asiatic Races Association
Others: Left to the discretion of the races concerned.
4 Invitations will be sent to each country (through the newspapers) or to public bodies representing the race, provided that in case such bodies are unknown, invitations may be sent to individuals for the sake of convenience.
5 The Executive Committee shall decide the following matters:
A Order and method of the meeting.
B All affairs concerning the proceedings of the meeting.
6 The resolution to be introduced at the Conference, names and addresses of delegates and their dates of birth should be sent to the Executive Committee before July 15th, when it is expected to meet.
7 The Pan-Asiatic Society of Tokyo will be responsible for all arrangements in connection with the boarding and lodging of the delegates; the securing of the conference hall, etc. . . .

Source 3 (translation from the Japanese original by Sven Saaler)
Provisional Statutes of the All Asian League (Zen Ajia Renmei Zantei Kiyaku). Gaimushō Gaikō Shiryōkan (Foreign Ministry Historical Archive, Tokyo), Gaimushō Kiroku (Diplomatic Records), MT I.4.6.0.1-1, Minzoku Mondai Kankei Zakken (Miscellaneous matters relating to the question of Asian nationalities), vol. 2: Ajia Minzoku Mondai (The question of Asian nationalities), 1925–1926, 273–75.

We establish the All Asian League with the objective of realizing eternal world peace based upon equality and justice, of sweeping away international [*sic*], racial and religious discrimination, and of ensuring the freedom and happiness of the same [Asian] race.

In order to accomplish these objectives, the League will engage in the following activities:

- The revival of Asia's spiritual and material culture
- The abolition of the existing unequal treaties in international relations and the abolition of discriminatory treatment for particular ethnic groups
- [The promotion of] cooperation between Asian peoples in the spheres of culture, the economy, and politics
- The promotion of the use of Asian products and [the promotion of] industry in Asian countries.

The League has its headquarters in Tokyo and will establish branches in areas where it is felt necessary.

The highest organ of the League is the Executive Board (*rijikai*) which shall consist of 25 members.

The Executive Board shall summon a General Assembly (*sōkai*) once a year to discuss important issues.

The Executive Board of the League will extend official recognition to organizations in Asian countries that share the objectives of the League, and will invite representatives [of these organizations] to the General Assembly.

The Executive Board will invite to the General Assembly individuals who have made notable contributions to the Asian cause.

The Executive Board will be elected by the General Assembly and its term of office will be one year.

The Chairman of the Executive Board will be elected by the Executive Board and his term of office will be one year.

Chapter Nine

Raja Mahendra Pratap: Indian Independence, Asian Solidarity, World Federation, 1930

Sven Saaler

Raja Mahendra Pratap (1886–1979) was an Indian freedom fighter, journalist, writer, and revolutionary social reformer. At the beginning of World War I, he went abroad to rally support for India's independence. In January 1915, when he was in Switzerland, Virendranath Chattopadhyay of the Berlin Club of the Friends of India (Deutscher Verein der Freunde Indiens) asked the German Foreign Ministry to invite Pratap to Berlin at the latter's request. He was indeed invited, and, at his insistence, he was also granted an audience with Kaiser Wilhelm II, who bestowed on him the Order of the Red Eagle and promised support for the Indian independence movement. During World War I, Germany became one of the most important non-Asian supporters of the pan-Asian movement in its quest for independence from colonial—that is, British or French—rule (see I:25).

Pratap was trained in a German military camp, and in April 1915, along with diplomat Werner Otto von Hentig, he left Berlin for Afghanistan with credentials from the Kaiser (Pratap 1947: 43; Hughes 2002). On the way the delegation met the Khedive of Egypt in Vienna and also Enver Pasha, the leader of the revolutionary Young Turks in the Ottoman Empire and the architect of the Ottoman-German Alliance during World War I. Enver Pasha provided the mission with a military adviser, and once in Afghanistan, they were able raise 2,000 troops (Pratap 1947: 43f).

On 1 December 1915, the first provisional government of India in exile, the Government of Free Hindustan, was established at Kabul (Pratap 1947: 51) with Pratap as president. The new government received support from Enver Pasha, who proclaimed a "holy war" against Britain. It also attempted to obtain assistance from tsarist Russia, Republican China, and Japan. Following the revolution in Russia, Pratap, ready to obtain support also from a communist government, approached the Bolsheviks. In 1919, he met Lenin and Trotsky in Petrograd (Pratap 1947: 60). In the meantime, under pressure from the British, Afghan cooperation was withdrawn from Pratap's Indian government, and the Indian mission in Kabul was closed down.

Following this setback, Pratap went to Japan in 1925 to continue to rally support for the Indian independence movement and engage in pan-Asianist activities. In later years, he visited Japan frequently. Between 1925 and 1945, he cooperated closely with Rash Behari Bose (I:24), the leader of the Indian community in Japan and an important figure in the pan-Asian movement. On the Japanese side, Pratap's supporters included eminent politician Viscount Gotō Shinpei; party politician Tokonami Takejirō; retired Lieutenant General Satō Tetsutarō; journalist and writer Murobuse Kōshin (the author of an early book on Pan-Asianism; Murobuse 1926); pan-Asian activists Ōkawa Shūmei, Nakatani Takeyo, and Mitsukawa Kametarō (see II:2 and II:4); Kokuryūkai-related Tōyama Mitsuru, Tanabe Yasunosuke, and Kuzuu Yoshihisa (see I:10); Miyazaki Ryūsuke (1892–1971, son of Miyazaki Tōten and cofounder of the Popular Socialist Party, Shakai Minshūtō, together with socialist Abe Isoo and Japan Federation of Labor founder Suzuki Bunji, 1885–1946); and Imazato Juntarō, the organizer of the pan-Asian conference held in Nagasaki in 1926 (see II:8). Despite these contacts, the government refused him entry to Japan in 1926 when he came to participate in the Nagasaki conference as the delegate from Afghanistan, as his passport had been stolen en route and he had no identification. Pratap returned to Japan a year later and continued expanding his network, attending meetings of the growing number of pan-Asian societies, such as the Greater Asia Association (Dai Ajia Kyōkai; see II:13) and the Jimmukai (Jimmu Society, founded by Ōkawa Shūmei in 1931) and giving numerous lectures throughout the country, in which he set out his pan-Asian goals and campaigned for Indian independence (Matsuura 2007a).

At the same time as fighting for Indian independence and promoting pan-Asian regionalism, Pratap also advocated some universal ideals—a characteristic of the thought and activities of many pan-Asianists, as in the ideology of the "eight corners of the world under one roof" (*hakkō ichiu*) popular in Japan. To this end, Pratap founded his World Federation Club in 1925 in Berlin and in 1929 launched the *World Federation Monthly Magazine* in Japan as the organization's official organ. His religious activities included cooperating with Japanese religious organizations such as the Ōmotokyō, which had a similar approach to promoting universal values hand in hand with pan-Asian ideals (Li 2007). In his speeches, Pratap advocated the creation of a world capital and a world government (Pratap 1947: 197). He also initiated the formation of a "black-shirt volunteer corps of the World Federation for the Province of Pan-Asia," with the objective of fighting "for the freedom of Asia" (Pratap 1947: 247, 255).

However, Pratap found himself in an awkward position, caught up between the visionary idealism of universal solidarity and humanitarianism on the one hand and the necessities of Realpolitik on the other. In order to secure the necessary Japanese support for his movement, he was forced to refrain from overt criticism of Japanese expansion into China—although he had previously opposed, for example, Japan's move into Manchuria in 1931 and the establishment of Manchukuo (Pratap 1947: 236, 252). His lack of enthusiasm for Japan's creation of a puppet state, which is evident in his recollections of his trips to Manchukuo (Pratap 1947: 252, 263), however, did not make him reconsider his cooperation with Japanese pan-Asianists, as his participation in the third pan-Asian Conference, held in February 1934 in Dairen, makes clear (Pratap 1947: 269; see also II:8). Although this conference was more clearly dominated by the aims of Japanese colonialism and imperialism than its two predecessors in 1926 and 1927, Pratap participated in it and described it as "on the whole a great success," even if he did "not agree with some of the details" (Pratap 1947: 269). His activities followed in the footsteps of Japanese expansion when, in 1935, he visited Inner Mongolia, which Japan had occupied in 1934, and met with local rulers such as Prince Te (Demchugdongrub, 1902–1966) who were cooperating with the Japanese authorities (Pratap 1947: 292f). Even in his autobiography he admits to thinking "that the present government of Japan, following the social system of Germany [*sic*], was trying its best to improve things" (Pratap 1947: 351). It was hardly surprising, therefore, that, just as during World War I, during World War II Pratap again chose to cooperate with Germany—and Japan—in pursuing his goals and that he vanished from the political stage with the defeat of the Tripartite Powers in 1945. Pratap returned to India in 1946 and, following Indian independence (1947), continued to work for radical social reform in India and the abolition of the caste system. He held a seat in the Indian parliament from 1957 to 1962 and died in 1979.

Source (English in the original; the original language has been kept, including grammatical errors)
Pratap, Mahendra (1947), *My Life Story of Fifty-five Years*. Dehradun: World Federation.

December Diary [1930]. The last month of the last year proved a very busy season. The 1st of December opened with a number of engagements. The most striking part of the day's menu was a dinner at the Soviet Embassy of Tokyo. The first secretary kindly invited Mr. Rash Behari Bose and myself to a sumptuous dinner table. . . .

The evening of the 4th became the red letter day of my present visit to Japan. A ceremonial reception was kindly given this day by my Japanese friends. Mr. Kuzu[u] [a leading member of the Kokuryūkai] was the chief organizer but Mr. Bose, as a Japanese citizen, was also on the reception committee. Group photograph was taken, fine dinner was served and full of feeling speeches were delivered. I thanked my hosts for their friendly regard. Afghanistan, Indian, Asian and World Federation questions were touched in my talk. To general satisfaction was passed by the representative gathering representing different sections of the Japanese society, sympathizing with the Indian fighters in their way of liberty.

The Chinese General Chen whom I had visited in the Imperial Hotel kindly came to see Mr. Bose and myself at our residence. I went to Mr. Miyasaki's [Miyazaki] home and met several Chinese gentlemen. His home is the meeting ground of many liberal minded persons. The meeting of the International Lodge Club at the home of Mrs. Omori was very interesting. The speaker of the evening was a Bahai preacher. She spoke on Persia. On account of my knowledge of that part of the world I was asked to say a few words. I chose to speak on religion. I enjoyed the international atmosphere and the hospitality of our hostess but I expressed my regret at the scanty audience. It is an international problem why such meetings are not better attended.

A swift, short but not unimportant visit could kindly be arranged to the Takushoku University. It is a colonial institution preparing students for colonial career. I was asked to speak to a group of students in their large gymnastic hall. I explained my views on the future of the colonial system. I believe that the idea of the colonial possessions must disappear from our society as individual slavery had to go. . . .

Another interesting meeting was a mid day lunch of the Daito Bunca [Bunka] College students. It is an institution for the development of Eastern Culture. . . . Late (*sic*) Count Oki [Ōki Enkichi, 1871–1926] kindly played the part of the chief host. I expressed my hearty thanks for their continued interest in my humble ideas. I recalled the generous hospitality of the late Count. I asked my friends to be true to the principles of renunciation and service, the watch words of all the ancient cultures of the East.

On the 7th December, afternoon, the World Federation branch was formally opened at the school of Mr. Mitsukawa [Kametarō]. I delivered a speech explaining my plan of the World Federation movement. A group photograph was taken with the flag of the World Federation as well.

I was fortunate enough to renew my acquaintance of Hon. Mr. Tokonami [Takejirō]. He is a great champion of the oppressed nations of Asia and Africa. . . .

On the 9th there were three engagements. I took lunch with Mr. M. Ogawa at Yokohama. He is an export-import merchant specially interested in porcelain articles. In the afternoon I spoke at the Chinese Y.M.C.A. Tokyo on the World Federation and in the evening threw was a large mass meeting. Here I also expressed my views on the unity of our human race, however, I made it quite clear that no unity is possible so long as such injustices prevail in society as the groupal slavery in India. Mr. M. Nakano [Nakano Seigō, 1886–1943; see II:1], vice minister of communication, took photograph together with me on the platform.

On the morning of the 10th I left Tokyo. Many kind friends kindly came to see me off. The same evening I arrived at Kobe. Here, Indian brethren received me at the Railway station. I drove to the residence of Mr. Futehally and took up my quarters there. . . .

I remained ten days at Kobe. During this time I spoke at several meetings. One of them was a mass gathering specially organized by the [daily newspaper] Kobe Shinbun at the Y.M.C.A. Hall. One another was a small dinner meeting arranged by Mr. Okami of the Kobe chamber of commerce. Once I went to Osaka to receive a kindly offering, in the form of a reception dinner, at the hands of some of my old friends, members of Kokoku Doshi Kai. Mr. T. [Takeyo] Nakatani, whom our readers know is one of the most active members of the party.

The Japan branch of the Indian National Congress kindly gave me a tea party. I spoke just a few words on the present situation of India and our duty at this juncture. After the party a debate was scheduled on Independent India versus India under the British. However not one Indian was found in the gathering to speak in favour of the British rule. Most moderate element of the Indian society positively declared that the time had long past to open mouth for the British rule! . . .

Our Diary for January [1931]. . . . The first of January found us at Peiping [Beijing], staying quietly in the Pan-Asia office of Mr. Hwang Kung Su, 70 Pa Tiao Hutung. We cared little for the new year. We set to work. We remained very busy for two weeks in preparing and publishing the three different editions of the World Federation. . . . During this time I could secure two opportunities to express my views in two different meetings. ONE MIDDLE SCHOOL kindly asked me to lecture to their students. I spoke on the World Federation. I related my plan of a world capital with five parliaments and a world cabinet. To accomplish our object I recommended immediate establishment of the World Federation Units and the World Federation Offices.

WORLD FEDERATION IN JAPAN

This is what they do and make appear Pro-Japan. Mr. Nakatani and the Director of the office of the World Federation Mr. Mitsukawa have brought out a fine pamphlet in the Japanese language with my speech and my photograph in the group inaugurating the World Federation office at Tokyo. Naturally such kindness impresses one's mind and makes on think and act a friend. We feel obliged. . . .

My Diary for the later part of May [1931]. . . . During my stay of twelve days at Kobe, I got two important opportunities to address two large gatherings. One was a public meeting specially organized by the Oomoto religious group and supported by all the leading press of the city. The attendance was variously estimated between four and five hundred. . . . In any case the audience was enthusiastic. . . .

When the Japanese army forced its way into Manchuria [October 1931] I was thunder struck. I was stunned with the turn of events. Every day since that I started my propaganda in the Far East I advised my Japanese brethren to move south and colonise the uninhabited islands in the South Sea. I strongly recommended closer friendship between China and Japan. But now all these hopes and desires were badly shaken. I felt more sorry for Japan which appeared to me in imminent danger of total destruction. The Shanghai incident brought another bomb shell or a series of bombardments. "Now comes war! Another great world war is [at] our door!" I thought. But so far the Japanese military is entirely successful in their main plan. It does not appear unlikely that they encroach further on Northern China. Where will it lead to? I have to admit that I have sustained a severe defeat in my program in the Far East. Japanese have every right to think that I have been pro-Chinese. And the Chinese to my astonishment believe that I have not opposed the Japanese. They say that my statements against the robber instinct can be equally applied to the Japanese as well as Chinese robbers. In spite of our temporary set back I do not mean to give up my struggle for the welfare of the Far East Asia and the World. . . .

Mr. Yasaburo Shimonaka [owner of the publishing house Heibonsha] is the moving figure of this newly formed society at Tokyo [the Great Asia Society, Dai Ajia Kyōkai; see II:13]. He was kind enough to invite me on behalf of his association to a dinner. I was also asked to give a little talk. I explained the position of Mahatma Gandhi in the great evolution of an All World Culture.

. . . THE GREAT ASIATIC LEAGUE

The soul of this movement is General Matsui [Iwane] (II:13). And we may call Mr. Nakatani, our old friend, the active hand of the association. They were also kind enough to invite me to their banquet. H.E. The *Charge de Affairs* of Turkey was also present. His witty remark that placed as he was between two revolutionaries, meaning Mr. Bose and myself, he found his position difficult, brought on a fit of laughter in the assembly. But the fact that the Turkish government of today which he honourably represents is itself a revolutionary government made us feel a little proud in his company.

Part II

PAN-ASIANISM AND JAPANESE RESPONSES TO FASCISM AND TOTALITARIANISM, 1930–1937

This section covers the first half of the 1930s, when pan-Asian discourse underwent a further radicalization as it fused with ultranationalism and militarism. In general terms, the perceived triumphs of fascism in Italy and national socialism in Germany provided an impetus for this radicalization, as did the apparent success of Soviet economic planning. Even in democracies, the doctrine of free trade was being undermined by talk of autarkic blocs and national unity cabinets. This kind of thinking found a receptive audience in Japan (II:11), where a series of events paved the way for the escalating militarism of the late 1930s.

In 1930 there was a campaign—supported by many pan-Asianists—against the government's signing of the London Naval Limitations Treaty, an instrument that, its critics alleged, fatally compromised Japan's security and jeopardized Japan's mission in Asia through a deal with Asia's Anglo-American oppressors. In 1931 an army-engineered coup resulted in the occupation of Manchuria and, a year later, in the formation of the puppet state of Manchukuo. When this act of aggression against China was censured by the League of Nations, Japan quit the League in 1933.

At home, Japan was rocked by a series of abortive coups d'état and assassinations that destabilized the system of government by party cabinets and led to their final demise in May 1932. In this period, the proponents of cooperation with the West gradually saw their influence eroded as liberals and other critics of militarism and expansionism were silenced through a series of political campaigns.

The silencing of liberal opinion left the field of public debate to extremists, and it was in this atmosphere that pan-Asian discourse was increasingly radicalized. The calls for Japan to assume leadership in Asia and exclude Western influence gained almost universal acceptance (II:10), as did demands for the realization of an Asian Monroe Doctrine.

Chapter Ten

Hosoi Hajime: "Japan's Resolve," 1932

Christopher W. A. Szpilman

Hosoi Hajime (1886–1934), a journalist and an expert on Korean affairs, was born in Tokyo. Because of financial difficulties, he did not go to university, but, at age eighteen, he found a job as a journalist at the daily *Nagasaki Shinpō*, where he covered Asian affairs. In 1907 he moved to Korea, where he was involved in Uchida Ryōhei's machinations to engineer a Japanese annexation of that country (see II:3). At that time Hosoi apparently espoused socialist views in spite of his connections to Uchida, the leader of the right-wing Kokuryūkai (see I:10).

Governor-General Terauchi Masatake's administration took a dim view of Hosoi's socialism and expelled him from Korea in 1911. Back in Japan, he worked as a journalist with the *Asahi Shinbun*, but in 1918 he resigned from this job to return to Korea, where in 1919 he witnessed the anti-Japanese (pro-independence) riots (the March 1 Movement). His experience in Korea—he reported on what he had seen there at a Rōsōkai meeting in 1919 (Mitsukawa 1935)—shocked him into the realization that Japan was confronting a "Korean problem." A "solution to this problem" (Kokuryūkai 1966b: 3:102), he concluded, could be found only if the Japanese could gain a better grasp of Korea's national character (*kokuminsei*). To promote this lofty goal, in 1920 he founded the Jiyū Tōkyūsha (Free Research Company) and began translating representative works of Korean history, classics, and literature into Japanese. At the same time, he lectured throughout Japan on Korea and its problems. Hosoi's achievements in promoting knowledge about Korea are impressive—a number of his books on Korea have been republished in the past thirty years.

As a pan-Asianist, Hosoi insisted on the reality of "one single spirit for the whole of the Great East (*Daitō isshin*)." This spirit was what, in Hosoi's view, made Asia one coherent entity in contrast to its antithetical nemesis, the West.

Though this spiritual doctrine was vague on details, from such pan-Asian premises Hosoi condemned Japan's foreign policy, which he dismissed as subservient to the Western powers, in particular Britain and the United States. Working from the same premises he also attacked the League of Nations, which he regarded—as did many of his contemporaries (see, e.g., I:32)—as a puppet of the Anglo-American powers and a symbol of Western domination over international relations. It was thus both as an advocate of a hard-line foreign policy and as a sworn enemy of the established parties that he joined Tōyama Mitsuru and his old associate Uchida Ryōhei from the Kokuryūkai in their campaign against the ratification of the pacifistic Kellogg-Briand Treaty in 1928.

To promulgate his hard-line and pan-Asian views to a wider public, Hosoi founded a publishing company called the Gettansha, which in the 1930s published the lowbrow monthlies *Hito no Uwasa* (Celebrity Gossip) and *Hito to Kokusaku* (People and National Policy). Such publications, which proved to be lucrative, in addition to the pamphlets and books Hosoi wrote and the lectures he gave, played a significant role in stirring up war fever among the Japanese public in the aftermath of the Manchurian Incident. As the consequences of this incident placed Japan on a collision course with the United States, it is no exaggeration to say that Hosoi's brand of Pan-Asianism (and that of his colleagues) probably influenced the course of history. But Hosoi did not live to witness what he had helped to unleash. He died in 1934 at the age of forty-eight.

Though largely forgotten today, Hosoi was well known in the 1920s and the early 1930s because of his work as a journalist, translator, and publisher. *Nihon no Ketsui* (Japan's Resolve), from which the excerpt here is taken, was written as part of Hosoi's efforts to propagate an aggressive foreign policy and, as such, encapsulates his pan-Asian views.

Nihon no Ketsui included prefaces contributed by four prominent figures—Admiral Viscount Saitō Makoto (1858–1936), the prime minister of the day; General Araki Sadao (1877–1966), the army minister; Murayama Tsurukichi (1883–1956), a retired senior official in the Home Ministry and director of the Chūō Kyōka Dantai Rengōkai (Central Federation of Ideological Guidance Associations); and Yasuoka Masahiro (see II:29). General Araki, a member of the Kōdōha (Imperial Way Faction), was known for his conservative and hard-line foreign policy views, so his endorsement was no surprise. The same was true for Murayama, a former Interior Ministry official known for his reformist zeal. But it seems unlikely that Saitō, who was known to support Prince Saionji Kinmochi's (1849–1940) moderate policies and who four years later would fall victim to the Kōdōha's assassins, supported Hosoi's pan-Asian and expansionist ideas. He probably endorsed the book out of friendship for Hosoi, not because he agreed with his extreme views. There is no doubt, however, that the prime minister's endorsement lent great authority to Hosoi's book.

Little is known about Nonami Shizuo, whom Hosoi quotes at great length in the excerpt reproduced here. Nonami was married to Yaeko, a niece of the nationalist Sugiura Jūgō (Shigetake, 1855–1924). He traveled extensively throughout Asia to collect information on behalf of the South Manchurian Railway Research Department. He seems to have specialized in the study of the opium problem, on which he wrote a number of books and pamphlets that appeared between 1918 and 1933. Some of them were published by the Heibonsha, with whose president, Shimonaka Yasaburō (1878–1961), renowned for his pan-Asian sentiments, he had close ties. He was also on friendly terms with pan-Asian journalist Mitsukawa Kametarō (1888–1936). Nonami's pan-Asian and anti-Western credentials are clear. He was a member of the Dai Ajia Kyōkai (Greater Asia Association; see II:13), which he joined in 1934. And throughout the 1920s he vituperated against the evils of British imperialism. The passage quoted by Hosoi reproduced here gives an accurate insight into his views.

Nihon no Ketsui was published in October 1932, a few months after the formation of the puppet state of Manchukuo (1 March 1932) in the wake of the so-called Manchurian Incident. In the book, Hosoi, drawing partly on Nonami, echoes the arguments already made more than a decade earlier by Kita Ikki (see I:27). Like Kita, he complains about the blatant injustice of the geopolitical status quo under which the white "races" are landlords whose landownership deprives the Japanese, other Asians, and indeed other peoples of color of their living space. Like Kita, he calls for this injustice to be redressed, if necessary by force of arms. Like Kita, he demands domestic reforms, including the formulation of an industrial policy and a controlled economy (Hosoi 1932: 346). More specifically than Kita, however, Hosoi addresses himself to the development of newly acquired Manchuria, rich in raw materials, such as iron, coal, and magnesium, and agricultural products, such as soybeans, which must be speedily integrated with Japan into one coherent, smoothly running, tariff-free, centrally controlled economic system (Hosoi 1932: 298–312).

Likewise, more specifically than Kita Ikki, Hosoi (elsewhere in the book) envisages a division of the world into blocs under which Japan would, among other things, be given a free hand in Asia in return for giving up its interests in the Americas to the United States. Now these visions of an Asian bloc under Japan's leadership and control are at odds with the kind of vague spiritual Pan-Asianism Hosoi advocated. However, it was a contradiction that he chose to ignore. Perhaps he thought (in a manner reminiscent of Henry Ford) that what was good for Japan would also be good for Asia.

It is difficult to assess the effect of *Nihon no Ketsui* on Japanese public opinion with accuracy, but it certainly made a stir. The Kokuryūkai praised it highly in 1936, and it was considered to be important enough as wartime propaganda for it to be republished at the height of the Pacific War (September 1942).

Source (translation from the Japanese original by Christopher W. A. Szpilman)
Hosoi Hajime (1932), *Nihon no Ketsui* (Japan's Resolve). Nihon Yūben Taikai Kōdansha, 322–25, 334.

. . . The White countries in fact occupy 87% of the world's land area and rule over 69% of the world's population. Sated with the blood and sweat that they have squeezed out of the people of color, they have left less than 13% of the world's land area and 31% of its population to independent countries inhabited by people of color. A country like Britain, with a small population of 46 million—that is, slightly over 9.5%, not even 10% [of the global total]—rules over 480 million people of color—a population ten times its own size—but it is still not satisfied, plundering rights and privileges in the east [Asian] region at will. Can international justice really condone this unquenchable greed? It is like having a person sitting in a crowded train, where there are people unable to get a seat, who stretches his arms and legs over the other seats and who, if anybody tries to sit even on the edge of a seat, immediately starts berating them as an "invader." Can mankind tolerate this kind of behavior? And even assuming that mankind does accept it, can God permit it?

Let me clearly declare on this occasion that, sooner or later, all such irrationalities must be resolved.

THE ASIAN FEDERATION: THE FIRST AND THE SECOND STAGE OF THE PLAN

We believe that, to complete our mission as mentioned above, we must set clear goals for an Asian federation. In other words, we believe that [we must] connect Samara to Constantinople and then descending south, draw a line that would include Egypt and Sudan, all the way down to Mozambique. In this way we will realize a greater Eastern sphere—but this will be achieved at the second stage of [our plan]. In the immediate future, we hope to link Hsingking [the capital of Manchukuo, present Changchun], Táonán, Ulan-Bator, Turfan [an oasis city in the present Xinjiang, or Sinkiang Uighur Autonomous Region, China], Yili [a city in the Xinjiang region], and

Tashkent with a single line connecting them all. The area contained within this line, from Afghanistan all the way down to Gwadar [a port on the Gulf of Oman in what is now Pakistan], is necessarily the goal of the first stage of the plan.

Rather than explain it here in detail myself, I will quote from a statement about the Asian Federation and a letter of intent concerning the establishment of a committee to study the means of control, domestic and foreign, by a pioneer of this problem, Mr. Nonami Shizuo. We hope that you will approve of it.

A Personal View by Nonami Shizuo

World Developments

1. With the Great European War as a watershed, three world trends have emerged in a striking way: a trend toward the formation of large states (*taikokushugi*), a trend toward planned economies (*tōseishugi*), and, at the same time, a trend toward national self-determination has also been promoted. To harmonize and adjust these three great and, at first glance, irreconcilable trends, it is an urgent and highly important task to formulate a national policy that would render the Japanese Empire's position in Asia impregnable.

2. Great Britain, which exemplifies old-style imperialism, is now inescapably in the throes of a decline and, though it is just about managing to maintain the status quo thanks to its hold on India, its future is doomed. Some believe that America has now passed its peak but, because of its vast territories and raw materials, the United States cannot be underestimated. However, the most serious issue at present is the revival of Soviet Russia, which, once its second five-year-plan is completed in 1937, will project enormous power throughout the northern hemisphere.

3. These are the reasons that our awareness of the world must transcend the realm of mere old-style imperialism; we must grasp the essence of international phenomena as they arise at each moment.

Greater Asianism

4. The trends toward the formation of large states and planned economies are clearly exemplified by arguments for a European federation, Pan-Americanism, the ideology of the Soviet Federation, etc. It is only natural that in Asia, too, there should arise the need for a Greater Asianism.

5. The underlying tone of this Greater Asianism must be the national (ethnic) freedom and national (state) independence of every Asian country. Based on the exhaustive inspection tours of Egypt, Turkey, Persia, Arabia, Afghanistan and other countries that I have undertaken in recent years, I conclude that

all these countries are on the road to reform based upon nationalism (*minzokushugi*). In fact, the recent independence of the mandated territory of Iraq positively proves it—as does the Indian independence movement, which is Britain's greatest concern. Likewise, the present revolutionary coup in Siam probably aims to eliminate French and British influence from that country.

6. Japan must now discard its existing foreign policy of subservience to the West; it must, in cooperation with these Asian countries, establish a new monolithic power under the umbrella of Greater Asianism; and, based on the so-called principle of autonomous diplomacy, it must help and guide the entire continent of Asia. . . .

TO THE LEADERS OF THE CHINESE REPUBLIC

. . . the mission of Japan, the land of the rising sun, is far-reaching. This is no time to waste our vital energy by arguing over insignificant short-term interests. As a first step toward the realization of an Asian league we wish, first of all, to guide and nurture the healthy development of the new Manchurian State. We must at the same time find a solution to the anti-Japanese sentiment that is filling the hearts of the four hundred million Chinese who are becoming "red" because of the Communist bandits, and strive to restore friendly relations between our two countries that share the same concerns. This is the only way to realize our great aspirations.

Chapter Eleven

Mori Kaku: "Extraordinary Means for Extraordinary Times," 1932

Christopher W. A. Szpilman

Mori Kaku (1882–1932) was born in Osaka and, after attending Tokyo Commercial College (present-day Hitotsubashi University), obtained a job with the Shanghai Branch of the Mitsui Trading Company (Mitsui Bussan). He soon rose to the position of manager of the Mitsui Bussan's Tientsin Branch, a position that enabled him to amass a substantial fortune. In Tientsin, he developed political ambitions, and in 1918 he joined the political party Seiyūkai. In April 1920 he retired from Mitsui Bussan and immediately (May 1920) was elected to the Diet on the Seiyūkai ticket. But it was only in 1927 when his party came to power that Mori was given the opportunity to formulate Japan's foreign policy. In the Seiyūkai cabinet (1927–1929), Mori occupied the relatively junior post of parliamentary vice minister in the Foreign Ministry. But as the Foreign Ministry portfolio was held by Prime Minister Tanaka Giichi (1864–1929), Mori was given a free hand in running the ministry. Mori had always detested Shidehara Kijūrō's policy of cooperation with the West and peaceful economic expansion in China. Shidehara's mistake, Mori complained, was to think of China as a state like Britain or the United States. Mori, in contrast, regarded China as a mere geographical expression, not as a state as such. China was divided into regions, each run by its own military clique or warlord; no responsible central government existed to negotiate with. The only way to deal with the Chinese, he insisted, was by military intervention.

In his new post, Mori took the initiative in launching a hard-line interventionist policy toward China. He was the moving spirit behind the "Eastern Conference" (*tōhō kaigi*, 1927), which formulated this new aggressive policy. After the collapse of the Tanaka cabinet over a matter relating to its China policy (the assassination of Marshal Chang Tso-lin, 1928), Mori found himself again in opposition. In 1930 he campaigned against the London Naval

Limitations Treaty, and, behind the scenes (after 1931), he worked to bring about a national unity government. At this point in his career, under the influence of developments in Europe, he had concluded that the era of party politics, democracy, and liberalism was over. After the fall of Wakatsuki Reijirō's (1866–1949) Minseitō cabinet in December 1931, Mori was appointed cabinet secretary in the Seiyūkai cabinet headed by Inukai Tsuyoshi (1855–1932); however, Inukai was assassinated on 15 May 1932 before Mori had the chance to distinguish himself in this post. Some months later, Mori's political career came to an abrupt end when he died at age fifty.

The speech reproduced here was made in June 1932. Over the previous nine months, the Japanese political scene had been in turmoil. In September 1931 the incident at Mukden marked the beginning of the Japanese annexation of Manchuria. In February and March 1932 former Finance Minister Inoue Junnosuke (1869–1932) and Baron Dan Takuma (1858–1932), president of the Mitsui zaibatsu (conglomerate), had been assassinated. And, although two military plots (October 1931 and March 1932) had been nipped in the bud before any physical damage was done, a third, also abortive, had resulted in the assassination of Prime Minister Inukai, thus putting an end to the era of party cabinets.

This political instability came hand in hand with economic difficulties. Like many of his contemporaries, Mori was increasingly impressed by the successes of fascism/national socialism in Europe, which appeared to offer a way out of the impasse, political and economic, that the existing political system based on liberalism had been unable to provide. Small wonder that some of Mori's views at the time had a distinctly fascist ring to them. Mori railed against the status quo, which, he insisted—using metaphors often employed by Western fascists—must be "smashed" or "surgically removed" (Yamaura 1941: 35).

The changes Mori proposed were wide ranging. The existing parliamentary system should be "smashed" on account of its slowness and inefficiency and because, in his opinion, it deprived the Japanese of their "freedom to act." The government should introduce a planned economy, adopt an active industrial policy, and impose stringent controls over banks and insurance companies and over the entire agricultural and fisheries sector, where a government rice monopoly should be introduced. He even recommended some (albeit limited) expropriation of private property. Only by resorting to such firm measures, Mori believed, would Japan overcome its endemic economic problems (Szpilman 2004).

Mori's proposed dismantling of the domestic status quo came in tandem with his advocacy of a continental expansion and an "Asian Monroe Doctrine." It would be tempting to put all this talk of expansion down to the charged atmosphere of 1932 with its rumored coups and assassinations, but that was not the case. Mori's tone may have become more strident in the 1930s, but the views he advanced were not new. As early as 1915 he had talked of an East Asian federation (*Tōa renpō*) and had advocated tough policies toward China even before he joined the Seiyūkai. Nor was there anything new or original about his view of China as a dysfunctional state with which it was a waste of time negotiating. That was essentially his position at the Eastern Conference of 1927. It was such long-held views that, prior to and during the Pacific War, earned Mori a reputation as a "pioneer of the New East Asian Order" (Abe 1980: 133–44).

But, at the core of Mori's Pan-Asianism—as in the case of many, perhaps most pan-Asianists—was anti-Westernism. This shows clearly in his insistence that Japan "should part company with the materialistic civilization of the Occident, which we have followed blindly for sixty years, and return to the old spiritual life of Japan and preserve Asia in accordance with the pristine culture and ideals of the Orient" (quoted by Hugh Byas, *New York Times*, 2 October 1932).

In his speech reproduced here, Mori's sounds very much like radical pan-Asianists such as Kita Ikki or Ōkawa Shūmei (see I:27 and II:4). Like them, Mori regarded the Western presence in Asia as the chief cause of Japan's and, by extension, of Asia's misfortunes. Like them, Mori called for Japan's "return to Asia," entailing the repudiation of the Versailles–Washington treaty system and the League of Nations. His dismissal of the League as at best irrelevant, if not downright harmful, to Asia also bears a striking similarity to Kita's (and other radical pan-Asianists') views on the subject, as does his insistence on drastic domestic reform as a necessary prelude to the liberation of Asia.

In 1932, as a starting point for his projected reforms, Mori singled out Manchuria, which was in the process of being annexed by Japan. It was in Manchuria, he thought, that Japan's experiment in domestic reform could be nurtured until it was ready for transplantation to Japan (a notion in keeping with the vision of Japan's so-called neobureaucrats). But once Japan had undergone reform, its mission to liberate Asia would begin. On the continent, this would in the first place take the form of saving China from the mess it found itself in. Once that was accomplished and (presumably) Chinese aid co-opted, the liberation of other areas would follow as a matter of course. However, this is more or less a tacit assumption, as Manchuria, Mongolia, and China were the priority for Mori, and his references to other areas were vague enough to amount to little more than rhetoric.

In Mori's thinking, the East Asian Monroe Doctrine—a reaction to an economic bloc system that Britain was attempting to form to overcome the effects of the Great Depression—was restricted in application to Manchuria, Mongolia, and China. But, as was also the case with America's Monroe Doctrine, Mori tacitly assumed a hierarchical relationship in the sphere where the doctrine would apply. Following liberation, Japan would provide regional leadership and protect the other states of Asia. However, the exigencies of politics forced Mori to limit the scope of his vision. For all his talk of Pan-Asianism and of an Asian federation, Mori—in contrast to, say, Ōkawa—focused his attention on the country he knew best, that is, China (with Manchuria and Mongolia thrown in). In the end he gave little attention to the broader version of Pan-Asianism. Mori's Eastern Monroe Doctrine, as his biographer Yamaura Kan'ichi (1941: 644) acknowledged, was later developed and expanded by his intellectual heirs into the ideas of the "New Order in East Asia" (see II:17) and the "Greater East Asian Co-Prosperity Sphere" (see II:24). That was the main significance of Mori's version of Pan-Asianism.

Source (translation from the Japanese original by Christopher W. A. Szpilman)
Mori Kaku, "Hijōji no hijō shudan" (Extraordinary Means for Extraordinary Times). *Diamond*, July 1932, reprinted in Yamaura Kan'ichi, *Tōa Shintaisei no Senku: Mori Kaku*. Mori Kaku Denki Hensankai, 1941, 26–29.

"Hijōji no hijō shudan," a talk given 18 June 1932 at the Conference to Discuss the Political Situation organized by the Diamond Publishing Co, and published in *Weekly Diamond*, 11 July 1932.

Our main goal is at least to ensure that the Japanese have freedom to act in the East (*tōyō*). This will ensure the right to survival for the Japanese. We are trying to restore this right. Once this is achieved, the Japanese will be able to act gloriously.

THE EAST ASIAN MONROE DOCTRINE.

The same goes for the League of Nations. Recently—I believe the date was 23 February during the Inukai administration—a response was sent to the Council of the League of Nations. Although this communication has an extraordinary significance for Japan's foreign relations, at the time people did not consider it particularly important. If anything, they were not even aware of it. To explain the situation—under the terms of both the Nine-Nation Treaty [1922] and the Kellogg-Briand Treaty [1928], all prerequisite conditions entailed the recognition of China as an organized state. That is, it was regarded as a state with real power equal to other states, a law-abiding state. However, in the rejoinder of 23 February [1932] Japan declared it would not recognize China as an organized state. In so doing, Japan clearly demolished the premises that formed the foundations of the Nine-Nation Treaty. . . .

The direction of our national policy (*kokuze*) has already been determined. To use the term that is fashionable these days, it is the Eastern Monroe Doctrine. Recently I made a radio broadcast under the title "Return to Asia" (*Ajia ni kaere*), which argued that Japan has no need to get involved in or meddle with the League of Nations. That should be left to those countries that have an interest in it. For a start, the League of Nations is not a league for maintaining world peace, but rather a league aimed at maintaining peace in Europe. Japan's divine task (*tenshoku*) is to withdraw rapidly from such an organization, return to Asia, and work hard to enhance the quality of life of seven or eight hundred million Asians. At the very least, in the East (*tōyō*) the Japanese must, by diplomatic means, secure a sphere where they have freedom to act. If Japan obtains freedom in this way, then as a result Japanese industry will be able to revive. And if Japanese industry revives, this new Japan, with its 70 million-strong population and a vigorous natural population growth, will be set to progress splendidly. But the way things are now, a solution to this problem will never be found by attempting to transplant to the United States and South America people of a different skin color. This is one of things I am aiming for.

However, if we strive to achieve such results by diplomatic means it is inevitable that forces bent on preventing our success will appear. We must oppose such forces. We must prepare for such resistance. Domestically, our financial and economic institutions no longer correspond to the reality of Japanese life. For example, what can be done about the recent five billion yen's debt accumulated by the rural sector (*nōson*)? What can be done to alleviate the problems of those below the middle class? There are many problems that require solutions. But these solutions cannot be found by relying on the existing financial and economic institutions. If something is to be done about it, pressure must be applied to these bodies and solutions obtained by applying new methods. If this is done, there will be an outcry from various quarters. But if we were to be alarmed by such a response and hesitate, we would never open up Japan's path to the future. To accomplish this, there is no other way but to reform the existing financial and economic institutions.

Chapter Twelve

Matsumoto Gaku and the Japan Culture League, 1933

Roger H. Brown

In 1933 Matsumoto Gaku (Manabu, 1886–1974) established the Nippon Bunka Renmei (Japan Culture League). Devoted to propagating Japan's culture and pan-Asian destiny, the League exemplifies the manner in which nationalist and pan-Asian ideologies reinforced each other during the 1930s. Matsumoto graduated from Tokyo Imperial University and entered the Home Ministry in 1911, embarking on a successful bureaucratic career culminating with service in the two positions coveted most by elite ministry officials: bureau chief and prefectural governor. Matsumoto headed the Shrines Bureau (1924–1925), Social Bureau (1931), and Police Bureau (1932–1934) and was governor of Shizuoka (1926), Kagoshima (1927–1928), and Fukuoka (1929–1931) prefectures. The job of governor, in particular, was synonymous with the ministry's elitist ideal of "shepherding the people," an archetype highly valued by Matsumoto and one he relied on in his nationalist and pan-Asian activities (Itō 2006; Brown 2009).

In the late 1920s, Matsumoto, increasingly critical of party-led cabinets, drew close to the nationalist ideologue Yasuoka Masahiro (see II:29) and like-minded officials such as Gotō Fumio (1884–1980) and Yoshida Shigeru (1885–1954; not to be confused with the diplomat and prime minister of the same name), joining them at the Kinkei Gakuin (Golden Pheasant Academy) to discuss political affairs and listen to Yasuoka lecture on East Asian theories of good governance. In 1931 Matsumoto worked with Yasuoka in creating the Nippon Nōshi Gakkō (Japan Agrarianist School) and, in 1932, participated in founding the Kokuikai (National Mainstay Society), a forum that became famous as the headquarters of reformist "new bureaucrats" (Otabe 1981; Brown 2009). When the cabinet of Admiral Saitō Makoto resigned in July 1934, Matsumoto retired from the bureaucracy, took a seat in the House of Peers, and devoted himself to cultural activism in support of national unity at home and national mission abroad. After the war, Matsumoto served as chief of the Central Police Academy from 1947 to 1948, founded and then oversaw the International Association of Ports and Harbors from 1947 to 1963, and served as head of the Japan Rivers Association from 1952 to 1972 (Itō 2006).

Matsumoto called for the creation of the Nippon Bunka Renmei in a short article in the Kokuikai's newsletter in July 1933, proposing it as the core of a "Fifth International" to offset the four "internationals" of the global socialist movement and to counter the recently established Nihon Puroretaria Bunka Renmei (Japan Proletarian Culture League) (Matsumoto 1933; Itō 2006). Consulting with Kokuikai associates and with business leaders such as Baron Gō Seinosuke (1865–1942), Matsumoto elicited financial support for his endeavor from the Mitsui, Mitsubishi, and Sumitomo conglomerates. Although Matsumoto failed in his effort to place the League at the center of the 1940 celebration of the country's founding, by 1938 the organization encompassed some 297 cultural groups involved in various traditional arts, martial arts, literature, theater, and international cultural exchange. Meanwhile, in 1937 the Nippon Bunka Renmei oversaw the creation of the associated Nippon Bunka Chūō Renmei (Central League for Japanese Culture), which supplanted the original League when that organization disbanded in December 1939 and which continued operation until 22 December 1945 (Furukawa 1998; Nihon Bunka Chūō Renmei 1938; Itō 2006).

Matsumoto brought the elitist outlook of a Home Ministry bureaucrat to his use of national culture to combat communist ideology and promote Japan's pan-Asian mission, envisioning the creation of a permanent, authoritative cultural organization for unifying government officials and the people. His writings exemplify how domestic political concerns and potent nationalism intersected with Japan's growing rejection of the Versailles–Washington order, ensuing drive for autarky, and expanding war with China. As was common with Japanese pan-Asianists in the 1930s, his invocations of Asian values consistently returned to Japan as the ultimate embodiment of those principles and the force by which they would become central to a new world order.

Matsumoto's efforts to convince foreign audiences of the justness of Japan's pan-Asian destiny are exemplified in the League's monthly English-language magazine *Cultural Nippon*. The excerpt reproduced here constitutes perhaps his most expansive, least Japan-centric and explicitly pan-Asianist perspective on the history of modern East Asia and its relations with the West, identifying the peculiar characteristics of the "Light of the East" with the imperative of realizing a new world civilization based on such Asian wisdom.

Source (English in the original)
Matsumoto Gaku, "Eastern Culture and Its Peculiar Features." *Cultural Nippon* 8:4, 1–15.

The East as distinguished from the West may be taken as comprising Japan, Manchuria, China, India, Southwestern Asia and territories of the South Seas, while the latter division of the world includes Europe, the Americas, and Africa, although the last named continent may be closer to the East than the West in cultural affinities. The extensive areas grouped as the East passed under the domination of Western countries at the dawn of the modern era and became for the most part colonies of the people who had come from Europe and elsewhere. It may be scarcely any exaggeration to say that the western civilization of the modern times was based in no small measure upon the exploitation of Eastern nations and the expropriation of material resources in their countries. The grasping hands that reached out of the west to Arabia, India and the South Seas finally fastened their hold on China and this hold was tightened in the years following the Opium War.

In China, however, the invading influences of the West found a country, unlike others of the East, more firmly knit by national sentiment and historical tradition. The fabric of its national life was found strong enough to maintain its unity in face of the process of western colonization. But China's protest and resistance were only partially successful. Many of its important ports, towns and islands were ceded or otherwise surrendered. Railways were built in the country with foreign capital and held under its control. The steadily expanding influence of European and other interests threatened to interfere even in the province of internal government and politics.

Japan was not overlooked by people who had come out from the west. Japan's modern history might have taken a course very much different from what it has but for the Imperial reign restored in good time and the national solidarity achieved under its direction. Japan not only successfully held its ground against the pressure from the West but in time came even to assume its position as a bulwark of the East against Western penetration and incursion.

It has always been the policy of Western countries, particularly of Britain, to extend their influence over other countries by the principle of "divide and rule." This principle was applied to the East and proved successful so far as to bring about dissension and conflict where countries had been held together by cultural understanding, ethnic affinity, geographic conditions and neighbourly sentiment. The East became a house divided. The hands that drove a wedge between Japan, China, India and other countries also brought them together like pawns moved in the games that were played by deep planning minds. The frequent clashes and costly disputes that were seen in the East in those times were due to the engineering of those minds. The peoples of the East who might have remained as kinsmen fought and killed one another only to serve the purposes of Western interests. This applies to the Sino-Japanese War, the Boxer Uprising, the Manchurian Incident and more recently the China Incident even as it does to the internal discord that kept Korea in turmoil for many years late in the last century, the civil wars of China and the trouble of Indians religiously divided.

Countries that had their own interests to advance in the East wished to see Japan at war with China. They knew that a war would weaken Japan and that a weak Japan and a weak China might easily be held under their control. It would have well suited their purpose to make Japan lose its position as the Far Eastern rampart against Western incursion. It was plain that with Japan reduced to a subordinate position, the whole of the Far East would easily and completely pass under European domination. Through the situations that developed under such conditions of international politics in China, by the multiform experiences that Far Eastern countries had to go through, and from the lessons they learned at their own expense, they now know who are their common enemies. Japan and China have fought and are still fighting, but they now know that they are truly friends and should have remained friends like kinsmen that they really are. It is a great tragedy of the East that these two nations who have so much in common between them have been in a death struggle when their true enemies stood elsewhere.

It is the duty of all Far Eastern peoples to recognize the indivisible unity of the East that was divided by Western peoples and win it back to them. This new sense of duty derives, not from pure speculation or aspiration, but from the happenings of historical moment that now indicate its possibilities and even its certainty. There is no lack of signs of the collapse of the so-called western civilization. It is almost equally evident that the principle by which mankind is to be saved from its fatal involvement in the ruin and wreck of western civilization must be found in the East. It is no longer the aspiration or the idealism of the East alone that the East should shake itself free from its colonial or semi-colonial conditions and turn to its own life and heritage and bring out the best that is in them and develop it in all its worthy aspects. We Eastern people should no longer bend our knees in worship of false gods. We should instead turn and look into our own life so as to recover its true soul. . . . For my present purpose I will take Japan, China, and India and look into their cultural life with regard to god, nature and man, the points on which their minds may be considered in relationship with world concepts of what forms the cardinal points of universal life.

The characteristic of the Eastern conception of god is that it is not regarded, as in the West, as an existence in contrast to man. European myths represent god as creator and man as his creation. . . . On the other hand, god and man are not conceived as at conflict in any of the Eastern schools of thought or philosophy. In the mythology of the Aryans who flourished in India the sun god Mitra, with Varuna, are represented as objects of affectionate worship. . . . In the Confucianism of China as well, heaven and earth are represented as being on intimate terms. . . . The native faith of Japan also conceives of divinity and man in harmonious relations. In Shintoism gods and men are parents and children. The gods are supreme beings but they are given human attributes. Men are shown as descendants of deities and as such destined later to be deities. In this faith the welfare of deities is thought the welfare of men. This relationship between deities and men as translated in terms of mundane life is seen in the relationship between the Emperor who is a personified deity and his subjects. It is from this principle that duty is stressed as between "the ruler and the ruled" and affection between "parent and child." . . . The world of the Verdic deities where light was given to all men and the nirvana which Buddha could promise only in the next world are found possible in Japan where all minds of men unite in one object of worship, the Emperor. . . . The rule of the Emperor who rules according to the will of his high ancestral deities is akin to the Chinese principle of emperors of high virtue ruling by representing the will of heaven. The only point of difference to be stressed is that the Japanese faith is quite free from the thoughts of usurpation of the throne and of revolution. . . .

The confronting positions taken by God and man in the thought of the West, to which I have already referred, are likewise seen in the conception of nature as against man. . . . Far different is the Eastern conception of nature and man; there is no thought of confrontation or conquest; no materialism as against spiritualism. Here nature and man are conceived as of one origin, born of gods and not created by them. . . . Instead of analyzing nature or arranging it in terms of abstraction, or dealing with nature as something inanimate, the Eastern effort was to become one with the life of nature itself.

This attitude is also discernible in architecture, land-scape-gardening, furnitures and paintings. . . . The same attitude is likewise shown in the provinces of industry and economics. . . . It may be said likewise with regard to government. The true principle of government is to give life to the people and to enable each of them to find his own proper place in society and fulfill his own destiny and purpose of life. It is therefore thought that only men of high virtue are capable of such government and as such are entrusted with government by the will of heaven. Hence the idea of the kingly way. The Emperor of Japan who rules by divine order and follows the will of heaven in doing so directs his government so as to enable every one of his subjects to find his proper place in communal life and fulfill his purpose in life.

Lastly, with regard to man, it is the rule of the modern school of the West to consider all things of creation from the standpoint of mankind. Men are emancipated even from men. Their emancipation signifies a complete negation of authority and status. Men are regarded as equal, as individual units placed in reciprocal relationships and generally confronting in outlooks and interests. As God stands confronting man, and also as nature exists in opposition to him so men stand against men.

But the Eastern school of thought conceives men only as forming a whole even as gods and men, nature and man, are considered to make a whole. Men are conceived either in moral relations as between the ruler and the ruled, parent and child, man and wife, brothers and sisters, or in social relationships of friends, of elder and younger, master and follower. There is no conception of men as individual units. They are always considered as units forming the whole. They are regarded as important only for the roles they play within the whole and the orders which are assigned to them within the same entirety of associate life. . . . This idea in Japan is expressed in the undivided allegiance that every subject owes to the Emperor. . . .

Where men are self-seeking and therefore confronting one another, and where they are free and equal, they will make use of others for their own interests. And when they make use of others, then only is there unity of interests or purpose. Even as nature is turned to good account, so men are turned to serviceable purposes. Where there is use for other men, there arises the thought of contracts and the relation of right and obligation. In the East, however, men never regard others in light of serviceable instruments or materials. There men are each their own absolute selves in the places that they fill. We make men live even as we make nature live. Men live when they live within the compass of the whole or, in other words, when they are active in public service. For this reason, when men make others live they themselves are enabled to live. The principle of the way of Bodhisattva as taught by Buddha means to serve other people to serve one's own interests. This conception of moral truth is possible because the interest of the self is considered as identical with, and indivisible from, that of others. The same principle underlies what Confucianism teaches as benevolence and loyalty. These thoughts attain a form of national morality, elevated and purified, in Japan where a strong structure of national life is seen under the one supreme ruler of the country.

From the preceding discussion, brief as it is, some idea will have been formed of the characteristics of the civilization of the East. These characteristics, taken as a whole, may be summarised into four attributes; namely, total, life-giving, harmonizing, and peaceful. These attributes are not seen in contrast but in blending or co-existent features that unite to make one whole, the features discernible only when observed from different angles.

By the term "total" is meant that attitude of mind which observes objects as entireties, and not analytical parts. . . . When an object is analyzed and observed in terms of abstraction, it is no longer alive, is deprived of its life. Men can be said alive only when they are conceived as whole entireties. However pretty a flower may be, or its colour or shape, its true soul is never caught unless it is considered as a whole. Hence, the characteristic attitude to give life to men and all things and to bring out the true life and quality of men and things.

The attitude to give life is harmonizing and non-confronting in nature. . . . It is true that the minds of Eastern people are not necessarily foreign to contrast or antithesis. In fact, there often are conflicts, opposition and contradiction, but they exist only until they are reconciled and harmonized. . . .

The peace that results from this [harmonizing] attitude is unlike what is attained by compromise, or by arbitration of those who wish to make use of one another, or what is sought by those who shirk action of any sort. The peace that is attained is the rhythmic harmony produced by units working in unison and fusing to form one complete whole. In the East importance is given to the art of war, but the word for martial art is represented by two ideograms meaning "suspension of arms." The idea is that arms are raised only against those who would break the harmony of the whole. The object of arms is to restore the harmony of the whole. Importance is given to the art of war but warfare itself is never sought or approved. But because the importance of arms is recognized in the East, its people have often been misunderstood to be warlike. The truth is that the East is alive to the importance of arms because it values peace in its truest sense. For history tells that the fate of those nations which court peace because they do not wish to take up arms under any circumstances is doomed. The present world war itself already affords cases in point.

And now the question may be raised, as to what position does the civilization of the East take with regard to the history of the world? The civilization of the East with all its peculiar characteristics would be worthless if it is left only as a relic of the past, arrayed on the shelves of a museum or catalogued in the archives of history. It would indeed serve no purpose to seek out such an obsolete order of life or thought. The civilization of the East should be relegated to the limbo of oblivion if it represented only a backward stage of cultural development or a stagnation of cultural work, as compared with the accomplishments of the West. By discarding their own, the peoples of the East would have to take the path lighted by the beacon of western civilization.

But we have faith in the civilization of the East. We find in its peculiar features an attitude of mind permanent, unshakeable and unbroken through the centuries of Eastern history. Under the tide of the western civilization that has swept over the East, our own cultural life although in no small parts yet superficially seems to have passed out of sight. But we do know that the stream from our old spring flows on continually and irresistibly. Those of us who thought their cultural attainment marked a backward stage of world civilization were not few. They had ill digested ideas of the streams of civilization that had come from the West. Many of these men strove to throw overboard what they had inherited from the past and hastened to delve in the books of the West. But it is now known that what was considered by them as a backward state of civilization or a condition of under-development of cultural life really represented the true values of the Eastern civilization. It is now realized that to discard what is the production of the East through centuries is to disown the East itself and to accept its fate as a colony of the West.

The ruin of the western civilization is now spoken of as it never has been. Its possibility is seen as never before. If the fabric of European civilization collapses, as it is threatening to do, it would mean the defeat of the intellectual achievement of the West, the collapse of the structure built by processes of analysis, formulation of abstract rules, subjugation of contradictory interests; the defeat of the minds that moved by tenets of individualism and liberalism. The fate that faces the West could only be averted by adoption of the cultural principle of Eastern life which is total in attitude, life-giving in purpose and harmonizing and peaceful in the working of intellectual forces. The scientific achievement of the West should be elevated by the principle of the East. Into the technical accomplishments of the West in the modern ages a new blood should be infused in the form of Eastern wisdom. The duty now imposed on the East is to negate the modern civilization of the West in its fundamental points, to give it flesh and blood anew from the deep wisdom of the East, and develop a new order of world civilization, higher in motive and greater in scope. This is the world mission with which the East is now charged. The oft-repeated dictum, "Light comes from the East," rings never truer than at present.

Chapter Thirteen

The Greater Asia Association and Matsui Iwane, 1933

Torsten Weber

The Greater Asia Association (Dai Ajia Kyōkai) was probably the single most influential organization to propagate Pan-Asianism between 1933 and 1945. Despite its prominence and its far-reaching activities, it received little attention in English-language research (the only comprehensive work in Japanese to date is Matsuura 2010). As a result, relatively little is known about its activities.

The Greater Asia Association was the successor organization to the Pan-Asia Study Society (Han Ajia Gakkai), which was founded in April 1932 by the founder-owner of the publishing house Heibonsha Shimonaka Yasaburō (1878–1961), the writers and activists Nakatani Takeyo (1898–1990) and Mitsukawa Kametarō (1888–1936), the Indian revolutionary Rash Behari Bose (1886–1945), and Vietnamese Prince Cuong De (1882–1951) (see previous chapters). The society's self-declared aim was to study the political, economic, and cultural problems of Asia. Unlike most other pan-Asian organizations, its focus was not limited to East Asia but explicitly included South, Southeast, and Central Asia. According to Nakatani, who later became the chief disseminator of Pan-Asianism within the Greater Asia Association, the society's name was inspired by existing pan-movements in other parts of the world (Nakatani 1989: 349).

Shortly after the society had been founded, Lieutenant General Matsui Iwane (1878–1948) of the Army General Staff proposed that the original study group be expanded into a larger organization (on Matsui's Pan-Asianism, see Matsuura 2010: chap. 9). Initially, the members of the Gakkai were reluctant to allow Matsui to join their group out of fear that it might be mistaken for an organization influenced or controlled by the army. But they changed their minds soon and permitted Matsui to join, although only as a private individual, and eventually they also agreed to Matsui's proposal to develop a more practically oriented organization with a view to initiating a popular Asianist movement. Thus, a new organization, named the Greater Asia Association, was founded in Tokyo on 1 March 1933, the "auspicious day of the first anniversary of the founding of Manchukuo," with the aim of promoting "the unification, liberation, and independence of the Asian peoples" (Murakawa Kengo in *Dai Ajiashugi* 1:1, 62).

The Greater Asia Association managed to attract as members leading representatives from the political, cultural, academic, and military worlds—figures such as Prince Konoe Fumimaro (president of the House of Peers future prime minister), Hirota Kōki (future foreign minister and prime minister), the writer Tokutomi Iichirō (see I:28), Yano Jin'ichi (1872–1970, professor of Sinology at Kyoto University), Murakawa Kengo (1875–1946, professor of history at Tokyo University), and Admiral Suetsugu Nobumasa (1880–1944). Shimonaka Yasaburō became the organization's president. Nakatani Takeyo assumed the duties as acting president, while Tanaka Masaaki (1911–2006), who would become notorious as a revisionist publicist in postwar Japan, became the editor in chief of the organization's publications, such as the bulletin *Dai Ajiashugi* (Greater Asianism), from which the founding manifesto of the association reproduced here is taken. *Dai Ajiashugi* was published from May 1933 through April 1942, and the topics covered ranged from "A History of the Republican Movement in India" (Subhas Chandra Bose, September 1936) and "Pan-Slavism and the Third Reich" (Imaoka Jūichirō, February 1935) to "The New Order in East Asia and in Europe" (Sugimori Kōjirō, September 1940) and "The Structure of Greater East Asian History and Japan's Historic Mission" (Yano Jin'ichi, April 1942). In its earlier volumes it also published translations of theoretical writings by Hans Kohn and Oswald Spengler, but contributions by non-Asians remained scarce. In addition, the Shanghai Greater Asianism Research Institute, a branch of the Dai Ajia Kyōkai set up in 1940, between 1941 and 1943 published an English-language journal called *Asiatic Asia*, which mostly reprinted articles from the *Dai Ajiashugi* in translation.

Nakatani, a "professional nationalist" (Storry 1957: 150), who was also a professor at Tokyo's Hōsei University, had been a member of various nationalistic and pan-Asian societies. Later he claimed that during his time with the Greater Asia Association he experienced the closest intimacy in thought, trust, and human relationships and named Shimonaka, Tanaka, and Matsui as forming the "central axis" of the organization (Nakatani 1985: 5). Judging by his copious contributions, Nakatani himself must certainly be included in the core of the group. In 1947, when Matsui was tried for war crimes at the International Military Tribunal for the Far East (also known as Tokyo Trials, 1946–1948), both Shimonaka and Nakatani appeared in court to testify for Matsui and emphasized the philanthropic character of their organization. Whereas Matsui was sentenced to death and executed in 1948, Shimonaka, following a three-year ban from public office under the American occupation, launched the movement for the World Federation of Nations (1951) and resumed his post as president of the Heibonsha. Nakatani dedicated himself to the cause of Afro–Arab–Asian solidarity.

Following the suggestion of Suzuki Teiichi (1888–1989), an army officer and later acting director of the Asia Development Board (Kōa-in), both the Dai Ajia Kyōkai and its bulletin *Dai Ajiashugi* were named after Sun Yat-sen's famous speech on "Greater Asianism" in 1924. In his memoirs, Nakatani insisted that the organization's name was changed from *Han Ajia* (pan-Asia) to *Dai Ajia* (Greater Asia) for this reason only and should not be mistaken for the adoption of an expansionist or imperialist agenda (Nakatani 1989: 349–53). In fact, the Greater Asia Association did appropriate some of Sun's key terminology, in particular when referring to the assumed distinctive features of "the West" and "the East." While, according to Sun, the former was culturally (and subsequently also politically) characterized by the unjust "rule of might" or "the way of the hegemon" (*badao*) based on force and aggression, the latter represented the virtuous "rule of right" or "Kingly Way" (*wangdao*), based on benevolence and virtue. The Greater Asia Association interpreted the founding of Manchukuo as the epoch-making first step in the revival of the Kingly Way on the Asian mainland. It declared that its aim was "to mediate communal and cultural cooperation between Japan and Manchuria and to promote the Greater Asianism movement on the continent" (*Dai Ajia Kyōkai Nenpō* 1934: preface).

On its first anniversary, the Greater Asia Association declared that, despite the fact that only the preparatory stages had been achieved in terms of the "great 100-year plan for Greater Asia," the organization had already "caused a remarkable stir both at home and abroad" and had sounded "an incredible echo throughout the world" (*Dai Ajia Kyōkai Nenpō* 1934: preface). As proof, in its first annual report it reprinted articles about the association and its activities that had appeared in English, German, Russian, Turkish, and Chinese newspapers. Interestingly, the leaders of the association seemed to care little about the negative responses it had received—some of which were included in the annual report—but appeared to be pleased that, unlike previous pan-Asianist organizations, its existence had been widely noted both at home and abroad. The organization's illustrious membership, its broad agenda, and the new political situation that developed following the Manchurian Incident and Japan's withdrawal from the League of Nations may have helped attract such wide attention. Tachibana Shiraki (1881–1945), a scholar-journalist based in Manchuria, where he published another journal with a strong pan-Asian bias, the *Manshū Hyōron* (Manchurian Review), conceded that the Greater Asia Association commanded the greatest authority among the existing pan-Asian organizations but went on to emphasize that, because of their theoretical immaturity and dullness, "it is not worth listening to their claims" (*Manshū Hyōron* 1933). The French journalist Marc Chadourne (1895–1975) was rather shocked by what he called a "quasi-official, detailed imperialistic program" when he read of the organization's aims during his travels in East Asia in 1934. However, he expressed little concern over the potential damage Japanese pan-Asian ambitions might inflict on other Asians. Instead, he criticized Nakatani's outspoken anti-Westernism, which threatened British and French possessions in Asia (*Tour de la Terre*, Paris 1935).

In addition to its publication activities mentioned previously, after its inauguration the Greater Asia Association began establishing branches outside Japan. Already in May 1933, the Da Yaxiya Xiehui (Greater Asia Organization) was set up in Guangdong (Canton) in southern China. In 1934, it was followed by a Taiwan branch, the Chōsen Dai Ajia Kyōkai (Korean Greater Asia Association) in Seoul and the Filipino Greater Asia Association in Manila. In December 1935, on a visit to Northern China, Matsui and Nakatani set up the Chinese Greater Asia Association in Tianjin (Tientsin) (for a list of Asian branches of the Association, see Matsuura 2010: 581). The main character of the association, however, remained that of "a group devoted to thought and culture" more than political action and it focused on publishing journals and pamphlets and holding lectures and seminars. Like a number of other pan-Asian organizations, in 1941 the Greater Asia Association was absorbed into the Greater Japan Alliance for the Revival of Asia (*Dai Nippon Kōa Dōmei*).

The most prominent figure in the Greater Asia Association was Matsui Iwane, who is today remembered chiefly for his role in the Japanese campaign to occupy southern China in 1937 and the subsequent Nanking Massacre. Matsui was born in Nagoya as the sixth son of an impoverished former samurai. He graduated from the Military Academy in 1897. His studies at the elite War College (Rikugun Daigakkō) were interrupted when he was appointed as a company commander in the Russo-Japanese War (1904–1905). He completed his studies after the war and, graduating in 1906, was immediately posted to the Army General Staff. Around this time he developed a strong interest in Asia, particularly China; he admired Arao Sei (1859–1896; see I:4), a "continental adventurer" (*tairiku rōnin*) and pioneer of modern Japanese research on China. However, as with most of the military highfliers, Matsui was sent to study in Europe (in his case France). On his return he requested to be stationed in China, where he served as a resident officer from 1907 to 1912 (and again from 1915 to 1919). There he met influential

Chinese political and military leaders, including Sun Yat-sen. In the army, Matsui was rapidly promoted becoming a full general in 1933. However, in the factional in-fighting after the assassination of the Army Ministry's Director of Military Affairs, Major General Nagata Tetsuzan, by Lieutenant Colonel Aizawa Saburō in August 1935, Matsui was placed on the retired list.

From the mid-1920s onwards, Matsui commented frequently on foreign affairs in the influential journal *Gaikō Jihō* (Diplomatic Review). Matsui's proposal for an Asian League (Ajia Renmei) dates to that time and was triggered by debates over the reform of the League of Nations. In particular, Matsui was influenced by a detailed reform plan proposed by Count Richard Coudenhove-Kalergi, the Austrian founder of the pan-European movement, whose writings were also published in Japan. But it was only after Japan's withdrawal from the League of Nations in 1933 that Matsui's proposal gained greater attention, as an Asian League was now more widely discussed as an alternative to the Western-dominated League of Nations. Several journals, including the popular *Kingu* (King), from which the text reproduced here is taken, published Matsui's writings and speeches.

After the outbreak of the Sino-Japanese War in 1937, Matsui was restored to active duty and appointed commander of the Japanese Central China Area Army (Naka Shina Hōmen Gun), which committed atrocities in Nanking in 1937–1938. The International Military Tribunal for the Far East held Matsui primarily responsible for these massacres, and thus he was sentenced to death and executed on 23 December 1948. While in China Matsui has become a symbol of Japanese wartime atrocities and Japan's war guilt, among rightist groups in Japan he is revered as a hero in Japan's "just war" for the "liberation of Asia" and an innocent victim of "victor's justice" at the Tokyo Trials. In the city of Atami (Shizuoka Prefecture) a statue of the goddess of mercy (Kannon) was built on Matsui's initiative in 1940 to commemorate the revival of Asia (Kōa). An issue of the English-language journal *Asiatic Asia* carried a photograph of this Kōa Kannon as "enshrined by General Matsui for the happiness and spiritual peace of the Asiatic peoples." (*Asiatic Asia* 1–2, March 1941) The Kōa Kannon still stands today and is now dedicated to the commemoration of the seven executed class A war criminals, including Matsui, as heroes devoted to the defense of Japan and Asia (Saaler 2005).

Like the founding manifesto of the Greater Asia Association, Matsui's speech reproduced here arose out of the increasing international pressure on Japan following the Manchurian Incident of 1931. China appealed to the League of Nations, which formed a commission that presented the results of its investigation in February 1933. The so-called Lytton Report acknowledged Japan's special interests in Manchuria but rejected Japan's claims that it was acting in self-defense in Manchuria and that Manchukuo was as an independent country. After the General Assembly of the League adopted the Lytton Report, the Japanese delegation walked out of the Assembly in protest. However, as Matsui notes, the solution to the crisis was hotly debated by the Japanese public. One month after Matsui's speech, Japan announced its formal withdrawal from the League on 27 March 1933.

Source 1 (translation from the Japanese original by Torsten Weber)
"Dai Ajia Kyōkai Sōritsu Shushi" (The reasons for the founding of the Greater Asia Association). *Dai Ajiashugi* 1:1 (May 1933), 2–5.

The reasons for the founding of the Greater Asia Association

1. In the wake of the Manchurian Incident, world politics are about to undergo an epoch-making transformation and conversion. The independence of Manchukuo, the world's youngest state, has already achieved the status of a major miracle in the postwar history of international affairs. Yet the emergence of an independent Manchukuo is merely a prelude to the historical transformation which is set to rapidly succeed it on the world stage. Following the independence of Manchuria, the autonomy of East Asia must be secured. The freedom and glory of Asia, the Mother of Civilization, must be revived, hard on the heels of the founding of the new state of the Kingly Way (*Ōdō shin kokka*). Once Manchuria was East Asia's final bulwark against the European conquest of the world. Now Manchuria itself has been strengthened and established as a state in its own right. With this new situation in the Far East as a model, we must begin working for the unity and reorganization of all of Asia.

2. We certainly believe that Asia constitutes a community with the same fate (*unmei kyōdōtai*)—culturally, politically, geographically and also racially. Real peace, welfare, and the development of the various peoples of Asia is only possible given Asia's self-awakening to its unity and its systematic unification. Mutual enmity and rivalry among Asian countries provides a favorable opportunity for foreign interference and can only aggravate the heavy burdens that Asia is presently being forced to bear. In order to eliminate this mutual rivalry among the countries of Asia and to halt foreign interventions and manipulation, it is vital to strive for the creation of a league (*rengōtai*) of the currently scattered and disorganized peoples of Asia. Moreover, the present chaos and disorder in Asia is not only the cause of Asia's own misery but, as it habitually stimulates the evil intentions and greed of Europe and America, it must also be seen as the greatest obstacle to world peace. The insecurity and unrest of the East are directly connected with insecurity and unrest in the world in general. Reforming Asia according

to the principles of autonomy and self-reliance for Asians is in fact the first step to stabilizing world politics.

3. Seen in this light, the heavy responsibility for Asia's reconstruction and reorganization rests on the shoulders of Imperial Japan (*kōkoku Nihon*). Once before, a quarter of a century ago, when our national destiny was at stake, we pushed back the angry waves of an invasion of East Asia by Imperial Russia, rescued all of Asia from defeat, and even began empowering the colored peoples of the world to raise their heads again. Now, on the occasion of the Manchurian Incident, the human race is again facing a wave of great historical change. It is now time for Imperial Japan to capitalize on the historical significance of the Russo-Japanese War and concentrate its entire cultural, political, economic, and organizational power on planning the next step in the revival and unification of Asia.

To be frank, as the leading player in the self-empowerment and uniting of the Asian peoples, Japan's efforts to improve the current international system dominated by Europe and create a new world order on the principles of racial equality and equal access to resources is the best way of propagating the founding ideals of our country and establishing the Imperial Way (*kōdō*) throughout the whole world. The formation of a "Greater Asian League" (*Dai Ajia Rengō*) is the great historical duty that the Japanese people are facing today.

4. Viewed from the perspective of the current evolutionary process in international politics, the formation of a Greater Asia Union is an extremely natural prospect. It is necessary for human societies to organize political and economic alliances based on geographical, cultural, and racial affinities. On the other hand, it is both unnatural and impossible to jump from a nation-state (*minzoku kokka*) to a world state (*sekai kokka*). Because the League of Nations was prematurely established as a pan-world union without waiting for important historical factors to mature—in fact, it was an unintended outcome of the European War—it is now undergoing fundamental revisions by pan-continental and pan-nationalist movements as a natural consequence. Despite efforts made in good faith by member countries, the League of Nations has remained almost powerless to solve international disputes and relieve ethnic conflicts. On the contrary, its efforts to solve conflicts have actually served to intensify them. Such weaknesses are the result of the League's conceptual basis in the notion of worldism (*sekaishugi*) and its ignoring of the evolutionary processes determining the realities of international politics mentioned above. The international politics and international economic structures of the present and future will in all likelihood be marked by a mix of opposition and cooperation among pan-continental and pan-national groups such as a European Union, Asian Union, American Union, Soviet Union and Anglo-Saxon Union. The structure of any new world peace must surely be based on the attitude of mutual co-operation.

5. Thus the organization of a Greater Asia Union is not only necessary for the Asia of today, but it is also the best and absolutely necessary step for securing real world peace. To this end we have together planned and founded the "Greater Asia Association" in the firm belief that there is no other or better way to bring about the realization of an Asian League, which will eventually bring together all the peoples of Asia, than through the study of the cultural, political, economic, and other affairs of the various Asian countries, the promotion of friendly relations and guidance between the Imperial nation and the Asian countries, and through efforts to introduce and spread the culture of the Imperial nation in those countries. This is also the best and only way of contributing to the progress of human culture and of securing world peace. It would be our greatest blessing if we could obtain the cooperation and approval of large numbers of well-informed people (*shikisha shoken*) in this endeavor.

1 March 1933
Greater Asia Association Founding Committee

Representatives (in no specific order):
Konoe Fumimaro, Hirota Kōki, Matsui Iwane, Suetsugu Nobumasa, Yano Jin'ichi, Kikuchi Takeo, Murakawa Kengo, Ogasawara Naganari, Tokutomi Iichirō (Sohō), Fujimura Yoshirō, Katō Keizaburō, Kanokogi Kazunobu, Shiratori Toshio, Tsubogami Teiji, Negishi Tadashi, Shiraiwa Ryūhei, Tozuka Michitarō, Yamawaki Masataka, Nonami Shizuo, Hiraizumi Kiyoshi, Shimonaka Yasaburō, Sumioka Tomoyoshi, Honma Masaharu, Sakai Takeo, Higuchi Kiichirō, Suzuki Teiichi, Ōta Kōzō, Mitsukawa Kametarō, Ishikawa Shingo, Shibayama Kenshirō, Naitō Chishū, Tsutsui Kiyoshi, Nakahira Akira, Ujita Naoyoshi, Shimizu Tōzō, Imada Shintarō, Imaoka Jūichirō, Nakayama Masaru, Handa Toshiji, Nakatani Takeyo.

Source 2 (translation from the Japanese original by Torsten Weber)
Matsui Iwane (1933), "Dai Ajiashugi" (Greater Asianism). *Kingu*, May Issue Supplement "Jikyoku Mondai: Hijōji Kokumin Taikai" (The Problems concerning the Current Situation: A People's Rally in Times of Emergency), 2–9.

MATSUI IWANE: "GREATER ASIANISM"

An Honorable Isolation

My friends! Japan has eventually arrived at the point where leaving the League of Nations has become unavoidable. Whether we should be happy or sad depends on the determination of our people from this point on. But there is one thing we must not forget: Japan has resolutely upheld the principle of justice. For the sake of international cooperation, it has ceaselessly continued to make every possible effort. Unfortunately, despite the sincere efforts made by the Empire over the past year and a half, it failed to make the League reconsider. As a result, Japan left the League and its international isolation has become inevitable. However, this is an honorable isolation. To stick firmly to right in this world of untruthfulness, one must occasionally be determined to defend an honorable isolation. This is my conviction, and I think it must also be the conviction of the Japanese people. It is at times when this belief is shaken that the danger comes, not from outside but from within. When the Manchurian problem reached its eleventh hour over the past twelve weeks, we sent a negative message to the League to the effect that public opinion was divided here. The atmosphere in Tokyo directly reflects the atmosphere in Geneva and has given the League reason for groundless suspicions.

> "Although Japan has taken an extremely resolute attitude, this is the response of only a section of the military and the government and not the opinion of the majority of the Japanese people. Consequently, is it not possible that Japan's management of Manchuria will fail halfway through the task for reasons of finance, economics, politics, and national opinion?"

This erroneous observation has influenced the League and was no doubt one reason why this unfair resolution was passed. Therefore I believe even more strongly that my 90 million Japanese compatriots must go forward, holding onto a firm conviction. The conviction of the people over the Manchurian problem is firm. Even more, our convictions on the Asian question are firm. Even if our homeland should be burned to the ground, we cannot sacrifice justice. It is precisely as a result of these firm convictions that justice was achieved in the first place and that, following the founding of the Imperial country, an honorable national policy could be established. . . .

For the Asian Nations

Ever since the great Meiji Emperor, the Empire's Asia policy has, through the two wars against the Qing (China) and Russia, become part of the spirit of our people. Looking back to forty years ago, we had to face the extremely demeaning and unbearable national crisis of the Triple Intervention [of 1895]. And, on that occasion, sparing no effort in struggling against difficulties, the Japanese people prevailed. The national crisis that afflicts the Empire today is several times more serious than the Triple Intervention. Given this situation, the people must again spare no effort in their struggle to overcome these difficulties and show their backbone to the world. It goes without saying that we must first strengthen the confidence and unity of the people and be determined to face the national crisis in perfect coordination.

The thirty million people of Manchuria were relieved by means of the Empire's sympathy and good faith. They stand to gain an honorable independence. But things must not stop there. Next we must also extend to the 400 million people of China the same help and deep sympathy that we have given Manchuria and relieve them from their miserable condition of political, economic, and intellectual subjugation by various countries of the world. This serious responsibility and mission is a double burden for the Empire. In this way we must relieve Manchuria and China, and then gradually extend our power to other countries in Asia and provide relief to the Asian peoples who share our race and stock (*dōshu dōzoku*). Starting from that very point, real freedom and peace will eventually come to the world and, at the same time, Japan will implement justice and shake off its present state of isolation.

Such opportunities have already started to make their presence felt in Asia. For example, the only countries that abstained from the unjust motion tabled in the General Assembly of the League were our fellow Asians from Siam. Moreover, there were over ten countries that were absent from the General Assembly and among them we counted with pleasure our Asian comrades from Iraq and Abyssinia (*sic*). Their abstention or non-attendance offers a few rays of hope for the creation of an Asian League in the future.

The Greater Asia Movement

In order to deal effectively with today's difficulties, from last summer we began propagating the Greater Asia Movement.

Needless to say, our Greater Asia Movement is not advocating the annexation of Manchuria. And we would never insist on ruling China or expelling all Westerners from Asia. The primary object of our association is to relieve the peoples of Asia from the political, economic, and spiritual suffering which the region is currently undergoing. I believe that this goal, pursued together with our fellow Asians, is the supreme destiny of Japan as the only fully independent country in Asia. Consequently, everyone who lives in Asia and binds himself to the mission of Asia and makes efforts for the welfare of Asia—be he British or American—is our comrade. It is precisely our hope that we will all strive together for the cause of Asia. Therefore we must first make sure that we have a firm foothold in Asia. Today, we must be like the European Federation in Europe or the Pan-American Movement in both American continents, where fellow Asians of the same stock (*dōzoku dōhō*) band together and take a firm foothold in their respective homes. In this way, pan-unions of Asia, Europe, America and the Soviets can harmonize their efforts and, beginning from there, proceed on the road to a genuinely just peace in this world.

In this time of unprecedented difficulty for the Empire and observing the world in terrible disorder, I firmly believe that there is only one path to a solution and that nothing else will do. My friends! Let's first observe the wide world, and then turn our attention to Asia on our doorstep. Then, I hope, our 900 million fellow Asians will wake up to Japan's vital mission and rise up as one man. In other words, "First return to Asia. Then return to Greater Asianism."

Chapter Fourteen

Kanokogi Kazunobu: "Imperial Asia," 1937

Christopher W. A. Szpilman

Kanokogi Kazunobu was born in 1884 in Yamanashi Prefecture into a prominent samurai family with roots in Kumamoto (on details of Kanokogi's life, see Miyamoto 1984). After graduating from the Navy's Engineering Academy, as a junior lieutenant he saw action in the Russo-Japanese War (1904–1905). A convert to Christianity, he was so shocked by the horrors of war that he resigned his commission to study theology and philosophy. After a short period of study at Kyoto Imperial University, Kanokogi went to the United States, where he pursued his studies at New York's Union Seminary College (BDiv) and at Columbia (MA). From New York, Kanokogi proceeded to Germany, where he wrote his doctoral dissertation under the supervision of the Nobel Prize laureate Rudolf Eucken (1846–1926). On his return to Japan in 1912, he taught philosophy at Keiō University (1912–1917), Tokyo Imperial University (1919–1923), and Kyushu Imperial University (1926–1939). Throughout the 1920s, he frequently traveled to Germany to teach and do research. He played a leading role in the founding of a Japan Institute in Berlin and a Japanese-German Association in Japan, and between 1929 and 1932, he edited *Yamato*, a German-language journal devoted to popularizing Japanese culture.

In 1939, while Japan's war against China was escalating with no victory in sight, he gave up his chair at Kyushu to help Japan's war effort. To this end, he assumed the duties of executive director of the Dai Nihon Genron Hōkokukai (Great Japan Patriotic Writers Association) as right-hand man to the president of that body, Tokutomi Iichirō (see I:28). He also traveled on a number of occasions to China to lecture in support of Japan's military policies.

After Japan's defeat, the importance of Kanokogi's activities was recognized by the Americans who arrested him as a class A war criminal, though he was spared prosecution. He was released on health grounds because of terminal tuberculosis. He died in 1949.

Kanokogi wrote a number of influential books as well as countless articles in specialist and popular journals. His books, most of which went through multiple editions, included *Bunmei to tetsugakuteki seishin* (Civilization and the Philosophical Spirit, 1915), *Eien no tatakai* (Eternal Struggle, 1915), *Sentōteki jinseikan* (The View of Life as a Struggle, 1917), *Risōshugiteki akusen* (Idealism's Uphill Struggle, 1926), *Nihon seishin no tetsugaku* (The Philosophy of the Japanese Spirit, 1934), and *Sumera Ajia* (Imperial Asia, 1937). But his writings account only partly for the spread of his ideas. Kanokogi had powerful links with members of Japan's political and intellectual elite (e.g., Viscount Gotō Shinpei, 1857–1929, and the Tokutomi brothers Sohō and Roka, 1868–1927) and used these links to propagate his views. Drawing on his access to members of the imperial family, for example, he introduced Emperor Hirohito's younger brother, Prince Chichibu (1902–1953), to pan-Asian and radical right-wing reform doctrines—exposure that marked the beginning of the prince's well-known radical sympathies that came to public notice in the 1930s.

Though the influence of such philosophers as Friedrich Nietzsche (1844–1900), Henri Bergson (1859–1941), and Georges Sorel (1847–1922) is clear, Kanokogi's thought was shaped in the main by philosophers Rudolf Eucken (1846–1926), Adolf von Harnack (1851–1930), and other nationalistic thinkers under whom he studied during his first sojourn in Germany. His thought, however, did not remain static: it kept pace with the intellectual and political developments taking place in Germany—developments that he, as an admirer of things German, followed closely (on Kanokogi and Germany, see Yō 2007). In the 1920s he was influenced by the geopolitics of Karl Haushofer (1869–1946). In 1930, Hitler's charisma and the successes of the Nazi Party inspired Kanokogi to found—together with former Yūzonsha comrades Nakatani Takeyo, Ayakawa Takeji, and Shimonaka Yasaburō—a party that was overtly formed on the Nazi model: Aikoku Kinrōtō (Patriotic Workers' Party). The Nazi successes merely reinforced Kanokogi's residual radicalism, which had been apparent as early as 1917–1918 when he had propounded a form of totalitarianism (*zentaishugi*) and talked of world revolution. Though he was no doubt influenced by World War I in Europe and the political upheavals in Russia, he was not a Marxist. Like the more well-known Kita Ikki (see I:27), whose ideas he anticipated in this case, he saw revolution in statist, nationalist, racial terms, envisioning the advent of a historic struggle between the "have" and "have-not" nations.

Kanokogi's visceral nationalistic radicalism formed an integral part of his Pan-Asianism. He began to formulate his ideas on the subject some time after his return from Germany in 1912. A few years later they were strong enough to stir him into action. Inspired by pan-Asian ideals, in 1917 he traveled to India, where, in addition to trekking in the Himalayas, he hoped to contact members of the Indian independence movement. But before he could meet anyone of consequence, the British arrested and deported him to Japan. Back in Tokyo, he joined the pan-Asian associations Rōsōkai and the Yūzonsha (see II:2). It was Kanokogi's departure for Germany in 1923 that served as the pretext for the dissolution of the Yūzonsha.

In 1933 Kanokogi participated, together with Prince Konoe Fumimaro (see I:32), General Matsui Iwane, and a number of other prominent figures, in the founding of the Dai Ajia Kyōkai (Greater Asia Association), an influential pan-Asian organization (see I:2).

Most of the chapters of *Sumera Ajia* had already appeared as separate articles in various journals between 1931 and 1936. Although in these writings Kanokogi addresses the general reader, his prose is full of philosophical terms that are not only difficult to translate but also difficult to understand even in Japanese. Kanokogi's pan-Asian ideas in *Sumera Ajia* appear to be especially strongly influenced by Haushofer's geopolitical ideas. Specifically, his vision of a vast Asian federation that would be capable of standing up to the Soviet Union, the British Empire, and the United States suggests the kind of regional bloc thinking characteristic of Haushofer's geopolitics (cf. Haushofer 1931). *Sumera Ajia* was also shaped by the climate of militarism and war hysteria of the 1930s brought about by the Japanese occupation of Manchuria (1931) and the creation of the puppet state of Manchukuo.

Kanokogi assumed in *Sumera Ajia* a certain historical and cultural commonality shared by all of Asia. At the same time he took for granted Japanese superiority over other Asian countries, for which he found the evidence in Japan's successful political, economic, and military modernization. Successful modernization, in turn, was rooted in Japan's unique national polity: Japan was a monarchy ruled by the same dynastic line, unbroken through ages immemorial. And just as the existence of Japan's imperial family accounted in his view for Japan's modern successes, so, Kanokogi believed, only such divine leadership would make it possible to realize the pan-Asian ideal of Asian unity. An Asian federation could arise only under the rule of the Japanese imperial line. This assumption of Japanese superiority is reminiscent of a strand of Japanese nationalist thought that stretches all the way back to the writings of the nativist thinker Hirata Atsutane (1776–1843) or even earlier. It clearly shows that, steeped as Kanokogi was in Western philosophy, he also drew on a venerable Japanese intellectual tradition that can be traced back to the nativism (*kokugaku*) of the Edo period (see II:14). It is from nativism that Kanokogi derived his concept of *Sumera* (the native Japanese lection of the character *kō*, or emperor). *Sumera* carried connotations of benevolent, virtuous rule by Japanese emperors in accordance with authentic Asian values and was, in his view, the very opposite of Western imperialism, which he saw as materialistic, rapacious, merciless, and violent and as such alien and unacceptable to Asia.

At the same time Kanokogi advanced another argument for Japan's superiority, which he may have borrowed from the writings of Okakura Tenshin (see I:7 and I:8). Japan, he contended, was superior not only because of its unique national polity but also because its culture represented a synthesis of Chinese, Indian, and Western cultures but without the flaws inherent in them, such as decadence or materialism. As such Japanese culture was better, loftier, and nobler than the original component elements. To save Asia, Japan must transplant its culture to Asia and prevent alien (Western) cultures from gaining a foothold there. Although Kanokogi was linked to radical pan-Asian members of the Yūzonsha such as Ōkawa Shūmei (see II:4) and Mitsukawa Kametarō, his Pan-Asianism—basically limited to China and India and paying scant attention to Western Asia and Islam—makes him closer to such traditional pan-Asianists as Okakura Tenshin and Tōyama Mitsuru than to his Yūzonsha comrades, as the following passages taken from *Sumera Ajia* make clear.

Source (translation from the Japanese original by Christopher W. A. Szpilman)
Kanokogi Kazunobu, *Sumera Ajia* (Imperial Asia). Dōbun Shoin, 1937, 118.

The decadence of China and the collapse of India are not necessarily man-made phenomena; rather they are the inevitable consequences that flow from their unique spirits. Their salvation therefore must begin by rectifying the flaws inherent in their spirits. Specifically, the spirit of China is attached to the world of "things that are," while the spirit of India is bound to the world of "things that are not." Only a synthesis can save China and India by rectifying the flaws of each. What lies between and forms a link between the world of "things that are" and the world of "things that are not" is the world of "things difficult to achieve." For that reason, a spirit capable of correcting the flaws in the spirits of China and India must first of all strive to realize in itself these "things difficult to achieve." However, it is clear right away that, among the spirits of Asia, only the Yamato spirit is striving to realize these "things difficult to achieve." . . .

Asia can only be saved from decadence and national ruin by a spirit that can rectify the flaws inherent in these two spirits. Such a spirit must be capable of rectifying these two extremes by combining them into one whole. No Asian spirit other than that of Japan can achieve such a synthesis. In fact, this is why Imperial Japan, that embodies this spirit [of synthesis], has been charged with the historic mission of savior of Asia.

But, needless to say, this mission can be accomplished only when our Japan becomes an Imperial Japan that truly represents the Yamato spirit. . . .

[To this end] a pro-Japanese government must first of all be set up in Northern China. Secondly, the whole of China must be made to cooperate with Japan. But to withstand the pressure from the three empires characterized by centralized planning (*tōsei*)—Soviet Russia, the British Empire and the United States—and to be able to protect Asia, we too must develop a central planning organization that is superior to theirs. At present, it is futile to keep talking about an Asian union that is nothing but a ramshackle agglomeration. It is time that we considered the idea of a great Asian federal state that is marked by control, order, instruction, and organization.

However, this great Asian federal state must be an Imperial (*sumera*) state. That is because, as you know, only the presence of the eternal Emperor—not only in Asia, but throughout the whole world—can provide the controlling principle for such a heroic federation.

When, in the depths of the night when people's voices die away, I contemplate the destiny of our imperial state, everything points clearly toward an Imperial Asian federation. Our domestic politics, economy, diplomacy, military issues, education, and intellectual endeavor must all be subordinated to this great ideal.

Chapter Fifteen

Nagai Ryūtarō: "Holy War for the Reconstruction of Asia," 1937

Roger H. Brown

On 14 October 1937, Nagai Ryūtarō, party politician and communications minister in the cabinet of Prince Konoe Fumimaro (see II:15 for details on Nagai and I:32 on Konoe), gave a speech on the "Holy War for the Reconstruction of Asia." Nagai characterized Japan's invasion of China as a noble effort to establish peace in East Asia by destroying a Nationalist regime that served the interests of Western imperialism and drummed up anti-Japanese sentiment while ignoring the threat posed to the region by the spread of communism. He also raised the stakes of the conflict by linking it to a Japanese national mission to create a more just and fraternal international order in Asia and, indeed, in the world at large. Speaking two months prior to the fall of Nanking (Nanjing), Nagai essentially outlined the pan-Asian definition of the war that would be made official through policy statements released by the Konoe cabinet during 1938 (see II:17). Likewise, Nagai gave his talk at the inauguration of the "Campaign for National Spiritual Mobilization" (*kokumin seishin sōdōin undō*), a government-directed undertaking that incorporated pan-Asian rhetoric into ever-expanding efforts to elicit popular support for national mobilization and total war.

In November 1937, the Cabinet Information Bureau appended the text of Nagai's speech to a pamphlet on "Preservation of Resources and the Cooperation of the People in Finance and Economics in the Period of Crisis" (*Shigen no aigo to hijōji zaiseikeizai e no kokumin no kyōryoku*), presenting both as reference sources for disseminating "awareness of current affairs." The following document is a translation of approximately two-thirds of Nagai's speech as printed in this pamphlet.

Source (translation from the Japanese original by Roger H. Brown)
Nagai Ryūtarō, "Ajia saiken no seisen" (Holy War for the Reconstruction of Asia). *Nihon Bunka* 10 (November 1937), 27–42.

Today . . . at the launching of the campaign for national spiritual mobilization, I join with all of you . . . participating in this profound national movement. As one who believes in the mission of the Japanese people, explaining our vital role in facilitating the opportunity for Asia's ascendance is a task after my own heart. . . . The purpose of this war is to crush the Nanking Government [of Chiang Kai-shek] and all anti-Japanese resistance forces that support that regime and that, ignoring the joint mission of Japan and China for Oriental Peace (*Tōyō heiwa*), are attempting to expel Japan from China. In addition to realizing the spiritual and powerful union of the peoples of Japan and China who share this ideal of constructing a newly emergent Asia, it is clearly true that the purpose of the war rests in the establishment of eternal peace in the Orient. Although wars are common in the world, I believe just and fair motivation such as that which lies behind our current dispatch of troops to China is exceptional. On the occasion of opening the Seventy-second Diet Session, His Majesty proclaimed, "Our soldiers are sweeping aside all obstacles and through their fidelity and bravery will spur reflection on the part of Republican China and rapidly bring about none other than the establishment of peace in East Asia." Likewise, Prime Minister Konoe has on numerous occasions in the Diet declared that "what our country seeks in China is not territory but partnership." In short, what the Japanese people desire dearly is that the Chinese people return to their true Asian mind, through alliance with Japan establish Oriental Peace, and, via the establishment of Oriental Peace, contribute to world peace and the welfare of humanity. Among foreigners there are those who look at this war and viciously attack what they see as Japan's territorial ambitions in China—but if there are those who see in our contemporary dispatch of forces to China an action the same as England's earlier Opium War [1839–1842] . . . to forcefully import opium into China, or Russia's use of the Boxer Rising [1900] to plot the occupation of Manchuria . . . well, to put it in a nutshell, those people are exposing their own ignorance.

Reflecting back on the period after the Great War, one sees that the weak peoples of the world who were oppressed by the military and financial strength of the Great Powers responded to the great postwar collapse of that strength by raising flags of revolt, and that there arose suddenly a fierce current bearing their efforts to achieve self-liberation from imperialist control, brutal oppression, and exploitation and to thereby construct independent new states. The oppressed peoples of our Asian continent also moved to the fore by declaring independence and abandoning unequal treaties. As fellow Asians we Japanese cannot repress heartfelt feelings of respect at the addition of these glorious new pages to the history of Asia. However, at this very moment China . . . submits before the imperialist hegemony of foreign countries that differ from China and its cultural system. What is this ugly state of affairs whereby the Bolshevization and colonization of all of China is ignored? Upon consideration, one sees that this is the result of the Nanking Government and the Chinese ruling classes connected with it being blinded by their desire to maintain political power and, in order to do so, unhesitatingly colluding with any and all foreign powers. The existence of such a government is China's one great shame. The establishment of Oriental Peace is the consistent national policy of Japan, and if people truly desire to work for the establishment of Oriental Peace, they will strengthen the partnership of the peoples of Japan, Manchukuo and China, countries that are Asian and that share a common culture, and establish the grand principle of mutual aid in national defense and industry. There is no other path than to resist stoutly those foreign powers bearing ambitions to dominate Asia and to construct for Japan, Manchukuo and China a New World of co-prosperity that is absolutely devoid of exploitation. Therefore, our dispatch of troops to China is part of a war of Asian reconstruction aimed at eradicating the anti-Asian and anti-independence ideology of slavery of a Nanking Government that is working to reject and hinder the realization of this grand ideal.

Japan, reflecting its long-standing position of leadership in Asia, has exerted itself fully to aid China in building a new country independent and autonomous. In Peiping [present Beijing], at the opening of the Conference on Tariff Reform, Japan led the nations of the world in endeavoring to recognize Chinese tariff autonomy. Likewise, at the Commission on Repealing Extraterritoriality, Japan exerted tremendous effort to improve China's position and, already full of sympathy, looked forward eagerly to the day when China would be reborn as a unified state. Nevertheless, the Nanking Government not only fails to understand Japan's true intentions, they moreover use anti-Japanism as a means to unify China and preserve their own power. . . . This vehement cultivation of hatred for Japan among all Chinese is truly an outrage that will destroy the foundation for Oriental Peace. The existence of such a government is completely incompatible with the idea of world peace. As a consequence, in recent years the trend toward viewing Japan as the enemy has spread throughout China [and incidents of anti-Japanese violence have escalated]. . . . On average there is a victim every four days, with the climax being reached in this July's incident at the Marco Polo Bridge [the beginning of the Sino-Japanese War of 1937]. . . . Under these circumstances, resolutely and fearlessly striking a crushing blow against the Nanking Government and its military, thus depriving them completely of fighting spirit, and explaining thoroughly effective ways for preventing any repeat of such untoward incidents, comprise Japan's mission for world peace and, at the same time, are an exercise of the Japanese people's inevitable right of self-defense.

However, the target Japan aims to strike is the Nanking Government and its military which continue implementing mistaken policies of anti-Japanese resistance—in no way is it the Chinese people. We of course bear no enmity toward the Chinese people; if anything, we cannot suppress our limitless sympathy for the Chinese people who, being oppressed by the Nanking Government and the foreign powers that pull its strings, even now are unable to achieve the true independence they so desire. . . . As Japanese, no matter what long-term resistance we confront, so long as the objectives of the Emperor's campaigning forces remain unattained, we must—with weapons in hand and with an uncompromising, indomitable and dauntless spirit—be resolved to continue the advance. For this reason, as well as so as not to cause anxiety in the minds of those officers and men on the front lines, those on the home front must also exert themselves to the utmost in their respective posts. All the people must arise and each and every one must awaken to the grand historical mission of the Japanese Empire and work to fulfill their duties on the home front. At the time of the Great War, Germany was surrounded at its borders by some two million enemy troops yet continued fighting for five long years and never allowed one enemy soldier to set foot on German soil, something at which the world truly marveled. Under those circumstances, the strenuous efforts of Germans on the home front and their vigorous determination to sacrifice their lives for their country were in no way inferior to that of German soldiers on the battlefield. . . . Today the Japanese government, in order to comfort the families of deployed soldiers and raise public bonds, is seeking ardently the cooperation of Japanese on the home front in reducing unnecessary expenses, curtailing overseas payments by limiting consumption of foreign goods, and preserving domestic resources with military uses by encouraging the use of substitute goods. Should the home front efforts of the Japanese people, who have been trained to lead through the grand spirit of patriotic devotion over the course of three thousand years, prove inferior to the German people in zeal, exertion and cooperation, the Japanese people would themselves bring shame upon Japanese culture. . . . Before the great purpose of national survival we must discard the narrow matters of the self and display our resolve to work for the greater good. Similarly, those Japanese on the home front through whose veins courses that grand spirit of patriotic devotion must teach the entire world that they are the equal of our officers and men fighting gallantly at the front. Ever since the occurrence of this incident, it is the brave and righteous actions of the officers and men of our army and navy on battlefields in north, central, and southern China that continue to surprise the world. Indeed, it is our national character tempered over three thousand years that, in the face of national crisis, emits a unique brilliance, and I believe it is on account of this unrivaled Japanese spirit that we display such profound *esprit* before the world. . . . In order to accomplish the task bequeathed by our ancestors we must exert ourselves strenuously so as to feel no shame before them, add yet more pages to the brilliant history of the glorious Japanese Empire, cultivate even more splendidly our proud national character, and feel keenly our heavy responsibility to pass this on to later generations. Should there be among Japanese charged with defending the home front those who do not awaken to this grave responsibility, who neglect their indispensible home-front duty to console the minds of officers and men giving their all at the front, and who begrudge cooperating with the current national campaign to realize Japan's historic mission in the world, one must say that such people relinquish their special rights as Japanese. When their time comes to die, I think they will be utterly unable to face our brave ancestors.

The point is that this war is not just the fight of the government, nor is it just the fight of the army and navy—truly it is the fight of all Japanese for the purpose of realizing the country's grand foundational ideal of *hakkō ichiu* ("the eight corners of the world under one roof") and a new world of human fraternity. Many will probably agree that the greatest source of instability in the world today is the widespread impoverishment accompanying the monopolization of resources in the international arena and the Bolshevik revolutionary schemes that, taking advantage of the resulting inequality and dissatisfaction, are being carried out around the globe. There is only one moral path that will liberate all of humanity from this global insecurity, reconstruct economic relations between nations on the basis of international justice, and lead to a world wherein all territory, capital, and labor are mobilized for the stable livelihood of all humanity. Namely, it is the moral mission of the Japanese people to carry forth the leadership principles for world reconstruction and, not just in the Orient but throughout the world, fight against exclusionism and communism. Therefore, this war—that is to say, Japan's eradication of exclusionist, communist forces in China—is truly the first step toward the grand moral and historical mission of realizing throughout the world *hakkō ichiu* and the great ideal of human fraternity.

Part III

PAN-ASIANISM AND THE QUEST FOR EMPIRE AND A "NEW ORDER" IN ASIA, 1937–1940

This part focuses on the period between 1937 and 1940. These years witnessed a second major resurgence of pan-Asian agitation in Japan that was echoed to various degrees in other parts of Asia. However, the outbreak of the Sino-Japanese War in 1937 had revealed the contradictions inherent in Pan-Asianism. In the eyes of most Chinese, Japan's profession of lofty pan-Asian goals in its "holy war" (a term used to refer to the war in China at least from 1934) was brutally contradicted by the rapid escalation of the conflict into total war and by the atrocities committed by Japanese troops against their Asian "brothers."

This wartime emergency situation required new strategies of legitimization. It was in this period that, for the first time, the Japanese authorities promulgated pan-Asian policy guidelines, drawing on slogans such as "Raising Asia" (Kōa). In 1938, the Agency for Raising Asia (Kōa-in) was founded, while the government issued declarations that proclaimed the establishment of a "New Order" in East Asia—an order that, in most cases, was linked to the pan-Asian ideals of an "East Asian Community" or an "East Asian League."

A number of organizations were founded, some of which were granted official status as advisory bodies to the government. Eventually, the various pan-Asian organizations were merged, under government guidance, into a single organization—the Dai Nihon Kōa Dōmei (Greater Japanese League for Raising Asia). Government involvement had the effect of making Pan-Asianism an important component of official doctrine. Thus, in contrast to the early pan-Asian societies in Japan, some of these new organizations attracted relatively large memberships.

Chapter Sixteen

Japanese Pan-Asianism in Manchukuo, 1935

Prasenjit Duara

Manchukuo (1932–1945), the Japanese puppet state in northeastern China or Manchuria, was the first major laboratory for the implementation of pan-Asian ideology of the Japanese military, in particular, of the Kwantung army, which controlled the region. The Treaty of Portsmouth, which concluded the Russo-Japanese War in 1905, acknowledged China's sovereignty in Manchuria, but it granted Japan the Russian lease on the Guandong (Kwantung) peninsula and the South Manchurian Railroad. From this time, Japanese interests and influence grew, particularly after the annexation of Korea in 1910 and during World War I. By 1927, 85% of Japanese foreign investment was in China, and of its Chinese investment, 80% was invested in Manchuria. The investment of the South Manchurian Railroad in 1920 alone was 440 million yen. By 1932, Japan's share of the total industrial capital in Manchuria was 64%, while the Chinese share was 28%. The Japanese controlled Manchuria through a tacit and rocky alliance with the warlord of the region Zhang Zuolin (Chang Tso-lin, 1875–1928), whom they assassinated in 1928. When his son and successor, Zhang Xueliang (Chang Hsüeh-liang, 1901–2001), declared his affiliation to the resurgent Nationalist Party (Guomindang/GMD, or Kuomintang) on the mainland, the Kwantung army engineered the Manchurian Incident of 18 September 1931 and established Manchukuo in 1932.

Although the establishment of the puppet state was an imperialist act, elements of the Japanese military were also swayed by the rhetoric of Pan-Asianism. While it became increasingly a front for Japanese expansionism, pan-Asianist ideals were pursued by several Japanese idealists and found institutional expression during the early period until 1937. The military learned of the necessity for some kind of compact with the Chinese communities from the settler communities of the area. The Japanese settlers, represented by such societies as the Daiyūhōkai (Great Majestic Mountain Association) and the Manshū Seinen Renmei (Manchurian Youth League), were painfully aware that Japanese interests and domination in Manchuria were doomed without a framework of Sino–Japanese coexistence.

The Manchurian Youth League developed the idea of *kyōwa* (*xiehe* in Chinese) or cooperation between races or nationalities and the rejection of colonialist attitudes. This idea was incarnated in a fascistic mass organization in Manchukuo known as Kyōwakai or Xiehehui and translated into English as the Concordia Society. The association was built on rhetoric of eternal peace embedded in East Asian ideals and a framework of mutual cooperation among the different peoples. It advocated anti-imperialism and even conceived of a new type of anticolonial state that would replace all imperialist powers—including the Japanese. Increasingly after 1937, however, the Kyōwakai became a propaganda machine for the Japanese army's expansion into mainland China and Asia. It was from these beginnings in Manchukuo that the *political* ideology of Pan-Asianism grew by the mid-1930s into the Tōa Renmei (East Asian League), the Tōa Kyōdōtai (East Asian Community), and still later the idea of the Daitōa Kyōeiken (Greater East Asian Co-Prosperity Sphere; see II:24).

The two pieces included here represent two essays from lower-school textbooks. They are written in classical Chinese—obviously for Chinese students—and expound on different aspects of Manchukuo's state-centered Pan-Asianism. Although the piece argues for a multinational state, there is a certain hierarchy of nationalities, with Manchus and Mongols, who were politically insignificant, given an originary status and the Japanese a special (and in other texts), leadership role. Although they represented over 80% of the population, the Chinese are not mentioned by name in this and many other texts. The second essay invokes Chinese traditions of loyalty and duty in order to foster these values for the Manchukuo State. The two figures referred to are legendary Chinese martial heroes, Guan Yu (?–219) and Yue Fei (1103–1142) and the state often drew on popular Chinese culture (including Confucianism) to represent itself as a "truly" Asiatic state in contrast to the GMD but especially to the communists. Indeed, Pan-Asianism in Manchukuo was closely intertwined with state building.

Sources (translation from the Chinese original by Prasenjit Duara)
Zhuji xiaoxuexiao xiushen jiaokeshu disice (Beginning Grade, Elementary School, Textbook for Self-Cultivation, vol. 4), December 1935.

LESSON 25: THE CONCORD OF NATIONALITIES

The nation is like a family. The people of a nation are like the members of a family. A family has brothers and sisters who are called siblings from the same womb (*tongbao*). In the case where a single nationality establishes a nation, the entire nation is like the brothers and sisters birthed by one mother. In the case where different nationalities establish a nation, it is like brothers and sisters birthed by different mothers. In brief, they are all siblings/compatriots.

Although the nationalities in our empire of Manchukuo are many, their unity lies in being the officers and people of the emperor. Their gains and losses, joys and sorrows are all held in common. They are like siblings from different surnames. For the security of our compatriots/siblings, we can only speak of the way of co-operation and concord.

The Manchus and Mongols are the original inhabitants of our country. The Japanese have especially conspicuous accomplishments in the establishment of our imperial state. As for the other nationalities, they have migrated to this land and lived among the people for a long time. Their feelings have melded together. The reason our nation is able to establish its independence in the world is entirely due to the spirit of co-operation and concord of the nationalities.

We ought to know that the great enterprise of establishing a nation-state is not the responsibility of a single nationality or a single name. The various nationalities currently residing in the land must cooperate. We must ensure that the knowledgeable plan thoroughly and the brave labor exhaustively. Only when we exert and arouse ourselves and each person achieves their goal, can we establish the basis of the nation for ten thousand years. Henceforth each nationality within the nation-state must make greater efforts.

Gaoji xiaoxuexiao xiushen jiaokeshu disice (Upper Grade, Elementary School, Textbook for Self-Cultivation, vol. 1), December 1935.

LESSON 28: EXERT LOYALTY AND SERVE THE COUNTRY

We are able to obtain our livelihood because we rely on society and especially upon the sovereign state (*jünguo*). Try to think; although I may be poor, the rich do not dare to bully me; although I may be weak, the strong do not dare to humiliate me. What is the reason? It is because our national laws protect us. Moreover, if we go abroad, we can find a place to live and plan a livelihood. We can gain people's respect and not meet with their disdain. What is the reason? It is because our nation's authority protects us. As a result, we entrust in our sovereign state and are showered by its favors. Is this not great?

Within the boundaries of our national territory, there is no land that is not our lord's land (*wangtu*). Within the boundaries of our territory, there is no person who is not our lord's officer. Since we receive the great benevolence of our sovereign state, there is none without the responsibility of duty to the country and there is none who may not keep loyalty and duty in their hearts. Loyalty and duty like that of Guan Zhuangmu and Yue Wumu are truly the best models for us.

Zhuangmu's personal name was Yu; his courtesy name was Yunzhang. He was engaged in a common mission with Zhang Fei. When Zhao Lie was pursued everywhere, he could not escape danger. At a time when Zhao Lie was not yet emperor, Cao Cao had sought to employ Yu. But because Yu had sworn a brotherhood pact unto death with Zhao Lie, he rejected the proposal. Cao sighed, saying, "He is truly a righteous warrior."

Wumu's personal name was Fei; his courtesy name was Pengju. He personally experienced over two hundred battles and had successively defeated the Jin [empire in northern China (1115–1234), ruled by the Tungus Jurchen tribes from Manchuria]. Qin Kuai [1090–1155] arrested him and falsely accused him of plotting rebellion, even to the sentence of death. At the moment of his trial, Wumu tore open his jacket to reveal the four characters that were deeply carved on his back "serve the country with dedicated loyalty."

Those who are loyal and righteous are rooted in heavenly nature. Today when people hear the stories of the loyal and righteous hearts of Guan and Yue, they cannot but well up with admiration and affection. It is evidence of the expression of heavenly nature. This is none other than the way of duty to the country and, moreover, heavenly nature is completed in loyalty and righteousness.

Chapter Seventeen

The Konoe Cabinet's "Declaration of a New Order in East Asia," 1938

Roger H. Brown

During the late 1930s, Japanese political and military leaders spoke increasingly of constructing a "New Order" within Japan and throughout East Asia. The key political figure in this development was the popular Prince Konoe Fumimaro (on Konoe's early career, see I:32), who assumed the position of prime minister for the first time in June 1937. Well-connected throughout Japan's governing circles, the prince received particularly staunch support at this time from those members of the political elite who sought to implement political and economic "renovation" (*kakushin*; cf. Itō 1978). Army officers seeking to realize a "high-grade national defense state" (*kōdo kokubō kokka*), reformist bureaucrats out to enhance their administrative authority, and various other advocates of comprehensive state control over the economy, politics, and society were convinced that Konoe was the one man who could help realize their objectives. For his part, Konoe sympathized with the objectives of renovating the domestic political order and enhancing Japan's position in East Asia, and the officials and intellectuals making up the premier's "brain trust," the Shōwa Research Association, busied themselves providing him with plans for a "New Order" that would promote political unity and national mobilization at home and Japan's pan-Asian destiny abroad (Berger 1977; Crowley 1971; Fletcher 1982; Itō 1983).

Although the prince eventually oversaw the establishment of the Imperial Rule Assistance Association (IRAA), the institution meant to serve as the centerpiece of the "New Order," during his second administration (July 1940–July 1941), the path toward that accomplishment was both facilitated and frustrated by the war with China that began in July 1937. On the one hand, the outbreak of the "China Incident" facilitated implementation of the "National Spiritual Mobilization Campaign" in late 1937 and, over time, did the same for the National General Mobilization Law passed in April 1938.

On the other hand, the inability of Konoe to bring the war with China to a successful conclusion undermined his first cabinet, convinced him to give up on IRAA-centered political renovation during his second term and brought his third administration to the brink of war with the United States, a prospect that resulted in his resigning the premiership in October 1941 (Berger 1977).

The first Konoe cabinet relied heavily on pan-Asian thought to explain the greater historical significance of Japan's military campaign in China, thereby articulating a foreign policy that paralleled the domestic drive to create a new political structure. While these ideas had already proliferated in the early 1930s, the Konoe government's employment of them nonetheless marked a watershed in the official use of Pan-Asianism to legitimize Japanese military actions and diplomatic policies. In the wake of the Manchurian Incident of 1931, pan-Asian ideals had helped justify Japan's growing dissatisfaction with the international system established through agreements concluded at conferences in Paris (1919) and Washington (1921–1922). When the capture of the Nationalist capital of Nanjing (Nanking) in December 1937 failed to force the regime of Chiang Kai-shek to sue for peace, the Konoe cabinet used pan-Asian ideals to legitimize a national mission to replace the "Anglo-American"–dominated status quo with a Japan-led "New Order for East Asia." For the government and numerous ideologues, successful prosecution of the "China Incident" henceforth became a "holy war" (*seisen*) to renovate international relations in Asia.

The year 1938 thus saw the Konoe cabinet announce three policy initiatives that set the course of Japanese relations with China in the years leading up to Pearl Harbor. In January, the cabinet declared the Chiang administration to be nothing more than a local regime and announced that "the Imperial Government would no longer deal with the Nationalist Government." Then, in November and again in December, the government issued statements redefining the war in China as part of a greater struggle on the part of Japan to create a "New Order" in East Asia. Henceforth, pan-Asian ideals served to frame Japan's war goals and foreign policy in relation to China (see, for example, the 1939 radio address by Premier Hiranuma in II:21), which was called on, under either a new regime or a chastened Nationalist government, to end its resistance and cooperate with Japan and Manchukuo in constructing the "New Order," resisting the spread of communism, and furthering regional economic development. Meanwhile, Japan's ongoing war with China, declaration of a "New Order" for East Asia, and deepening ties with Germany and Italy worsened relations with the United States and Great Britain. In August 1940, the second Konoe cabinet expanded the vision of a "New Order" in East Asia to encompass a "Greater East Asia Co-Prosperity Sphere" (see also II:24) and, the following month, a formalized alliance with German and Italy via the Tripartite Treaty. From December 1941, the government of General Tōjō Hideki used the same pan-Asian rhetoric to legitimize expansion of the "China Incident" into the "Greater East Asia War."

The following sources exemplify the use of Pan-Asianism by the first Konoe cabinet to legitimize Japan's invasion of China and to mobilize the energies of the Japanese people in support of this war. The first document is the English version of the "Declaration of a New Order in East Asia" (*Tōa shinchitsujo seimei*) released by the Japanese Foreign Ministry on 2 November 1938. The second document, taken from an official English translation distributed by the Dōmei News Agency, is part of a radio address given by Konoe on 3 November explaining his government's policy to the public and underscoring the need for their full support in realizing Japan's destiny as the leader of Asia. The third document, released by the Foreign Ministry on 22 December, is the official declaration of the Konoe government's "three principles" for realizing Sino–Japanese relations in line with the proposed "New Order" in East Asia.

Sources: The following three texts are reproduced in U.S. Department of State, *Papers relating to the foreign relations of the United States, Japan: 1931–1941: Volume I (1931–1941)*. Washington, DC: U.S. Government Printing Office, 1931–1941, 477–81. Statement by the Japanese Government, November 3, 1938.

By the august virtue of His Majesty, our naval and military forces have captured Canton and the three cities of Wuhan; and all the vital areas of China have thus fallen into our hands. The Kuomintang Government exists no longer except as a mere local regime. However, so long as it persists in its anti-Japanese and pro-communist policy our country will not lay down its arms—never until that régime is crushed.

What Japan seeks is the establishment of a new order which will insure the permanent stability of East Asia. In this lies the ultimate purpose of our present military campaign.

This new order has for its foundation a tripartite relationship of mutual aid and co-ordination between Japan, Manchukuo and China in political, economic, cultural and other fields. Its object is to secure international justice, to perfect the joint defence against Communism, and to create a new culture and realize a close economic cohesion throughout East Asia. This indeed is the way to contribute toward the stabilization of East Asia and the progress of the world.

What Japan desires of China is that that country will share in the task of bringing about this new order in East Asia. She confidently expects that the people of China will fully comprehend her true intentions and that they will respond to the call of Japan for their cooperation. Even the participation of the Kuomintang Government would not be rejected, if, repudiating the policy which has guided it in the past and remolding its personnel, so as to translate its rebirth into fact, it were to come forward to join in the establishment of the new order.

Japan is confident that other Powers will on their part correctly appreciate her aims and policy and adapt their attitude to the new conditions prevailing in East Asia. For the cordiality hitherto manifested by the nations which are in sympathy with us, Japan wishes to express her profound gratitude.

The establishment of a new order in East Asia is in complete conformity with the very spirit in which the Empire was founded; to achieve such a task is the exalted responsibility with which our present generation is entrusted. It is, therefore, imperative to carry out all necessary internal reforms, and with a full development of the aggregate national strength, material as well as moral, fulfill at all costs this duty incumbent upon our nation.

Such the Government declare to be immutable policy and determination of Japan.

RADIO SPEECH BY THE JAPANESE PRIME MINISTER (PRINCE KONOYE)

It is my great pleasure, on this occasion of the birthday anniversary of the late Emperor Meiji and once more remembering the high virtues of the Emperor, to enunciate the views of the Government in connection with the establishment of peace in the Far East the work of which has been bequeathed to us from the late Emperor. Following closely on the heels of the fall of Canton, Hankow, which forms the heart of the interior of China came under Japanese control. . . . There is a well-known saying that 'those who control the vital areas of China control whole China.' The Chiang Kai-shek administration has practically been reduced to a mere local regime. . . .

Japan holds the key to the disposal of China. However, what Japan sincerely desires is the development and not the ruin of China. It is China's cooperation and not conquest that Japan sincerely desires. Japan desires to build up a stabilized Far East by cooperating with the Chinese people who have awakened to the need of self-determination as an Oriental race. No country desires or understands as Japan does perfection of China as an independent state and China's racial aspiration and sentiment. History shows that Japan, Manchukuo and China are so related to each other that they must bind themselves closely together in a common mission for the establishment of peace and order in the Far East by displaying their own individuality. It is a matter for deep regret, not only for the sake of Japan but also for the sake of the Far East, that the realization of this ideal between Japan and China was hampered by the wrong policy pursued by the Nationalist Government. The keynote of the policy pursued by the National Government is very superficial because it was based on the trends of the temporary reactionary period following the termination of the World War. This policy was not based on the tradition and intuition which are so characteristic of the Chinese nation. The National Government did everything in order to maintain its power and did not care for steady bolshevization and colonisation of China. This is not in accordance with the way pursued by China's zealous patriots who have fought at the sacrifice of their own lives for the construction of a new China. This is the reason why Japan which is so closely affiliated with China as one of the two greatest races in the Orient has risen in arms to crush the Chiang Kai-shek administration although she does not want to have a tragedy of fighting with the brother nation China. Japan sincerely desires that China will awake. Those who are jealous of the future in China should rise up for the execution of the common mission of the Far East by pointing the Chinese people to their destined path and guide the rejuvenated China. . . . The Chinese race which on many occasions during its history extending over five thousand years held a guiding torch for the civilization of the world should leave behind it a history compatible with the great deeds left by China's forefathers by bringing a new light to the civilisation of the world and sharing with Japan in the mission for the construction of a new Far East. If the National Government regains the original spirit of the Chinese race, effects changes in the policy it has pursued and the personnel and emerges as a new administration for the reconstruction of China, Japan would not reject the participation of the National Government. All countries of the world should have a clear recognition regarding the new situation in the Far East. History shows clearly that peace and independence in China have been frequently menaced as the result of the struggle for supremacy among foreign powers which was based on imperialistic ambitions. Japan sees the necessity of effecting a fundamental revision in this situation and desires to establish a new peace fabric in Far East on the basis of justice. . . . If the Powers understand the real intentions of Japan and devise a policy in accordance with the new situation in the Far East, Japan does not grudge to cooperate with them for peace in the Far East. The world knows that Japan is earnestly determined to fight it out with communism. What the Comintern intends to do is bolshevisation of the Far East and disturbance of world peace. Japan expects to suppress in a drastic manner the sources of the evils of bolshevisation and their subversive activities behind the so-called long-term resistance of the Chiang Kai-shek administration. Fortunately, both Germany and Italy which are our allies on the anti-Comintern front understand the intentions of Japan in the Far East and have extended their moral support in the current incident which has greatly encouraged the Japanese nation. In this respect we extend our deep gratitude to these countries. The current incident had convinced us of the necessity of further tightening the bonds. Japan is determined also to cooperate in the reestablishment of world order guided by a common view of the world. What the world at present needs badly is the establishment of peace on a fair balance of power. There is no denying the fact that various principles in the past have forced the maintenance of the status quo marked by an unbalanced state. That the international treaty such as the covenant of the League of Nations has lost its prestige is fundamentally due to this irrationality. . . .

Japanese history shows that the vicissitudes of the country have always depended on the people's self-consciousness about the national structure. When we realize that the Imperial Throne is concerned about the establishment of permanent peace in the Far East we subjects cannot but feel that our moral mission is indeed heavy. The Japanese people at this very juncture must face their respective duties solemnly. They must also have a clear understanding and should not err in their recognition about what kind of sacrifice and preparation is necessary for the construction of a new fabric on a moral basis in the Far East. . . . Japan which is entrusted with the task of constructing a new Far East has entered upon a new stage of creation in all fields of human life. In this sense, the actual fighting has just started. In order to be a great nation we must proceed with the perfection of various preparations for reconstruction both at home and abroad with a firm faith and determination.

STATEMENT BY THE JAPANESE PRIME MINISTER (PRINCE KONOYE), DECEMBER 22, 1938

The Japanese Government are resolved, as has been clearly set forth in their two previous statements issued this year, to carry on the military operations for the complete extermination of the anti-Japanese Kuomintang Government, and at the same time to proceed with the work of establishing a new order in East Asia together with those far-sighted Chinese who share in our ideals and aspirations.

The spirit of renaissance is now sweeping over all parts of China and enthusiasm for reconstruction is mounting ever higher. The Japanese Government desire to make public their basic policy for adjusting the relations between Japan and China, in order that their intentions may be thoroughly understood both at home and abroad.

Japan, China and Manchukuo will be united by the common aim of establishing the new order in East Asia and of realizing a relationship of neighbourly amity, common defence against Communism, and economic co-operation. For that purpose it is necessary first of all that China should cast aside all narrow and prejudiced views belonging to the past and do away with the folly of anti-Japanism, and resentment regarding Manchukuo. In other words, Japan frankly desires China to enter of her own will into complete diplomatic relations with Manchukuo.

The existence of the Comintern influence in East Asia can not be tolerated. Japan therefore considers it an essential condition of the adjustment of the Sino-Japanese relations that there should be concluded an anti-Comintern agreement between the two countries in consonance with the spirit of the anti-Comintern Agreement between Japan, Germany and Italy. And in order to ensure the full accomplishment of her purpose, Japan demands, in view of the actual circumstances prevailing in China, that Japanese troops be stationed, as an anti-Communist measure, at specified points during the time the said agreement is in force, and also that the Inner Mongolian region be designated as a special anti-Communist area.

As regards economic relations between the two countries, Japan does not intend to exercise economic monopoly in China, nor does she intend to demand of China to limit the interests of those third Powers, who grasp the meaning of the new East Asia and are willing to act accordingly. Japan only seeks to render effective the co-operation and collaboration between the two countries. That is to say, Japan demands that China, in accordance with the principle of equality between the two countries, should recognize the freedom of residence and trade on the part of Japanese subjects in the interior of China, with a view to promoting the economic interests of both peoples; and that, in the light of the historical and economic relations between the two nations, China should extend to Japan facilities for the development of China's natural resources, especially in the regions of North China and Inner Mongolia. The above gives the general lines of what Japan demands of China. If the true object of Japan in conducting the present vast military campaign be fully understood, it will be plain that what she seeks is neither territory nor indemnity for the costs of military operations. Japan demands only the minimum guarantee needed for the execution by China of her function as a participant in the establishment of the new order. Japan not only respects the sovereignty of China, but she is prepared to give positive consideration to the questions of the abolition of extra-territoriality and of the rendition of concessions and settlements—matters which are necessary for the full independence of China.

Chapter Eighteen

Rōyama Masamichi and the "Principles of an East Asian Cooperative Community," 1938

Jung-Sun N. Han

In November 1938, the first Konoe Fumimaro cabinet declared that Japan would establish a "new order" in East Asia (see II:17). Confronting intensifying nationalist resistance in China to the Japanese invasion of 1937, the Konoe cabinet oscillated between nonrecognition and recognition of the Chinese Nationalist government. At a time of increasing confusion and disorder, the concept of an "East Asian Cooperative Community" (*tōa kyōdōtai* or *tōyō kyōdōtai*) was introduced to the world of politics and journalism as a guiding principle for the policymaking process regarding China. The term was popularized by Rōyama Masamichi (1895–1980), who at the time was a member of Konoe's "brain trust," the Shōwa Kenkyūkai (Shōwa Research Association).

A Tokyo Imperial University graduate, Rōyama was one of the leading political scientists in wartime Japan. Under the influence of his mentor Yoshino Sakuzō, a liberal and internationalist intellectual, Rōyama developed research interests in China within the context of a growing internationalism in the aftermath of World War I. In this period he was interested mainly in understanding the development of internationalism in global politics and assessing its repercussions in regional politics. Rōyama understood the contemporary development of internationalism from an evolutionist point of view. He regarded the formation of an international society as the culmination of an inevitable global historical process of evolution that advanced from "tribal society," through "ethnic society," and "national society" before it reached the final stage of "international society." While this evolutionary process was inevitable, it could be slowed by various factors, such as nationalism, which Rōyama regarded as a major obstacle to the development of international society. This was a particularly pernicious problem in the "Far East," which, in his view, lagged behind the rest of the world in terms of historical development and was still stuck in the age of nationalism.

The concerns over nationalism led Rōyama to join the Japan Branch of the Institute of Pacific Relations in 1927. The Institute of Pacific Relations (IPR) was an international nongovernmental organization established in Hawaii in 1923 to promote cooperation and secure peace in the Asia-Pacific region. Alarmed by intensifying anti-Japanese nationalism and frustrated by the ongoing political confusion in China, Rōyama reasoned that the "China problem" would leave Japan no option but to devise a new political order applicable to the "special" state of political development that marked the region.

Paradoxically, Rōyama's experience with the IPR and its internationalist experiments led him to formulate a pan-Asianist regionalism characterized by the central notion of an "East Asian Cooperative Community" (EACC). Arguing that the world order created after World War I, with the League of Nations at the center, could not be applied to Sino–Japanese relations following the Manchurian Incident, Rōyama called for a new order that would rationalize relations between the two countries in the name of cooperative development and reciprocal progress. The EACC was different from other pan-Asianist concepts that called for an "East Asian League" in the sense that it did not emphasize a racial and cultural affinity between Japan and the rest of Asia. Rather, the EACC was based on an economic and developmentalist rationale. Translating political problems into the terms of mutual economic development, Rōyama proposed the notion of a regional bloc that was designed to promote Sino–Japanese economic cooperation while at the same time maintaining Japanese control over the developmentalist agenda. Propounding this self-serving scheme, Rōyama remained blind to China's aspirations to regain its national independence and international respect. In the end, Rōyama's notion of a regional economic community failed to resolve the conflict between China and Japan that ultimately led to the demise of the Japanese Empire.

Source (translation from the Japanese original by Jung-Sun N. Han)
Rōyama Masamichi, "Tōa Kyōdōtai no Riron" (The Principles of an East Asian Cooperative Community). *Kaizō*, November 1938, 6–27.

The recent China Incident [the Sino-Japanese War] has assumed the status of a holy war. Upon the outbreak of war, the government explained that "(Japan) does not have territorial ambitions" and that "what (Japan) seeks is Sino-Japanese cooperation." Unlike the case with most international conflicts, (we have to) make it clear that the rationale for the China Incident does not lie in material motivations. The fact that enormous sacrifices have been made signifies that (the motives for) the incident lie beyond the calculation of gains in territory, resources, or markets. Even if such motives exist, they must only be secondary ones.

Yet the meaning of the holy war does not simply lie in the fact that material interests are not its primary goal. That would be too passive an explanation and fail to explain the true meaning of this holy war. As has been often repeated on all fronts, the [true significance of the war] lies in the moral goal of establishing a new order in East Asia. In other words, [the goal] is to establish and guarantee a permanent peace. For that purpose, [we are] making huge sacrifices and are prepared to endure great difficulties. . . .

The recent incident differs in essence from the wars undertaken in the pursuit of lesser goals. Such wars are characteristic of modern Europe, which has experienced the Great War and is now restricted by the League of Nations and the General Treaty for the Renunciation of War [Kellogg-Briand Treaty, 1928]. We can judge this from the fact that the incident does not allow a simple application of the principles of international law created in the aftermath of the Great War. This is because, as the recent incident shows, for the first time the Japan of the Orient has become aware of its mission to the world, independent of the guidance and intervention of the Western powers. In a nutshell, the reason for this situation is the awakening and unification of the Orient—two phenomena of global historical significance. Therefore, far from being a war of minor and restricted [importance], from a global historical perspective [the China Incident] displays an all-encompassing significance. . . .

However, the time for "the awakening of the Orient" at last has arrived. . . . Although on the one hand this turning-point represents the materialization of Western ideas by the League of Nations, meaning the continuing domination of the major powers, it is also the result of the Orient having found its place within a global system. If it had not been for the Great War and the postwar League of Nations, which led to a concrete conceptualization of the world, the Orient could not have awakened as the Orient. . . .

Ideally, the greatest significance of the recent incident should lie in an enhanced awareness by the peoples of the Orient toward the "unification of the Orient." Yet, in reality, there are obstacles [to this unification] in the form of tragic conflicts between different ethnic groups and the confrontation with Western imperialist structures. As mentioned above, the lack of the single cultural order necessary for unification has hindered the unification of the Orient. However, the new unified cultural order and associated thinking cannot [yet] be realized in concrete terms as a result of the major obstacles that persist between different peoples. These obstacles are deformations produced by nationalism—the organizing principle of the Western world. Here lies the fundamental problem that has to be resolved first of all. That is, the East

Asian problem needs to be crystallized in the form of war and politics before it can be crystallized in the form of culture and thought. The new order in East Asia must be created before the formation of a new Oriental ideology, in the smoke of powder and the hail of bullets. The Orient, baptized with fire and sword, will rationalize East Asian thought. . . .

In this respect, the unification of the Orient must begin by doing away with nationalism. But where will the engine needed for this process come from? The main engine for this task is to be found in the advancement of Japanese nationalism on the Asian mainland. . . .

However, the principle at the heart of the Japanese advance onto the [Asian] mainland is not imperialism, but regionalism pursued for reasons of security and development. . . .

In this respect, the theory of a regional cooperative community—Asia's destiny—which is already reflected in the actual process of Japan's advances on the Asian mainland, is the only principle that will awaken the Orient to embrace its world mission and realize the unification of the Orient. There is no doubt that this principle represents an ideology powerful enough to overcome the tragedy of the Orient created by perverse nationalisms. . . .

There are a few theoretical characteristics that mark [this regional cooperative community]. . . .

First, the Oriental regional cooperative community (*tōyōteki chiiki kyōdōtai*) must embrace a single new system. . . . This system should not be a territorial empire in which one ethnic group or one state dominates the others, but it should rather be a regional cooperative community whose natural political structure is a confederation.

Second, this Oriental regional cooperative community should respect existing differences among the various ethnic cultures represented, acknowledge different ethnic backgrounds, recognize its global cultural mission in relation to Western culture, and make an effort to creatively unify all these elements. . . .

Third, the Oriental regional cooperative community must implement rational plans and policies to guarantee and improve the welfare of its peoples. . . .

Fourth, the economic system of the regional cooperative community should reflect a collective economy and not an imperialist economic system. . . .

Fifth, its final but most important characteristic is that the theory of a regional cooperative community does not assume an autarkic or bloc system but a global system, and thus embodies the principles of the international political and economic system.

Chapter Nineteen

Miyazaki Masayoshi: "On the East Asian League," 1938

Michael A. Schneider

Miyazaki Masayoshi (1893–1954) was a minor bureaucrat who came to wield considerable influence over draft plans for Japan's wartime mobilization (on Miyazaki's life, see Kobayashi 1995). Associated with prominent military figures, most notably Ishiwara Kanji (see II:22), Miyazaki reached a wide audience with his sharp critiques of laissez-faire capitalism blended with a vision of pan-Asian economic unity. As such, he offered a clear link between pan-Asian idealism and the formulation of concrete policies to implement a union of Asian nations. His career trajectory paralleled Ishiwara's, however, and he too became a marginal figure during the war years. Nevertheless, his ties to the Manchurian development project during the 1930s gave him influence in postwar discussions for reinvigorating Japan's economy.

Miyazaki was one of the few Japanese to witness the early stages of the Russian Revolution first hand. He was born in Kanazawa, Ishikawa Prefecture, to a former samurai family that had successfully made the transition into the rice trade business. Having earned a prefectural scholarship to study the Russian language in Harbin in 1914, he obtained another scholarship to continue his study in St. Petersburg (Petrograd at the time), where he earned a college-level degree. As a student, he witnessed the February Revolution (March 1917) and the ensuing chaos under the Provisional Government. He left Russia in July before the Bolshevik (October) Revolution, but the experience of the revolution shaped his views on political leadership and economic policy.

On his return, Miyazaki parlayed his expertise on Russia into a position with the Southern Manchurian Railway (SMR), eventually landing in its Research Section (on the history of the SMR's research section, see Kobayashi 2005). During the 1920s, he carried out a number of studies of the postrevolutionary Soviet economy. He was particularly interested in Soviet central planning as pursued under the New Economic Policy and the Five-Year Plans. While certainly no Marxist, Miyazaki developed an appreciation for the role of state central planning for the economy.

In 1930, he met Lieutenant Colonel Ishiwara Kanji, then serving on the general staff of the Kwantung army. Introduced to Ishiwara's vision of an impending global confrontation between regional economic blocs, Miyazaki perceived intellectual common ground over the importance of long-term economic development as essential to putting Japan and northeastern Asia on a firm wartime footing. For his part, Ishiwara subsequently credited Miyazaki with providing the intellectual rationale for his vision of regional development. After the outbreak of the Manchurian Incident in September 1931, Miyazaki sided decisively with the militarists. He moved from the Research Section to the newly organized Keizai Kenkyūkai (Economic Research Association [ERA]), taking the directorship of its First Division. This division held responsibility over general economic planning, thus appealing to Miyazaki's desire to establish the broad outlines of a new command economy. The move made him understandably unpopular within the SMR, as it led to a hollowing out of the existing Research Division while compelling the civilian bureaucrats to work with the military advocates of territorial expansion. In his new position, Miyazaki was the principal author of the ERA's 1932 proposal for state management of Manchurian industrial development. The proposal argued that the rise of regional economic blocs during the Great Depression was a direct response to the mismanagement of Japan's economy. In place of the bungled laissez-faire, export-oriented development of the 1920s, he insisted, Manchurian development must focus on long-term growth in heavy industry.

With the state of Manchukuo established in 1932 and the ERA's planning complete, future planning for continental development shifted to Tokyo. By 1935, both Ishiwara and Miyazaki found themselves there. Miyazaki joined the Japan-Manchukuo Finance and Economics Research Association, a think tank backed by the Army General Staff and populated with young economists mostly from Tokyo Imperial University. By 1937, the association under Miyazaki's leadership had crafted a detailed blueprint for the development of the Japanese economy in such a way as to give it the industrial might to confront the great powers in East Asia. As with Miyazaki's earlier proposals, this five-year plan included a sweeping vision of economic development to place the economy on a war footing, with centralized planning, production targets in heavy industries, controls on financial institutions and foreign exchange, and constraints on the activities of private entrepreneurs. It also called for dramatic changes to the domestic political structure in order to manage these policies.

Miyazaki and Ishiwara viewed the slide into full-scale war with Chiang Kai-shek's Nationalist government in 1937 as premature. Predictably, the immediate needs of war prosecution derailed many of the broadly conceived, long-term prescriptions for centralizing economic planning. Their prescriptions for reform of existing government institutions had many powerful critics. Reflecting Ishiwara Kanji's gradual alienation from the official course of continental policy, Miyazaki reoriented his activities to support Ishiwara's vision for organizing a community of allied states liberated from Western imperialism: an East Asian League (on Ishiwara's role; see II:22). To this end Miyazaki played a leading role in forming the Tōa Renmei Kyōkai (East Asian League Association) in October 1939. The organization boasted fifty-two branches with some 6,600 members (Kobayashi 1995: 194). It had sister organizations in China, in Beijing the Zhonghua Dongya Lianmeng Xiehui (Japanese: Chūka Tōa Renmei Kyōkai, Chinese East Asian League Association, 1940), whose president was Miao Pin (1899–1946) and the Dongya Lianmeng Zhongguo Tongshihui (Japanese: Tōa Renmei Chūgoku Dōshikai, Association of Chinese Comrades of the East Asian League, 1941) in Nanjing headed by Wang Jingwei (Wang Ching-wei; see II:23), the premier of the collaborationist Nanjing (Nanking) regime (Kobayashi 1995: 194).

Miyazaki published his own views in 1938 in a book titled *Tōa Renmei Ron* (On the East Asian League). The appearance of the book coincided with the formation of the Wang Jingwei regime in Nanjing. It was a rare opportunity for Miyazaki to give a public voice to ideas he had been promoting within bureaucratic circles for years. As indicated in the translation here, the tract, with its sharp, clear prose and an unflinching critical tone, reads as an ideological call to arms on behalf of his command economy proposals. The work thus anticipates the reasons why the subsequent movement for an East Asian League, led by Ishiwara, would be a largely oppositional one. Although steeped in pan-Asianist themes and sustaining the image of Japanese moral leadership in Asia, Miyazaki and the movement for an East Asian League argued that East Asian unity must be formed by politically independent states, even if that requirement meant political independence for colonies like Korea. This quasi-internationalist stance was viewed as critical of the continental strategy of the Konoe Fumimaro cabinet. Ishiwara's nemesis Army Minister Tōjō Hideki ultimately suppressed the movement in 1941.

Miyazaki spent the remainder of the war years in occupied China working on local economic development projects. He was in Shanghai at the war's end and escaped close scrutiny by the American occupation authorities on his repatriation. He joined the Nihon Keizai Fukkō Kyōkai (Japanese Economic Recovery Association), a private think tank devoted to postwar reconstruction. Given his contacts with noted political figures, he might have achieved greater status in the postwar era, but he died of liver cancer in 1954 before achieving a prominent position.

Source (translation from the Japanese original by Michael A. Schneider)
Miyazaki Masayoshi, *Tōa Renmei Ron* (On the East Asian League), Kaizōsha, 1938, 44–53.

The policy of an East Asian League means turning away from our emulation of European imperialist and colonial polices and eventually repudiating them. . . .

I cannot emphasize enough that, in abandoning our imperialist policies, our nation must not vacillate. Today, the ambition to justify all of Japan's deeds has a strong grip over the nation. A posture of ruthlessly defending every one of our policies in the past, however, does not demonstrate the magnanimity of a great nation. Although our continental policy brought peace and prosperity to Korea and achieved a perfect merger of the Japanese and Korean peoples, we should not lose sight of the fact that we have lost supporters for our policies in East Asia. Japan must revert to its own course. It must reestablish a position of leadership in East Asia. For this reason, it is essential that we drive out any vestiges of imperialist thought remaining in our public discourse. As long as these attitudes persist in Japan, it will be difficult for East Asians to grasp the East Asian League framework, but moreover its policies will lose their moral force. In this sense, Japan, as the advocate for the League, must investigate the psyche of oppressed peoples thoroughly at every stage of the League's formulation. We must be ever mindful that the structure of the League not replace the system of Western exploitation with a system of Japanese oppression and must further be resolved not to give the impression that it will.

With the League taking as its goal the liberation of East Asian peoples, the right of political independence of liberated peoples must be guaranteed unconditionally. As Japan and its allies cooperate with the liberation movements of other East Asian peoples, it must be left to voluntary decision whether they join the League or whether they remain completely independent nations. Further, we must recognize a right of withdrawal after joining. The East Asian League is a union of autonomous East Asian nations, which should be bound closely by the sinews of mutual political and economic interdependence between Japan and its allies. It is not a system of coercion. The ultimate will to independent statehood cannot be suppressed. I believe that, with Japan and its allies assuming this stance, centrifugal forces will be very weak and the chances of a people distancing themselves from the League would be extremely small. From the perspective of the development of national economies generally or from the perspective of the benefits for ordinary individuals, the fact is that advantage is gained by being part of a big nation or a big bloc. During this recent period of quasi-warfare among competing blocs, this holds especially true for a small, weak country in the corner of East Asia. The historical significance of an East Asian League to East Asians could be most easily understood were Japan to adopt such a stance. . . .

[Miyazaki goes on ascribe the oppressive race relations under European empires to the liberal, free trade ideology of the West.]

The White man's system of rule over East Asia was, at root, shot through with liberal thought. Those who think my words are extreme need look no further than the cases of natives of India, the Annamites of French Indochina, the blacks of South Africa or the present state of the blacks and native Indians of the United States. . . .

It is emotionally stunning to think back to the days before the Manchurian Incident—when a segment of the Japanese intelligentsia longed for free trade, held out hope for the potential of a global economy, and even advocated abandoning Manchuria—that the day had arrived when the thought and systems of Western liberalism held such potency that Japanese would abandon their own East Asian-ness (*Tōyōsei*). . . .

The establishment of an East Asian League is a comprehensive renovationist policy, combining the renovation of our policy on the continent with the establishment of a new domestic order. Its renovationist character becomes increasingly clear, as evidenced by our comprehensive global policy through the Anti-Comintern Pact [concluded with Germany in 1936], and presents powerful testimony that Japan is entering a new epoch.

Chapter Twenty

Ozaki Hotsumi: "The Ideal of the 'East Asian Cooperative Body' and the Objective Basis for Its Formation," 1939

Eri Hotta

Ozaki Hotsumi (1901–1944), best known for his association with Richard Sorge (1895–1944), the German spy who passed on vital strategic intelligence to the Soviet Union on the eve of the Pacific War (cf. Johnson 1964), was a journalist and political analyst with an expertise in Chinese affairs. In the 1930s, he gained prominence through his activity in the research unit of the South Manchurian Railroad, the Shōwa Kenkyūkai (Shōwa Research Association [SRA]), a brain trust for Prime Minister Konoe Fumimaro, as well as in the exclusive Asameshikai (Breakfast Club), an informal policy discussion group formed by the closest aides and friends of Konoe's in 1937.

Ozaki's ideological composition was complex. He was at once a communist, internationalist, Japanese nationalist, and, above all, pan-Asianist. Indeed, his Pan-Asianism facilitated his undercover work for Sorge, as a common concern for the future of Asia drew Ozaki close to his unwitting sources of information. The piece reproduced here is important since it mirrors Ozaki's ideological commitment, which was nuanced at best and ambiguous at worst. What might have contributed to the development of his Pan-Asianism, among other worldviews? Key answers lie in his biography.

Ozaki Hotsumi was born in Tokyo in 1901 but was raised mostly in colonial Taiwan, where his father was a newspaper journalist. At age eighteen, he came back to Japan to attend the elite First Higher School and Tokyo Imperial University. From 1928 to 1932, he lived in Shanghai as a correspondent for the daily *Asahi Shinbun*. On the Asian continent he observed at close range the turmoil of China, torn apart by warlord factionalism, the rise of modern Chinese nationalism, and Japan's expansionism. Seeing China's chaos firsthand deepened his sympathy for Chinese communism. He sought contact with local communists, a communist student group of the the East Asia Common Culture Academy (Tōa Dōbun Shoin), and Shanghai's cosmopolitan residents with leftist sympathies. Sorge, who was then on a fact-finding mission for Moscow, was one of them.

Sorge described his relationship with Ozaki from this period as "impeccable, both personally and professionally" and Ozaki's departure for Tokyo in 1932 as "a terrible loss" to the execution of his mission (Obi 1962c: 160). Ozaki, for his part, related that

> . . . my chance meeting with those people [Sorge and his partner Agnes Smedley] in the end determined my ensuing narrow path. Those people were both loyal to their ideologies and profound in their principles, as well as being devoted to and talented in their work. If those people were in any small way motivated by self-interest, or acted as if they were trying to use us, I at least would have refused and parted company. But they, especially Sorge, continued to be kind and loyal colleagues. (Obi 1962b: 8)

In light of such mutual admiration, it is no surprise that Ozaki promptly agreed to cooperate when he was approached again by Sorge in Japan in 1934. Certainly, the two men had much in common. Their analytical skills, scholarly penchant for and love of history, as well as their passionate and gregarious nature all combined in a way that enabled both to become successful reporters for major newspapers (Sorge wrote for the *Frankfurter Zeitung*) and indeed skillful espionage agents. In spite of the remarkable overlap of these two characters, however, there was a significant gap in how they perceived the role of Soviet communism for the future of the world. This is where Ozaki's Pan-Asianism comes in. His experiences in Taiwan and mainland China were very important to the development of his ideology. Ozaki himself reflected that his experience of coming in close contact with Taiwan's Chinese residents, and seeing the "ruler-ruled" dynamic of imperialism in "everyday life and in very specific forms" was "the only extraordinary experience" in his otherwise "ordinary" childhood (Obi 1962b: 5).

Of his later experience in Shanghai, Ozaki commented that it stiffened his already strong ideological position, which revolved around his interest in nationalist movements in general and the national liberation of China in particular. Thus, his ideological trajectory began from his "doubt, from the humanistic standpoint" as the basis of his sympathy for and interest in the "China problem." His exposure to Japanese colonialism in Taiwan at an early age aroused his humanistic concern for China and its liberation from exploitation, which turned him to communism as a possible answer for countering oppressive forces. This finally led to his view of the Soviet Union as the proponent of principles that would help to strengthen nationalism in Asia.

There was another important aspect to Ozaki's ideology: his Japanese nationalism. On his return from China, he detected an overwhelming crisis of values in Japan's domestic life, plagued by a deteriorating economy and rising terrorism. Such pressing political developments at home led a "conceptual and formulaic theorist" like him to face the problems of contemporary Japanese politics head-on (Obi 1962b: 9). He said as much in his prison cell:

> I myself remained an internationalist and a communist. Nonetheless, my specific understanding of Japan, its politics, or its nation grew more practical. . . . My writings mainly dealt with the issues of national policy, critiques written from a Japanese standpoint, the China problem as well as the reorganization of the nation . . . my enthusiasm for these problems was after all a reflection of my second side [as an analyst of Japanese politics and as a nationalist] and never a camouflage for my other side [as a communist], nor a convenient means to earn money from my writing. . . . Certainly in recent years, I have been an internationalist as well as a Japanese nationalist . . . , the two did not seem to contradict one another. Or, at the very least, they managed to co-exist within me for a very long time. (Obi 1962b: 9–10)

In Ozaki's mind, communism was not opposed to nationalism, either. As a result, the nationalisms of Japan and China and their places within the "East Asian Cooperative Body" are at the heart of the selected article. His admission could be one answer to the venerable question whether communists could consistently believe in national self-determination, evoked by the famous but often misinterpreted declaration by Marx that "the working men have no country. We cannot take from them what they have not got." As the history of the twentieth century suggests, there are in fact very few examples of active nonnationalist communists. Like Mao Zedong, Ho Chi Minh, and Josef Tito, among numerous others, Ozaki inclined toward communism not because he thought nationalism and other variants of nationalist ideology, such as Pan-Asianism, did not exist or were unimportant. Rather, he was attracted to communism precisely because he believed it could reconcile at least some aspects of emerging and clashing "national" and "state" interests on which the existing international order, however deplorable and unjust it might be from the Asian standpoint, was predicated. And he hoped that such a reconciliation could be reached within a broader-than-nation-state, international, and possibly and eventually transnational, pan-Asian framework based on the cooperation of his two homes, China and Japan.

To be sure, Ozaki's nationalism had its limits. Unlike his SRA colleague Miki Kiyoshi (1897–1945; on Miki, cf. Kim 2007), whose concerns for Japan's domestic situation were coupled with the goal of Japan's securing Asian leadership position, Ozaki's vision was truly more communistic and egalitarian, aspiring to cooperativism in a very literal sense. And here, a closer look at his view of East Asian Cooperative Body is called for.

Published in the January 1939 issue of *Chūō Kōron* (The Central Review), the article reproduced here followed the opinion pieces penned by Ozaki's SRA colleagues, the philosopher Miki Kiyoshi (Miki 1938) and political scientist Rōyama Masamichi (1895–1980; Rōyama 1938; on Rōyama, see II:18). They all aspired, with limited success, to explain and interpret Prime Minister Konoe's "New East Asian Order Statement" of 3 November 1938 (reproduced in II:17). Konoe's radio broadcast proclaimed that the ultimate objective of Japan's military engagement in China was the construction of a new East Asian Order and that the Japanese Empire would welcome Chinese support in that endeavor. The statement was an attempt to reverse the adverse effects of Japan's earlier policy of trying to bully Chiang Kai-shek's Nationalists into suing for peace. It highlighted the need for East Asia to develop its own regional bloc in which a new order would be established to resist other potent forces of international relations, such as communism and imperialism.

But the statement fell short of explaining what the "new order" was to be about, how it was to be achieved, and how it was to be managed. In their respective articles, Miki, Rōyama, and Ozaki all gave variations on the same theme, which was that the idea of East Asian Cooperative Body constituted the very essence of this new, moral, and just international order that would benefit not only Asia but also possibly the rest of the world. Ozaki said as much in the selected article: "Most of those who argue for the 'East Asian Cooperative Body' do not see 'East Asia' as a stand-alone, closed unit. For them, 'East Asia' is a regional, racial, cultural, economic, common-defensive unit that precedes the trend of a general world order."

Moreover, prevalent among the proponents of East Asia Cooperative Body was the idea that the rise of such a Japanese-led regional framework was a historical inevitability. For the moral goal of establishing a "New Order in East Asia," they insisted that "even with enormous sacrifices," Japan "had to keep on fighting with dogged perseverance" (Rōyama 1938: 7). To a certain degree, Ozaki shared such sentiments with his colleagues, who were from the right and left of the political spectrum. He did believe that Japan was uniquely placed in Asia to undertake a reconstruction of Asia. He also believed, like his colleagues, that Japan required a drastic domestic reform. It was the extent of this reform and the ultimate future he saw for Japan as well as for the rest of Asia that made his case exceptional.

We now know from his post-arrest reflections and interrogation records that his vision of the future lay in a collaborative union of a postcapitalist Japan and a communist China backed by the Soviet Union. Revolving around this union was the "cooperative body of various East Asian nations" consisting of "India, Burma, Thailand, the Dutch and French East Indies, and the Philippines" as well as what he regarded as ethnic and religio-national communities, such as "the Mongolians, the Muslims, the Koreans, and the Manchus" (Obi 1962a: 203–4). Ozaki believed that Japan and China were ready for socialist hegemony. However, he did not regard the establishment of communist governments as an absolute necessity in the immediate future for all the countries concerned. Sticking to the Marxist principles of developmental stages, he felt that they should choose "the most suitable form of governance themselves" in accordance with the objective of creating a "New East Asian order, which in turn should not be disruptive of the larger world order" (Obi 1962a: 204).

Precisely because Ozaki was "not a simple communist" (Obi 1962b: 11), his view of internationalism too was far from simple. He decisively rejected the naïveté of either Wilsonian internationalism, the Versailles–Washington treaty system, or even the utopian internationalism of Comintern persuasion. Rather, his internationalism always revolved around the pressing questions of what to do with Japan internally and externally and, by extension, China. Because Ozaki recognized the force of nationalism in China and its ramifications for Japan's position in the wider world, he was reluctant to embrace those optimistic brands of internationalism wholeheartedly. He stated that "the 'world' only exists conceptually and abstractly. Realistically and specifically, there are only 'international' relations as consisting of various nation-states," citing the dissolution of the Comintern as a clear evidence of how state interest usually overrides universalistic claims (Obi 1962b: 34). Given Ozaki's complicated ideological allegiances, therefore, the selected piece should not be read simply as a piece of writing disguising his single-minded wish for the Soviet takeover of the whole of East Asia, as some have tenuously done in the past. It should be approached with a full awareness that his concerns for Asia were "a reflection" rather than a "camouflage" for his "other side" (Obi 1962b: 9–10).

Ozaki's more celebrated espionage partner in fact lacked such an awareness of the hard-nosed realities of international politics. Sorge regarded the Soviet Union as paving the way directly for a "world" society, the possibility of which Ozaki flatly rejected. All the same, the two embraced the same fate. In October 1941, the Japanese police arrested the key members of the Sorge Spy Ring. Declared guilty of violating the Peace Preservation Law and National Defence Security Law, both Ozaki and Sorge were executed nine months before Japan's defeat on the anniversary of the Bolshevik Revolution, 7 November 1944.

Source (translation from the Japanese original by Eri Hotta)
Ozaki Hotsumi, "*'Tōa Kyōdōtai' no rinen to sono seiritsu no kyakkanteki kiso*" (Principle of the "East Asian Cooperative Body" and the Objective Basis for Its Establishment). *Chūō Kōron* (January 1939).

[Ozaki begins the article by linking Konoe's "New Order" statement to the idea of an East Asian Cooperative Body. He also asserts that the construction of such a regional entity serves as the *jus ad bellum* of Japan's military engagement in China.]

. . . We should not be focusing our attention simply on the evolving state of Sino-Japanese relations resulting from the war, or the war's objective realities. To do so is to deliberately ignore the emergence of a new order. The outlines of the new order concept can be detected in Prime Minister Konoe's radio broadcast [of 3 November], which was presumably made to make the government's proclamation of the same day known more widely to the public. That is to say, [Japan intends to]:

"cooperate with China, not to conquer China"
"lead the rehabilitated China to carry out the common mission of East Asia"
"let the Chinese nation share in the great task of building a New East Asia"
"establish a new peaceful state of affairs in East Asia"
"lead various East Asian nations in the construction of a new autonomous federal entity based on a truly moral foundation."

Owing to such words, the character and parameters of the "New Order" became clear in the government's top-level policy proclamations. They indeed point to the features of "East Asian Cooperative Body." . . .

I actually believe that the "East Asian Cooperative Body" ideal emerged inevitably, and I believe in its potential for future development. Nevertheless, in reality the "East Asian Cooperative Body" has a series of weaknesses and problems of feasibility. . . .

[Ozaki points out that some Japanese are concerned with Japan's pursuit of its exclusive material gains. He also sees Chinese nationalism as a tremendous obstacle to defeating Chiang Kai-shek and realizing the cooperative body.]

Most Japanese did not begin the war hating the Chinese. Rather, they tried to deal a blow to the Nationalist government because of its wrong-headed policies and to facilitate its repentance. However, the Chinese from the beginning saw this conflict as a national struggle with its national destiny at stake, and they behave accordingly. We could forcefully divide China into enemies and allies. But even then, the divided blocs would continue to present this same problem of nationalism regardless. In all likelihood, even if the war were to end as Japan wishes, that is to say, even if Japan were to score a complete victory, it is inevitable that we would still be faced with serious problems connected to this question of nationalism. . . .

We need to reflect quietly on the meaning of "holy war." Today, in certain Japanese quarters, some argue that Japan must demand clear, concrete concessions from the continent. [If Japan were to gain nothing], they say that those brave fighters who have spilt their noble blood would not rest in peace, and those soldiers in the field who are, as we speak, fighting for Japan, will not be satisfied. Their argument is utterly wrong. . . . We are convinced that those who have sacrificed their lives for the country did not spill their precious blood to demand [material] compensation. Absolutely not. Rather they longed to become human pillars of the "New East Asian Order" that would bring about ultimate peace to East Asia. . . .

The theory of a "New East Asian Order," observed as a principle, is a grand ideal that anyone can agree upon. However, when it is applied to practical politics, it naturally runs into numerous problems. One must be aware of such foreseeable difficulties and still have the will to carry out the task. Otherwise, the theory of an "East Asian Cooperative Body" will end up as a modern myth, a dream. At present the "East Asian Cooperative Body" concept, because of the difficulty in dealing with the China conflict, is regarded by some as a panacea for Japan's exit policy. That is far from the truth. I have reiterated that there are bound to be problems of nationalism. On 1 November, Chiang Kai-shek wrote to the whole nation: "China's battle is not an ordinary war of conquest between two countries. It is a national, revolutionary war. Moreover, the prolonged war of nationalism and revolution will certainly be concluded with a final victory." Seen from the light of competing nationalisms, we must be aware of how miserable and petty this argument of "East Asian Cooperative Body" really is. . . .

With China in the East Asian Cooperative Body, the future question remains whether such a body takes a federalist or a union format. We suspect that on the one hand, there is a yearning for a centralized state. On the other hand, there is an increasing need for a regionalist approach, where regional differences [within the cooperative body] are stressed. In the latter case, Japan's economic ties with North and Central China would have to become something fundamentally different. That is one point of consideration. . . .

The question of whether the principle behind the "East Asian Cooperative Body" could develop empirically is of course dependent on the power equation between Japan and China as well as on the state of international relations. But the biggest obstacle lies within Japan, where forces must gather to realize such an effort. . . .

Whether or not the "East Asian Cooperative Body theory" would be able to liberate East Asia from its plight depends on several factors. The theory must in the end gain Chinese support, from those who are willing enough to embrace the proverb of "suffering now and flourishing later." The success also depends on whether it can resolve tensions between different nationalisms. Finally, the "cooperative body theory" must gain support from within Japan itself, where an internal reorganization must be carried out. The theory's future depends on all these factors.

Chapter Twenty-One

Hiranuma Kiichirō: "The New Asiatic Order," 1939

Christopher W. A. Szpilman

Hiranuma Kiichirō was born in 1867 into a middling samurai family in what is now Okayama Prefecture. He graduated from the prestigious Law Faculty of Tokyo Imperial University in 1888 and entered the Justice Ministry the following year. In 1910 he distinguished himself during the successful prosecution of Kōtoku Shūsui (1871–1911) and other anarchists on charges of conspiracy to assassinate the Meiji emperor (the High Treason Incident). In 1912, he was promoted to the post of procurator general, in which he remained for an unprecedented period of nine years (1912–1921). After a brief stint as president of the Great Court of Cassation, Hiranuma accepted the portfolio of justice minister in the second Yamamoto Gonnohyōe Cabinet (1923). Shortly after the fall of that cabinet in the wake of the Toranomon Incident (an assassination attempt on the crown prince), he was appointed a privy councilor (1924).

Hiranuma served in the Privy Council until 1939, becoming vice president in 1926 and president in March 1936. The crowning achievement of his career was his appointment as prime minister on 5 January 1939, though his term in office turned out to be disappointingly short. Hiranuma, who had spent most of his time as premier in negotiating an anti-Soviet pact with Germany, resigned when he heard the news of the conclusion of the Soviet-German Non-Aggression Treaty (28 August 1939). But even after his resignation, Hiranuma continued to play a powerful role in Japanese politics. As one of the nation's elder statesmen (*jūshin*), he participated in choosing prime ministers; he was a cabinet minister in the second and third Konoe cabinets (July 1940–October 1941), and in the last days of the Pacific War (February 1945), he was reappointed as president of the Privy Council, in which capacity he took part in debates on Japan's surrender and in forming the first postwar cabinet of Prince Higashikuni. After Japan's defeat,

Hiranuma, arrested as a class A war criminal, was sentenced to life in prison by the International Military Tribunal for the Far East. He died in prison in 1952. Hiranuma's political power came from his position in the Privy Council, but he also wielded a considerable influence through his followers in the Justice Ministry. However, the main source of Hiranuma's power was the Kokuhonsha (National Foundation Society), an organization that he founded (1921), sponsored, and (after 1924) led. The Kokuhonsha included a large number of Japan's best and brightest: senior bureaucrats, generals, admirals, privy councilors, peers, and leading scholars, as well as a handful of party politicians. Its members believed that their future political prospects depended on the success of Hiranuma's political career, and they supported him whenever they could. This helps explain why Hiranuma invariably emerged as a candidate for the post of prime minister during every cabinet change after 1927. That it took twelve years to become prime minister is indicative less of the impotence of the Kokuhonsha than of the opposition to his candidacy by the last *genrō* (elder statesman), Prince Saionji Kinmochi (1849–1940), and by a number of powerful court officials who viewed Hiranuma, in the words of Prince Saionji, as a Japanese equivalent of Mussolini (Szpilman 1998a: 127).

Whether this assessment was accurate is open to doubt. Hiranuma himself strenuously denied that he was a fascist—as do most historians, who regard Hiranuma not as a fascist but as a conservative. They also on the whole agree that the Kokuhonsha was, like its leader, an ideologically conservative body. Nevertheless, in spite of its conservative reputation, the Kokuhonsha managed to attract a large number of right-wing radicals and pan-Asianists (e.g., Nakatani Takeyo, 1898–1990; Ayakawa Takeji, 1891–1966; and Kasagi Yoshiaki, 1892–1955) who contributed to the Kokuhonsha's flagship publication, the monthly *Kokuhon* and, in some cases (e.g., Mitsukawa Kametarō), even had an input into the editorial policy. Their presence in *Kokuhon* suggests some sympathy for these radicals' pan-Asianist views, as does the support that Hiranuma gave to the Muslim pan-Asianist Kurban Ali (Mantetsukai and Shimano Saburō Denki Kankōkai 1984: 458–59; on Kurban Ali, see also I:23).

The statement reproduced here must be seen in the context of Japan's China policy. It was published at a time when Japan's seemingly invincible armies advanced deeper and deeper into China without, however, managing to score a decisive victory that would put an end to Chinese resistance. Japan, in effect, was embroiled in a "holy" war it could not win.

Although this 1939 statement expressed the official cabinet policy of the day, it does appear to reflect Hiranuma's personal views to a high degree (on these views, see Hiranuma Kiichirō Kaikoroku Hensan Iinkai 1955). For Hiranuma's was a traditional, conservative variety of Pan-Asianism, and in accordance with Hiranuma's convictions, the statement condenses pan-Asian unity down to the sphere of Sinitic civilization. This was clearly different from the approach of other, younger and more radical pan-Asianists, such as Ōkawa Shūmei (see II:4) and Kanokogi Kazunobu (see II:14), who did not limit the scope of their Pan-Asianism to East Asia and liked to talk of revolution—anathema to Hiranuma.

Hiranuma was a great admirer of Chinese classics and culture. He even founded a library, the Mukyūkai (Eternal Association), to house his (and his friends') enormous collection of Chinese classics. His own writings reflected this taste, being invariably replete with references to Chinese history and classical literature. It was his conviction that the Chinese classics provided a moral foundation for individuals and society alike and thus were indispensable for good government. These classics, as well as the script in which they were recorded, were the shared heritage of all the nations of East Asia. In other words, Hiranuma sincerely believed that the Chinese classics formed the cement that united China, Japan, Korea, and neighboring areas within the broad sphere of Chinese civilization. Although many of the younger radical pan-Asianists also had good knowledge of the Chinese classics, in contrast to Hiranuma and other conservatives, they were unlikely to see in them the solution to China's (or Asia's) problems.

For all the differences between Hiranuma's "old" Pan-Asianism and its "new" variety as espoused by Ōkawa and Kanokogi, it is possible to detect a point of convergence. Specifically, both conservatives like Hiranuma and radicals like Kanokogi (who also spoke of India) and Ōkawa (who paid much attention to Islam) agreed that modern China, mired in political and social turmoil, had degenerated and needed to be saved from itself.

It was, Hiranuma argued (like Kanokogi or Ōkawa), this degeneracy that had caused China to be split into the mutually hostile fiefdoms of petty warlords supported by their private armies; it was this degeneracy that had allowed the communists to become a power to be reckoned with within China; and it was this degeneracy that had given Chiang Kai-shek's Nationalist government recognition as the legitimate government of China even if, in Hiranuma's eyes, Chiang's regime was just another military clique headed by yet another petty warlord. China, which had betrayed the magnificent ideals of Confucianism, the statement insists, must "return to its true nature" and recover its proper "oriental morality." But as the Chinese government had failed to restore these ideals, it was Japan's heaven-mandated duty to restore them for the sake of China, sparing neither "lives" nor "money." So, with or without Chinese cooperation, Japan would forge "a new East Asiatic system unparalleled in the world" that would comprise the territories of China, Manchuria, and Japan (including Korea). This system, under Japan's leadership, would then become "the cornerstone of Far Eastern stability."

Hiranuma's claim that Japan was waging a war to prevent peoples of "the same race [from] shed[ding] each other's blood" can be seen as a concession to radicalism—but the traditional emphasis on a common culture and common letters is preponderant in the statement.

It would surely be wrong to interpret the professions of "the deepest sympathy for the Chinese people" in the text here as stemming from Hiranuma's admiration for the Chinese classics. They must be seen as propaganda designed to justify Japanese aggression as is made obvious, for example, by the reaffirmation of Japan's steely resolve "to attain the goal of the holy war." Nevertheless, Hiranuma's love for the Chinese classics can be detected in the claim that the "goal of this holy war" is to return China to its "true nature," that is, to a nature faithful to the values specified in Chinese classics as Hiranuma understood them.

Source (English in the original)
"The New Asiatic Order," Speech broadcast by Baron Hiranuma Kiichirō on 4 March 1939 (translation by the Domei News Agency, Tokyo), Appendix 1, *Japan's Diplomacy and Its Aims as Outlined in Speeches and Remarks by Hachiro Arita, Foreign Minister, at the 74th Session of the Imperial Diet, 1938–39* (The Japan Times and Mail, 1939), 24–27.

The forces for construction of the new East Asia are rearing their heads with a strength that nothing can resist. I am glad to be given an opportunity of saying a word or two at this most important period of renovation. Everlasting peace is the common ideal of the world. The endeavors of Japan to make East Asia a Utopia of everlasting peace with the China incident as the turning point are aimed at completion of the Heaven-ordained task to fulfill the aspirations of the entire people of East Asia. Japan, Manchoukuo and China, joined by common letters and racial ties, are geographically and historically situated together in such a way that the relationship of coexistence and coprosperity among them is inevitable. They have a common destiny to rely on one another, to help one another and to work together for the common prosperity of East Asia. It is of the first importance for the three nations clearly to take cognizance of this inseparable friendship. The policy of the Empire [of Japan] for the construction of a new order in East Asia remains precisely as stated by the former Premier, Prince Konoye, and is aimed ultimately at assuring the eternal stability of East Asia by the three nations working hand in hand. For this purpose, the three nations must establish relations of mutual linkage in politics, economics and culture and must collaborate for the establishment of international justice, achievement of joint anti-Comintern defense, creation of a new civilization and realization of economic combination.

Manchoukuo, as you already are aware, has more and more regulated and strengthened its structure as a new, rising State and now is discharging its important responsibility as a wing of the construction of a new East Asia. In China, too, we feel the rising tide of renovation. The Empire is most desirous that a new central regime be established and develop soundly, such as would be capable of cooperating with the Empire for the great task ahead.

History shows clearly that the Empire and China, placed in an inevitable relationship of coexistence and coprosperity, have grown and developed within a common civilization. Consequently, unless the Empire and China strive in united efforts for the building up of this new order in East Asia, it will be impossible to bring about everlasting peace and prosperity in this part of the world. This peace and prosperity is something which the Chinese people, victims of severe maladministration, have desired above all for many years. The Empire has the deepest sympathy for the Chinese, people who have borne suffering and hardship during such a long period. It is the ardent desire and goal of the Empire to rescue the Chinese people from such suffering and misery by constructing a bright and cheerful new order on the Continent. It is for this purpose that, since the outbreak of the China Affair [the Sino-Japanese War, 1937–1945], the Empire has paid such sacrifices in lives and money and is prepared to continue its untiring effort to attain the goal of the holy war. It is fighting so that China may return to its true nature and East Asia may come back to its own. It is fighting to uproot once and for all such sources of evil as would make peoples of the same letters and same race shed each other's blood. This relationship of coexistence and coprosperity is, of course, one in which the Empire and China mutually reserve their positions of independent nations. For this purpose, the Empire is bearing sacrifices in the China Affair which ordinarily could not possibly be borne. Japan desires the revival of China even at such a cost because it feels its mission to lie in making China a China of East Asia. The Empire and a rejuvenated China must join in strong linkage in politics, economy and culture, and each must supply what the other lacks. For this purpose, any such materialistic thought based on reliance on Europe and America as would make China a colony of a Western Power must absolutely be banished from China. In order to do this, it is vitally important to enforce a thought policy common to Asia, to promote the revival of Oriental morality and to strengthen the anti-Comintern front.

The great evil and harm being wrought by the doctrine which the Comintern [the Third Communist International founded in Moscow in March 1919] is spreading throughout the world and its incompatibility with this Oriental morality need not be expatiated upon. The National Government [under Chiang

Kai-shek, in Chongqing/Chungking], which has forgotten the Chinese people, under the pressure of the Communist Party, has adopted a policy of admitting Communism into China and is being more and more submerged under the pressure of the Communist Party. If nothing is done to check the tendency, China will be brought under the control of the Comintern, and the entire Chinese territory will be Bolshevized. Intelligent Chinese are aware of this and keenly feel the need for rescuing their country and innocent people from the talons of Communism.

If the life of misery and oppression under the exploitation of bandits and warlords and the new order which Japan proposes to construct are compared and examined, the justice of Japan's intentions must become quite clear. The very fact that numerous Chinese are living in peace in Japan eloquently attests to the sentiment of the Japanese Government and people.

The National Government, which led the entire Chinese people astray, has already fled to the hinterland and has been reduced to a mere local regime, but it is continuing its anti-Japanese operations with ostensible vigor. It has lost any real fighting strength and is continuing hopeless resistance. This is partly due to the fear of the mistaken leaders of the Nationalist Government that they may lose their positions and partly to expectation of foreign aid. But even among Nationalist leaders there not a few Chinese who are said to be in sympathy with the real intentions of Japan. It is not difficult to imagine that in time third Powers will be compelled to understand the real intentions of Japan and abandon their mistaken anti-Japanese policy.

On the other hand, if the National Government, failing to appreciate the real value of the movement of reconstruction of a New East Asia which is spreading over the Continent, is relying on the assistance of third Powers to continue its anti-Japanese operations merely for the sake of preserving its own position, its shortsightedness must be called pitiable and likened to a drowning man clutching at a straw.

But against a National Government which has destroyed the life of innocent people by its war of 'scorched earth' and which is selling its own country to third Powers in its foolish attempt to make use of these third Powers, the Imperial fighting force cannot diminish the intensity of its expedition. For, if the maladministration of the exploiting warlords is merely to be superseded by the tyranny of Communism, the Chinese people must forfeit their happiness forever. It is precisely because of this that the Empire is concentrating on defense against Communism with so much energy. For a new order to be established in East Asia, Japan, Manchoukuo and China must unite into one body to keep Communism out.

The Empire is prepared to complete this great task, whatever the difficulties in its path. . . . I am firmly convinced that the strength of spirit which the

Yamato race has maintained ever since the founding of the Empire will be fully equal to the task.

I most earnestly hope that the people of China will understand the ardent wish of the Japanese Empire, sympathize with this spirit and rise with a bold heart to join hands with Japan and Manchoukuo for the completion of a new East Asiatic system unparalleled in the world and become with us the corner-stones of Far Eastern stability.

Chapter Twenty-Two

Ishiwara Kanji's "Argument for an East Asian League," 1940

Roger H. Brown

In May 1947, Ishiwara Kanji (1889–1949) testified before a special military court convened as part of the International Military Tribunal for the Far East. While not under indictment himself, Ishiwara responded with indignation at what he viewed as American hypocrisy in trying Japanese for aggression and atrocities. Accusing prosecutors of being ignorant of their own country's history of expansionism in East Asia, he neatly shifted responsibility for Japanese aggression to the Americans and other Westerners who set the aggressive example, bluntly suggesting that, if they wished to try someone, they should subpoena the American Commodore Matthew Perry, who, with his flotilla of "black ships," forced the opening of Japan in 1853–1854. Disingenuous and evasive on the question of Japan's militarism and expansionism, Ishiwara's outburst illustrates aptly the manner in which Pan-Asianism served to both motivate and rationalize Japanese actions during the 1930s. Indeed, few individuals could match Ishiwara's degree of personal involvement in setting Japan's militarist quest for autarky in motion or close association with the pan-Asian ideology that accompanied that pursuit.

Ishiwara spent all but twenty-one years of his life in uniform (on Ishiwara's life, see Aoe 1997; Peattie 1975). He received his commission with the Twenty-First Class of the Military Academy in 1909 and served as an infantry field and staff officer before being retired at the rank of lieutenant general in 1941. Ishiwara was one of the key conspirators in the Manchurian Incident of 1931, which he viewed as a first step toward gaining the resources necessary for Japan to mobilize for a coming global war. While calling for formation of a New Order for East Asia based on Japanese, Manchurian, and Chinese cooperation, he sought an early end to the "China Incident" that began in July 1937 so as not to undermine preparations for total war against the West. This view brought him increasingly into conflict with other officers on the Army General Staff, who saw the war as an opportunity to destroy Chinese resistance at one blow and, as their position gained ascendance, Ishiwara's star began to fade. Leaving the General Staff for assignment with the Kwantung army in Manchukuo, Ishiwara made no secret of his unhappiness with the army's corrupt dominance over that puppet state. Criticizing those he held responsible for this state of affairs—including Major General Tōjō Hideki—he soon returned to Japan in 1938.

Although Ishiwara's army career was in eclipse, the years from 1939 to 1941 afforded him an opportunity to refine his thoughts regarding Japan's pan-Asian destiny and preparations for a "final war" against the West (cf. Ishiwara 1993), ideas that found institutional expression via the East Asian League Association (Tōa Renmei Kyōkai). A former lecturer at the Army War College, he perceived in his study of military history a tale of technological progress and strategic alternation between protracted wars and decisive wars. A follower of Nichiren Buddhism since 1919, he drew inspiration from this ethnocentric and apocalyptic form of Buddhism, which reserved for Japan the central role of combining government and religious truth in order to regenerate the world and bring about peace and harmony. Under the influence of the Nichiren revivalist Tanaka Chigaku's (1861–1939) blend of religious doctrine and emperor-centered ideology, Ishiwara conceived his theory of a "final war" (*saishū sensō*) between the champions of East and West, roles to be filled, respectively, by Japan and the United States.

Ishiwara envisioned a reorganization of domestic politics into "one country, one party" beneath "direct imperial rule," which would in turn facilitate increased industrial production and the creation of the national defense state that would provide Japan with military superiority in relation to prospective future foes, including the Soviet Union and, ultimately, the United States. Ishiwara sought to extend this renovation to the rest of East Asia, thereby securing the independence and modernization of the region while simultaneously fulfilling Japan's pan-Asian destiny. Japanese national mobilization would occur in tandem with the establishment of an alliance of East Asian nations to be led by Japan, harmonized through the creation of a new Asian morality rooted in the Kingly Way (*ōdō*) and animated by the spiritual qualities of the Japanese emperor. Facilitated through Japan's foundational spirit, the resulting material preparedness and ideological and political unity would enable Japan to successfully prosecute the final world war against the West. Japanese victory in this decisive conflict, which he believed would occur some thirty years hence, would result in the realization of world peace in the form of *hakkō ichiu* ("the eight corners of the world under one roof").

Although Ishiwara's personal interest in pan-Asian thought developed early in his life and the idea of an alliance of East Asian nations took shape shortly after the creation of Manchukuo in 1932, the East Asian League Association was not founded until 1939. At its peak, the organization boasted numerous branches at home and abroad and at least 100,000 members. Among the League's supporters were army officers in China, such as fellow Manchurian Incident conspirator and later Army Minister General Itagaki Seishirō (1885–1948), and members of the Japan-backed government in Nanjing, including President Wang Jingwei (Wang Ching-wei; see II:23). The New Order envisioned by the League resembled an East Asian commonwealth of nations under Japanese leadership and, in theory, held out the possibility of a regional system less coercive than the New Order being pursued by the Japanese government. Nevertheless, it was clearly to be a league not only led by Japan but also formed in the service of Japanese mobilization for war with the West.

Whatever ultimate form the East Asian League may have taken must remain speculative since the organization quickly ran afoul of General Tōjō, who, first as army minister in the second and third cabinets of Premier Konoe Fumimaro and then as prime minister in the successor administration, oversaw the League's suppression and ultimate disbanding. Tōjō's antipathy arose from both personal and political differences with the League and its leader. First, the League, reflecting Ishiwara's personal outlook, advocated a less hard-line approach to relations with China, something that Tōjō viewed as defeatist and antithetical to his own hard-line policy. Second, there was the obvious potential of the League to serve as a political base from which Ishiwara might challenge both Tōjō personally and government policy in general. Indeed, it was his perception of the League as a tool for getting at him personally that led Tōjō to initiate a crackdown in the fall of 1940. On the receiving end of this attention, Ishiwara fought back vigorously and publicly, his efforts culminating in a speech at Kyoto Imperial University in which he identified Tōjō and his allies rather than the Chinese as the true enemies of Japan and as men who should be arrested and executed. Nevertheless, it was a losing battle, and in March 1941, Ishiwara was placed on the retired list. A brief stint lecturing at Ritsumeikan University also ended under pressure from the authorities, and Ishiwara returned to his hometown for the remainder of the war.

It was there that occupation authorities later found him, outlawing his early postwar efforts to update and spread his ideas and deposing him for the war crimes tribunal. Meanwhile, the East Asian League Association was dissolved in 1942, then reorganized under the name East Asian League Comrades Association (Tōa Renmei Dōshikai), and finally purged by American occupation authorities in 1946.

The following translation is comprised of the East Asian League Association's manifesto and an explanation of the historical necessity for forming the

League and realizing a "New Order" for East Asia. These passages are taken from the association's *Tōa Renmei Kensetsu Yōkō* (Prospectus for Constructing the East Asian League), which goes on to enunciate the League's ideals and plans in greater detail before ending with an appended essay by Satomi Kishio (1897–1974)—the son of Tanaka Chigaku who was an Ishiwara associate—arguing for the compatibility of the Confucian Kingly Way with Japan's Imperial Way.

Source (translation from the Japanese original by Roger H. Brown) "Sengen" (Manifesto) and "Tōa Renmei no Hitsuzensei" (The Inevitability of the East Asian League), Tōa Renmei Kyōkai (ed.) (1940), *Tōa Renmei Kensetsu Yōkō* (Prospectus for Constructing the East Asian League). Ritsumeikan Shuppanbu, 1–7.

MANIFESTO

The final world war that is the great pivot of human history will arrive in the coming few decades. The Shōwa Restoration is none other than the unified application of the total abilities of the East Asian peoples in expectation of certain victory in this decisive battle.

Specifically, the aims of the Shōwa Restoration are as follows:

1. Out of the various states of the region form an East Asian League capable of eliminating the oppression of Euro-American imperialism.
2. Through assertive and reformist construction within the League rapidly increase true strength and prepare the conditions for certain victory in the decisive war.
3. En route to constructing the above, establish the leadership principles of a new age rooted in the Kingly Way.

11 February 2600 [1940]
East Asian League Association

THE INEVITABILITY OF THE EAST ASIAN LEAGUE

Establishing absolute world peace has long been humanity's ideal. That so long as humanity exists there will be no end to war is contemporary common sense. According to theoretical and idealistic thinking, eradicating war is fundamentally impossible; however, progressive development in perfecting the art of war will, through a final world war giving full play to mankind's capacity for strife, ultimately bring about the end of war itself. Bringing an end to war is the realization of global unity, the first step toward absolute world peace.

In the "New Thesis on the Shōwa Restoration" we have already made the case that the final world war will arrive within about the next thirty years and that global unity ought to be realized within about fifty years.

Looking at the development of human society it is clear that the spheres of states grow ever larger even as their number grows ever fewer and that the inevitable trend of history is that there will soon be unification into a world state. Through the rapid development of communications, transportation, culture, and industry the world's space is being increasingly reduced and regional contiguous states are drawing together. Following the first great European war the world evolved from the era of states confronting states to the age of state alliances confronting state alliances; however, through the second great European war, the world is now dividing into four groups, namely, Europe, the Soviet Union, South and North America, and East Asia. In this manner one can imagine the world henceforth will ultimately divide into two groups of states representing the civilizations of the Kingly Way and of the Despotic Way, and that these two groups of states will then deploy for the final world war centered on the Pacific, the result of which will be the unification of the world.

In this way, following the inevitable tendency of world history, it is most natural that the various East Asian peoples who adjoin regionally, approximate racially, and are similar culturally must unite as one.

The idea of East Asian Unity is not necessarily new. There were among our Meiji predecessors more than a few who called for the unification of the three countries of Japan, Korea and China, and Sun Yat-sen also advocated Great Asianism. However, in their day, the objective conditions in East Asia did not yet allow for East Asian unification. As an idea, the case for an East Asian community has existed previously, but when it came to connecting this to the realities of East Asia, the time was not yet right. However, today that is no longer the case. The objective conditions are ripe for realizing the unification of the various peoples of East Asia and for forming the East Asian League. If so, then what are those objective conditions?

First, Japan has obtained the capability to strike back from East Asia against the forces of Euro-American imperialism. Following the Meiji Restoration, Japan first endeavored necessarily to free itself from the shackles of the unequal treaties imposed by the Euro-American countries. After the Sino-Japanese War, she at long last succeeded in treaty revision and then fought and won against Russia which was seeking to occupy Manchuria and annex Korea. At that time Japan was respected by the various races of Asia as a liberator and Japanese, too, thought of East Asian revival; however, regrettably Japan was then incapable of rivaling the forces of Euro-American imperialism and thus imitated the forms of imperialism, cooperating especially with the various Euro-American countries and, moreover, we must admit the truth here, oppressed the various races of East Asia who should have been our allies. However, having availed itself of the opportunity presented by the Manchurian Incident, Japan's capabilities increased rapidly. At the same time self-confidence in that power unconsciously stirred moral instinct that attained the conscious awareness to liberate the races of East Asia from the bonds of Euro-American imperialism. The unity of East Asia takes as its prerequisite the liberation of East Asia. Japan, availing itself of the opportunity presented by the recent [China] incident, has secured the capability to expel the forces of Euro-American imperialism and this, we must say, is the most important condition for the formation of the East Asian League.

Second, there is the decline of Euro-American imperialist power in East Asia. Led by Great Britain, the first country to complete the industrial revolution, the Euro-American countries advanced into East Asia during the nineteenth century by means of cannons and goods. In the age of imperialism, through banks and railways they invaded East Asia and, except for Japan, placed virtually all the races of East Asia under their control. However, rule over East Asia by Euro-American imperialism was shaken in the wake of the first great European war and is now collapsing because of the China Incident and the second great European war. In particular, Great Britain, the pioneer of aggression against East Asia, is now experiencing its downfall. Construction of the New Order for East Asia, i.e., formation of the East Asian League, will be accomplished only through the expulsion from East Asia of the political and military power of the Anglo-American countries that fail to cooperate with this venture. Today, the three countries of Japan, Germany, and Italy, who share the objective of constructing a New World Order, have concluded an alliance, and both Germany and Italy now recognize the leadership of Japan in East Asia. Thus, with the liberating of East Asia and its victimized peoples from the bonds of Anglo-American financial and military control, one can consider the objective conditions demanding the formation of the East Asian League to be ripening.

The third vital factor is the decline of liberal thought and the rise of a new East Asian world view originating in the Kingly Way. As we all know, liberalism has its origins in Great Britain and accompanied the establishment of Great Britain's global hegemony and, from the eighteenth century through the early twentieth century, constituted the *zeitgeist* that dominated the world. Thus, the world order of this age was established with this spirit as the foundation. Therefore, it is no exaggeration to call this order that existed in indivisible relation to the development of Great Britain, the British Order. Nevertheless, this liberal order must now conform to the general trend of the world. Since the first great European war, totalitarian systems have been set up in the Soviet Union, Italy, and Germany. In particular, the overwhelming victory of Germany and Italy in the second great European war is a triumph of the totalitarian world view. In East Asia, as well, liberalism is being increasingly liquidated and, furthermore, on the basis of traditional spiritual culture there is developing a new world view refining modern thought. Beneath this new East Asian world view originating in the Kingly Way is a general trend demanding the construction of a New Order for East Asia.

As stated above, following the progressive development of humanity, advancement from small regional states to large regional state alliances is an historical inevitability. The current shifting from the age of state confrontations to the age of state unions is the inevitable advance of world history. No power can avert this inevitable current of world history. At this moment the objective basis is being constructed for unification of the East Asian states, i.e., for the necessary formation of the East Asian League. However, the East Asian League will never be realized if things are allowed to naturally take their own course. Formation of the East Asian League will only come about through the endless cooperative efforts of the three peoples of Japan, Manchuria, and China who must be the core and each work tirelessly for that construction. In other words, as argued above, the East Asian League will be constructed atop the foundation of various objective relations in accord with world historical necessity, but only by directing our subjective will to work toward this can that construction be realized.

Chapter Twenty-Three

Nanjing's Greater Asianism: Wang Jingwei and Zhou Huaren, 1940

Torsten Weber

The concept of Asianism in China was a principal instrument in the justification of official Chinese collaboration with Japan during the Sino-Japanese War (1937–1945). However, the Asianism proposed by the main Chinese collaborators—Wang Jingwei (Wang Ching-wei, also Wang Zhaoming, 1883–1944) and his followers—was neither an invention for propaganda purposes nor a mere adoption of Japanese wartime rhetoric. Instead, it was part of an integrated attempt at seeking political legitimacy by claiming the intellectual heritage of Sun Yat-sen (1866–1925; see II:5), the "Father of the Republic" (*guofu*). Wang's Asianism, therefore, was a "restoration of Sun Yat-sen's Asianism" (So 2007: 189), particularly as expressed in his famous Kobe speech of 1924. It was "primarily in this speech that Wang Ching-wei claimed to find the justification for his cooperation with Japan" (Jansen 1954: 213). By adopting Sun's Asianism, Wang managed to combine his claim to Sun's legacy with appeasing the Japanese on the one hand and offering a political alternative in the domestic arena to the united front of Mao Zedong's Chinese Communist Party and Chiang Kai-shek's Nationalist Party (Guomindang [GMD], or Kuomintang) on the other. Eventually, Wang's balancing act between pleasing the Japanese and appealing to the war-torn Chinese failed under the combined pressure of anti-Japanese resistance and the military success of the Allied forces. Before Wang died in 1944, he realized that his attempts to create an anticommunist and pro-Japanese China under his leadership had failed.

Wang Jingwei was born in Guangdong (Canton) and first visited Japan in 1904 as an exchange student at Hōsei University. In 1905, when Sun Yat-sen founded the Chinese Revolutionary League (Tongmenghui or T'ung-meng-hui; Japanese: Chūgoku Dōmeikai) in Tokyo, Wang became an editor of its party bulletin, the *Minbao* (People's Paper). In 1910 Wang returned to China to assassinate the regent and father of the child-emperor Puyi but was arrested and sentenced to death before he accomplished his mission. Following the Republican Revolution of 1911, he was freed and became one of Sun's closest followers. In the 1920s, he held several posts in Sun's Revolutionary Government in Guangdong.

When Sun Yat-sen died in 1925, he left behind not only a war-torn and disintegrated China but also a vacancy in the succession to the GMD leadership. At first, Wang appeared as the most likely candidate. However, lacking military support at a time when China was de facto ruled by regional warlords, Wang was quickly outstripped by Chiang Kai-shek, then head of the Whampoa Military Academy. The military expedition to unify northern China with the south from 1926 onward further strengthened Chiang's position. Subsequently, Wang—as the leader of the GMD's left wing—became Chiang's main inner-party rival, and the claim over the prerogative to Sun's legacy became an important instrument in his challenge to Chiang's leadership. Wang was eventually reconciled with Chiang after the Manchurian Incident (1931) and became premier of the GMD's Nationalist Government (1932–1935). His rivalry with Chiang, however, continued. When Chiang was again forced to cooperate with the communists after the Xi'an Incident of 1936, Wang's anticommunist and pro-Japanese stance estranged him further from the GMD leadership. Although Wang, together with Chiang and his GMD government, fled the Japanese invasion of China to Chongqing (Chungking) in 1938, he soon turned away from Chiang and began to look toward the Japanese.

Premier Konoe's announcement of a new China policy ("New Order in East Asia"; see II:17) in November was interpreted—both in Japan and in China—as an implicit invitation to Wang to become the head of a pro-Japanese administration in occupied China. Just one month later Wang and his followers left Chongqing. After a period of refuge in Hanoi and Hong Kong, Wang decided to move to Shanghai, where he would directly negotiate the conditions of his collaboration with Japan. It is important to note that almost a year and a half passed between Wang's defection and his assuming the leadership of a Japanese-sponsored government in Nanjing (Nanking) in March 1940. Studies that portray Wang as a traitor (*hanjian*)—still the predominant view in mainland China and Taiwan—overlook the fact that an appropriate political response to the situation was hotly debated within the Wang group. Once the decision to collaborate had been taken, Wang negotiated with the Japanese over the exact terms of his cooperation, which included the demand for a Japanese troop withdrawal. Seen in this light, Wang appears to have been much less of the passive toy in the hands of his Japanese masters than the frequent characterizations of his government as a "puppet regime" imply.

In order to legitimize his government in Nanjing, to appear to the Chinese as an attractive alternative to Chiang, and simultaneously to please the Japanese, Wang employed a number of striking political symbols and slogans (Cheung 1995). He adopted the same name and structure as Chiang's Chongqing government and built his political program around the cornerstones of peace (*heping*), anticommunism (*fangong*), and national reconstruction (*jianguo*). These three slogans were usually displayed together with the national flag, the same one that had been adopted by the unified Nationalist government in 1928 ("blue sky–white sun–red earth"). Wang also insisted that his assumption of the leadership of the government in Nanjing would be publicized not as the creation of a new regime but as a "return to the capital" (*huan du*). Equally important, Wang linked the legitimacy of his government largely to the person of Sun Yat-sen. Together with Zhou Fohai (Chou Fuhai, 1897–1948), a close follower of Wang, he visited Sun's tomb in Nanjing prior to the official inauguration of his new government. Sun's birthday (12 November) was also used as a symbol of Wang's self-proclaimed succession of Sun's leadership. For example, the opening of Nanjing's Central Bank in 1940 was delayed to coincide with 12 November, and Wang's speech, translated here, explicitly noted Sun's birthday as the occasion on which it was written. While Wang openly embraced Japan's pan-Asian rhetoric, he explicitly linked his pro-Japanese and antiresistance positions not to Japanese but exclusively to Sun Yat-sen's Asianism. References to Sun soon became ubiquitous in Wang's speeches and articles. In the foreword to a collection of Sun's writings, which was published in 1941 and which included the text of Sun's Greater Asianism speech, Wang wrote,

> Racially, geographically and historically, as well as in respect of environment, culture and material development, it is natural for China and Japan to be friends, unnatural for them to be enemies. Any dispute which arises between the two nations should be regarded as a transitory aberration, and should be settled in an appropriate manner so that the natural relationship may resume its permanent and natural course of peace and friendship. This point has been expounded most clearly and most thoroughly in the teachings bequeathed us by our late Leader, Dr. Sun Yat-sen. There are occasional passages to be found in those teachings in which he blames China for her errors; there are others in which he takes Japan to task for her mistakes; but at no time and in no place did he ever suggest that the two countries should be or remain enemies. Rather it was his constantly proclaimed hope that they would become friends, joining wholeheartedly in a united effort to promote the glorious cause of Greater Asianism. (Tang 1941: ix)

In order to solidify his claim to Sun's legacy and to justify his collaboration with Japan, a number of journals were published in Japanese-occupied China that promoted Wang's adoption of Sun's Asianism, including the monthlies *Da Yazhouzhuyi* (Greater Asianism), *Da Yazhouzhuyi yu Dongya lianmeng* (Greater Asianism and an East Asian League), and *Da Dongya* (Greater East Asia). While these publications clearly functioned as instruments of propaganda, it should not be overlooked that Wang himself and many of his followers held sincere pro-Japanese sentiments. In addition, humanitarian and idealistic motives, such as putting an end to the ongoing slaughter on the battlefield and his well-known anticommunism, were among the reasons that led Wang to his betrayal of Chiang and to his cooperation with the Japanese. As Dongyoun Hwang points out, the nature of the differences between Chiang Kai-shek and Wang Jingwei was "not merely political factionalism, but ideological" (Hwang 1998: 15).

In addition to Sun's Greater Asianism, Wang and his supporters also adopted Sun's Three People's Principles (*Sanminzhuyi*; cf. Itō 1989) as theoretical underpinnings of the new Nanjing regime—and took considerable pains to convince the Japanese of the compatibility of these principles with Asianism. Reportedly, the nationalism (*minzuzhuyi*), democracy (*minquanzhuyi*), and livelihood (*minshengzhuyi*) that Sun had extensively lectured on in the summer of 1924 were viewed as "a menace" in Japan (Boyle 1972: 246). In this context, Zhou Huaren's text reproduced here can be read as an attempt to assuage Japanese concerns over the Three Principles, in particular nationalism. Although Zhou paid great attention to showing the conformity of the principles with the ideals of Greater Asianism, the text had to be edited to fit the Japanese rhetoric before it appeared in translation in Japan. For example, the Japanese version explicitly affirms Konoe's declaration of a New Order ("to share the responsibility for erecting a New Order in East Asia"), whereas Zhou's original text does not mention the "New Order" but speaks only of "the responsibility for building a stabilized East Asia." Wang's writings were similarly altered to remove any references to Chinese nationalist aspirations that ran counter to the official Japanese political rhetoric. The fact that such editing was necessary further demonstrates that condemnations of Wang as a Chinese quisling who "perverted Sun's Greater Asianism . . . in search of a theoretical basis for his own disgraceful behavior or treason" (Shi 2002: 217) are, at best, greatly exaggerated (see Hwang 1998: 2–6).

Zhou Huaren (1902–?) was vice minister of transportation in the Wang government. He represented Nanjing-China at the first of three Greater East Asian Writers' Conferences (see II:25), which was held in Tokyo in November 1942 to obtain the support of writers for the Greater East Asian War and "to create a Greater East Asian Literature." Zhou was also vice chairman of the Propaganda Committee of the All-Chinese Society for an East Asian

League and chairman of the China branch of the Tōa Renmei Kyōkai (East Asian League Association; see II:22), founded in February 1941. Though he did not belong to the innermost circle of Wang's confidants, he quickly emerged as the regime's main propagandist, in particular with regard to propagating the concept of Greater Asianism as a means of justifying Sino–Japanese collaboration. Zhou contributed numerous articles to *Da Yazhouzhuyi* from 1940 onward and authored the 168-page *Da Yazhouzhuyi Gangyao* (Outline of Greater Asianism, 1940), which set out the guiding principles of Wang's collaborationist politics according to the template provided by Sun's theoretical heritage. Zhou's writings in Japanese translation appeared mostly in *Dai Ajiashugi* (Greater Asianism), published by the Greater Asia Association, while some were also reprinted in magazines such as *Kaizō* (Reconstruction) and *Nihon Hyōron* (Japan Review).

Source 1 (translation from the Chinese original by Torsten Weber)
Wang Jingwei, "Minzuzhuyi yu Da Yazhouzhuyi" (Nationalism and Greater Asianism). *Da Yazhouzhuyi* (Greater Asianism), 1:4 (November 1940), 1–5.

On the occasion of the anniversary of President Dr. Sun's birthday, 12 November, 29th year [of the Republic, 1940]

"For about forty years I have devoted myself to the cause of the People's Revolution (*guomin geming*), with the aim of gaining freedom and equality for China," said Dr. Sun Yat-sen. There can be no doubt that China's national consciousness derives from the great work of Dr. Sun. Ever since there have been national groups in China there has also been a national consciousness. This has displayed itself to some extent over a history spanning more than 4000 years. But it is really only as a result of the life-long efforts of Dr. Sun that a concentrated form of this national consciousness—a combination of a sophisticated contemporary national consciousness with the nationalism of the past—could be established theoretically and was also pushed forward practically. In his last moments he passed this task on to his surviving comrades and compatriots.

This year marks the centenary of the Opium War [1839–1842]. In the hundred years from 1840 to 1940 the imperialism of economic penetration, assisted by military invasion, has been the main factor in the ceaseless repression of China's national consciousness. We must say that this repression has caused considerable suffering to the Chinese nation. But, as China's national consciousness had already been formed, this kind of repression could never be lethal. On the contrary, the more attempts at disintegration, the greater the unity, and the more pressure, the greater the solidarity.

Apart from the fact of this repression [of national consciousness], its exploitation is also deplorable. This is the new method used by the Communist Party. While openly claiming that the worker has no fatherland, it exploits China's national consciousness when demanding national salvation. While openly advocating class struggle, it employs China's national consciousness by loudly insisting on a national united front. This tactic of using a sheep's head to sell dog meat brings suffering to the Chinese people, which is even greater when added to the reality of repression. But this tactic will not prove fatal either, because it can only be temporary and before long the people will wake up and then they will not be deceived again.

At the time of Dr. Sun's death, the true character of the Communist Party had not yet become apparent. . . . The target of Dr. Sun's national revolution was an end to the outrage of Imperialism. He was born in 1866, 22 [*sic*] years after the Opium War. He started his efforts to achieve a national revolution in 1885, 45 years after the Opium War, and when he died in 1925, 85 years after the Opium War, he said: "In *Yiyou*, the year of our defeat in the Sino-French War, I made up my mind to overthrow the Qing [Ch`ing] dynasty and create a republic." *Yiyou* is the year 1885, when Sun was 23 [*sic*] years old. He had witnessed this foreign threat and decided to turn against the Qing court and strive for the People's Revolution.

The foreign threat was mainly economic penetration backed up by military invasion. It was not easy for China to resist this kind of foreign threat. Without nationalism it could not achieve the self-awakening of the Chinese masses and unify their strength. And without the concept of Greater Asianism, it was impossible to bring about the self-awakening of the masses of East Asia and to unify the strength of its peoples. For this reason, after he had delivered his lecture on the Three People's Principles on 24 August of the 13th year [of the Republic, 1924], he lectured in Kobe on 28 November of the same year on Greater Asianism.

In his will, Sun Yat-sen stated: "Through the experiences of the past 40 years I have come to understand that in order to achieve this goal, we must raise the masses and ally with those peoples who treat us as equals and fight jointly with them." Many people have interpreted the phrase "those peoples who treat us as equals" as denoting the Soviet Union, but in his will no particular country is specified. If Japan is treating us as equals, then this is exactly what is envisaged by Greater Asianism. Why must we—apart from awakening the masses—also ally ourselves with those peoples who treat us as equals and fight alongside them? Because the power of imperialism, based on economic penetration backed up by military invasion, has already put down deep roots. The red race in America, the brown race in Australia, and the black race in Africa have all gradually been oppressed and conquered and have all either been subjugated or enslaved. For China to resist this kind of force, it is fundamental to achieve the self-awakening of the people and unify the power of the Chinese masses.

But merely to draw attention to this situation while disregarding the wider context is not only insufficient but also impractical. Formerly, a country did not undertake alliances lightly because alliances meant sharing another's fate, experiencing some good fortune together and then dying together in misery. To avoid such an outcome, it was considered better to remain isolated. But as regards the general international situation, seen both economically and militarily, there is a trend away from unilateral action to the formation of blocs. Already powerful countries can no longer avoid resorting to alliances, let alone countries that have only just started to rise or those planning their reconstruction after having fallen behind. This is exactly where Greater Asianism originates from. As I have said above, one after another, the three continents of America, Australia, and Africa have gone under and the threat has now come to the yellow races of Asia. After the Opium War, the imperialist invasion did not stop at China, but Japan was also threatened at the same time. However, Japan escaped this threat of invasion and thus achieved freedom and equality some decades before China. However, unless the aggressive forces of imperialism are extinguished, there is the danger that Japan will one day be subjected to invasion again. This is the very point that makes the destinies of the two countries of China and Japan identical. It is a great pity that we have neglected this fact of our identical destinies, but rather antagonized each other. After a process of reflection, we are now working hard to face our common destiny together. Fifteen years after the death of Dr. Sun, the ideals of Greater Asianism gleam with new splendor and illuminate the future path of two great peoples who are going forward together.

When, in the past, the destinies of China and Japan were in conflict, it appeared that nationalism and Greater Asianism were incompatible ideals. Now, in the age of a joint Sino-Japanese future, they are not only intertwined but one could say they have even melded into one. If China fails to acquire its independence and freedom it will not be qualified to share responsibility for East Asia, and if East Asia is not liberated China's independence and freedom cannot be achieved or guaranteed. This is what every Chinese must bear in mind. Since Japan expects China to shoulder its share of responsibility for East Asia, it will naturally treat us on the basis of equality. Ever since the Konoe Declaration [of a "New Order in East Asia," November 1938; see II:17], this has been Japan's unyielding national policy and the expression of a unified public opinion.

Source 2 (translation from the Chinese original by Torsten Weber)
Zhou Huaren, "Da Yazhouzhuyi yu Sanminzhuyi" (Greater Asianism and the Three People's Principles). *Da Yazhouzhuyi* (Greater Asianism), 1:2 (September 1940), 11–15.

1

Greater Asianism and the Three People's Principles are essentially identical. President Sun said: "The Three People's Principles are the principles of national salvation." Mr. Wang [Jingwei] says: "If we can realize the Three People's Principles, we will naturally achieve the status of freedom and equality and at the same time we will increase our strength and share with Japan the responsibility for creating a stable East Asia. Thus, speaking from the perspective of China, the Three People's Principles relate to saving the nation and from the perspective of East Asia, the Three People's Principles are equivalent to Greater Asianism" (from Wang's "The Theory and Reality of the Three People's Principles") [Zhou's remark in the original text]. To be sure, Japan is the strongest country in Asia and China is the largest country in Asia. If we cannot direct the power of both countries to become the driving forces behind a revival movement, Asia cannot possibly be saved. Japan has already gathered up its strength. As China is currently in the process of building a modern nation state, China's present ambitions are twofold—to save China itself but also at the same time to save Asia. It is for precisely this reason that we can say that the Three People's Principles are equivalent to Greater Asianism.

. . . The Japanese [politician] Kōno Mitsu [1897–1981] reviewed the Three People's Principles and Greater Asianism as follows: "Sun Yat-sen's philosophy of the people's livelihood as an element of nationalism will strengthen the independence of the Chinese people and assist the revival of all Asian peoples. And it also informs the World Principle of Great Harmony (*Datong de Shijiezhuyi*), to be achieved through Greater Asianism. . . . We can confidently say that, at a profound level, Sun's ideals envisioned first creating a strong new China and then, building on policies of neighborliness and cordiality, planning the revival of Asia and the liberation of the Asian countries from oppression by the Whites through the realization of Greater Asianism."

What he observed was correct. We must realize the Three People's Principles to demand equality for ourselves and, at the same time, we must implement the ideals of Greater Asianism to demand equality for other nations. This way of thinking corresponds with the philosophical ideals of ancient China, in particular, with the concept of "taking responsibility for the welfare of the people" and "having a constant concern for the suffering of the people." Through promoting and expanding these ideals, we will find the spirit of Greater Asianism. Dr. Sun's principle of Greater Asianism is wholly derived from these ideals.

In addition, when we analyze the practical contents of Greater Asianism, we see that they correspond to the Three People's Principles. The key point of nationalism is the demand for the indiscriminate equality of all people within one country. It then involves raising the international status of the Chinese nation to a position of equality and, finally, pursuing equal status for Asian nations with those on other continents. It demands the independence and liberation of the Chinese nation and—taking matters one step further—aims at the independence and liberation of the peoples of East Asia. The final ideal of nationalism is a great union of the world (*shijie datong*). These ideals form the consistent expression of Dr. Sun's spirit and thought.

2

The methods to be used in realizing the ideals of Greater Asianism and of nationalism are identical. The President [Sun] has said that, in order to make Greater Asianism a reality, the traditional culture of the East must be revived. This culture embodies the Kingly Way (*wang dao*), or the ideals of benevolence and virtue (*renyi daode*). Only if we succeed in creating a union of the Asian peoples on this basis can Greater Asianism be realized. And the key point for the realization of nationalism is the unity of the Chinese people themselves and the revival of the traditional morality of the Chinese people, as well as the revival of benevolence and virtue and the promotion of the Kingly Way. . . .

In his lecture on nationalism he stated: "To take up the issue of culture again, the culture of China predates European culture by some one thousand years. The finest period of European culture was in the heyday of Greece and Rome, and with Rome it reached its zenith. However, the Roman Empire was contemporaneous with China's Han dynasty [206 BC–AD 220]. From this we can see that at the time of the Han dynasty China's ideals of peace were already well established, as China did not advocate war against foreigners" (4th Lecture on Nationalism). In subsequent passages, Sun gave examples of countries and regions such as the South Seas [Pacific Islands], Nepal, and Siam to illustrate the similarities with the Kingly Way in Greater Asianism.

The culture of the East (*dongfang*) has always been very strong. But in order to resist the material civilization of Western Europe, virtue and benevolence are not enough on their own. Thus the President encouraged the study of Western science, a point which he also stressed in his lectures on nationalism. In his lecture on Greater Asianism, he argued that one should study science on the basis of virtue and benevolence, and again in his lecture on nationalism he stated that Asians must make an effort to catch up with developments in Western science. However, when China becomes strong again, the traditional duties of the Kingly Way "to relieve the weak and help the needy" must not be neglected (6th Lecture). In sum, we can say that the methods of realizing Greater Asianism and of achieving nationalism are identical and can be compared as follows:

Greater Asianism:

1. Revive Eastern culture, with an emphasis on benevolence and virtue
2. Create an alliance of the peoples of East Asia
3. Study Western science, but with benevolence and virtue as a foundation; promote industry as a means of self-defense

Nationalism:

1. Revive China's traditional virtues, including benevolence and virtue
2. The unification of the different peoples within China should result in the creation of a nation (*guozu*)
3. Make efforts to catch up with developments in European science, but with the ideals of the Kingly Way as the foundation

The individual elements of this three-point structure correspond to one another. The scope of the second point in the first list separates East Asia from China but, as it involves the union of the same race, it resembles the watery element of blood. The substance is the same.

. . .

4

As the ideals underpinning Greater Asianism and the Three People's Principles are substantially identical, can we not simply promote Greater Asianism and set aside the Three People's Principles? As the principles explained above range from the intimate to the unfamiliar and from the close to the distant, we clearly cannot do this.

On the other hand, if we affirm the Three People's Principles, why must we also advocate Greater Asianism? The reasons for this are also very simple:

1. China is just one among the countries of Asia and its political, economic, and social structures are closely linked with those of its neighbors. Without forming alliances with other Asian nations, the independence and liberation of any one country cannot easily be achieved.

2. The twentieth century is the age of national alliances. The continents of Europe and America have formed various blocs and the Pan-American alliance has already achieved some notable results. (Although the Pan-American Alliance deserves some criticism, without it many countries in America, in particular the small countries of Central America, would be unable to maintain their independence.)

Economic alliances are even more important than political alliances. It was because the League of Nations paid no attention to economic problems that it failed. Following the current European War, the European nations will certainly form an alliance. In the future, Europe will present itself to the world in the form of an alliance, and the Americas have already formed an alliance as a means of resistance. Therefore, the Asian peoples must also inevitably form a grouping based on their common beliefs and practices.

In conclusion, insofar as we are Chinese we advocate the Three People's Principles, but insofar as we are East Asians, we support Greater Asianism. In substance, both are identical and have the same goals. For this reason we must first of all strive for the independence, equality and freedom of China, to the best of our ability. At the same time, because China is a part of Asia and thus China and Asia possess an inseparable character, and also because the objective situation requires it, we must also work for the independence and liberation of all of Asia.

The Three People's Principles and the ideals of Greater Asianism are not only mutually inclusive, but in fact are reciprocal and complementary. To our own people we recommend the Three People's Principles and to the Asians we advocate Greater Asianism. Both go back to one common root; they are the two sides of the same coin. These are the teachings of President Sun and should not be interpreted as two separate concepts. This point should not be overlooked when researching Greater Asianism.

Part IV

PAN-ASIANISM AND WORLD WAR II, 1940–1945

After Japan's attack on the United States, Britain, and the Netherlands in December 1941, the war in China merged into World War II. Japan officially named this new conflict the "Greater East Asian War." The adoption of this term reflected Japan's official interpretation of this conflict as the final stage in the long drawn-out struggle to expel the Western colonial powers from Asia. By adopting this name and by resorting to pan-Asian rhetoric as part of its strategy to legitimize the war, Japan attempted to garner support from other Asian nations for the war against the West. The creation of the Greater East Asian Co-Prosperity Sphere (II:24 and II:27) was a direct outcome of these attempts and the clearest expression so far of pan-Asian policies formulated by the Japanese government.

However, it soon became obvious to most Asian peoples in territories occupied by Japan that the Japanese representation of the conflict as a war of "Asian liberation" was no more than propaganda. In China, a brutal war of wanton destruction continued unabated until 1945. Southeast Asia was exploited as ruthlessly under Japanese governance as under Western colonial rule. Mobilized to assist Japan's war effort, many "Asian brothers" lost their lives through fatigue, disease, and starvation as food supplies were commandeered by the Japanese authorities for their military needs. Even at the height of the war, the Japanese continued their appeals to pan-Asian solidarity; however, the gap between the lofty pan-Asian ideals professed and the brutal reality of Japanese rule became unbridgeable. Although pan-Asian publications proliferated once again during the wartime years, they were largely dominated by hollow phrases.

But even in those desperate years and notwithstanding the harsh treatment meted out by the Japanese occupation authorities, some Asians still clung to the hope that Japan would liberate Asia from Western colonial rule. Such hopes found expression in articles in newspapers and journals published throughout East and Southeast Asia. Although some of these publications were unquestionably produced by local propagandists in the pay of the Japanese (or by Japanese propagandists themselves), there is no doubt that many others were genuine and spontaneous expressions of pan-Asian ideals. But no amount of such material could prevent the collapse of Japan's war machine and Japan's unconditional surrender on 2 September 1945.

Chapter Twenty-Four

Matsuoka Yōsuke and the Greater East Asian Co-Prosperity Sphere, 1941

Sven Saaler

Matsuoka Yōsuke (1880–1946) was born in Yamaguchi Prefecture in western Japan, a region that many influential politicians of modern Japan have called home. Matsuoka went to the United States at the age of twenty. After graduating from Oregon University's Law School (Ano 1997), he returned to Japan and after 1904 pursued a diplomatic career at the Foreign Ministry. In 1921 he became a director of the state-owned South Manchurian Railway Company (Mantetsu). In 1930 he was elected to the House of Representatives on the Seiyūkai ticket. As a politician, he continued to advocate Japanese expansion in Manchuria and the creation of a Japanese puppet state there.

Matsuoka gained international notoriety in 1933 when he announced, as Japan's representative to the League of Nations in Geneva, that his country would resign from the League after the League condemned the establishment of Manchukuo as an act of aggression. Between 1935 and 1939, Matsuoka was back in Manchuria as president of the South Manchurian Railway Company, but he quit this important position when, in July 1940, he was appointed foreign minister in the second Konoe Fumimaro cabinet. During his tenure, he signed the Tripartite Pact with Germany and Italy (27 September 1940) and the Neutrality Pact with the Soviet Union (13 April 1941) but was forced out of the government in July 1941 after the German attack on the Soviet Union. After Japan's defeat in 1945, he was arrested as a class A war criminal but died in prison of tuberculosis before receiving his sentence.

As a vocal advocate of Japanese expansion in Manchuria, Matsuoka had from early on envisaged a scheme of regional integration in East Asia under the leadership of the Japanese Empire (Eizawa 1995: 88–94). In January 1933 he claimed, in an interview reported in a two-page feature in the *New York Times* (8 January 1933), "a world spiritual mission" for Japan as well as a leadership role in East Asia. In 1941, in a speech to the Japanese Imperial

Diet (reproduced here), Matsuoka called for the establishment of "a *sphere of co-prosperity* throughout *greater East Asia* with Japan, Manchukuo and China as its pivotal point." This idea of a Greater East Asia Co-Prosperity Sphere (*Daitōa kyōeiken*), which he also advocated in his popular book *Kōa no Taigyō* (Matsuoka 1941b), would become one of the major wartime slogans, aiming at legitimizing Japanese leadership in East Asia, shutting out Western interests in Asia, and mobilizing manpower and raw materials to support Japan's war effort (see also the following chapters).

The concept was rooted in older forms of Pan-Asianism and was directly linked to Konoe's proclamation of a "New Order in East Asia" in 1938 (see II:17), Konoe's attempts to form a pan-Asian core by installing a Japan-friendly government in China under Wang Jingwei (Wang Ching-wei; see II:23), and the reaffirmation of these policies by the Hiranuma cabinet (see II:21). Matsuoka had been an early advocate of the concept of Greater East Asian Co-Prosperity and used the term as early as 1938 when he was president of the Mantetsu. The concept continued to be prevalent after the end of Matsuoka's tenure as foreign minister and was, once again, reaffirmed as official policy by the third Konoe cabinet in July 1941 (*New York Times*, 20 July 1941). It became of pressing importance when the government utilized Co-Prosperity rhetoric in order to justify Japan's occupation of French Indochina. As the Japanese government declared,

> French Indo-China and Japan have from olden times been closely bound in cultural, historical and economic relations. Prior to the closing of Japan to foreign intercourse [in the 1630s] . . . , there were two Japanese towns each in Annam and Cambodia and very prosperous trade was carried on with Japan. . . . In recent times Indo-China has re-established her old relations with Japan in a new sense as a source of materials for the industries of Japan. Relations of late steadily have become closer and more cordial, with Indo-China constituting an important link in the sphere of common prosperity in Great East Asia which Japan is endeavoring to establish. (quoted in the *New York Times*, 27 July 1941)

The idea of the Greater East Asia Co-Prosperity Sphere eventually reached its zenith with the creation of a Ministry for Greater East Asia (Daitōashō) in November 1942 and the calling of an "Assembly of the Greater East Asiatic Nations" in Tokyo in November 1943 (see II:27). However, it was not an idea of Asian solidarity only. At least in Matsuoka's case, it implied universal validity—and the long-term political aim to extend the benevolent rule of the Tennō to the whole world. In this sense, the idea of East Asian Co-Prosperity overlapped with the concept of "The Eight Corners of the World Under One Roof," or *hakkō ichiu* (Eizawa 1995: 94f).

Certainly, these concepts found some support among the Japanese and also among some of the peoples of the region. Many Japanese soldiers who fought in Southeast Asia testify in their diaries and recollections that they believed that they were fighting for a pan-Asian cause, that is, for the liberation of Asian peoples (Yoshimi 1987: 189). The previously mentioned Tokyo Conference of November 1943 was accompanied by a "People's Mass Meeting for Solidarity with Greater East Asia" in Hibiya Park, which was reportedly attended by over 120,000 people (Go 1944). However, the idea of a Greater East Asia Co-Prosperity Sphere lost its attraction after Japan's defeat in World War II. Ever since, it has been associated with Japanese expansionism, and thus even today the idea remains an important and problematic historical legacy for Japan—a legacy that is considered by many as a major obstacle to regional integration in contemporary East Asia.

Source (English in the original)
Address by the Foreign Minister of Japan, Yosuke Matsuoka, delivered before the 76th session of the Imperial Diet, 21 January 1941. *Contemporary Japan*, February 1941.

It gives me great pleasure to have this opportunity of explaining at the reopening of the 76th session of the Diet the recent course of our country's foreign affairs.

Needless to say, the aim of Japan's foreign policy is that of enabling all nations of the world each to take its own proper place, in accordance with the spirit of the Hakko Ichiu ["The Eight Corners of the World under One Roof," a wartime slogan used to justify Japanese territorial expansion], the very ideal which inspired the foundation of our Empire. The object of the Three Power Pact, concluded between Japan, Germany and Italy on September 27 [1940] last, is none other than the realization of the same great ideal. . . .

The Three Power Pact stipulates that Germany and Italy recognize and respect the leadership of Japan in the establishment of a new order in Greater East Asia. It is our avowed purpose to bring all the peoples in greater East Asia to revert to their innate and proper aspect, promoting conciliation and co-operation among them, and thereby setting the example of universal concord. . . .

Of the nations in greater East Asia, Manchukuo has special and inseparable relations with this country [Japan]. As you are aware, during the ten years which have already elapsed since her emergence as an independent nation, her national foundations have become strong and secure while her international position has been greatly enhanced, her teeming millions ever enjoying an increasing measure of prosperity. In June last year, the Emperor of Manchukuo paid a visit to Japan to offer his felicitations personally to our Imperial House on the auspicious occasion of the 2,600th anniversary of the foundation of our Empire. This is a source of genuine congratulation for the peoples of Japan and Manchukuo as it is a conspicuous manifestation of the unique relations subsisting between the two nations, sharing, as they do, common aims and aspirations. By the Sino-Japanese Basic Treaty concluded with the National Government at Nanking, and through the Joint Declaration made by Japan, Manchukuo and China, the Republic of China recognized Manchukuo, with the result that an exchange of ambassadors has been arranged between them.

Inasmuch as an early settlement of the China Affair [Sino-Japanese War, 1937–1945] is desirable in the interests of the creation of this sphere of common prosperity throughout greater East Asia, the present Government ever since its formation, has urged the Chiang Kai-shek regime to reconsider and reverse its attitude, with a view of bringing about its amalgamation with the Nanking Government, but it remains still struggling against Japan. . . .

In the light of such an international situation, the Japanese Government, in pursuance of their fixed policy, recognized the National Government at Nanking and on November 30 of last year concluded with the latter the Sino-Japanese Basic Treaty. This treaty embodies the three basic principles of good neighbourliness, economic co-operation and joint defence against communist activities. It stipulates that both Japan and China respect each other's sovereignty and territorial integrity, and undertake close economic co-operation on the basis of equality and reciprocity, and that Japanese forces be stationed in certain specified areas in Mengchiang [also transliterated Mengjiang, an autonomous region in Inner Mongolia, 1936–1945, under the control of the Mongol United Autonomous Government, informally under the control of the Japanese army] and North China. Not only does Japan demand no territorial cession and no indemnities, but she has willingly pledged to China a policy of abolishing extraterritoriality and also of restoring the "concessions" to China. This is an eloquent testimony of her sincere desire for the attainment of a moral union of the Asiatic peoples. . . .

We have thus maintained an attitude to surmount all obstacles for the purpose of establishing a sphere of co-prosperity throughout greater East Asia with Japan, Manchukuo and China as its pivotal point.

Let me now make a brief survey of our relations with the Netherlands East Indies, French Indo-China, and Thailand, which lie within the abovementioned sphere of common prosperity.

The Netherlands East Indies and French Indo-China, if only for geographical reasons, should be in intimate and inseparable relationship with our country. Therefore, the situation which has hitherto thwarted the development of this natural relationship must be thoroughly remedied, and relations of good neighbourliness secured for the promotion of mutual prosperity. . . .

As regards French Indo-China, it formed the most important route of supply for Chungking since the beginning of the China Affair. Consequent, however, upon the sudden change in the European situation last June, a change has occurred in the relations between Japan and French Indo-China, resulting in the closure of the border between French Indo-China and China itself, and the entry by agreement, of Japanese armed forces into French Indo-China. . . .

In June, last year, a Treaty of Amity and Neutrality was concluded by Japan with Thailand. With the exchange of ratifications, completed on December 23 at Bangkok, the bonds of friendship between the two countries have been drawn still closer. . . .

The relations between Japan and Near Eastern countries have recently increased in cordiality. Our ratification of the Treaty of Amity with Iran is only one of many proofs that illustrate this happy state of affairs. . . .

In establishing a sphere of common prosperity in greater East Asia, and ensuring the peace of the Orient, it is not desirable that the present diplomatic relations between Japan and the Soviet Union should be left as they are. The utmost efforts are being made, therefore, to remove mutual misunderstandings and, if possible, to bring about a fundamental and far-reaching adjustment of diplomatic relations. . . .

The prevailing confusion of the international situation shows no sign of subsiding, but, on the contrary, it tends to increase. Should the United States unfortunately become involved in the European war, and should Japan, too, be compelled to participate in the war, another great World War both in name and reality would ensue, precipitating a situation which would defy all attempts at saving it. Should the war take its furious course, unleashing formidable new weapons which have not hitherto been used, no one could guarantee that it would not develop into a war spelling the downfall of modern civilization. The Three Power Pact has been concluded for the purpose not only of making sustained efforts for the establishment of a sphere of common prosperity throughout greater East Asia, but of preventing, in its course, any further extension of the present disturbances.

Chapter Twenty-Five

The First Greater East Asia Writers Conference, 1942

Eddy Dufourmont

The First Greater East Asia Writers Conference (Dai Ikkai Daitōa Bungakusha Taikai) was held from 1 to 13 November 1942. It was a major event in terms of the mobilization of intellectuals during the Asia-Pacific War (1931–1945) and was also the very first occasion that Asian writers met at an official gathering in Japan.

The conference was made possible only as a result of the concurrent Japanese military victories in East and Southeast Asia and the wartime mobilization of Japanese writers that resulted in the formation of the Patriotic Association for Japanese Literature (Nihon Bungaku Hōkokukai) in May 1942. This organization, headed by the novelist and playwright Kikuchi Kan (Hiroshi, 1888–1948), included more than 3,000 members. In July of the same year, the association was sent a proposal for a conference of writers from throughout East Asia from the Information Service of the Cabinet, the body that controlled wartime propaganda (cf. Keene 1964).

However, the collaboration of Kikuchi and other writers with the Japanese government went back much earlier: in 1937, Kikuchi had organized a delegation of writers to China, and in 1940 he was the moving spirit behind the formation of the first Japan-wide writers' organization. The foundation of the Patriotic Association for Literature of 1942 was simply a reaffirmation of the leading role Kikuchi's earlier body played among writers in Japan. Alongside the Great Japan Association for Patriotic Arts (Dai Nihon Bijutsu Hōkokukai) and the Great Japan Patriotic Writers Association (Dai Nihon Genron Hōkokukai), the Patriotic Association for Literature in Japan was just one of many tools utilized by the government to achieve the total mobilization of the nation's cultural life for its wartime objectives (cf. Shillony 1981). The government's decision to mobilize the cultural sector for the war effort reflected its understanding of the conflict as a "total war" that necessitated the involvement of the entire Japanese population, without exception. The origins of the notion of total mobilization can be traced back in Japan to the end of World War I, when senior Japanese army officers had been strongly influenced by German efforts to mobilize the whole population and the complete resources of the nation for wartime needs. Thus, the "thought war" (*shisōsen*) and "spiritual mobilization" (*seishin dōin*) represented elements of "total war" that were seen as of equal importance with industrial mobilization. As part of these efforts, in 1937 and 1941 the Ministry of Education issued a number of ideological manifestos, including the "Cardinal Principles of the National Polity" (*Kokutai no hongi*) and "The Way of the Subject" (*Shinmin no michi*).

While the decision to hold the Greater East Asia Writers Conference must be seen in the context of these developments, its effectiveness was greatly increased by the dispatch of some of Japan's most famous writers to Southeast Asia as members of various propaganda corps: in 1942, for example, the novelist Takami Jun (1907–1965) was attached to the propaganda corps in Burma, the philosopher Miki Kiyoshi (1897–1945) served in the Philippines, and the novelist Ibuse Masuji (1898–1993) was sent to Singapore. These propaganda corps were very active in presenting Japan's expansion into Southeast Asia as a "liberation of Asia" and the establishment of a "Greater East Asia Co-Prosperity Sphere" (*Daitōa Kyōeiken*; see II:24 and II:27); their goal was to convince the populations of the occupied territories of the merits of cooperation with the Japanese military. They were also instrumental in inviting authors from the occupied territories to visit Japan and thus in bringing together a diverse group of writers as a literary manifestation of East Asian cultural cooperation during wartime.

Despite these efforts, in the end no writer from Southeast Asia attended the conference. Apart from the Japanese participants, which included poet Noguchi Yonejirō (1875–1949) and novelist Kume Masao (1891–1952), a number of authors from northeastern Asia attended—including thirty writers from Korea, Taiwan (at that time both part of the Japanese Empire), Manchukuo (a Japanese puppet state), China, and Mongolia—some of whom were Japanese living in these territories. The other delegates were members of literary organizations created by the Japanese and specialists in Japanese literature. For example, Gu Ding from Manchukuo belonged to the Manchurian Writers' Association (Manshū Bungeika Kyōkai), founded under Japanese "guidance." Yi Gangju and Yu Chin-o were members of the Korean Writers' Association (Chōsen Bunjin Kyōkai), also founded by Japanese authorities. The Chinese delegates included Qian Daosun, an expert on Japanese classical literature who specialized in *Manyōshū* (The Collection of Ten Thousand Leaves, a compilation of classical poetry dating from the eighth century), and Yu Bingxi, a graduate of the Imperial University of Tokyo, well known for his research on the Edo period. Another Chinese, Chang Wojun, had translated the novels of Natsume Sōseki (1867–1916) and was a teacher of the Japanese language.

During the three days of the conference proper, Japanese and English were used as official languages, and the writers organized workshops on ideological themes with titles like "the establishment of the spirit of Greater East Asia" or "winning the Greater Asian war through literature." These efforts, however, produced no concrete results in terms of publications.

The final declaration translated here was written by Yokomitsu Riichi (1898–1947), a novelist and poet close to Kikuchi Kan, who had been sent to Rabaul, New Guinea, in 1942 and again in 1943. In the final days of the conference, the writers went on a tour of historic sites in the Kansai area, with Yoshikawa Eiji (1892–1962) and Tanizaki Jun'ichirō (1886–1965) serving as their guides. Two further conferences were held in August 1943 in Tokyo and in November 1944 in Nanjing (Nanking), with Chinese being the only non-Japanese participants.

The declaration reproduced here shows the ways in which Pan-Asianism was drawn on to mobilize writers and representatives of the cultural sector in a wartime context. As the document shows, these writers, who often claimed after 1945 to have had no responsibility for the war or to have been victims of the military, were active and enthusiastic supporters of the war effort.

Source (translation from the Japanese original by Eddy Dufourmont)
Final Declaration of the First Greater East Asia Writers Conference (1942), reproduced in Sakuramoto Yoshio: *Nihon Bungaku Hōkokukai*. Aoki Shoten, 1996.

We have gathered here in hopes of establishing, strengthening and perfecting the spirit of Greater East Asia. We are truly delighted that, after debating the essence of this spirit and discussing the urgent tasks which confront us, we have been able to confirm that our convictions are immovable.

The outbreak of the Greater East Asia War gave all of us, the writers of the Orient (*tōyō*), a stimulus that penetrated to the bottom of our hearts; it gave us a steely resolve to strive for the reconstruction of the Orient. This is the result of the great heroic thrust of the Japanese nation, on which, it could be said, everything depends. We open our hearts to the radiant Oriental tradition, we appeal to the spirits of our ancestors, and from the depths of eternal subjugation and stupor we swear and proclaim that we will make a fresh start.

The foundation for a new life of the Orient has been laid; our hearts and spirit are strongly united. We declare to all those countries that are our enemy that we are now marching on with intrepid determination. Any remaining problems concerning literature and thought must be resolved through firm belief and long and arduous work. We will retain in our hearts a profound impression of this conference and, in the spirit of ardent faith and love, we will zealously endeavor to extol to the world our great Oriental life. But the success of all this depends entirely on our victory in the Greater Asian War; indeed, the fate of the East as a whole also hinges on the successful completion of this Great War. With Japan in the vanguard, we, the writers of all Asia, facing life or death together, will spare no effort to ensure that this great day will come to the Orient. We swear to the above.

5 November 1942
Greater East Asia Writers Conference

Chapter Twenty-Six

Indonesian Nationalism and Wartime Asianism: Essays from the "Culture" Column of *Greater Asia*, 1942

Ethan Mark

The three short essays introduced here pack a startling punch, even today. The two authors are Indonesian, the time of publication mid-1942. All three essays appeared within little more than a month of each other in the "Culture" column of the Japanese-sponsored Indonesian-language newspaper *Asia Raya* (Greater Asia), which premiered in Batavia (Jakarta) on the Japanese emperor's birthday of 29 April 1942. Each glitters with the rhetorical power and assurance reflective of the sense of a radical transition to a new and better, post-Western order. Less than two months earlier, after a whirlwind nine-day campaign, Japanese forces had conquered Java, wresting it along with the rest of the Indonesian archipelago from centuries of Dutch colonial domination. At the time of writing, Japanese, Americans, Europeans, and Southeast Asians remained stunned and radicalized by the suddenness of this development and the vastness of its implications. Japan, perennially viewed not only by Westerners but by most Indonesians as little more than a distant, second-class Western copycat, now seemed to have beaten the West at its own game. Not just for Japanese but for Indonesians as well, both past and future were suddenly bathed in a new, "Asian" light.

How far indeed Japan seemed to have come from where it had been just a few months before: bogged down for more than four years in a brutal, stalemated war of attrition in China against an enemy that Japan insisted was really its friend but that refused to heed its continued calls for "Asian brotherhood," albeit at the point of a gun. Against the presumably much more powerful West, however, things had gone all Japan's way. Indeed, not only could Japan now claim to be the only Asian society modern enough to compete with the West, but the ease and scope of its three-month string of military victories even suggested that Japan might have a better recipe for national strength than its Western competitors.

Brimming with newfound confidence, Japanese spokesmen in Java and elsewhere proclaimed that the secret of Japan's modern success lay precisely in its remaining faithful to its indigenous, non-Western traditions amidst the modern Western capitalist-imperialist onslaught or, more precisely, in Japan's retention of its indigenous racial and cultural traditions even as it adopted and mastered Western material civilization and its benefits, finely balancing the two for optimum results. The result was the pioneering of a genuinely alternative, "Asian" route to modern nationhood that could avoid the pitfalls of Western experience—individualism, social division and confrontation, exploitation, and bloody revolution—while enjoying its undisputed benefits of scientific progress and material prosperity. Japan's aim in expanding into Asia was not selfish imperialism of the Western variety but rather to create a "Greater Asia" by leading the same sort of rejuvenation among its downtrodden Asian brethren. In order to finish the job against a common Western enemy that remained powerful and determined, however, Asian cooperation and sacrifice was essential. The Indonesian-language *Asia Raya* newspaper, sponsored and overseen by civilian Japanese members of the Sixteenth Army Propaganda Squad and staffed by Indonesian nationalists who had volunteered their services to the perceived common cause, was meant to propagate this message of Asian unity and resolve among the Indonesian public.

In Japan, this rhetoric of a "Greater Asia" had taken shape in the decade since the Great Depression in the context of an increasingly uncompromising confrontation with Chinese nationalism that flared into full-scale war from 1937. While claiming to represent a uniquely "Asian" perspective, however, Japanese wartime discourses of a "return to tradition" and heralding of a "decline of the West" shared much with those in other contemporary places, notably those of its wartime allies Italy and Germany. Although pointing to the past, here as elsewhere, this rhetoric was nothing if not modern—reflecting and responding to the modern social tensions engendered by rapid industrial capitalist development within a unique interwar context of profound crisis in the global status quo that was at once social, economic, political, and cultural. As in Italy and Germany, the rhetoric gained currency against a backdrop of depression and accompanying global crisis of "Anglo-American" liberal capitalism and heightened interimperial rivalry. Reflecting this, in Japan as elsewhere, the discourse was generally combined with calls for a much-expanded role for the state as ultramodern, transcendent organizer and mediator of social life. Drawing on the social Darwinism still globally dominant in an age of high imperialism, it also shared with its Italian and German counterparts a tendency to resort to viewing social problems through the essentialist prism of race and culture and to the policing of their "purity" as social prescription.

In Japan as elsewhere, this revolutionary yet conservative ideology held its strongest appeal to Japan's rapidly expanding, ambitious middle class, hungry to cash in on modernity's promise. Members of this class felt a particular sense of frustration at the persistence of Japan's "old order," a domestic power structure perceived to be dominated at the top by a "semifeudal" political and economic oligarchy from which they felt excluded. They also felt threatened "from below" by the rise of an increasingly restless, politicized, and chaotic "mass society," symbolized by activist workers and audacious modern women. A renovated, unified, virile nation-state, cleansed of the "Western" scourges of individual and class interest, efficiently implementing and distributing the benefits of technological progress, regimented and mobilized for battle in the ruthless international struggles of the day, was the only way forward. Here too as in Italy and Germany, Japan's interwar spokesmen for national renovation saw an expanded and rejuvenated empire as key to the success of their domestic program. But convinced of the Western origin of Japan's—and Asia's—modern woes, many Japanese saw this expansion as a genuine mission of "Asian liberation" that might appeal to its neighbors as well.

While the ideology of a "Greater Asia" thus held an extremely potent appeal to many Japanese, however, Japan's increasingly aggressive attempts to export it to China met only with increasing suspicion and resistance. Yet while most Japanese resented and misunderstood Chinese resistance and feared its implications for their restless Korean and Taiwanese colonies as well, Japanese responses to the broader global trend of anticolonial nationalism in fact ranged from ambivalent to sympathetic. Globally, nationalism was the trend of the times, and imperialism, by contrast, was becoming increasingly difficult to defend. Themselves long treated as racial and cultural second-class global citizens according to the Western scale of measure, furthermore, interwar Japanese were inclined to sympathize with the nationalism of fellow Asians—so long as it did not impinge directly on Japan's own imperial security. In China, proclaiming a mission of Asian liberation, Japan's spokesmen sought in effect to transcend the contradiction inherent in these two fundamentally conflicting agendas, seeking to co-opt Asian anticolonial nationalism and its appeals within a Japanese imperial framework.

While this maneuver saw little success in China, the Indonesian essays that follow reveal that under different circumstances, receptivity to such discourses could in fact cross the political and boundaries normally assumed to separate colonizer from colonized and imperialism from anticolonial nationalism. Both authors comfortably and confidently embrace the Japanese-sponsored notion of a "return" to an "Asian" identity, tradition, and model of society as a natural, indigenous recipe for overcoming the modern crisis visited by "Western" modernity not only on Asia but now on the West itself. Both proclaim that this "return to tradition" does not represent going backward but is in fact the only workable way forward. For only through a rediscovered and restored "Asian" spirit could the social and moral decay that was the inevitable product of a fragmented, chaotic, "soulless" Western modernity be forestalled. In the most radical of the three essays, "One Ancestry, One Race," author Sanoesi Pané (1905–1968) goes so far as to question the very legitimacy of "Indonesia" itself as an unnatural, tainted concept derived and inherited from the self-centered interests of Western imperialism. In contrast, Asia appears in the form of a natural, organic order defined by similarities in race, culture, and language, product of a unity dating to ancient times, transcendent of national, religious, or other modern divisions. Pané even identifies this "natural" Asian order with the ancient imperial Japanese term *Sumera mikuni* (Imperial Country) in popular usage among Japanese military and civilian spokesmen in the late 1930s and early 1940s. These positions located Pané at an extreme of embrace of the Japanese and their legitimacy as Asia's leaders, surpassing that of most of his nationalist colleagues—indeed even for Pané himself, this was the only occasion on which he openly questioned the legitimacy of Indonesian nationalism itself. But as I have argued in more detail elsewhere (Mark 2006), to read this essay or the countless other Indonesian wartime writings in approval of a "return to Asia" either as simple, shallow "collaboration" or as purely strategic posturing in the face of overwhelming Japanese power is to miss the broader transnational appeal of "Asia" to would-be nation builders across the region—and not only during the war but before and after it as well.

The Indonesian readiness to embrace an "Asian" identity and Japanese promises of "Asianization" exemplified so vividly in these 1942 newspaper essays was the result of a distinctive and complex mix of practical, historical, sociological, and ideological factors. Foremost among these was the fact that unlike in northeastern Asia, Southeast Asia's experience of colonial oppression had come not at the hands of Japan but at the hands of the West. This encouraged a perception of the West and "its" capitalism and imperialism as a common enemy. To a certain extent, shared ambivalence toward China and the Chinese represented another point of intersecting perceptions and interests: whereas Japan's attempts to gain Chinese sympathy had been undermined by a history of competition and confrontation, Southeast Asia's native populations themselves often perceived local ethnic Chinese as rivals and as handmaidens of Western imperialism. Further potential practical incentives to cooperation with Japan included eventual national independence, education, military training, and—in an occupation period of high unemployment and material insecurity—a steady income and food on the table. For

Indonesia's struggling nationalists and Islamic leaders in particular—up to now largely denied political influence and access to the masses by the Dutch and the native nobility through whom they ruled—collaboration with the Japanese, whatever the risks, promised increased political and social influence and perhaps a chance to lessen the suffering of the people.

But as vividly revealed in these essays, for many among these very same groups of ambitious Indonesians, the interest in working with Japan went beyond these sorts of purely pragmatic, strategic considerations and into the realm of ideology. This receptivity was expressed in particular in notions of a common "Asian" identity on whose basis a new, improved Indonesia, Japan, and Asia, liberated from the legacies and problems of Western modernity, might finally be built. In occupied Indonesia, those most captivated by this missionary vision of a "new Asian order" were men occupying a domestic social position roughly corresponding to that of the most enthusiastic of their "Asianist" counterparts in Japan: ambitious, frustrated members of the Western-educated indigenous sub-elite or nascent middle class. Poised between Indonesia's tiny feudal colonial upper nobility and its impoverished, uneducated agrarian masses, it was from among this class that Indonesia's anticolonial nationalist movement had emerged in the preceding decades. In the period preceding World War II, Indonesian nationalists, along with counterparts in many parts of the colonial world, had puzzled with increasing urgency over how to westernize and modernize and yet avoid being a mere cultural copycat of the West. The Great Depression and the associated crisis of capitalism encouraged not only intensified opposition to Western imperialism but also increased speculation over the weaknesses of Western modernity and the possibilities of its transcendence through a rediscovery and "revival" of local cultural traditions. For the nationalist class in particular, the notion of a non-Western, indigenous modernity seemed to offer a "third way" by which the power of the masses could be mobilized in a shared national battle against the illegitimate interests of the old colonial order, including the old native aristocracy, while promoting social harmony and avoiding a Western-style social revolution. In sum, it appears the radical yet conservative promises of Japanese wartime Asianism found a particular resonance with preexisting Indonesian nationalist political and social concerns.

With its direct ties to Japan's Sixteenth Army Propaganda Corps, the *Asia Raya* newspaper has been remembered largely as a mouthpiece for the Japanese. Its editing and writing staff was mostly Indonesian, however, and its Japanese supervisors were not military men but civilian writers of pedigree and some repute drafted into the service to win Japanese as well as local hearts and minds. According to the most important of these, Tomizawa Uio, the idea for the newspaper itself came from the prominent Indonesian Arab businessman A. S. Alatas. Many of *Asia Raya*'s editorial staff came over from the prewar newspaper *Berita Oemoem*, journal of the *Parindra* nationalist party, whose membership represented the more conservative, elite wing of the movement, known for a prewar willingness to cooperate with the Dutch rulers but also close prewar leanings toward Japan. Strikingly, however, *Asia Raya* also featured contributors hailing from the more "radical" factions of the prewar nationalist movement, usually farther to the political left and lower down the ranks of the social elite, who had refused to cooperate with the Dutch rulers and had more popular support but were also—at least until the Pacific War began—more ambivalent toward Japan and its imperialism.

Among the latter were the authors of the texts that follow. Sanoesi Pané was a prominent poet, playwright, scholar, and outspoken journalist and cofounder of the left-wing *Gerindo* nationalist party in 1937. Asmara Hadi (1914–1976), who replaced Pané as *Asia Raya*'s regular culture columnist in June 1942, was prewar editor of the influential *Pemandangan* newspaper and an energetic nationalist ideologue who had undergone cadre training with Sukarno before the latter's exile at Dutch hands in 1934. In the intervening time he had married Sukarno's daughter and emerged during the occupation period as one of Sukarno's most loyal spokesmen and protégés.

To some degree, the enthusiasm for Japan as Asian leader and model expressed in these essays can be seen to have represented a wartime conversion undergone by many Indonesians, prompted in large part by astonishment at Japanese achievements and mutual optimism regarding future prospects. For Pané, in the years before the war, it was decidedly *not* Japan but rather India that was looked to as a model for Indonesia's own national struggle in light of its powerful nationalist movement and its ancient cultural-historical links with Indonesia. In a 1930 newspaper dispatch while journeying in India, Pané had even observed, "Japan has secured a significant place among the great powers, but does not appear capable of bringing changes to the world political or economic structure; in fact, where the lighting of new paths and the opening of new perspectives is concerned, it has achieved little. The task of leading a searching mankind, of laying new social foundations in the light of the eternal, falls to India" (Pané 1930). Yet as suggested in this same passage—published more than eleven years before Japan invaded Southeast Asia—the appeal of an "Asian" alternative for the "searching mankind" of the interwar years was a notion with a lengthier history and a wider appeal across the region, rooted in the experience of Western colonial domination, the perception of a "decline of the West," and the ambitions of nation building common to Asia's middle classes in particular.

The Japanese–Indonesian honeymoon that fostered the mutual embrace expressed in these essays was to prove short lived. As Japan's occupation progressed toward a situation of what might be called colonial normalcy, the mutual enthusiasm so evident in these early essays was to cool significantly and irrevocably. It was only in September 1944, when the tide of the war had turned decisively against Japan, that Tokyo finally issued a promise of Indonesian national independence, and only then at some undetermined point in the future—a point that still had yet to be reached when Japan surrendered to the Allies in August 1945. In the meantime, what most Indonesians had experienced was a Japanese wartime regime that combined escalating demands for labor and resources with a military-colonial arrogance, ignorance, and oppression that made the former Dutch rulers appear tolerant and brotherly by comparison. While the appeal of Japan as Asia's rightful leader was thus irrevocably undermined, however, the ideological and sociological appeals of a "return to Asia" remained potent, particularly among the region's nation-building elites. Herein lies the fascinating and troubling contemporary significance and resonance of the essays that follow.

Source 1 (translation from the Indonesian original by Ethan Mark)
Sanoesi Pane, "'Nihilism,' Nature's Enemy." *Asia Raya* (Jakarta), 4 May 1942.

When Hermann Rauschning wrote *Revolution des Nihilismus (The Revolution of Nihilism)* [1939] to combat National Socialism, he forgot about nihilism in the demo-liberal spirit and order.

The spirit of the West is based upon egotism, which prioritizes the ego, the "seed" of man as a complete unity. The Western man feels as if he stands on his own, in opposition to nature and society. Was it not indeed in the West that the idea appeared that society is the product of reconciliation between individuals—human beings who are always competing with one another out of their natural impulses—that society is based upon a "social contract"?

The Western man does not feel his ego as a part and product of nature, and its connection with its compatriots is considered a "compromise," with as its pivotal point the promise not to destroy one another.

The translator of Rauschning's book into Dutch, Menno ter Braak [1867–1940], is himself truly unaware that he himself is ruled by nihilism, only prioritizing his ego, his own person.

"Menschelijke waardigheid" (human dignity/respect for humanity), which he adores, is merely respect for egotism, not respect for humanity in an environment of shared interests, and not at all as a product of the soul of nature.

Herman Rauschning and Menno ter Braak do not see the disorder in the fields of politics, economics, society, do not see the boundless competition, to the point that the world is starving, even though it is in truth profoundly rich.

It is the obligation of us, the ranks of Greater Asia, to bring man back to the realization that he is the product of the soul of nature, that all men are brothers in essence, and must be brothers outwardly as well.

In the face of demo-liberal nihilism, we present regulation. Nature is always regulated, and in the society of man too there must be rules, which give shape to the desires of nature.

What rebels, what carries out revolution, that is the demo-liberal movement, which is born of this egotism, which rebels against God's will and the desires of nature.

The darkness that was predicted by Oswald Spengler will not arise in the West if the West is willing to examine *Der Aufgang des Morgenlandes—The Rise of the Land of the Rising Sun*—and learn from this supremely important development.

The educated of Indonesia must also be able to free their spirits and thinking from the spell of Western writers, who wallow in the mud of nihilism, until they are able to take part in building a new order on an old basis, which arises once again in Greater Asia.

Source 2 (Translation from the Indonesian original by Ethan Mark)
Sanoesi Pané, "One Ancestry, One Race." *Asia Raya* (Jakarta), 13 May 1942.

Anyone who studies the story of the Pacific Ocean, who compares the cultures of Japan and Indonesia together with the Japanese language and the languages of Indonesia, no longer doubts that the Japanese race and the Indonesian race share a common ancestry and that their cultures share a common basis.

The question automatically arises: If this is the case, is it possible for the Japanese race and the Indonesian race to become one race, to inhabit one blood?

The answer cannot be other than: [Yes,] they surely can.

If we do not believe that the Indonesian race can enter *Sumera Mikuni* and become *Sumera Mitami* (Imperial Subjects), then we are denying the true story and the true situation.

For thirty years we have aspired to a unified Indonesia, to a great Indonesia (*Indonesia Raya*), such that it is understandable that there are Indonesians who are startled to hear of *Sumera Mikuni* and *Sumera Mitami*. But when we think deeply, we must admit that what we considered our homeland for the last thirty years, and what we call Indonesia, is only a coincidence, merely the area corresponding to that under Dutch control.

It may be assumed that if the [Malay] Peninsula, the Philippines, Madagascar, and New Zealand too were included within the realm of Dutch control, we would view these areas too as a part of our homeland! In truth the original inhabitants of the [Malay] Peninsula, Madagascar, and New Zealand are [indeed] of the same ancestry and the same race as us. The Malay language of the Peninsula, the Malagasi language and the Maori language belong to the same family as the Indonesian language. It is easy for us, too, to feel as one race with the Japanese—suppose that Japan and Indonesia had both been under the rule of, for example, the English. Under these circumstances, we would have [already] been aspiring to *Sumera Mikuni* from before. It is thus clear that our denial of the possibility of being the same race as the Japanese and becoming *Sumera Mitami* is in essence completely hollow (*kosong belaka*), based only upon an unnatural situation, that is, upon Dutch hegemony.

The desire for *Sumera Mikuni* and *Sumera Mitami* is based not upon facts of coincidence, but upon facts that are visible and real. The fact that we share the same ancestry with the Japanese race is not something merely temporary like Dutch rule. The wall that for so long kept us apart from Japan has now collapsed, and in this era the unification of the region of the Pacific Ocean—our ocean—is no longer simply a dream. Is it still appropriate that we nurture the old ideals, that we aim for Great Indonesia (*Indonesia Raya*), when we can now aim for ideals more in harmony with the desires of nature, more pure, that is to unify the *Sumera Mitami* once again and to purge foreign power from our homeland, from the Pacific Ocean? We understand that it is difficult for the inhabitants of Indonesia, who have for so long struggled to free themselves from imperialism, to immediately return to these proper ideals, to suddenly expand their aims. But the principles of *Sumera Mikuni* and *Sumera Mitami* must begin to be realized in Indonesian society, must become a guideline for us in all fields.

Source 3 (Translation from the Indonesian original by Ethan Mark)
H. R. (Asmara Hadi), "Static and Dynamic." *Asia Raya* (Jakarta), 8 June 1942.

We often used to hear: The Eastern spirit is a static one, the Western soul dynamic. Meaning that the East never changes, while the West constantly changes, advancing forward in its history. If there happened to be any change in Eastern society, it was the dynamic of the West that made this happen. This is what we often heard before.

This is indeed untrue. Dynamic is not the monopoly of Western society, dynamic plays out in the East as well. In fact there is no thing nor situation in this world that is static in its nature; everything changes, advances, develops.

In the West, Hegel began to bring to light and truly express awareness of dynamic through his triad: Thesis, antithesis, and synthesis. Every situation gives rise to a new situation at odds with the preexisting one. From this opposition arises a synthesis, a new fusion that represents a new thesis, and this will in turn give rise to its antithesis. This, Hegel said, is the law that moves history and human culture.

And in the East? Thousands of years before Hegel was cleverly suckling, thousands of years before Europe had the word "modern," when all of Europe was still a great forest, it was the heart of the East that was illuminated by divine inspiration, that already knew that the face of the conditions of the world is not fixed, but always changing, advancing, developing.

Thousands of years before Hegel, the Hindu religion taught that the entirety of nature is possessed by Brahma, Vishnu, and Shiva. Here it must be emphasized that this Brahma, Vishnu, and Shiva are not the three gods as often taught in elementary or middle school in the past. According to Hindu philosophy, profoundly broad and deep for those inclined to plumb it, this Brahma, Vishnu and Shiva are the attribute of the one and only Substance (Zat).

Brahma creates, Shiva returns what is to its origins, and Vishnu always comes to renew. They do not oppose one another, but complete one another, work together, carrying out their respective duties like the supreme Brahma (God). It is through their interworkings that the face of the world changes, advances, and develops.

The difference between the Western dynamic and the Eastern dynamic is this: the dynamic of the West is restless (not fast!), and the dynamic of the East is calm (not slow!). The Dynamic of the West may be compared with Faust, who searches and works continuously because he has lost a definite aim in life and lost his spiritual tranquility. We can compare the dynamic of the East with [the *Bhagavad Gita* warrior] Arjuna, who is strong yet calm because he is sure of Dewata's guidance and knows life's aim. What is more, the East is also sure that what changes is only the appearance, the outward shape, while the basis, the soul, the essence remains. Because of this, the culture of Greater Asia may change its pattern or its shape, culture in the time to come may have a different appearance and pattern from those of past ages, but the basis, the soul is unchanging, fixed, everlasting.

If Eastern society appeared over the past four centuries as if it were no longer alive, it is Western imperialism that is to blame, because this imperialism shackled the spirit of progress. Proof that the countries of the East can develop their existence if they are not shackled, if they are free, stands before us: Japan.

Chapter Twenty-Seven

The Assembly of the Greater East Asiatic Nations, 1943

Li Narangoa

The Assembly of the Greater East Asiatic Nations (*Daitōa kaigi*) was held in the National Diet building in Tokyo on 5 and 6 November 1943. It marked a turning point in Japan's relations with other Asian nations and was an attempt to construct a form of Pan-Asianism in which Japan's leadership was less obtrusive than it had been previously.

The main agenda of the conference was to discuss "measures for a successful prosecution of the War for Greater East Asia and the plan for the construction of Greater East Asia." The Assembly was intended to strengthen solidarity among Asians in the Greater East Asia Co-Prosperity Sphere (GEACS) in the fight against the Western powers. While it affirmed the pan-Asian idea of "Asia for Asians" as the ideology of GEACS, the process of preparation for the Assembly and the "Joint Declaration of the Greater East Asia Conference" revealed that the Japanese were playing a subtle diplomatic game with their Asian allies. The Declaration, to be sure, talked about "respecting one another's sovereignty and independence." However, Japanese ambitions for preserving leadership were reinforced, although they were framed in the rhetoric of "mutual cooperation" and "mutual assistance." The Assembly was hailed as the climax of the concept of Pan-Asianism in which all Asian countries were to coexist on an equal footing. In reality, Japan remained the dominant power in East Asia, but for the first time the Assembly gave Japan's Asian partners grounds to claim an equal role.

The Assembly was held in the context of two developments in the international situation that were working against Japanese interests. First, the Pacific War had turned against Japan. Since mid-1942, the Japanese advance in Southeast Asia and the Pacific had been halted, and Japanese forces were being pushed back. The military setbacks made access to natural resources more difficult, so mobilizing the occupied regions to boost Japan's war effort became more important than ever before. Second, the Japanese were aware of the Atlantic Charter, proclaimed in August 1941 by the United States and Britain, which set forth a number of principles for the postwar world, including the renunciation of all aggression, the right to self-government, access to raw materials, freedom from want and fear, and the disarmament of aggressor nations. They knew that the United States and Britain regarded the Republic of China as an important ally in the war against Japan and even promised to renounce their rights of extraterritoriality in China (Sanbō Honbu 1985: 320–22).

To compete for the hearts of local populations against the Atlantic Charter, Japan was forced to rethink its policies toward the occupied regions. The promises made by the Allied powers, especially the promise of self-government, appealed to Asians who had been striving to form their own nation-states. Many Asians had collaborated with the Japanese in the hope of gaining independence with Japanese help. But the reality had been that the Japanese were unwilling to promise them self-government or the kind of independence they desired. Instead, the Japanese, seemingly forgetting their initial promises of liberating Asians, offered excuses such as "the time is not yet ripe." By 1943, however, Japan needed to go beyond rhetoric and show Asian peoples that it was indeed promoting their national interests. In these new circumstances, Japanese leaders began planning a conference that would demonstrate their commitment to a new role for Japan in Asia and to equality with other Asian countries. The Assembly of Greater East Asiatic Nations was the outcome of these plans.

On 31 May 1943, the Japanese government issued "The Greater Asiatic Policy Guidelines" (*Daitōa seiryaku shidō daikō*), which outlined a number of concessions to Japan's Asian partners. Putting these guidelines into effect, Japan had negotiated with the Nanjing government headed by Wang Jingwei (Wang Ching-wei; see II:23) a revision of the unequal treaty with China that also included the abolishment of extraterritoriality of Japanese nationals in China; Japan had returned the former Burmese Shan states of Kengtung and Mongpan as well as four Malay states to Thailand, and finally it had recognized the independence of Burma and the Philippines. Japan also abandoned its policy of setting up separate administrations in the Mongol region and northern China and now emphasized the unity of China. The Assembly of Greater East Asiatic Nations, the first official gathering of the leaders of all these "new" countries, was the climax of the new Greater East Asian policy that was to demonstrate the solidarity of the Asian countries involved.

To show how important the Assembly of Greater East Asiatic Nations was for Japan, on 2 October 1943, that is, a month before the conference, the Imperial Headquarters (Daihon'ei) confirmed that it would consult the

Assembly on how to "successfully prosecute the Greater East Asian War and strengthen solidarity between the East Asian countries." The countries that were invited to participate were Thailand, Manchukuo, China (represented by the Nanjing government), Burma, and the Philippines. The provisional government of Free India was allowed to participate as an observer and was represented by Subhas Chandra Bose (1897–1945).

The "Joint Declaration of the Greater East Asia Conference" was the most important item on the conference agenda because it officially reaffirmed solidarity between the participating Asian countries. At the same time, it also aimed to show the world that Japan had waged the Pacific War not for its own benefit but to liberate East Asia from the yoke of Western imperialism and establish "world peace." The wording of the declaration was thus considered very important. Japanese political and military leadership, however, was not unified on the question of what message the declaration should convey. The Japanese were split roughly into two groups. Some held that the declaration should emphasize the "equality of the Asian nations" and economic cooperation in the postwar period and promise that after the successful conclusion of the war the Japanese army would withdraw from the territories it now occupied. This view originated within the Japanese Foreign Ministry and was represented by the foreign minister, Shigemitsu Mamoru (1881–1957). Others argued that it was important to emphasize the need for cooperation among the Asian nations in order to achieve military victory. This viewpoint was, above all, advocated by the Army Ministry led by General Tōjō Hideki (concurrently prime minister and army minister) and by the recently established Ministry for Greater East Asia (Daitōashō). The Foreign Ministry viewpoint reflected an understanding that the ideology of the GEACS under Japanese leadership had failed to mobilize Asian nations, which were aiming for full sovereignty based on equality. The Foreign Ministry thus suggested a new policy that would appeal to the subject Asian nations by respecting their political and economic "equality." Shigemitsu proposed setting up a Greater East Asiatic Alliance that would work like an international institution and would be able to make decisions about political and economic questions within the region based on equal voting rights, as in the League of Nations. By contrast, the Army Ministry's position still conceived of the GEACS as being under Japan's control. Its ultimate aim was to mobilize Asians for the Japanese war effort. What would happen after the war was another matter.

The final draft, subsequently accepted by the Assembly, was a compromise between these two positions. The main text indicated that the declaration should aim at friendly neighborly relations based on equality—that its main concern was not just mobilization of Asians for the war against the West but also the development of an economic and management policy for

Asian countries after the war. There was, however, an additional introduction, drafted in the Ministry of Greater East Asia, that emphasized the history of the colonization of Asia by the Western powers, the inevitability of Japan's mission to liberate Asia from Western oppression, and East Asia's contribution to eternal world peace (Hatano 1996: 167–72). The declaration of the Assembly of Greater East Asiatic Nations marked an ideological retreat from the doctrine of a GEACS under Japanese leadership (Kawahara 1979: 317) for the sake of winning more active support from Japan's Asian partners.

The representatives of the Asian countries that participated in the Assembly were united in supporting Asian unity and praising Japan's assistance to their own countries and to the region. In reality, for all these representatives the conference was first of all an opportunity to proclaim their newly obtained independence (except for Thailand, which had never been colonized) to the world and to their own people and to participate as sovereign states in regional affairs. The Provisional Government of Free India was recognized by Japan just a few days before the opening of the Assembly but at that time had no territory under its control. To remedy this problem, during the conference Prime Minister Tōjō Hideki announced the transfer of the Andaman and Nicobar Islands, at the time under Japanese occupation, to the Provisional Government.

Second, the Assembly provided the participating Asian countries with an opportunity to send Japan a message that it must not attempt to construct its own colonial system in Asia. By using Japan's own rhetoric they aimed to limit Japan's actions. They all emphasized the ideal of recognizing each other's "autonomy and independence" and offering mutual assistance. As President Jose P. Laurel (1891–1957) of the Philippines stated in his speech at the Assembly,

> The Greater East Asia Co-prosperity Sphere is not being established for the benefit of any integral unit of that Sphere. According to His Excellency [Tōjō Hideki], the starting point of the establishment of the Sphere is recognition, respect for the autonomy and independence of every integral unit, so that, with that recognition of political independence and territorial integrity, each nation may develop in accordance with its own institutions, without any particular member monopolizing the resulting prosperity of any given country or nation. . . .

Here Laurel was clearly emphasizing his own country's rights and used Tōjō's own words to warn Japan against "monopolizing" the benefits of the pact. Although the Asian delegates praised their host highly in their speeches, they were all concerned about the effect of Japanese policies in their home countries. Although Japan nominally recognized their "independence," in major matters of state they were guided by the Japanese, and in foreign relations and military affairs they were still closely tied to Japan by treaty obligations. Within these limitations, at the conference Japan's Asian partners tried to mark out as much space as possible for their own freedom of action and asserted their independence as much as they felt they could. The Philippines was reluctant to declare war on the Allies. Thailand was reluctant even to take part in the Assembly because it felt that participating alongside governments that were merely Japanese "puppets" would reduce its standing as a genuine sovereign state. Thai Prime Minister Pibun Songkhram (1897–1964) excused himself from the Assembly, claiming ill health, and sent a replacement delegate.

In sum, the Assembly of Greater East Asiatic Nations was convened by Japan to mobilize the peoples of East Asia for the Pacific War and establish friendly cooperative relations in the name of "building Greater East Asia." To achieve this latter aim, Japan recognized newly independent governments and stressed the principle of mutual respect for sovereignty. These pronouncements amounted to a retreat from the doctrine of the GEACS under Japanese leadership. Without the dominant leadership of any one country, the new GEACS appeared to be the materialization of the pan-Asian ideal, which Asian nationalists such as Sun Yat-sen had advocated earlier (see II:5).

Following the Assembly, Japanese Foreign Minister Shigemitsu began laying plans for a second Greater East Asiatic Conference for April 1945. This, however, never materialized because of the deteriorating war situation and the collapse of infrastructure in Asia. In early April 1945, the cabinet of General Koiso Kuniaki (1880–1950), in which Shigemitsu served as foreign minister, resigned. Shigemitsu was no longer in office. The new government, headed by Admiral Suzuki Kantarō (1868–1948), convened a Conference of Ambassadors of Greater East Asia (*Daitōa taishi kaigi*) on 23 April 1945. The conference issued a common declaration, similar to the declaration by the Greater East Asiatic Assembly, which placed stronger emphasis on respect for the "political equality" of the Asian nations (Kajima Kenkyūjo 1971: 492–99), but this had no effect on the outcome of the war.

Source 1 (English in the original)
"Joint Declaration of Greater East-Asiatic Nations." Go [Gō] Toshi (ed.) (1944), *The Assembly of Greater East-Asiatic Nations*. The Nippon Times.

THE ASSEMBLY OF GREATER EAST-ASIATIC NATIONS (NOVEMBER 5–6, 1943)

JOINT DECLARATION OF GREATER EAST-ASIATIC NATIONS
Unanimously Adopted by the Assembly of Greater East-Asiatic Nations, Nov. 6, 1943

It is the basic principle for the establishment of world peace that the nations of the world have each its proper place, and enjoy prosperity in common through mutual aid and assistance.

The United States of America and the British Empire have in seeking their own prosperity oppressed other nations and peoples. Especially in East Asia, they indulged in insatiable aggression and exploitation, and sought to satisfy their inordinate ambition of enslaving the entire region, and finally they came to menace seriously the stability of East Asia. Herein lies the cause of the present war.

The countries of Greater East Asia, with a view to contributing to the cause of world peace, undertake to cooperate toward prosecuting the War of Greater East Asia to a successful conclusion, liberating their region from the yoke of British-American domination, and assuring their self-existence and self-defense, and in constructing a Greater East Asia in accordance with the following principles:

1. The countries of Greater East Asia through mutual cooperation will ensure the stability of their region and construct an order of common prosperity and well-being based upon justice.

2. The countries of Greater East Asia will ensure the fraternity of nations in their region, by respecting one another's sovereignty and independence and practicing mutual assistance and amity.

3. The countries of Greater East Asia by respecting one another's traditions and developing the creative faculties of each race, will enhance the culture and civilization of Greater East Asia.

4. The countries of Greater East Asia will endeavor to accelerate their economic development through close cooperation upon a basis of reciprocity and to promote thereby the general prosperity of their region.

5. The countries of Greater East Asia will cultivate friendly relations with all the countries of the world, and work for the abolition of racial discriminations, the promotion of cultural intercourse and the opening of resources throughout the world, and contribute thereby to the progress of mankind.

Source 2 (English in the original)
Hideki Tojo, "The construction of Greater East Asia and the establishment of world peace." Go [Gō] Toshi (ed.) (1944), *The Assembly of Greater East-Asiatic Nations*. The Nippon Times.

THE CONSTRUCTION OF GREATER EAST ASIA AND THE ESTABLISHMENT OF WORLD PEACE

By
H. E. PRIME MINISTER GENERAL HIDEKI TOJO
(Address delivered before the Assembly of Greater East-Asiatic Nations, November 5, 1943)

Your Excellencies and Gentlemen:

During the past centuries, the British Empire, through fraud and aggression, acquired vast territories throughout the world and maintained its domination over other nations and peoples in the various regions by keeping them pitted and engaged in conflict one against another. On the other hand, the United States which, by taking advantage of the disorder and confusion in Europe, had established its supremacy over the American continents, spread its tentacles to the Pacific and to East Asia following its war with Spain. Then, with the opportunities afforded by the First World War, the United States began to pursue its ambition for world hegemony. More recently, with the outbreak of the present war, the United States has further intensified its imperialistic activities and has made fresh inroads into North Africa, West Africa, the Atlantic Ocean, Australia, the Near East and even into India, apparently in an attempt to usurp the place of the British Empire.

The need of upholding international justice and of guaranteeing world peace is habitually stressed by America and Britain. They mean thereby no more and no less that the preservation of a world order of their own, based upon division and conflict in Europe and upon the perpetuation of their colonial exploitation of Asia. They sought to realize their inordinate ambitions in Asia through political aggression and economic exploitation; they brought on conflict among the various peoples; they tried to destroy their racial integrity under the fair name of education and culture. Thus, they have to this day threatened constantly the existence of the nations and peoples of Asia, disturbed their stability, and suppressed their natural and proper development. It is because of their notion to regard East Asia as a colony that they harp upon the principles of the open door and equal opportunity simply as a convenient means of pursuing their sinister designs of aggression. While constantly keeping their own territories closed to us, the peoples of Asia, thus denying us the equality of opportunities and impeding our trade, they sought solely their own prosperity. The Anglo-American ambition of world hegemony is indeed a scourge of mankind and the root of the world's evils.

Movements for emancipation have occurred from time to time among the nations and peoples of East Asia, but due to the ruthless and tyrannical armed oppression by America and Britain, or due to their malicious old trick of division and alienation for ruling other races, these patriotic efforts ended largely in failure. Meanwhile, Japan's rise in power and prestige was looked upon by America and Britain with increasing dislike. They made it the cardinal point of their East Asia policy, on the one hand, to restrain Japan at every turn and, on the other, to alienate her from the other countries of East Asia. It was obviously unwise for them to permit either the rise of any one country as a great Power or the banding together of the various nations and peoples. These American and British methods became more and more sinister and highhanded, especially in the last several years.

For example, they made a tool of the Chiang Kai-shek regime and so aggravated Sino-Japanese relations as to lead to the unfortunate China Affair [*Shina Jihen*; contemporary term for the Second Sino-Japanese War, which had begun in 1937]. Furthermore, they resorted to every possible means to obstruct a settlement. Following the outbreak of the present war in Europe, they interfered with free commerce under the pretext of wartime necessity and even resorted to the severance of economic relations with Japan, an act tantamount to war. At the same time, they augmented their military preparations in East Asia in an effort to force Japan's submission. Despite such an attitude on the part of the United States and Britain, Japan, in her desire to prevent war from spreading into East Asia, endeavored to the last to find a solution by peaceful negotiation. However, the United States and Britain, not only failing completely to manifest an attitude of reflection and mutual concession, but intensifying instead their threats and pressure, endangered the very existence of our nation. Japan at last was compelled to rise in self-defense and to fight for her existence, and thus she accepted the challenge that was hurled against East Asia. Staking her national fortune, Japan marched forth to battle in order that permanent peace might be established in East Asia.

With the outbreak of the War of Greater East Asia, the Imperial Army and Navy fought with heroic courage under carefully laid plans and within less than half a year expelled America and Britain from the entire region of East Asia. The various countries of Greater East Asia have either declared war to fight with us, or are closely cooperating for the prosecution of the war to a successful conclusion. Today, the ardor and enthusiasm of the peoples of

Greater East Asia have spread throughout our region. With mutual trust and harmony among our nations, we are valiantly marching forward together to secure our existence and to establish permanent stability in Greater East Asia by crushing the counteroffensives of America and Britain.

It is my belief that, for all the peoples of Greater East Asia, the present war is a decisive struggle upon whose outcome depends their rise or fall. It is only by winning through this war that they may ensure forever their existence in their Greater East Asian home and enjoy common prosperity and happiness. Indeed, a successful conclusion of this war means the completion of the very task of constructing the new order of Greater East Asia.

The United States and Britain may naturally repeat their counter-offensives against Greater East Asia with all their material might upon which they rely, but we, the nations of Greater East Asia, must summon up our total strength to repel these attacks. We must deal out crushing blows to our enemy and thereby finish the war victoriously and secure to East Asia an enduring peace and stability.

At this moment, Japan is carrying out extensive operations from her position of strategical advantage acquired by her early victories in the war. On the home front, the internal structure, in parallel with these operations, has been steadily improved. Especially through the recent re-organization it has been so adjusted as to meet fully the needs of decisive warfare. Her one hundred million people with but a single mind, with a firm conviction in sure victory and with an inflexible fighting spirit are marching forward to triumph in this Great War. I firmly believe that the other Greater East Asiatic Nations, whom you represent here, are also grimly resolved to shatter the counter-offensives of their age-old enemies, America and Britain, by throwing their full weight into the field in concert with the Japanese nation and thereby to secure lasting stability for Greater East Asia.

Next, it is my desire to express to you the fundamental views of the Japanese Government regarding the construction of Greater East Asia.

It is my belief that to enable all nations each to have its proper place and to enjoy the blessings of common prosperity by mutual efforts and mutual help is the fundamental condition for the establishment of world peace. And I must furthermore say that to practise mutual help among closely related nations in one region, fostering one another's national growth and establishing a relationship of common prosperity and well-being, and, at the same time, to cultivate relations of harmony and concord with nations of other regions is the most effective and the most practical method of securing world peace.

It is an incontrovertible fact that the nations of Greater East Asia are bound, in every respect, by ties of an inseparable relationship. I firmly believe that such being the case, it is their common mission to secure the stability of

Greater East Asia and to construct a new order of common prosperity and well-being.

This new order of Greater East Asia is to rest upon the spirit of justice which is inherent in Greater East Asia. In this respect it is fundamentally different from the old order designed to serve the interests of the United States and Britain who do not hesitate to practice injustice, deception and exploitation in order to promote their own prosperity.

The construction of Greater East Asia is being realized with grim steadiness in the midst of war. In contrast, what are America and Britain doing in India? Britain's oppression of India grows in severity with every passing day. More recently, America's ambition there has asserted itself and discord and friction between Britain and America on the one hand and the Indian masses on the other are being aggravated; and the Indian people are being subjected to indescribable hardships and tribulations.

The famine of unprecedented magnitude, which such a situation has recently brought about in India, has even been admitted by Britain and America. All patriots of India are imprisoned, while the innocent masses are starving. This is a world tragedy—a calamity of all mankind. The peoples of Greater East Asia could never let it go unattended. Happily, Mr. Subhas Chandra Bose responded to the call of the hour and with him rose the Indian patriots both within and without their country. Thus was the Provisional Government of Free India created and the foundation of Indian independence laid. The Japanese Government have already declared to the world that they will extend every cooperation and assistance for the independence of India. I am confident that the other nations of Greater East Asia will also give wholehearted support for the realization of Indian independence.

By no logic and reason could America and Britain possibly reconcile what they advocate under the so-called Atlantic Charter with what they are actually doing in India. But we are not even surprised at the contradictions between the beautiful signboards which they put up and the evil designs which they harbor within. We know too well that deception and camouflage constitute their very nature. However, regardless of what the enemy may do, Japan is determined to follow, together with the other nations of Greater East Asia, the path of justice, to deliver Greater East Asia from the fetters of America and Britain and, in cooperation with her neighbor nations, to strive toward the reconstruction and development of Greater East Asia.

Today, the unity of the countries and peoples of Greater East Asia has been achieved and they have embarked upon the gigantic enterprise of constructing Greater East Asia for the common prosperity of all nations. This surely must be regarded as the grandest spectacle of human effort in modern times.

As regards the situation in Europe, we are very glad that our ally, Germany, has still further solidified her national unity and, with conviction in sure victory, is advocating to crush the United States and Britain and to construct a new Europe.

The War of Greater East Asia is truly a war to destroy evil and to make justice manifest. Ours is a righteous cause. Justice knows no enemy and we are fully convinced of our ultimate victory.

Japan is grateful to the nations of Greater East Asia for the whole-hearted cooperation which they are rendering in this war. Japan, is firmly determined, by cooperating with them and by strengthening her collaboration with her allies in Europe, to carry on with indefatigable spirit and with conviction of sure victory in this war, the intensity of which is expected to mount from day to day. Japan, by overcoming all difficulties, will do her full share to complete the construction of Greater East Asia and contribute to the establishment of world peace which is the common mission of us all.

Chapter Twenty-Eight

Women Leaders and Pan-Asianism in Wartime Japan: Ichikawa Fusae (1940), Takamure Itsue (1940), and Inoue Hide (1944)

Michael A. Schneider

Women were actively mobilized in support of Japan's aggression on the Asian continent. They joined patriotic associations; took on "home-front" roles as laborers, nurses, and community leaders; worked to accommodate households to wartime austerity controls on consumption; and endured personal sacrifices as mothers and wives. Their contribution to the war effort has been recognized. Women, however, do not appear in public discourse as important theorists of Pan-Asianism. To be sure, many contributions in this volume show that, even among its male proponents, Pan-Asianism lacked a unified philosophical vision. Women's roles as pan-Asian ideologues were similar to those played by men: weaving pan-Asianist garb pragmatically in response to the changing international situation. But, as this chapter shows, women's role in shaping pan-Asianist discourse was not negligible.

To appreciate the distinctive role of women in pan-Asianist discourse, one must consider women's relationship to a countervailing discourse on internationalism. A notion of transnational brotherhood among all Asians is not entirely antithetical to internationalism. Many recurring themes in pan-Asianist writings—acquiring knowledge of other Asian societies, respect for local cultures, criticism of Japanese parochialism, and opposition to imperialism—were fully compatible with the views of internationalists. Other themes, most notably the presumption of a world divided along racial lines and the rejection of the West as a source of universal values, clashed sharply with core internationalist themes. Women who emerged as leaders in political and foreign policy commentary in 1910s and 1920s Japan were, broadly speaking, internationalists. Women's commentary on foreign policy issues, therefore, often followed from internationalist themes: the universal experiences of motherhood, the promotion of women's suffrage and other elements of a transnational feminist movement, and, more broadly, an economic and cultural transformation of Japanese domestic society that rendered Japan similar to other modern consumer societies around the globe.

As the documents introduced here show, politically active women did not automatically oppose Japanese continental expansion on the grounds that it constituted a breach of the principles of international sisterhood or an obstacle to the advance of women's interests. On the contrary, many viewed the Sino-Japanese War (1937–1945) as an opportunity to expand their claims to political activism. They did not foresee how the war would undercut these ambitions, eroding the very social and economic foundations of their newly found political expression. Wartime controls on consumption frustrated urban women who had shaped their lives and careers around the burgeoning consumer economy. Many women leaders had succeeded because of their foreign educations and international knowledge, but the conservative discourse, hostile to Western cultural influences, increasingly identified women's independence as an example of foreign pollution. Wartime government policies, thus, sought to co-opt and stifle the independent activities of these women.

Ichikawa Fusae (1893–1981) was the most politically prominent of the women presented here. Born into a peasant family in Aichi Prefecture, she was educated at Aichi Prefectural Women's Normal College and worked for a time as a schoolteacher before turning to journalism and political activism. In 1919, she worked to establish the New Women's Association with noted feminist Hiratsuka Raichō (1886–1971). By the 1920s, Ichikawa had emerged as the most articulate proponent of women's suffrage, participating in the formation of the Women's Suffrage League of Japan in 1924. She also participated, along with Inoue Hide (Hideko, 1875–1963), in the Pan-Pacific Women's Conference of 1928.

The outbreak of the Sino-Japanese War in 1937 prompted Ichikawa to push forward with the women's suffrage movement. In 1938, the Women's Suffrage League began publishing an English-language newsletter describing the group's activities to foreign audiences. In this newsletter, Ichikawa defended Japan's actions in China, claiming that one of Japan's war aims was to build unity among Japanese and Chinese women. She placed high hopes in the possibility of Sino–Japanese accommodation through educated Chinese women under the collaborationist Wang Jingwei (Wang Ching-wei; see II:23) government founded in 1940 in Nanjing (Nanking). However, as the text reproduced here demonstrates, Ichikawa failed to distinguish between Pan-Asianism and Japanese expansionism, assuming that the goals of Japanese aggression were compatible with the advancement of Chinese in some (unspecified) union with Japan in which women would enjoy full equality or, at least, the ability to achieve self-realization. It was from this premise that she argued for cooperation among "Asian women" and campaigned for the establishment of an East Asia Common Culture Academy (Tōa Dōbun Shoin) for girls that would provide them with an appropriate pan-Asian education.

The second writer introduced in this chapter, Takamure Itsue (1894–1964), was one of the most complex and controversial figures in the prewar feminist movement. Takamure was born in Kumamoto Prefecture. At one point in her highly unconventional life, she tried to escape the humdrum existence of her childhood by running away to work in a factory only to be discovered and hustled back home by her family. Having attended (but not completed) Kumamoto Women's Normal School, Takamure became a schoolteacher for a time but in 1920 moved to Tokyo, where she achieved prominence as a poet and journalist during the next few years. Takamure argued that women's closeness to nature through motherhood meant that their liberation could not be achieved through political achievements within a modern state or through material advances within an industrialized society. Takamure reasoned that a return to smaller, agricultural communities would elevate women's status, in effect returning women to the high position that she believed they had held in Japan's ancient past. She reviled the urban, androcentric home; the capitalist system on which it rested; and the conventional marriage and nuclear family that attended on it. Despite finding common cause with key elements of the prewar feminist movements, Takamure did not believe the progress of Japanese women should be tied to the industrial, cosmopolitan city. Instead, she sought "Asian values" in Japanese history and the Chinese classics.

Despite her reclusive nature, she maintained a keen interest in international affairs. In her commentaries, she departed from the conventional stance that women should be united across national boundaries in their opposition to war. Her endorsement of the Japanese invasion of Manchuria in 1931 was eager and early, as compared to other women radicals. After 1938, she completed studies of matrilineal aristocracies in ancient Japan, complementing the official history of an unbroken and single line of imperial succession and national unity. She employed her history to rationalize the position of the emperor as the head of an all-encompassing family state, substantiating the intellectual underpinning to the Greater East Asian Co-Prosperity Sphere. After government decrees forced adult women to register in the Greater Japan Women's Association, she wrote articles for its organ *Nihon Fujin* (Japanese Woman), contributing her considerable literary talents to the rhetorical comfort of the wartime state.

The third author, Inoue Hide, was the daughter of a prosperous farmer in central Japan. She was educated at Kyoto First Higher Girls School and Japan Women's College, then at Columbia University and the University of Chicago, where she studied between 1908 and 1910. Back in Japan, she took a post at Japan Women's College (at present Japan Women's University) as professor of household management studies (*kaseigaku*), known idiomatically in English as "home economics." In 1919 she was promoted to head of that department. She became the first female president of Japan Women's College in 1931, a post she held until 1946.

Inoue's English-language skills, her international experience, and her prominent academic position brought her to the attention of the organizers of the International Women's Disarmament Conference, held in Washington, D.C., at the same time as the Washington Naval Limitations Conference, 1921–1922. After attending the conference, she traveled around the world, recording her impressions of postwar Europe and Asia in *Fujin no Me ni Eijitaru Sekai no Shin Chōryū* (The World's New Currents as Seen through the Eyes of a Woman, 1923). She continued to be active alongside other prominent internationalists in informal advocacy on behalf of international peace, leading a twenty-five-woman Japanese delegation to the Pan-Pacific Women's Conference in 1928. Though Inoue wrote little on international politics in this period, her embrace of internationalist principles was unmistakable.

Throughout the Asia-Pacific War from 1931 to 1945, she contributed commentaries to the college's organ *Home Weekly*, becoming increasingly supportive of Japan's war in China, its propaganda efforts, and the rise of a new order in politics and society. She visited China twice (1939 and 1942) as an official consultant to promote Chinese women's education in occupied territories. For her services to the state, she was decorated with the Order of the Sacred Treasure, Fifth Class, during the celebration of the mythical 2,600th year of imperial rule in 1940. After Japan's defeat, her support for Japan's aggression resulted in her being purged from public life in 1946.

Inoue's essay reproduced here was published in 1944. It displays an element of consistency with her earlier position on the importance of educating women but also contains a stunning repudiation of the central features of her own education and career through the vocabulary of Pan-Asianism. The essay appeared in the journal *Kōa Kyōiku* (Education for a Rising Asia), published by the Tōa Kyōiku Kyōkai (East Asian Education Society). The East Asian Education Society was not an official government body, but its board was studded with leading educators, Education Ministry officials, and representatives of semiofficial pan-Asianist groups. As the name of the journal and the content of the article suggest, Inoue and other Japanese women leaders had enthusiastically embraced the rising popularity of the pan-Asian ideal of *Kōa*.

Source 1 (translation from the Japanese original by Michael A. Schneider)
Ichikawa Fusae, "Mite Kita Shin Shina" (The New China I Saw). *Fujō Shinbun*, no. 2080 (21 April 1940), 2, and no. 2081 (28 April 1940), 8.

I arrived in Nanjing (Nanking) two or three days before the establishment of the new Central Government [under Wang Jingwei in late March 1940]. Shortly after my arrival I went to Hankou (Hankow) and then returned to Nanjing, which was now, to my delight, pulsing with a new exultation. . . .

Whether the new government in fact has the sufficient ability to rule or, and this is a key point, whether Japan will fully support it is yet to be determined. On this point, I have high hopes, plus it must succeed. The people in government have vitality, so there are some grounds for optimism.

[During my stay in the city] I met frequently with women and was able to talk and listen widely. The assembled women were the spouses of city, prefectural, or provisional government figures and school teachers and were individuals currently supporting Japan. I felt that the things they said were no doubt accurate, but that in speaking with them the level of candor was comparatively low. Their political consciousness, however, was relatively strong. . . .

At the same time, there must also be greater awareness about Japan. When listening to questions about Japan, it seemed that many people thought that all Japanese women were slaves. They [Japanese and Chinese] must get to know each other better and develop good points of mutual acquaintance. . . .

As regards the education of intellectual women [of Shanghai], [Chinese women] have been almost exclusively educated in European or American schools or have studied overseas and received very strong influence from Europe and the United States. These women, as individuals and as citizens, have enormous ability beyond what one might usually think. Even in the Chongqing (Chungking) Government [under Chiang Kai-shek], some women are active, but the new government also tries to esteem women. I asked Mr. Wang [Jingwei] about this point. He replied, "I am a democrat and thus believe in women's political rights and the equality of the sexes. However, the number of people with political consciousness is very small. I have always wondered what we should do about the large mass of women whose level is extremely low." There are a few women who have joined the new government but they remain in very low positions.

In any case, women are being accorded equal political rights. Both the Wang and Chongqing governments face the important problem of establishing constitutional government and are trying to have their entire nation participate in politics. When voting rights are granted, women will not be left out. This means they will be ahead of Japan. . . .

From now on, Japan cannot fail to deal with Chinese women. In that, it is essential that Japanese women take the lead. This message must get to people at the highest reaches of the military. We must commit heavily to the study of the Chinese language. To this end, we must establish a school for girls similar to the East Asian Common Culture Academy.

When military power is withdrawn, we must not end up back where we started. Rather, Japanese must set down roots culturally and work in concert based on a heartfelt respect of each individual for each other. This is not something that can be achieved quickly.

Even as time goes by and great efforts are being made, we must do everything to achieve a hundred year peace in East Asia. For these reasons, I think an enormous responsibility devolves upon Japanese women.

Source 2 (translation from the Japanese original by Michael A. Schneider) Takamure Itsue, "Shin Shina no Kensetsu to Nihon Fujin" (The Establishment of a New China and Japanese Women). *Josei Tenbō* 14:4 (April 1940), 5.

1. Reflections on the Founding of a New Central Government [in China]
In the West, "Asian" is essentially synonymous with "primitive." The fact that a global revolution is beginning in this place of the primitive, is something that I have not yet accepted intellectually, but I can feel it intimately. Casting a cold eye across the words "communalism" and "new order," I glimpse a part of it, but I think it is one of many spontaneously-generating, new modes of thought. Various things will spring from it here and there. In this sense, the founding of this new government will be a highly profound and momentous occasion.

2. How should Japanese women contribute?
Initially, we must show restraint. First, we must call back Japanese prostitutes from China. Because of their presence, the Chinese view of Japanese women is exceedingly low. Second is the task of ensuring that upper-class Japanese women in China are well educated; this matter is one we simply must not neglect. Shouldn't we feel self-reproach that Chinese women are more advanced than we are? This is a matter of greatest concern especially now at a time when the Sino-Japanese partnership is entering its crucial stage as well-educated women return from [Nationalist leader Chiang Kai-shek's capital] Chongqing [to Nanjing].

Source 3 (translation from the Japanese original by Michael A. Schneider) Inoue Hide, "Joshi Kyōiku no Dōkō" (Trends in Women's Education). *Kōa Kyōiku* 3:3 (1944), 18–24.

. . . The extraordinary string of national events—the Manchurian Incident, withdrawal from the League of Nations, the China Incident, the Greater East Asian War—have led to a wholesale return to the Imperial Way in national thought and life, while also compelling deep reflection on women's essential mission. The desperate phase of the Greater East Asian War, in particular, demands a transformation in women's views of the state, lifestyles, and accordingly, education. . . .

A trend toward practical education aligned with the needs of the state must predominate. The majority of the country's men are fighting weapon-in-hand on the front lines in areas of Greater East Asia. In particular, this necessitates increasing productive capacity on the home front, deploying male students from schools to the battlefield, further increasing the national material livelihood, and shifting women's labor and effort in industrial, agricultural, and other productive sectors to administrative and transportation bodies. Therefore, we no longer can allow women to indulge in aimless, self-indulgent academic pursuits. In girls' middle schools, education must follow the path of cultivating laboring women to meet the highest needs of the state. We must reorient toward foundational training directly useful to laboring and daily life issues, turning away from the many hours set aside for foreign language study as in the past. By taking a path of reducing English-language education, while emphasizing material, scientific, agricultural, and physical training, home management studies will be elevated and the study of Japanese language and history strengthened, we will be able to establish the foundation of girls' middle school education that truly encompasses the spirit of Japan's national polity, brings home a Japanese spirit, and instills in spirit, body, and skills the ability to serve the needs of the state. . . .

[Inoue goes on to describe the importance of greater participation of women in leadership roles in educational and other institutions.]

As we consider the future management of the Greater East Asian Co-Prosperity Sphere, we must develop educational content sufficient to allow Japanese women to work collaboratively in men's foundational and developmental projects. As stated in the Joint Declaration of the Greater East Asia Conference [in 1943; see II:27], the establishment of the Greater East Asian Co-Prosperity Sphere . . . must be grounded in mutual economic and cultural prosperity and united in broad solidarity. Thus, I do not think these things can be achieved through the cooperative efforts of men alone. This broad solidarity manifested in the guiding spirit of "Eight Corners under One Roof"—connecting household with household, binding child to child, melding blood and spirit—must be rooted in cooperation and harmony among women. Accordingly, one half of the heavy burden of this great undertaking must be borne on the backs of women. The solidarity of East Asia's 500 million women must first see the rise of Japanese women and the expression of their leadership talents.

Chapter Twenty-Nine

Yasuoka Masahiro: "Education for Japanese Capable of Being Leaders of the Greater East Asia Co-Prosperity Sphere," 1942

Roger H. Brown

The nationalist ideologue Yasuoka Masahiro served as a private adviser to members of Japan's governing elite from the 1920s through the 1980s. During the prewar and wartime period, he combined his enthusiastic call for restoring Japanese political morality and realizing Japan's pan-Asian destiny with abiding concern for preserving the *kokutai* (national polity) against radical ideological threats and the destabilizing effects of a protracted war (for details of Yasuoka's career, cf. Brown 2007, 2009). Born Hotta Masahiro in Osaka in 1898, precocious academic ability and adoption into the Yasuoka household facilitated his entry into the elite world of the First Higher School and Tokyo Imperial University. Once there, he inquired into the philosophy of neoidealism and built on childhood lessons in classical Chinese learning, laying the foundations for a nationalist discourse on personal cultivation and the political obligations of "men of character" (*jinkakusha*) that would constitute the core of his writing and speaking. Associations formed through the university facilitated his entry into the nationalist movement, where he cooperated with fellow pan-Asianists Kita Ikki and Ōkawa Shūmei (see I:27 and II:4) until issues of personality, ego, and ideology split the right-wing movement in the mid-1920s. By that point Yasuoka had likewise formed ties with members of the aristocracy, bureaucracy, and business world that would sustain his activism in the years ahead.

Yasuoka's nationalist "personalism" (*jinkakushugi*), his belief in the need for political leadership by capable moral elites, and his fear of political instability are essential characteristics of his Pan-Asianism. From the outset of his career, Yasuoka argued that the materialism of modern Western civilization left individual Japanese with confused personalities and divorced from the "Japanese spirit" (*Nihon seishin*). It was thus imperative that they and their fellow Asians awaken to their true ethnic identity and personally reconnect with the "Oriental spirit" (*Tōyō seishin*), an accomplishment indispensable for reviving "Oriental civilization" (*Tōyō bunmei*). He argued that Asians should neither reject nor worship Western civilization, nor should they practice the lifeless, rote methods of classical Chinese scholarship. Instead, they should combine understanding of the modern West with an embrace of the wisdom offered by Confucianism, Daoism, and Buddhism. For instance, he invoked the critique of materialism offered by European idealism, the placing of moral self-cultivation before material pursuits stressed in Confucianism, the devotional spirit of Buddhism, and the complementary Daoist dualism of yin and yang in order to assert that the spiritual proclivities of the Orient complemented the materialist inclination of the Occident and, consequently, that revival of the former was imperative for returning balance to world civilization (Yasuoka 1922, 1933).

As was common with Japanese pan-Asianists, Yasuoka assigned Japan the leadership role in this renaissance of East Asian civilization and connected the project to the imperative of domestic spiritual and political renovation. Nevertheless, he differed in his heavy reliance on Confucian principles of moral self-cultivation and virtuous governance in theorizing renovation both within Japan and throughout East Asia. Echoing the advice offered by the military theorist and Confucian scholar Yamaga Sokō (1622–1685), Yasuoka argued that Japanese officials must cultivate themselves properly in order to fulfill the role of moral exemplar to the general population. Likewise in line with Sokō, he presented Japan, rather than China, as the country where Confucian principles of virtuous governance, or the Kingly Way (*ōdō*), had been best realized in the form of the Imperial Way (*kōdō*). As Japanese expansion accelerated in the 1930s, Yasuoka drew on his blend of Confucian principles and Japanist nationalism to insist that it was only through moral justness and upright behavior that Japanese would elicit the cooperation of other Asians in the creation of a Japan-led New Order in East Asia. Just as successful renovation at home depended on the leadership of farsighted men of ability and virtue, fulfilling Japan's "divine destiny" (*shinmei*) to lead Greater East Asia required demonstration of these traits by all Japanese before the peoples of Asia and, indeed, the rest of the world (Brown 2007; Kawai 2006).

However, whether making his case for national renovation or Asian renaissance, Yasuoka consistently demonstrated conservative anxiety over any development that might endanger the emperor-centered *kokutai*. Thus, while Yasuoka supported the creation of Manchukuo in 1932 and the realization of Japanese leadership of East Asia, he also advocated rapid conclusion of the Sino-Japanese War that had begun in 1937 and opposed the Tripartite Alliance as provocative and unnecessary for fulfilling Japan's pan-Asian destiny. By early 1943, as variously motivated anti-Tōjō Hideki factions struggled, first, to cooperate with each other and, second, to force the Tōjō cabinet's resignation, Yasuoka was publicly expressing concern over the unforeseen consequences that wars, even when successful, bore for political and social stability (Brown 2007; Yasuoka 1943b).

Early indication of such trepidation appears in the following speech given by Yasuoka in July 1942 before the Keimeikai (Morning Star Society), a study group founded in 1918 by Count Makino Nobuaki (1861–1949) and bureaucrat Hirayama Narinobu (1854–1929) with money provided by entrepreneur Akaboshi Tetsuma (1883–1951). While welcoming the realization of the Greater East Asia Co-Prosperity Sphere, Yasuoka nevertheless warned of the potential consequences of such rapid expansion for racial harmony and political stability. Worrying that Japanese were not up to the challenge of governing Greater East Asia effectively, he displayed his customary emphasis on proper moral cultivation as the key to producing Japanese capable of eliciting the allegiance of their fellow Asians. The attention he pays to the issue of education reform, to differences among *minzoku* (translated here variously as "ethnic people," "race," or "people"), and to the need for elite leadership illustrates how for some Japanese enthusiasm for their country's pan-Asian mission existed in tension with the prejudices of ethnic nationalism and anxieties of political conservatism.

Source (translation from the Japanese original by Roger H. Brown)
Yasuoka Masahiro, *Daitōa Kyōeiken no Shidōsha taru beki Nihonjin no Kyōiku* (Education for Japanese Capable of Being Leaders of the Greater East Asia Co-Prosperity Sphere), Keimeikai, 1943.

LESSONS TO BE DRAWN FROM THE WEAK POINTS OF THE BRITISH EMPIRE

As a result of the Greater East Asia War . . . Japan has arrived at its destiny of having to lead a great territorial expanse encompassing more than one billion people. . . . It is natural to welcome this as an auspicious example of Japan's prosperity, expansion, and glory. However, it is often the case that danger lurks not within conditions of human adversity but rather within circumstances of prosperity. It is at this moment when Japan has achieved sudden, largely unforeseen development and expansion that those truly thinking of Japan must reflect deeply. The ignorant masses may freely welcome this sudden expansion and development with a chorus of praise, but it is at this time more than ever that men of discernment must think deeply about the long-term future of the state. . . .

JAPAN'S FUTURE PROSPECTS AS THE LEADER OF ASIA

[Consideration of the British case] should for various reasons make us reflect and learn. It goes without saying that we must maintain racial purity and, as the word Yamato indicates, advance without losing Japan's racial harmony. The more the Japanese state expands and the more it brings in numerous races, [the more we] must think seriously about how to simultaneously preserve the purity of the Japanese while realizing harmony with these various peoples and, furthermore, how to sustain the authority necessary to be the leader of these various ethnic and racial groups. Simply celebrating expansion and the fact of ruling many people is exceedingly childish and shallow. Indeed, I think it is clear that, for Japan's sake, Japanese statesmen and intellectuals must exercise great vigilance in regard to the undesirable omens that are appearing everywhere. . . .

NEIGHBORING PEOPLES' FEELINGS TOWARD JAPAN

The Koreans . . . are a magnificent people in no way inferior to the peoples of such Europeans countries as Czechoslovakia, Poland, and Holland. Having returned home to the New Japan they now go out into the world anew as Japanese (*atarashiki Nihon minzoku toshite*) in no way inferior to any race. In terms of physical strength and such they are now of the same level as homeland Japanese (*Nihon naichijin*), and possibly possess unsurpassed energy and ability. To the north of Korea, Japan is assisting in the establishing of Manchukuo. The majority of the people of that nation (*kokumin*) are, of course, members of the [Chinese] Han race. . . . These people have experienced four thousand years of repetitive rise and decline and great change, yet remain vigorous. . . .

The Chinese people possess what is, from the perspective of Western history, philosophy, and ethnographic science, a rather inscrutable vitality and spirit. The Western notion of culture sees culture as separate from the condition of simplicity, vulgarity, and primitivism. However, unlike those of the West, China's civilization and culture have not separated from simplicity and primitivism, and no matter the extent to which [China's] culture develops, it will retain within it that harmonious simplicity and primitivism. . . . From the Western way of thinking, anyone with such a history of being repeatedly invaded and conquered by other peoples, of having experienced repeated rebellions and revolutions, and of being plagued with eruptions of banditry should have long ago lost their racial vitality. Or, alternatively, like the Ainu or the slaves of Europe, they should be on their last legs or, at best, have become global wanderers like the Jews. Nevertheless, the Chinese remain serenely in possession of that large country, an inscrutable presence maintaining their unique culture. In addition to the Chinese, the current Greater East Asia War will integrate within our sphere the Indonesians [*Indoneshia minzoku*], Indians, Thais and others. If these ethnic masses (*minzoku taishū*) truly make Japan their leader and in that way harmonize and construct the Greater East Asia Co-Prosperity Sphere, [the result will be] a sturdy co-prosperity sphere unparalleled in the world, and the complete transformation of contemporary world civilization will be no mere dream. Conversely, should these masses, these different races (*iminzoku*) not follow Japan—not only not follow but harbor thoughts of intrigue or incite feelings of animosity and engage determinedly in acts of resistance—then of course Japan will confront a gravely dangerous and deplorable situation.

. . . [A]s you all know, and as is also pointed out by Sun Yat-sen in his three democratic principles, until recently the Chinese masses, while possessing a sense of individuality, family, and religion, largely lacked a conception of themselves as members of a nation, of a state. . . . [However] as a result of long-term anti-Japanese education . . . nowadays their ethnic consciousness and spirit of resistance is truly formidable. . . . Recently, an official returned from Manchuria and earnestly related how, following a talk at an assembly on the unity of Japan and Manchuria, one passionate youth stood and said, "Japanese-Manchurian unity is fine, however, while we are Manchurians, the graves of our ancestors are in republican China—in China. More than the unity of Japan and Manchuria, for us there is the unity of China and Manchuria—the unity of Manchuria and Nationalist China!" Although there had been no reaction from the audience following the speech on the unity of Japan and Manchuria, from this same audience there arose now applause such as to raise the building's roof. This, the official felt, should tell us something. Once, while traveling in Manchuria, I participated in a discussion with young officials of Manchukuo and one fellow pointed out that in the capital of Xinjing [Hsingking; Japanese: Shinkyō, present-day Changchun] there were 70,000 Japanese . . . and that it was thanks to Japan that this grand state had been created. Therefore, [he continued], one would expect to find everywhere in Xinjing Manchurians (*Manshūkokujin*) and Japanese on good terms and engaging in pleasant conversation, but for some reason one hardly ever sees them together conversing. Not only that, even at the city office one finds Chinese with Chinese, Koreans with Koreans, and Japanese with Japanese, all clearly segregated and not getting along at all. Why on earth is this so? Since this is the Japanese Empire, certainly Koreans, but also Chinese and Mongolians, should all joyously and naturally gather wherever there are Japanese. . . . Why is it, he implored, that Japanese do not possess that kind of charisma? Likewise, when I returned to Korea and spoke with representatives of the Korean people, there was the same problem.

. . . There are many statesmen who hate hearing these things, but true statesmen and true intellectuals must open themselves to reports of these phenomena and respond with calm, deliberate foresight. . . .

FOREIGNERS' VIEWS OF JAPANESE

As to why it is that a people with such an inviolable *kokutai* and glorious history should witness, as the backside of rapid expansion and development, such unwelcome phenomenon and reports, my own personal experience suggests the following: Through modern civilization Japan clearly has made remarkable strides and truly progressed far in knowledge and technology. However, most would also admit that the charms and strengths of Japanese as human beings have declined in comparison with those of our ancestors from the days of the Shogunate or Meiji. . . . Somehow, Japanese have become uninteresting, boorish, hurried, grim, and irritable. It is undeniable that as human beings Japanese have declined and become, in the words of [foreign observers], desolate. However, Japanese were not originally such a people. Certainly, when considering this grand *kokutai*, history, and ethnic spirit, we contemporaries are by any measure an extremely promising, delightful race. . . . Why is it that Japanese today receive such censure and ill will from other races? Ultimately, I think the problem is one of education and learning, and, broadly speaking, education and learning are about realizing personal cultivation (*kyōyō*). Certainly, if possible, from numerous peoples bring about joyful submission; if joyful submission is not possible then respectful submission; if that is not possible, then at least submission. At any rate, in order to bring about submission Japanese cannot rely only on mere violence, military force, and economic power. They must greatly cultivate virtue (*toku*). And, after all is said and done, that can only come from personal cultivation. . . .

. . . [W]hen we consider how [the British] have been able to successfully oversee so many different territories and peoples and to preserve their authority for so long, we cannot overlook the force of British education, of British personal cultivation. . . . [W]hen it came to the personal cultivation of the class of their countrymen charged with overseeing and controlling their colonies, Englishmen exerted unparalleled pains and efforts.

PROBLEMS RELATING TO EDUCATION

What one notices travelling around Britain or France, and this is true also in Germany, is that the common masses are truly beastly. From the perspective of both daily life and popular customs, the Japanese masses are by far the more refined and moral. However, in these countries there is a clear difference between the general masses and the leadership class. In terms of both wealth and personal cultivation, leaders clearly possess their own particular dignity, personal cultivation, and ability. Accordingly, the masses, recognizing this difference of ability, respect and readily submit to them. Similarly, leaders appropriately take responsibility and fulfill their leadership role well. If one looks at Japan, the ordinary masses come off very well in comparison with their Western counterparts in regards to spirit, popular customs, and human qualities; however, there is utter failure to recognize the difference between the ordinary masses and the leadership class. In short, [society] is being leveled. Therefore, the relations of trust and responsibility between the leadership class and the general masses are becoming ambiguous. I think this is a point requiring profound consideration. In particular, when it comes to shouldering the destiny of the national masses (*kokumin taishū*) [and to] leadership education for the purpose of guiding many different races, one realizes that there are many points of regret [and that these extend to] education for leaders, for young people, for virtuous gentlemen (*shikunshi*), for political leaders, for mastering the self and for governing village and country. . . .

LACKING THE SPIRIT OF EDUCATION

. . . [U]ntil the Meiji period, people were educated in order to make them superior human beings. . . . Of course, becoming superior means a lot of things, but it means first of all becoming a person who possesses splendid personal character. Completion as a great man, this is the most important thing. . . . Namely, the spirit and zeal of the superior man has faded greatly from the Japanese. Therefore, while there have appeared many who are useful for having mastered some knowledge and technology, overall a gradual decline has occurred when it comes to serving the state, doing something for people, charming the masses, or any other such essential matters relating to the rise and fall of the ethnic nation-state (*minzoku-kokka*). . . .

THOROUGH PERSONAL CHARACTER EDUCATION

Henceforth, in order to produce real Japanese truly capable of leading people, of eliciting from other peoples willing allegiance, [contemporary] education must be reformed. We must return to the proper path of education. Returning to the proper path of education means implementing compulsory education that to the degree possible cultivates great men [and that] thoroughly inculcates [self]-understanding as someone's child and as a subject of the state. For instance, what of human conviction, discernment, and etiquette? People need to receive thoroughly the kind of education found in the Five Relationships and Five Cardinal Virtues [of Confucianism], moral education as to how one should one behave toward parents, toward siblings, toward friends, and in relations between superiors and inferiors. . . . Regarding the cultivation and education of men of great character, I would like to introduce a few of the criticisms of Japanese being made by intellectuals of other countries.

PERSONAL CULTIVATION AND MAGNANIMITY AS A GREAT PEOPLE

Whether one goes to Korea, Manchuria, or China, or to Europe, you will hear from old and young alike the following evaluation of Japanese. First, Japanese gentlemen are strangely ill-mannered. They are said to lack etiquette. This is the world's established opinion. There is no one in the world as awkward in greeting others as Japanese. . . . No place lacks decorum as much as the Japanese Club. There are three bad things about Japanese clubs: drunkenness, arguments, and public urination. Also, when Japanese speak with others they do so without compassion [and] nonchalantly say things that hurt others. Once when dining at a Chinese restaurant in Beijing, a close friend who was accompanying me explained intently . . . [how], rather than calling out in a kind voice, Japanese yell "Boy!" When riding in a rickshaw they will, as if angry, speak roughly toward the driver. This appears in all facets of life. . . . Next, Japanese like to argue and are impractical. Likewise, they recklessly play with the law and turn their back on human feelings. As you all know, ever since the Manchurian Incident, Japanese have been viewed as lawbreakers, as bandits, and such. . . . Next, Japanese are often said to be rash, impetuous, and lacking stamina and tenacity. . . . Finally, while in times of emergency Japanese have the habit of pulling together and acting loyally and bravely, in ordinary times of prosperity there is no nationality more jealous and divisive than the Japanese. . . .

If Japanese fail to redeem these weak points they will be unable to erect true authority [in Asia]. . . . They will be unable to become leaders capable of commanding one billion people. . . . Henceforth, the vital virtue of Japanese must be cultivated thoroughly through education. This matter will decide Japan's fate. If this is not done, Japan's expansion will become Japan's peril. . . .

Chapter Thirty

Hirano Yoshitarō: "The Historical Basis of Greater Asianism," 1945

Mutō Shūtarō

Hirano Yoshitarō (1897–1980) was born in Tokyo. His maternal grandfather Hirano Tomiji (1846–1892) was an industrialist who founded Ishikawajima Hirano Shipyard, the present IHI Corp. After graduating from the First Higher School (Ichikō) in 1918, he studied at the Faculty of Law, Tokyo Imperial University, graduating in 1921. As an assistant at the Law Faculty, in 1924 Hirano published *Minpō ni okeru Rōma Shisō to Jeruman Shisō* (Roman and German Thought in Civil Law), in which he advocated the necessity of a civil code based on local manners and customs. Following the German legal scholar Otto von Gierke (1841–1921), who had criticized the first draft of a new German civil law code for its neglect of "Germanic" principles, Hirano attempted to identify problems in the Meiji civil code, which was modeled on the German draft. His preference for "communal" Germanic thought over more "individualistic" Roman thought comes across clearly in his comments on the problems of the countryside. He regarded the rural commune as an ideal and believed that an injection of communal values into the civil code would make it more in tune with the traditional values of Japanese society.

In his second book, *Hōritsu ni okeru Kaikyū Tōsō* (Class Struggle in the Law, 1925), Hirano changed his stance diametrically. He now interpreted communitarian rules such as commonage as a hangover from feudal times that needed to be set aside. Quoting directly from the *Communist Manifesto* that "the history of all hitherto existing societies is a history of class struggle," in this book Hirano assumed a clearly Marxist stance. One reason for this sudden change may have been his involvement in the Industry and Labor Research Institute (Sangyō Rōdō Chōsajo), which had been founded in 1924 by the Marxist Nosaka Sanzō (1892–1993).

Hirano studied abroad at government expense from April 1927 to January 1930. While in Paris, Hirano met the Sinologist Karl August Wittfogel

(1896–1988), whose books *Economy and Society in China* (1931), *The Theory of Oriental Society* (1938), and *New Light on Chinese Society* (1938) he subsequently translated into Japanese. Moving from Paris to the Institute for Social Research (Institut für Sozialforschung) in Frankfurt am Main on the advice of Wittfogel, Hirano began to consider Marxism in earnest. He also participated in socialist meetings, such as the Second World Congress of the League against Imperialism in Frankfurt.

After his return to Japan, Hirano taught a course in "kinship law." According to his lecture handouts, Hirano embarked on the task of explaining the historical transformations of kinship relations. First of all, he rejected the common view that marital and parent–child relationships were natural and universal, insisting that the bonds of kinship were restricted or conditioned by the relations of production. "Blood bonds" were weakened in proportion to the strength of a society's productive forces. With the demise of the extended family system, the nuclear family had arisen as a societal unit in accordance with the capitalist mode of production. Therefore, he argued, in a normal capitalist society, kinship law must correspond to the requirements of the nuclear family.

Three months after he had commenced his lectures, Hirano was arrested under the Peace Preservation Law (Chian Ijihō) on charges of providing funds to the Japanese Communist Party. Though he avoided a prison sentence, he was forced to give up his post at Tokyo Imperial University. The following year, Hirano participated in meetings preparatory to the publication of *Nihon Shihonshugi Hattatsushi Kōza* (Lectures on the Historical Development of Japanese Capitalism, 1932–1933, usually abbreviated as *Kōza*), a project conceived and developed by Noro Eitarō (1900–1934), a member of both the Industry and Labor Research Institute and the Japanese Communist Party. Although these meetings apparently lacked specific goals, the participants, who were later known collectively as the Kōzaha (Lecture Faction), agreed to conform to the so-called 1932 thesis—the Comintern view that Japan after the Meiji Restoration was still an absolute monarchy that represented semi-feudal Asiatic-style rule over its rural communities. This analysis implied that Japan must first experience a bourgeois revolution as a precondition for a communist revolution, which was considered to be a second stage.

Hirano wrote five essays for the *Kōza* project, which were subsequently reprinted in a single volume, *Nihon Shihonshugi Shakai no Kikō* (The Structure of Japanese Capitalist Society, 1934). This is considered one of the most important works to be produced by a Kōzaha scholar. In the following years, a major debate on the nature of Japanese capitalism and revolutionary strategy broke out between the Kōzaha and the rival Rōnōha (Worker-Farmer Faction), another informal group of academics influenced by Marxism. The latter, in opposition to the Kōzaha, regarded the Meiji Restoration as an already completed bourgeois revolution and, as a result, argued that Japan was ready to undergo an immediate communist revolution. Hirano made a number of contributions to this debate in popular magazines, attacking the views of the Rōnōha.

In July 1936, while planning a series of new lectures on Japanese feudalism, Hirano was arrested again, this time on charges of being involved in the formation of communist organizations. In prison, Hirano eventually renounced Marxism and "converted" (*tenkō*; see Steinhoff 1991) to the nationalist state ideology that had come to dominate political and ideological discourse in the 1930s. Hirano's stated reason for this "conversion" was his remorse at his failure to fulfill his filial obligations toward his mother-in-law, who had died while he was in prison (Ishidō 1985). Such an argument was not unusual in prewar Japan, where many Japanese scholars renounced Marxism ostensibly as a result of family obligations.

After his release from prison in 1939, Hirano became a member of the Sixth Inquiry Committee of the Tōa Kenkyūjo (East Asian Institute), alongside Suehiro Izutarō (1888–1951) and other former faculty members from the Faculty of Law at Tokyo Imperial University. The East Asian Institute fell directly under the control of the government's Planning Bureau (Kikaku-in) and was charged with undertaking research on the East Asian region to provide information required for the formulation of national policy as the Sino-Japanese War (1937–1945) expanded in scale. The Sixth Inquiry Committee had been set up specifically to study "living law"—local manners and customs—in rural northern China. Committee members traveled to China in August 1940 to meet representatives of the Research Division of the South Manchurian Railway Company (Mantetsu Chōsabu), which was in charge of information gathering for the Japanese government. In the course of an inspection tour of rural areas in both northern and southern China, Hirano concluded that the concept of mutual family and neighborhood assistance was the key to understanding Chinese society.

On his return to Japan, Hirano analyzed the data from Hebei (Hopei) Province in northern China provided by the Mantetsu Chōsabu and, on the basis of this information, argued for the existence of a "natural" village that was an entity distinct from the "administrative" village. However, based on the same materials, Kainō Michitaka (1908–1975) had concluded that Chinese people lacked any concept of a village because no clear boundaries between communities were defined and, in contrast to Japan or Germany, in China there were no cooperatives with freeholding farmers as central figures. Although Hirano partly acknowledged Kainō's views, he stuck to his own ideas. In an attempt to demonstrate the existence of the natural village in China, Hirano began to elaborate his own version of Pan-Asianism—the notion of a pan-Asian commonality based on similarities in *rural lifestyle* and the centrality of the village community.

In 1941, Hirano toured the South Seas area, from Xiamen (Amoy) to the Celebes in the Dutch East Indies, publishing the results of his tour as *Taiheiyō no Minzoku Seijigaku* (Ethnopolitics of the Pacific Ocean, 1942). At the outset of this work, he declared that "we are now striving for the construction of a Greater East Asia Co-Prosperity Sphere." This was the first book in which Hirano openly advocated the ideology of Pan-Asianism, with the goal of justifying the Greater East Asia Co-Prosperity Sphere. He continued to promote pan-Asian ideas in four subsequent books: *Minzoku Seijigaku no Riron* (The Theory of Ethnopolitics, 1943), *Minzoku Seiji no Kihon Mondai* (Basic Problems of Ethnopolitics, 1944), *Hokushi no Sonraku Shakai* (Village Society in North China, 1944), and, finally, *Dai Ajiashugi no Rekishiteki Kiso* (The Historical Basis of Greater Asianism, 1945).

Based on these writings, the three main characteristics of Hirano's Pan-Asianism can be summarized as follows:

1. Emphasis on the rural community

It is clear from the preface to *Dai Ajiashugi no Rekishiteki Kiso* that Hirano considered rural village communities as the social essence of Asia. The "natural" village he had discovered in China was generalized to form the common basis of daily life in Asia. While his high regard for rural community entailed a complete conversion from Marxist thought to an Asianist ideology, logical similarities between his early work on civil law and his later Pan-Asianism can be detected.

2. Views on the family system

Hirano's views on the family system were as complex as his views on the importance of rural communities. As a pan-Asianist, Hirano advanced a stark dichotomy between "individualistic," "commercial" Europe on the one hand and "communal," "communitarian," and "rural" Asia on the other. Moreover, he considered the ability to transform different "blood" relationships into a familial relationship an important characteristic of the Japanese family system, and, based on this insight, he advocated a new Asian order centering on Japan as a *pater familias*, acting as a benevolent "guide" for the "Asian brothers and sisters."

3. German intellectual influences

Hirano borrowed the concept of *Minzoku seijigaku* (ethnopolitics) from Karl Haushofer's (1869–1946) influential works on geopolitics published in the 1920s and 1930s. The central dichotomy in Hirano's thinking was between Asian rice farming, based on irrigation, and European wheat farming, dependent on rainwater—a concept that he apparently developed under the influence of Karl Wittfogel. The strong and consistent influence of German thought is apparent in Hirano's work throughout his entire scholarly career up until his conversion to Pan-Asianism. Hirano translated the multivolume work titled *Grundlagen, Aufbau und Wirtschaftsordnung des Nationalsozialistischen Staates* (Foundations, Structure, and Economic System of the National Socialist State, 1936–1938) edited by two leading Nazi economists, Hans-Heinrich Lammers (1879–1962) and Hans Pfundtner (1881–1945) into Japanese. It was published under the title *Shin Doitsu Kokka Taikei* (Outline of the New German State, 1939–1941).

A year after Japan's surrender, Hirano took office as head of the Institute of Chinese Studies (Chūgoku Kenkyūjo)—a reconstituted Institute of East Asian Studies. Hirano was also appointed vice president of the Japan-China Friendship Association (Nitchū Yūkō Kyōkai), thus becoming a central figure in postwar Sino–Japanese relations at the nongovernmental level. Hirano reverted to Marxism and became involved in the peace movement. He failed, however, to repudiate or in any way explain both his wartime pan-Asianist writings and his sudden political "conversion" (*tenkō*), that is, his wartime renunciation of Marxism and his turn toward Pan-Asianism. These inconsistencies were harshly criticized by Takeuchi Yoshimi (1963b; cf. II:35) and others.

Despite such inconsistencies, Hirano's writings are of great importance because they exemplify the development of Pan-Asianism during the later war years when the influence of the ideology was at its strongest—as reflected in the flood of pan-Asianist works produced by former leftists such as Hirano.

Source (translation from the Japanese original by Mutō Shūtarō)
Hirano Yoshitarō, *Dai Ajiashugi no Rekishiteki Kiso* (The Historical Basis of Greater Asianism). Kawade Shobō, 1945.

PREFACE

1

Traveling to many parts of Europe and Asia as an emissary of our enemy, American President Roosevelt, in 1942, Wendell L. Willkie [1892–1944] wrote the book *One World*. In it he noted the awakening of powerful nationalist movements throughout the whole East Asian region, observed Asian aspirations to break the fetters of American and British imperialism and their colonial rule, and acknowledged the rapid rise of Asian national consciousness.

The national liberation movement that is bringing these various Asian peoples together and creating the Greater East Asia Co-Prosperity Community under the banner of Greater Asianism now constitutes a great menace to our enemies, Britain and America. . . .

However, the Chongqing (Chungking) government has taken advantage of the notable rise of these Asian nationalist movements to approach the Indian Congress Party, while the Yan'an government is making an appeal to West Asia, drawing on Lenin's theory of self-determination. As I have already noted in "The Indian Independence Movement and the Chongqing Government," the Chongqing regime, with its isolated and narrow-minded nationalism, opposes both the international tendency for the formation of economic blocs and the creation of regional economies and the Co-Prosperity Sphere based on the Eastern moral principle of civility. Instead, it clings to a facile universalism centered on American and British imperialism advocated by the old League of Nations, which is no more than an international forum for promoting American and British interests. It [the Chongqing government] merely signifies submission to the Anglo-Saxon world hegemony. That is not all. The Chiang [Kai-shek, Jiang Jieshi] government has ceded its own territory to the United States for use as air bases, has renounced the principle of Chinese independence, and has become a mere subject of America and Britain who are both conspiring against the nationalist movement that intends to revive the Asian homelands on a cooperative basis. The Chiang government is at present not a "national government," but rather a "greedy government" controlled by Kong Xiangxi [K'ung Hsiang-hsi, often known as H. H. Kung, 1881–1967], Song Ziwen [Soong Tzu-wen, 1894–1971, a brother-in-law of Sun Yat-sen] and Chiang Kai-shek's family. As this regime degenerated into the "comprador government" of American and British imperialism, it abandoned the Asian nationalist movement. At the same time, the Yan'an government—whose goal is to destroy the thriving nationalist movement of our Asian brothers in the Asian homeland—is a running dog of Russia, just as the Chongqing government is the stooge of America and Britain. In addition, the facile universalism of Sun Yat-sen, to which they are now obliged to conform, has been denied them in the end.

In contrast to those who prostrate themselves before America, Britain and Russia, Japan's construction of a Greater East Asia represents a genuine emancipation of Greater East Asia by Asians, for Asians. For this reason, we must smash the Anglo-Saxon invasion of the Orient as well as Russia's intrigues. In particular, we must form a union in the Orient with the two most numerous peoples with ancient traditional cultures—namely, China (*Chūgoku*) and India. But at present, the realization of Greater Asianism by effecting a union between Japan and China is the most urgent necessity.

2

Japan, Manchuria and China form the core for the construction of the Greater East Asia Co-Prosperity Community.

Before the outbreak of the Greater East Asia War [1941], a joint communiqué by Japan, Manchuria, and China declared that "the three nations mutually respect one another's natural characteristics, and under the shared idea of constructing an ethically based new order in East Asia, pledge to cooperate closely with each other as good neighbors to form an axis of lasting peace in East Asia. With this axis at the core, we will contribute to peace for the whole world." At present, the "East Asia" made up of the three nations of Japan, Manchuria, and China has expanded into a "Greater East Asia" that includes the southern regions. In addition, the six main independent nations [in the grouping] have published a joint Greater East Asia Charter based on co-existence, co-prosperity, independence, friendship, the promotion of Asian culture, the moral economy of co-prosperity, and our contribution to world progress in the Orient [*sic*], including India. At the present stage of the construction of Greater Asia, Japan is the central force and Japan, Manchuria, and China still remain both its starting point and axis.

In particular, the Japanese and Chinese races—which are related historically, culturally, geographically, and economically—share the same eternal destiny. As Sun Yat-sen has already said, the security of Japan is inseparable from that of China. "Just as Japan cannot exist without China, so China cannot exist without Japan. Therefore, if we want to plan a hundred years' peace for both nations, there can be no discord." And even if discord should occur between the two nations, whether they like it or not they will have no choice but to cooperate with each other to achieve the development of the Orient, as they share one eternal destiny. As we are neighbors and brothers with the same script and of the same race, sharing the same economic interests—as we share the particular burden of destroying the fetters of Anglo-Saxon oppression in Asia and of waging a war of independence to recover Asian autonomy, so we will come to the realization that in order to guarantee the security of Greater East Asia and carry out the great task of Raising Asia (*kōa*), a cooperative union of Japan and China not only forms the very core of the movement to construct a Greater Asia—it is also an historical inevitability for which the two nations share a joint responsibility. . . .

3

As Asia was originally one, it cannot exist and prosper without being unified. The nations of Greater East Asia share an inseparably close relationship as a result of geography, blood, culture, and history. The realization of this unity and the construction of a morally based order of co-existence and co-prosperity that is united in terms of politics, economics, and defense are the shared duties of all the Asian nations. These duties cannot be accomplished without respecting each other's independence and establishing friendship within a Greater East Asian region. This respect for independence and friendship can never be realized in the way that the anti-Axis powers are going about it—through international conferences that serve to promote their own interests. We must create an order based on the principles of harmony and respect (*wakei*) which [in turn] is based on the original civility of Oriental morality, because the essential character of Oriental society is based on this principle.

Okakura Tenshin [cf. I:7 and I:8] once said that "Asia is one," and I too assert that the Orient is one. But until now, the Orient has been unable to overcome its disunity on account of the nature of its internal relations—regional self-sufficiency in terms of geography, commerce and economic life—and as a result of external pressures in the form of the European and American invasion of the Orient.

However, Oriental unity has been slowly developing throughout the long history of the region. First of all, absorbing the cultures of China (*Shina*) and India, the Japanese race perfected its national polity (*kokutai*). It perfectly merged and assimilated both Chinese and Indian cultures while preserving its original national culture. On this point, it is in stark contrast to the Chinese race which completely lost touch with Indian culture, for it had assimilated Buddhism so voraciously that it turned it into a branch of Taoism. In addition to the Chinese race having a poor record at merging Chinese and Indian cultures, it also has a poor understanding of Japanese culture. Needless to say, the Indian race is almost completely ignorant of the cultures and thought of China and Japan, having been attracted to Western culture for centuries. Historically speaking, this confirms the fact that the Japanese race is the only one that has [successfully] merged the various Oriental cultures.

I have here established the exemplary role of the Japanese race in the unifying of Oriental cultures and thus pinpointed the way forward for the Oriental axis, which should offer favorable cultural and ideological prospects for the construction of a Greater Asia.

Having assembled the races of East Asia (Japan, Manchuria, and China), the races of Greater East Asia and the South Seas, and the races of the Orient including India, and having swept aside the American and British invasion of the Orient, how should we then create the common foundations for a Greater Asia? Japan has embodied the essence of Oriental culture for three thousand years and is located at the center of exchange between the continental civilizations of China and India and the oceanic cultures of the Pacific (including the smaller oceans, the Indian Ocean and "Southern Ocean"). In the early modern period, Japan—which in addition has absorbed Occidental culture and science—emerged as the center of power in the Orient by merging Oriental and Occidental cultures. For this reason, Japan has the kind of qualifications that inspire optimism about the future prospects for the modern unification of Oriental cultures and for the propagation of the Way. . . .

4

When [Okakura] Tenshin stated that Asia is one, he was referring to the community of culture and the arts. However, we must also acknowledge the existence of a remarkable community of the spirit (*seishin*) and everyday life (*seikatsu*), as well as in social and economic life, social institutions and the basic character of society.

Traditional Oriental society, based on the Asian system of economic organization, is best represented by rural village society (*nōson kyōdo shakai*) based on the family system and ancestor worship. It exhibits a communal character which is the social essence of Asia, expressing a morality based on the values of harmony and respect. Moreover, it stands united as one against the common enemy, invaders of the homeland, and courageously sacrifices itself for the public good.

From ancient Greece and Rome to the modern era, European and American society has been characterized by individualism, free competition, conquest, and conflict—whereas the essence of Asian society could be described as the living unity of the family from the *pater familias* and chief family of the clan on down, in addition to friendship and civility. The whole system supports and fosters the individual. Centered on its head, the whole and its various parts are united in one. The chief moral maxim is not the rule of might but the rule of right, not conflict but friendship. Centered on the chief family, the various branch families, united as they are by familial ties, transform even people of different blood into people of the same blood. This last point—the transformation of a people of a different stock into a people of the same stock—is one of the chief characteristics of the Japanese family system and the Japanese spirit.

The reason for this is that, whereas the ancient Mediterranean civilizations of Greece and Rome and the modern societies of Europe and America have been characterized by profit-driven commerce based on free competition, Asian societies are founded on the values of the rural community (*nōson kyōdōtai*). The impact of a rice-based agricultural economy on the mutual assistance that marks family and neighborhood makes the home the foundation of social life and also turns community and friendship into key principles of village life (*kyōdo seikatsu*). Thus, it can be said that the flourishing of the various Asian cultures is founded on these rural village communities (*kyōdoteki nōson kyōdōtai*).

The natural conditions that permit the Asian style of agriculture are the warm and humid climate produced by the East Asian monsoon. The vast region with its difficult terrain that extends from Manchuria to India—more specifically, the continental areas and islands below a line stretching from the Tumen River estuary all the way to the Persian Gulf—form the core region of our homeland, where the Orient flourishes as the Orient. . . .

Moreover, this warm and humid Asian region has always been connected to the larger world through its two climatic corridors, the northern dry zone and the southern ocean. The dry zone is a vast continental region stretching from Mongolia to Central Asia covered with desert plains, where migrating stock-farming societies have developed. Linked to both West Asia and South Russia, these societies have enjoyed considerable historical influence through their trade routes into Western Europe, symbolized by the famous "silk road."

Furthermore, it is common knowledge that not only was the Southern Ocean a route along which the Arabs and Islam made their gradual progress towards the East, and along which the mercantile mariners of China traveled back and forth during the Middle Ages, but it has also served as the route for the European invasion of East Asia in modern times.

Although exotic cultures were transmitted along these northern and southern routes to reach the very core of East Asia, Japan and China, East Asia did not lose its identity. On the contrary, by absorbing these various cultures it enriched itself and has gradually created a brilliant and original Oriental civilization. It is not without reason that our Nara Court [eighth century AD] and China's T'ang Dynasty [seventh to tenth centuries AD], which were established at around the same time, both embraced the ideal of a cosmopolitan world-state.

The seeds of a cosmopolitan East Asia grew and developed in the home villages (*kyōdo*) of East Asia over several thousand years. Constantly refined and growing in sophistication, this distinctive culture was based upon solid social ethics seen in the discipline of the rural village community (*nōson kyōdōtai*), with its values of common life and mutual self-help based on the family unit. This culture, which was connected to the outside world through the northern and southern corridors, is responsible for creating the unshakable social morals of rural village communities with their emphasis on mutual aid within families and neighborhoods, which is based in turn upon the rice-growing economy of Asia, with its warm and humid climate. . . .

Part V

PAN-ASIANISM DURING THE COLD WAR, 1945–1989

Although in the end pan-Asian ideals proved a total failure, World War II nevertheless led to a weakening of Western power in Asia. The prestige of the Western colonial powers had been permanently damaged by their initial easy defeat at the hands of the Japanese, and a return to the status quo ante proved impossible after the war's end. In the following decade India (1947), Burma (1948), Vietnam (1954), and Malaya (1957) all became independent, among many other new nations in the region. By 1950 China, a semicolony before the war, had become a communist state, free of imperialist presence. Another consequence of the war was a protracted period of confrontation between the United States and Soviet Russia known as the Cold War, a standoff that continued for almost forty-five years. The bipolar world order of the Cold War, with the search for alternatives to this division, constitutes the setting for this section.

In Japan, following its defeat, Pan-Asianism was discredited by its wartime associations and disappeared from mainstream public discourse for many years. It was only in the 1960s that a resurgence of pan-Asian rhetoric took place in Japan, when the word was rehabilitated by those at the political extremes—it was used by some leftists as a term of abuse and also by unrepentant right-wing nationalists (II:34) who were keen to justify the war Japan had waged as a war of "Asian liberation" (*Ajia kaihō sensō*).

Pan-Asian sentiments also appeared, unexpectedly, in the writings of some Japanese Marxists who emphasized the importance of Asian solidarity in the face of what they regarded as a renewed threat of Western colonialism and imperialism (II:32). In a similar fashion, the Japanese peace movement also appealed to notions of solidarity in strikingly pan-Asian terms. It was in this climate that the first scholarly analysis of Pan-Asianism was published in 1963. Takeuchi Yoshimi's (II:35) famous article took a relatively balanced view of the ideology behind the movement without condemning it outright. His work has been a source of inspiration for scholars dealing with Pan-Asianism down to the present day.

Outside Japan, Pan-Asianism fell into total disrepute, especially in China, Korea, and the Philippines, where it was regarded as synonymous with collaboration with the Japanese occupiers. In India, however, which had not been occupied by the Japanese, Pan-Asianism retained some of its prewar appeal. From the Indian perspective, the war waged by Japan had brought forward Indian independence by years, if not decades. This "positive" assessment of the war against the British Empire was reflected, for example, in the dissenting opinion of Indian Justice Radhabinod Pal (1886–1967) at the International Military Tribunal for the Far East; in the elevation of Subhas Chandra Bose, who had cooperated closely with Japan during the war (II:27), to the status of a national hero; and in the writings of the prominent historian and diplomat K. M. Panikkar (II:31). Pan-Asianism was also the inspiration—at least in part—behind initiatives to launch the nonaligned movement by so-called Third World countries, notably at Bandung (II:33).

Chapter Thirty-One

K. M. Panikkar: "Asia and Western Dominance," 1953

Christopher W. A. Szpilman

Kavalam Madhava Panikkar (1895–1963), born in what is now Kerala State, southern India, was educated at Oxford University, where he studied history, and at the Middle Temple (London), where he read for the bar (for Panikkar's biography, cf. Banerjee 1977). On his return to India he had a varied career. In his twenties, he lectured at Aligarh and Calcutta universities, then turned to journalism as editor of the nationalist newspapers *Swarajya* (Own Land) and (after 1925) *The Hindustan Times*. Subsequently he served as a senior bureaucrat in various Indian states. After India became independent in 1947, Panikkar's involvement in the nationalist movement, and his personal links with India's first prime minister, Jawaharlal Nehru (1889–1964), led to appointments as India's ambassador to China (1948–1952), Egypt (1952–1953), and France (1956–1959). Although a stroke forced him to retire from the diplomatic service in 1959, he made enough of a recovery to resume a career in education. Toward the end of his life he served as vice-chancellor of Kashmir and Mysore universities.

Panikkar was a prolific writer whose publications included poetry, novels, newspaper articles, and even translations of classical Greek plays into Malayalam verse. In 1955 he published *In Two Chinas*, an account of his experiences as India's ambassador before, during, and after the communist takeover, in which he adopted a sympathetic stance toward the Chinese Communist Party. His autobiography was published posthumously in 1977.

Although Panikkar's writings ranged over many subjects, his main passion was history, and it is for his achievements in this field that he is best known. While he published works on various aspects of Indian history (e.g., *Sri Harsha of Kanauj: A Monograph on the History of India in the Frst Half of the 7th Century A.D.*, 1922, and *Gulab Singh: 1792–1858, Founder of Kashmir*, 1930), Southeast Asia, and even Africa, his primary interest as a historian lay in East–West relations. On this subject he published a number of specialized monographs with self-explanatory titles—such as *Malabar and the Portuguese* (1929) and *Malabar and the Dutch* (1931)—for which he had done extensive archival research in Portugal and Holland. However, his many years of research on relations between East and West were summarized in his *Asia and Western Dominance: A Survey of the Vasco da Gama Epoch of Asian History, 1498–1945*, published in 1953, a highly popular work that went through at least sixteen editions and from which an excerpt is reproduced here.

Panikkar's book was written in the political climate of the Cold War. Western colonialism was in its last throes, communism had triumphed in China, Asian nationalism was on the rise, and plans were being made to hold what was to be known as the 1955 Bandung Conference (see II:33). The West and Western civilization appeared discredited. This context perhaps accounts for the fact that, in the book, Panikkar plays down the West's impact on Asia. Unlike Ōkawa Shūmei (see II:4), who perceived relations between Asia and Europe as an enduring, destructive, but also mutually enriching conflict between equals, Panikkar insists that it was Asia that by and large had shaped Western culture and civilization, not vice versa. Even in the three centuries that followed the voyage of Vasco da Gama in 1498, he contended, Europe exerted no significant impact on India or China. As he saw it, the West began to shape Asia only after the advent of the industrial revolution, which for the first time in history provided the West with overwhelming material advantages. This material superiority enabled the Western powers to oppress and exploit Asia, and it was in turn this oppression that, by breeding resentment, gave rise to Pan-Asianism.

On this basis one might assume that Panikkar regarded Pan-Asianism not as an independent ideology but as a reaction to Western oppression, without which no Asian solidarity could have arisen. However, that would not be an accurate assessment. For, although he indeed stressed this reactive character of Pan-Asianism, Panikkar believed that there existed certain values shared by all of Asia, including East Asia and India. These values, however, were not shared uniformly. In an argument vaguely reminiscent of Rousseau's "noble savage" myth, Panikkar took the view that only the cultures of the "common people" shared a substratum of values that accounted for (or perhaps more accurately had the potential to create) Asian unity (particularly in East Asia), whereas the highly sophisticated cultures produced by India and China, Hinduism, and Confucianism, peculiar to their countries of origin and mutually incompatible, hindered the emergence of Asian unity.

The political climate of the Cold War, combined with his hatred of Western imperialism, informed Panikkar's positive assessment of the Bolshevik

Revolution in Russia and his sympathetic attitude toward the communist revolution in China. The October Revolution, he asserted, was authentic and in accordance with Asian values. In the Asian part of Russia, he regarded it as the "work of Asian people themselves" (Panikkar 1953: 250). Moreover, the Russian Revolution had undermined the moral and intellectual authority of the West over Asia and contributed to the collapse of Western colonialism. Before the revolution, "the moulding of the Asian mind . . . was almost exclusively [achieved] by Western Europe and America." (Panikkar 1953: 253). By the end of the 1920s, however, "new [nationalist] movements had begun to develop in Asia reflecting the revolutionary trends which had their origin in Russia," movements that "gained moral strength by the mere existence of a Revolutionary Asia" (Panikkar 1953: 251).

This positive assessment of the Russian Revolution is a point that Panikkar shared with Japanese pan-Asianists such as Ōkawa Shūmei and Mitsukawa Kametarō and the Chinese revolutionary leader Sun Yat-sen, who went so far as to see in Soviet Russia a potential ally against Western and specifically Anglo-Saxon imperialism (see I:25). While this similarity was probably a coincidence (in both cases, hatred of Western imperialism led to the idealization of its antithesis, Soviet communism), there is no doubt that Panikkar was to some degree influenced by Japanese Pan-Asianism. This is evident in his references to Okakura Tenshin (Kakuzō, 1862–1913, see I:7 and I:8) and the Japanese poet Noguchi Yonejirō (Yone, 1875–1949).

Like Japanese pan-Asianists, Panikkar regarded Japanese aggression on the Asian continent as a reaction to Western power and expansionism, for which the West was ultimately responsible. From this perspective, he saw the Pacific War as "the logical outcome not only of [Japan's] own aggressive policy but the policy followed by America after the First Great War of forcing Japan into a diplomatic isolation" (Panikkar 1953: 308) and the tragic events in China following the Sino-Japanese War as not wholly the result of Japanese aggression but also of the Western presence. He asserted that the responsibility for what had happened in China "rests squarely on the shoulders of the [Christian] missionaries" (Panikkar 1953: 453).

His anti-Western attitude did not prevent Panikkar from condemning Japanese imperialism. For Panikkar, Japan was an "aggressor" in Asia, just like the Western powers, whose ranks it had joined. Japan's Asian policy, he noted, "suffered from a fundamental contradiction. Her first object was the exclusion of European authority from Asia in which she had the support and sympathy of Asian people. Side by side with this, she had also been an apt pupil of the Great Powers in their policy of expansion, and the promulgation of the Imperial Way over the peoples of Asia seemed to her to be a divine mission" (Panikkar 1953: 282).

It was this aggressive Western-style aspect of Japanese foreign policy that, in Panikkar's view, motivated Japanese reaction to Russia's October Revolution, which "instead of raising any hopes in Japan caused it the greatest alarm. Japan had joined the ranks of 'aggressors' and her interest naturally was that any revolution in Asia against the West should be solely for national independence and not for radical changes in society" (Panikkar 1953: 254). This fear of the Soviet Union was partly responsible, he contended, for driving Japan into an alliance with Germany and Italy in the 1930s.

The great importance Panikkar attributed to the October Revolution accounts for a major difference between him and most other Pan-Asianists, for, unlike them, Panikkar did not regard the Russo-Japanese War (1904–1905) as the decisive event in the collapse of Western colonialism in Asia. Consequently, Japan's triumph over Russia receives little treatment in his book.

Source (English in the original)
K. M. Panikkar, *Asia and Western Dominance: A Survey of the Vasco da Gama Epoch of Asian History, 1498–1945*. London: George Allen & Unwin, 493–95.

When the Asian peoples recovered from the "first intoxication of the West," as Yone Noguchi called it, they were able to fall back and find sustenance for their intellectual self-respect in a culture which had attracted some of the superior minds of the West. In fact, while resistance to political domination of Europe provided the motive force of the new nationalism, its justification and strength lay in a growing appreciation of its own culture to which European scholarship had also materially contributed.

If nationalism developed directly by resistance and indirectly by the recovery of historical sense and pride in cultural achievement as a result of Western contact, the sense of Asianism is exclusively the counterpart of the solidarity of European feeling. Before the end of the nineteenth century there was no such feeling as Asianism. But in the beginning of this century we find the great Japanese artist Okakura Kakuzo opening a book with the startling declaration "Asia is one." Undoubtedly there is much that is common in the tradition of non-Islamic Asia, in religious approach, social organization, art and so on. From Japan to India the civilizations of Asian countries are united by certain common features which cannot be explained solely by the influence of Buddhism. Ancestor-reverence, family relationships, both of which are outside the sphere of Buddhism, are common features of the social organization of the non-Islamic East. . . .

The idea that there is no common social or spiritual background for an attitude of Asianism to develop is therefore not wholly correct. In any case, if it did not exist, the common experience of a hundred years has created a political background. All the Asian countries have had to go through the same suffering, fight the same battles and meet the same enemy. This evolution towards political freedom has been, generally speaking, on parallel lines. The racial arrogance of the Europeans, their assumed attitude of intellectual and moral superiority, and even the religious propaganda to which all the Asian countries were subjected, gave rise to a common political outlook in the Asia of the twentieth century. Books like the *Futurism of Young Asia* by the Indian socialist, Benoy Kumar Sarkar (see I.21), were indicative of this change of attitude.

It should also be remembered that the European nations in emphasizing their solidarity, their European-ness in dealing with Asian countries, inevitably gave rise to a common feeling of Asian-ness. Even in India, where nationals of other European countries enjoyed no political rights, the division was between Europeans and Indians and not between Englishmen and Indians. The exclusive clubs in India were not for Englishmen, but for Europeans. Special schools and educational facilities that existed were also for Europeans. In China, where all European countries enjoyed political privileges, the European communities went to great lengths to present a united front. Even when the Franco-German War was being fought in Europe, the pressure of the doctrine of European solidarity against Asians compelled the German Minister to line up behind his French colleagues in the affair of Tientsin. Similar was the attitude of the Powers to Japan during the period of negotiations for treaty revision. Japanese efforts to sign bilateral treaties were frustrated on numerous occasions by the desire of the Western countries to stand together. From 1880 to 1914—during the period of imperialism—the Europeans were united against Asia, and this attitude, in its turn, gave birth to a sense of Asianism which even the aggressive actions of Japan and its proclaimed policy "of standing in with the West" did not seriously undermine.

Chapter Thirty-Two

Eguchi Bokurō: "Asia in World History," 1953

Curtis Anderson Gayle

During much of his lifetime Eguchi Bokurō (1911–1989) sought to fuse history writing with larger events taking place in both Japan and Asia. Born in Saga Prefecture, Eguchi attended Tokyo Imperial University and in 1953 became a professor in the history department at the University of Tokyo. After retiring in 1971, Eguchi moved to Tsuda College, where he continued to teach until 1988. For many Marxists like Eguchi, particularly during the early postwar years, being a historian meant not only writing history but also taking part in mass movements that located history writing within the changing subjectivity and consciousness of everyday life. During the 1950s, he was one of the organizing members in the Movement for a People's History (*Kokuminteki rekishigaku undō*), which mobilized factory workers, women, students, and farmers to put both pen to paper and feet to the pavement (Gayle 2003). Eguchi subsequently became an important member of the Japan Council against the Hydrogen and Atomic Bombs (*Nihon Gensuikyō*).

Eguchi looked at the relationship between Japan, Asia, and the postwar world in a very profound way. Shortly after World War II, he began to explore the relationship between Marxist ideas, Asia, and the history of the modern world. Inspired by sweeping but not always smooth movements toward decolonization in China, India, and Southeast Asia, he stood at the crossroads of a new generation of progressive historians in Japan who saw in Asia the key to both modernity and a new international system they hoped would emerge in the second half of the twentieth century. Inspired far more by Mao Zedong's (Mao Tse-tung, 1893–1976) China than by the United States, the United Kingdom, or even the Soviet Union, Eguchi sought in much of his work to rethink the postwar historical and political position of Japan. Unlike the wartime Kyoto School, which essentially concurred with the imperial policy of creating a new kind of Japan-centric world history at the expense of

Asia and for the purpose of colonial domination (Heisig and Maraldo 1995), Eguchi envisioned a new phase of world history based on the very decolonization of those nations that had borne the brunt of Japanese imperialism and its "assimilation policies" to linguistically and culturally Japanize places like Taiwan and Korea. Thus, although the question of "Asia" was paramount to both the Kyoto School and to postwar historians such as Eguchi, their historical outlooks and indeed the historical environment from which they gazed out on Asia operated within vastly different modalities. Rather than taking it as the ordained nexus of an imperial-centric Asian hierarchy, Eguchi saw Japan as a peripheral presence in postwar Asia, especially when taken together with a new China that had finally awakened to independence and socialism as well as with an independent India. Asian independence and its future were issues taken up at the Bandung Conference, held in Indonesia in 1955 (see II:33), the latter taking as its objective the articulation of a new world independent of the two superpowers.

Written in 1953, the same year as the Korean War came to a conclusion, Eguchi's "Asia in World History" both anticipates and seeks to push forward an age of Asian decolonization from European and American colonial rule. Since decolonization brought with it independence, the real question for Eguchi was whether this new Asia would work as an integrated space of cooperation or whether it would produce a new series of inter- and intraregional conflicts in the aftermath of colonial domination. Would Asia become a place for regional networks of integration, or would it decompress into local and regional conflicts that made a mockery of the ideals of decolonization? Eguchi certainly hoped that the rise of China would help answer this question: although he argues in the source passage for the United Nations to recognize the People's Republic of China (PRC), which only took place in 1971, Eguchi also claims that the founding of the PRC was itself something that had already begun to shift the international balance of power in the aftermath of World War II.

Eguchi wrote "Asia in World History" just as this question was coming to have immediate yet ever complex relevance for Japan itself. Although the Cold War had become a reality in Japan with the Reverse Course of 1948 and the subsequent suppression of Japanese labor unions and other voices of dissent, the outbreak of the Korean War in 1950 suggested for Eguchi and others that America's geopolitical strategy in East Asia included trying to "roll back" communism on the Korean peninsula and eventually in China as well. This brought a resounding hue and cry from the left in Japan for a number of reasons. First, it signaled the possibility that America was intent on overthrowing an independent, socialist China. Second, Eguchi and others feared this would in turn lead to a larger attempt to obfuscate decolonization in Asia.

Third, the Korean War also placed the pacifist Article 9 of the postwar Japanese Constitution in jeopardy by bringing Japan into the war effort. Fourth, Japan's participation in rebuilding heavy industries for military production to aid U.S. and UN forces on the Korean peninsula also meant the further consolidation of Japanese capitalism within a conservative government seen as unfit to bring Japan into a new age of independence and democracy in Asia.

Perhaps most tellingly, Eguchi feared that the onset of the Cold War and its penetration into Asia brought with it the possibility that China, Japan, India, and Southeast Asia might once again become pawns of empires, whether capitalist or socialist. Eguchi thus feared that the long-awaited age of cooperation among Asian nations could very well degenerate into the (bi) polarization of Asia at the hands of both the United States and the Soviet Union. Just as Mao Zedong eventually cast an eye of suspicion on Moscow, Eguchi and like-minded historians in Japan often had mixed feelings about the Soviet Union. Needless to say, they did credit the Bolshevik Revolution of 1917 with bringing the doctrines of Marxism-Leninism into the purview of the nation-state, and they were influenced by Lenin's and Stalin's theories of nationhood and independence (Forman 1998). At the same time, however, Marxist historians such as Eguchi were wary of both parties to the Cold War and, conversely, saw in the PRC and in India strong beacons for Japan and for East and Southeast Asia.

At the time he wrote "Asia in World History," Eguchi was therefore quite interested in how Asia might make its mark on the world stage and, from this perspective, discussed the issue of Asian colonization and how it had been historically thrust into a long series of colonial relationships with Europe. In his discussion of European and Asian history, Eguchi often utilizes Marxian historical terminology and in particular the stage theory of history. He likewise often refers to a synthesis of historical events to suggest their synthesis in a more advanced historical epoch. What is clear from the text translated here, moreover, is that he saw the end of World War II not just as a time for Japan to rebuild but also as an age in which both Japan and Asia could help redefine world history itself. In this important sense, Eguchi represents an early example of thinking about the relationship between Japan and Asia in a way that could take stock of the postcolonial world and the manifold contributions (or sacrifices) made by colonized nations to the development of imperial metropoles. In this sense, he realized that an age of postcolonial nations in Asia carried with it the potential to write a new history from the non-West and in the voices of ordinary people in places like Japan, China, and India.

Eguchi and other historians in the 1950s, however, tended to focus more on European colonialism than on Japanese colonialism. This was because they wanted Japan to arrive at its own particular "postcolonial moment" just like China and India. Although clearly cognizant of how Japan had colonized Asia in previous decades, through their historical narratives Eguchi and others also emphasized the present moment of Japan's "colonization," or subordination, to the United States in order to elide the historical trajectory of Japan with those of newly independent nations. If Asia was to claim its rightful place within some kind of postwar world history, Japan would have to be rendered historically as a victim of Western empire much in the same way that other Asian nations had been. Thus, even though Eguchi did elsewhere give attention to the Meiji era (1868–1912) and how Japan had set the stage for its own age of empire, he also spent ample time—especially during the early postwar era—theorizing how the Japanese *minzoku*, or nation, might go about shaking off the yoke of American imperialism. In this crucial sense, a progressive kind of cultural nationalism worked in tandem with the belief in a new form of Asian internationalism and mutual cooperation in a new era.

The text translated here, written in 1953, reflects Eguchi's firm belief that postwar Asia could finally take charge of its own destiny. For Eguchi, the rise of Asia in aftermath of the Japanese Empire would have to avoid the mistakes of the past whereby one hegemonic nation sought to dominate the rest. It was for this very reason that he and other Marxist historians at the time attempted, through both their own history writing and helping to organize populist-oriented history-writing campaigns, to write Japanese history into an extended and indefinite postcolonial moment. The history written by Eguchi and others sought to elide Japan's own past and present into the historical trajectories of China, India, and all those whose time for national liberation had come. Thus, Eguchi's references to the Asian nations in the source passage and in many of his other writings during the early postwar period refer not only to those peoples who could begin to claim their own historical moments but also to a Japan that might join in a new version of "Asianism" based on different historical grounds and telos from prewar imperialist versions. Although in the source passage Eguchi does take ample note of Asian liberation from prewar Japanese imperialism, as I have pointed out elsewhere (Gayle 2003) Japan existed for Eguchi and some of his colleagues as both a former imperial power and, simultaneously, a clean slate on which to write a new history of the present as an Asian nation.

The more fundamental problem of origins is, however, never far from hand. Eguchi does not really tell what he means by "Asia." As Edward Said and others have amply shown (Said 1995), Orientalist designations of Asia from the seventeenth century onward have included parts of the Middle East in an expanded conglomerate of imperial terrain that covered vast and heterogeneous swaths of the globe. What Eguchi seems to mean by "Asia" are those regions referred to today as East, Southeast, and South Asia. Yet there is no discussion in this passage of the historical grounds for calling a certain space "Asia." Eguchi ends up utilizing historical and geopolitical generalizations to make the point that the national liberation of non-Western peoples should not just take place in a space of emotive dissonance but might actually convene around nations like China and India in order to forge the basis for a more balanced international order. Although this is certainly not what has happened in either the postwar or the post–Cold War era, Eguchi's focus on Asia in a postcolonial age is something that remains as valid now as it was then.

Source (translation from the Japanese original by Curtis Anderson Gayle)
Eguchi Bokurō, "Sekaishi ni okeru Ajia" (Asia in World History), reproduced in Eguchi Bokurō, *Eguchi Bokurō Chosakushū* (Collected Works of Eguchi Bokurō). Aoki Shoten, 1953, vol. 4, 121–27.

1.

Asian history, particularly in the modern era, is no longer something that can be confined to the region which we ordinarily think of as "Asia." The population of Asia constitutes more than half of the entire world and by virtue of this fact alone Asia does have an important role to play in the larger development of the modern world today.

From the history of the modern world we can see that human society has made much progress, as evidenced by the development of modern industries, traffic organization and medical facilities. Individuals in the modern world have also reached new heights of self-consciousness and we have seen the overall development of societies from feudalism to civil society. Here we might ask what these kinds of modern developments have meant for Asia. In order to answer this question, it is first necessary to acknowledge that Asian development has come relatively late. It is, however, also important not to overlook the fact that the epoch of modern European progress has brought with it dramatic change to and has cast a dark shadow over Asia. The dawning of modern Europe during the Renaissance and age of exploration was a time in which colonialism began to appear at the barrel of a gun. The period of the Industrial Revolution was, likewise, one in which Britain possessed the power of industrial development and established its international status. It was during this period, during the latter half of the eighteenth century, that the British East India Company staked its claim in India and beat out the French in efforts to undermine Indian society from its very roots. From the age of colonialism onward, industrialization in Asia brought with it everything from foreign consumer goods to new rail links in remote farming villages. Modern architecture also began to line city streets in Asia as poverty and social unease became widespread. In Europe and America, modern civil society, the basis of capitalist development, began to take hold. This also meant, however, the start of the subjugation of foreign countries and along with it the perpetuation and even strengthening of feudal systems.

Looked at in this way, we can see that what is often referred to as the "late development" of Asia is not simply that but has instead been an attempt to catch up with the level of capitalist development in European countries. It is even possible to say that without its conquest of Asia, modern Europe would not have been able to develop in the way that it did. Of course, it was not only Asia that became a victim of Western imperialism. This kind of thing also took place in America and Europe as certain states established capitalist systems, such as in Eastern Europe nations and in Spain, where quite anomalous societies were created. As a result, within these capitalist societies' revolutionary forces critical of capitalism also began to grow. Here the most basic lesson to be learnt from Asian history is that the brunt of capitalism has been borne by ordinary people (*minshū*) and as a result these nations (*minzoku*) have often been forced to live under harsh economic conditions.

If we consider the heavy burden borne historically by Asian societies amidst such conditions of poverty, it is possible to objectively say that popular resistance to and critiques of the modern capitalist world led by European powers are completely natural. During the period when socialist theory was established, through the industrial revolutions of 1848 and in response to the development of European societies, various movements of strong popular resistance, such as the 1850s Taiping Rebellion in China and the Sepoy Revolt in India, began to threaten European empires and, in particular, the British Empire. Within late-developing societies in Asia nascent forms of national resistance, even though they were important internationally, nevertheless came to face many difficulties and were eventually quashed. As the push of imperial powers into Asia grew and what is often called the age of empire took off, various peoples who were feeling the brunt of imperialism even began to turn against one another. First, both Japan and China were forced into unequal treaties with the West and subsequently both began to target smaller countries in their geographical neighborhood. For instance, the Sino-Japanese War of 1895 was the result of Korea's being forced into colonization and dependency toward both Japan and China simultaneously. The 1900 Boxer Rebellion in China also shows in a microcosm how these conditions served as a driving force in modern Asian history. This incident began in Shandong and spread to Tientsin, eventually reaching railroad facilities built with foreign capital and leading to an anti-foreign popular movement that was eventually put down by Western and Japanese military power, solidifying the semi-colonial status of China and in a most obvious way bringing to light relations between modern imperial powers that had divided up Asia and indeed the world. Secondly, although this event also led to the Russo-Japanese War and an age where modern imperial powers began to fight against one another, in Asia Japan subdued China militarily and used its military power to join forces with the United Kingdom and thus garner an important place within the larger confrontation between empires. Finally, this same year (1900), a fledgling popular resistance movement took shape in Northern China and, in a separate development, revolutionary figure Sun Yat-sen established contact with the Governor of Taiwan through Southern China and worked with him to help bring about the overthrow of the Qing [Ch'ing] Dynasty in the Huizhou Incident.

Amidst the difficulties facing these movements during the next half century, the question of how these kinds of fledgling popular resistance movements developed, how they were organized, and how they brought with them the desire for a new awakening toward liberation in Asia constitute seminal issues in Asian history. Asian history during the twentieth-century, moreover, cannot be fully understood without taking into consideration World Wars I and II. World War I brought huge changes to Asia and in the process caused great suffering among various Asian peoples. Yet it was also at this time that the economic leverage of Western countries—preoccupied with domestic military production— over Asian colonies began to weaken and, through the spread of capitalism into Asia, the desire for liberation among Asian peoples began to grow remarkably. The Russian Revolution of 1917, which occurred during the final stages of World War I, likewise gave a boost to anti-imperialist movements and had a very concrete impact on Asian movements for national liberation.

If we look at the May Fourth Movement of 1919 and the actual founding of the People's Republic in 1949, we can say that revolutions in China have encouraged international aspirations for independence which signalled the dawning of a new era in world history. In this regard the Moscow-based Comintern, which was established in 1919, paid particular attention to the possibility of revolutions in Asia. Within such an environment, Sun Yat-sen, who had about twenty years' experience working toward revolution, became pro-communist and pro-Russia.

World War I brought huge changes to Japan's own place in the international system as well. Japan was, without a doubt, able to become a stronger and more independent state as a result of the war. But the leaders of Japan chose not to utilize this opportunity to move toward democracy at home and instead chose the path of continuing to build military superiority in order to bring most of Asia to its knees. The Japanese state wanted both domestic and international crises through which it could steadily increase its tight-grip over Asia. Yet the deterioration of conditions in Asia, as witnessed by events such as the Manchurian Incident, war with China, and the Pacific War, brought the kind of international pressure to Asia that eventually led to the greater organized awakening of Asian peoples. These events themselves helped to gradually set in motion a process of resistance by subjugated peoples to Japanese imperialism. In this way, then, a new stage of Asian liberation from Japanese imperialism became a reality.

2.

It is also clear that the establishing of the People's Republic of China in 1949 has been something relevant not only to the liberation of Asian peoples, but has also made its mark on what might be called the "two worlds" of the bi-polar order. China's emergence has in fact brought with it a monumental shift in the entire international balance of power.

It is already well known that the post–World War II world has seen both the emergence of the American Marshall Plan in 1947 and the formation of the Cominform by the Soviet Union, events which led to the start of the Cold War. The Paris Peace Conference in April of 1949, on the other hand, banned atomic weapons, created the North Atlantic Treaty Organization (NATO), and declared its formal opposition to oppressive measures against popular movements for liberation in Greece, Indonesia, Indochina (Vietnam and Cambodia) and Malaysia. In this sense, Asian nations have not been afforded the luxury of remaining on the sidelines of the Cold War, a development that has meant various kinds of popular resistance that had been simmering for a long time were now finally able to rise up and take advantage of the anti-imperial climate to make their mark on the world stage. Both the policies of America, which has an overwhelming influence in the post-war capitalist system, and the problems of Asian nations themselves have now, however, become key international concerns. By 1947, United States trade and investment in Asia was growing in a remarkable way, but it was also just at this time that the United States implemented the Truman Doctrine and Marshall Plan for Europe. In Asia, it likewise set up the Far Eastern Economic Commission and put forward an Asian version of the Marshall Plan geared toward strengthening anti-communist regimes. The United States then announced its Plan for the Development of Late-Developed Areas (*Kōshin Chi'iki Kaihatsu Keikaku*) in January of 1949. Such policies were designed to counter the rise of revolutionary movements in China and, even though they were met with negative reactions by Asian nations, it was clear that such events were helping to set the Cold War into place in Asia. It was within this environment that the People's Republic of China became a reality.

From 1945 until 1949, China had been one of the five Permanent Members of the United Nations Security Council and thus the establishment of the People's Republic of China impacted upon the internal power balance of this most important international institution in the post-war era. The new government formally demanded that it be recognized by the United Nations and officially replace the Republic of China regime which had been recognized as the legitimate government in China. Since the new government in Peking was now in a position to economically and politically gain the support of non-aligned and small to mid-sized countries, its formal recognition by the United Nations became a very serious issue. Although in the beginning of 1950 Peking once again demanded that it be formally recognized by the United Nations as the sole legitimate representative of China, no solution could be found and the problem was deferred. It was at this point that the Soviet Union began to oppose the attendance of the Taiwan representative at various United Nations committees and it subsequently refused to attend important committee meetings. In late June of 1950, just as the Soviet Union was boycotting the United Nations, the Korean War broke out.

Here it is important to remember that even before these events the United Nations was already caught up in the Cold War and was thus facing considerable challenges. With the outbreak of the Korean War and the passage of various resolutions by America and the United Nations Security Council in the formal absence of the Soviet Union, the use of military force by United Nations troops was officially sanctioned on the Korean Peninsula. The Soviet Union eventually returned to its seat and began to once again assert its views and the United Nations was able to at least give the appearance of stability to the world. Yet it must also be pointed out that these machinations at the United Nations in 1950 reveal its limits as a forum in which disputes can be solved through the rule of law. These limitations in the function of the United Nations soon also became apparent to peoples in Asia. Asian nations thus saw fit to assert their own claims to independence and autonomy even without the formal support of the United Nations or recognition for their cause under international law. In this sense, democracy was in deep crisis. . . .

3.

The history of modern Asia does, however, also show us in stark terms the limits of today's world. As mentioned earlier, even though Asia comprises more than half of the world's population, Asians continue to be victims of the development of the modern world. When talking about Asia from an Asian position, it is essential to pay attention to this important point. It is also particularly necessary for Japanese people to reflect with contrition upon their own position in modern Asian history. It thus seems reckless for Japan either to say that it is the centre of Asia, or to talk of racial or cultural commonalities with Asia, in order to foster its claim to speak for all of Asia [i.e., to lead Asia].

Looking at Asia within the history of the modern world, we might also ask what paths of historical development have been historically possible. It is hard to deny that in terms of modern development, especially in the formation of capitalism and the establishment of democracy, Asia has been late on the scene. The real problem, however, is not that Asia has been behind, but that its late development has placed it on the receiving end of exploitation in modern world development, leading the development of Asian societies to become more and more warped.

It is within these kinds of conditions, moreover, that peoples once left out of modern democratic politics are now seeking to stand on their own two feet. Various Asian leaders are utilizing European models in order to gain independence from Europe or to protect their independent existence. Although the external pressure coming from modern imperial powers on these countries is strong, in Asia democracy and nationalism have already moved away from issues affecting the concrete interests of the nation, marking an age in which both democracy and nationalism have become hollow ideas without any real substance. Only in the case of Japan has an Asian country, though imperfectly, resisted the West and gone on to become an imperial power. But there is not much chance that Japan will repeat, either at home or in Asia, the wholesale victimization of peoples and nations. Nevertheless, movements seeking Asian independence and development have continued to seem like grasps in the dark. With this historical reality in mind, it is necessary to rethink theories about modern society so that they can better reflect things happening in everyday life and speak to the overwhelming interests of the people. This means looking at communism not as an ideology, but first and foremost as something that can develop as the starting point for solutions to the concrete problems of the people (it is perhaps more correct to say that from the beginning communism has been just this).

The modern world has produced many hardships and many victims in Asia and during the past three years the Korean War has seen many casualties. The truce declared in this war by no means, however, suggests a final resolution to the conflict. On the contrary, during the war itself various forms of military action, diplomatic negotiations, and attempts by the United Nations and member countries to mediate illustrate the desire for peace and in concrete, historical ways also suggest how peace may be brought about. This desire can also be seen in the growth of the people's power not only in Asia, but in the world more generally. In either case, the kinds of things experienced in twentieth century Asia thus far have been crucial to the independence of Asians themselves and stand on their own as important moments within the larger advance of world history itself.

Chapter Thirty-Three

The Bandung Conference, 1955

Kristine Dennehy

In April 1955, representatives from twenty-nine countries gathered in Bandung, Indonesia, for the landmark Asian-African Conference, hosted by the prime ministers of Burma, India, Indonesia, Pakistan, and Ceylon. While the participants hailed from a diverse array of countries in Asia, Africa, and the Middle East, the origins of the conference can be traced to the early post–World War II ideas of Pan-Asianism expressed at the First International Asian Relations Conference held in New Delhi in 1947. In this context, Pan-Asianism was closely tied to the anticolonial struggles of Asian peoples, such as the Indians who were on the verge of gaining independence from Britain after centuries of Western domination. One of the most significant achievements of the conference was its success in paving the way for the subsequent development of a nonaligned bloc in the context of ongoing decolonization in the midst of the Cold War. After Bandung, newly independent nations and those that were still struggling for independence now had a viable alternative to alignment with the global superpowers, the United States and the Soviet Union. One of the other major successes of the conference was the moderating role played by Zhou Enlai (Chou En-lai, 1898–1976) in bringing communist China to the table to negotiate with other Asian countries, including neighboring Southeast Asian countries like the Philippines that were fearful of Chinese communist influence within their own national borders.

The agenda for the conference focused on the following five points: economic cooperation, cultural cooperation, human rights and self-determination, problems of dependent peoples, and world peace. As noted in the opening remarks by the president of Indonesia, Achmad Sukarno (1901–1970), the cohesive force uniting the countries gathered was the common experience, as "colored peoples," of material and spiritual suffering at the hands of white Western imperial powers in the modern era. In addition to the five sponsoring countries, the other participants included Afghanistan, Cambodia, the People's Republic of China, Egypt, Ethiopia, Gold Coast, Iran, Iraq, Japan, Jordan, Laos, Lebanon, Liberia, Libya, Nepal, the Philippines, Saudi Arabia, Sudan, Syria, Thailand, Turkey, Democratic Republic of (North) Vietnam, State of Vietnam, and Yemen. Although Japan was exceptional in having emulated Western military and diplomatic tactics to maintain its own sovereignty and then, in turn, colonize other Asian peoples, it still shared the geographic proximity, the racial characteristics, and the historical experience of having been a victim of gunboat diplomacy in the mid-nineteenth century. Furthermore, only three years before, in 1952, it had regained its full sovereignty with the end of the Allied occupation. In this sense, the pan-Asian commonalities were based primarily on geography, race, and subjection to Western military dominance.

In his opening speech to the conference delegates, Sukarno spoke from his personal experience as a nationalist who had been imprisoned by the colonial Dutch government in the 1920s and 1930s and lived in exile for a time before returning to Indonesia in 1942 and working under the Japanese occupation authorities during wartime. He was then elected the first president after Indonesia had gained independence from the Netherlands. At the Bandung Conference, Sukarno stressed the newfound historical agency of formerly colonized peoples who had struggled under such dire and violent circumstances for their independence. This emphasis on the efforts of Asian and African peoples themselves was meant to bring attention to the new moral and ethical responsibilities that Asians and Africans had to take up in the postcolonial age of Cold War tensions.

The participants at Bandung saw themselves as uniquely positioned to reject a restrictive alliance with either of the superpowers. Instead, they preferred to join together with other formerly colonized countries in search of a less confrontational approach to international relations and seek mutual economic development, as stated in the Ten Principles of the Final Communique of the Conference (see source 1). They were also critical of the current workings of the United Nations, which they saw as perpetuating the big-power politics of Western nation-states. In his opening speech the delegate of the Philippines, Carlos Romulo (1899–1985) stresses that the nation-state is not adequate to the task of solving global problems in the nuclear age:

> . . . for the primary goals of economic transformation and well-being and peace, the nation no longer suffices. Western European man today is paying the terrible price for preserving too long the narrow and inadequate instrument of the nation-state in an epoch when nationalism, as such, can solve only the least of our problems and leaves us powerless to meet the more serious ones. . . . Indeed, the great travail of the Western world, its conflicts, rivalries, and wars have

derived in no small degree from the fact that the nation, as such, has outlived its usefulness as an instrument of progress. (Holland 1955: 15–18)

Ironically, while leaders like Sukarno were distinguished by their nationalist fervor, at the Bandung Conference they emphasized the limitations of the nation-state political framework inherited from Western powers in the modern era. Instead, they strove to form new alliances and open channels of communication that would provide an alternative model for mutual progress and prosperity on a wide-scale regional basis. Both Sukarno and Romulo were quick to point out that the legacies of colonialism were still formidable in 1955, particularly in the form of economic underdevelopment. By stressing the exploitative nature of the global economy in the age of empire, they were also making links to the contemporary legacies of those uneven economic relationships even after former colonies like Indonesia had achieved political independence.

They also distinguished Asian countries in general as being ahead of their African brothers in the process of decolonization while also being poised to serve as a model in this historically inevitable transition to independence. Just before the Bandung delegates met in 1955, the Vietnamese triumphed in their anticolonial struggle against the French, and this situation in Indochina provided the immediate backdrop for the calls from the conference organizers to support such independence movements in Asia and beyond in places such as Tunisia. The positive contributions of Asian leaders at the 1954 Geneva Conference on Indochina also served to bolster their legitimacy as proponents for a new kind of Asian leadership in global conflicts, particularly those of an anticolonial nature. In this sense, the vision of Pan-Asianism that was being promoted at Bandung in 1955 transcended geographic boundaries, with its emphasis on overcoming the inherently problematic underpinnings of nation-state rivalries backed by military force. This kind of Pan-Asianism shared, above all, its anticolonialism with prewar forms of Asian regionalism, but with a special emphasis on nonalignment in the context of Cold War division of the world in the American and Soviet camps.

Source 1 (English in the original)
Excerpts from the Speech by President Sokarno of the Republic of Indonesia at the Opening of the Asian-African Congress in Bandung, Indonesia, on 18 April 1955, The Ministry of Foreign Affairs, Republic of Indonesia (ed.), *Asia-Africa Speaks from Bandung*. Djakarta: Ministry of Foreign Affairs, 1955, 19–29.

It is my great honor and privilege on this historic day to bid you welcome to Indonesia.

. . .

As I survey this Hall and the distinguished guests gathered here, my heart is filled with emotion. This is the first intercontinental conference of coloured people in the history of mankind.

. . .

For many generations our peoples were the voiceless ones in the world, disregarded and living in poverty and humiliation. Then our nations demanded—nay fought—for independence and achieved independence, and with that independence came responsibility.

. . .

In the last fifty years there have been more developments and more material progress than in the previous five hundred years. Man has learned to control many of the scourges which once threatened him. But has man's political skill marched hand-in-hand with his technical and scientific skill? The answer is "no." The political skill of man has been far outstripped by his technical skill, and what he has made he cannot be sure of controlling. The result of this is fear and man gasps for safety and morality. Perhaps now in the history of world society, governments and statesmanship need to be based upon the highest code of morality and ethics. And in political terms, what is the highest code of morality? It is the subordination of everything to the wellbeing of mankind. Many who are in places of high power think, rather, of controlling the world.

. . .

How is it possible to be disinterested about colonialism? For us, colonialism is not something far off and distant. We have known it in all its ruthlessness and we have seen the immense human wastage it causes, the poverty it causes and the heritage it leaves behind when it is eventually and reluctantly driven out by the inevitable march of history. We have experienced all this. We cannot yet say that all parts of our countries are already free. No people can feel themselves free so long as part of their motherland is unfree. There is no such thing as being half free, as there is no such thing as being half alive. We are often told that "colonialism is dead." How can we say it is dead so long as vast areas of Asia and Africa are unfree? Colonialism also has its modern dress in the form of economic control, intellectual control and actual physical control by a small but alien community within a nation. Wherever, whenever and however it appears, colonialism is an evil thing and one which must be eradicated from the earth!

. . .

What can we do? We can do much! We can inject the voice of reason into world affairs and mobilize all the spiritual, all the moral, all the political strength of Asia and Africa on the side of peace. Asia and Africa 1,400,000,000 strong—far more than half of the human population—can mobilize what I have called the moral voice of nations in favour of peace. We can demonstrate to the minority of the world, which lives on the other continents that we, the majority, are for peace, not for war. In this struggle, some success has already been scored. I think it is generally recognized that the activities of the five Premiers of the sponsoring countries had a not unimportant role to play in ending the fighting in Indochina. The peoples of Asia raised their voices and the world listened. It was no small victory and no negligible precedent. Why were these five successful? Was it because they were Asians? Maybe that is part of the answer, for the conflagration was on their doorstep. But I think that those five Premiers brought a fresh approach to bear on the problem. They were not seeking advantage for their own countries.

. . .

Let this Conference be a great success. In the spirit of diversity that exists among its participants—let this Conference be a great success. Yes, there is diversity among us. Small and great nations are represented here, with people professing almost every religion under the sun—Buddhism, Islam, Christianity, Shintoism and others. We encounter here almost every political faith—democracy, monarchism, theocracy, with innumerable variants. And practically every economic doctrine has its representative in this Hall—marhaenism, socialism, capitalism, communism—in all their manifold variations and combinations. But what harm is there in diversity, when there is unity in desire? It is a Brotherhood Conference, not an Islamic nor a Christian nor a Buddhist Conference. It is not a meeting of Malayans nor of Arabs nor one of Indo-Aryan stock. Neither is it an exclusive club or a bloc which seeks to propose any other bloc. Rather it is a body of enlightened, tolerant opinion, which seeks to impress on the world that all men and all countries have their place under the sun—to impress on the world that it is possible to live together, meet together, speak to each other without losing one's individual identity; and yet to contribute to the general understanding of matters of common concern and to develop a true consciousness of the interdependence of men and nations for their wellbeing and survival on earth.

Source 2 (English in the original)
Excerpt from the Final Communique of the Bandung Asian-African Conference, The Ministry of Foreign Affairs, Republic of Indonesia (ed.), *Asia-Africa Speaks from Bandung*. Djakarta: Indonesian Ministry of Foreign Affairs, 1955, 161–69.

. . .

The Asian-African Conference was convinced that among the most powerful means of promoting understanding among nations is the development of cultural co-operation. Asia and Africa have been the cradle of great religions and civilisations which have enriched other cultures and civilisations while themselves being enriched in the process. Thus the cultures of Asia and Africa are based on spiritual and universal foundations. Unfortunately, contacts among Asian and African countries were interrupted during the past centuries. The peoples of Asia and Africa are now animated by a keen and sincere desire to renew their old cultural contacts and develop new ones in the context of the modern world. All participating Governments at the Conference reiterated their determination to work for closer cultural co-operation. . . .

The Asian-African Conference gave anxious thought to the question of world peace and co-operation. It viewed with deep concern the present state of international tension with its danger of an atomic world war. The problem of peace is correlative with the problem of international security. In this connection, all States should co-operate, especially through the United Nations, in bringing about the reduction of armaments and the elimination of nuclear weapons under effective international control. In this way, international peace can be promoted and nuclear energy may be used exclusively for peaceful purposes. This would help answer the needs particularly of Asia and Africa, for what they urgently require are social progress and better standards of life in larger freedom. Freedom and peace are interdependent. The right of self-determination must be enjoyed by all peoples, and freedom and independence must be granted, with the least possible delay, to those who are still dependent peoples. Indeed, all nations should have the right freely to choose their own political and economic systems and their own way of life, in conformity with the purposes and principles of the Charter of the United Nations.

Free from distrust and fear and with confidence and good will toward each other, nations should practice tolerance and live together in peace with one another as good neighbors and develop friendly cooperation on the basis of the following principles:

1. Respect for the fundamental human rights and for the purposes and principles of the Charter of the United Nations.
2. Respect for the sovereignty and territorial integrity of all nations.
3. Recognition of the equality of all races and of the equality of all nations, large and small.
4. Abstention from intervention or interference in the internal affairs of another country.
5. Respect for the right of each nation to defend itself singly or collectively in conformity with the Charter of the United Nations.

6A. Abstention from the use of arrangements of collective defense to serve the particular interests of any big powers.

6B. Abstention by any country from exerting pressure on other countries.
7. Refraining from acts or threats of aggression or the use of force against the territorial integrity or political independence of any country.
8. Settlement of all international disputes by peaceful means such as negotiation, conciliation, arbitration or judicial settlement, as well as other peaceful means of the parties' own choice in conformity with the Charter of the United Nations.
9. Promotion of mutual interest and cooperation.
10. Respect for justice and international obligations.

Chapter Thirty-Four

Hayashi Fusao: "Affirmation of the Greater East Asian War," 1963

Kristine Dennehy

The following excerpts are from Hayashi Fusao's (1903–1975) controversial text, *Dai Tōa Sensō Kōteiron* (Affirmation of the Greater East Asian War), first published as a series of articles in *Chūō Kōron* (The Central Review) in 1963. Hayashi was born Gotō Toshio in Oita Prefecture in 1903. Growing up in poverty, he showed academic promise and proceeded to attend the Fifth Higher School in Kumamoto, where he came under the influence of Marxism and socialism. As a student at the Faculty of Law, Tokyo Imperial University, in the early 1920s, he was an active member of the Shinjinkai (New Men's Association). In 1930 he was imprisoned for his association with communism. He is known as a member of the Proletarian Literature Movement, but later he renounced his communist ideals (*tenkō*; see Steinhoff 1991) and in the postwar period went on to become a seminal figure among nationalists with a revisionist historical agenda (Gluck 1993: 84). Hayashi's ideas continue to resonate with Japanese nationalists, particularly in their calls to "correct" the view of history that portrays Japanese modernization and expansionism in a critical light (McCormack 2000: 57).

Hayashi's central argument in this text is that the 100-year period from the mid-nineteenth century to the mid-twentieth century (approximately 1845–1945) was one long, continuous war, characterized by Asians led by the Japanese trying to defend themselves from the aggressive actions and strategies of Western imperialist powers like the United States and Britain. He contrasts Western aggression with the fundamentally defensive posture of Japanese leaders who, he argues, had no other choice but to pursue an equally aggressive course of action so as not to fall prey to Western domination and to protect and liberate other Asians from the yoke of Western imperialist powers. Hayashi explains that the initial inspiration for this argument came from the independence movements that were spreading throughout Asia and Africa in the late 1950s and early 1960s. He wanted to situate those movements in a historical trajectory that had begun in the mid-nineteenth century, with the imperialist expansion of Western countries into areas such as Indochina. In this sense, he implies that there was a kind of solidarity between the Japanese and the people of other Asian and African countries based on the shared historical experience of victimization at the hands of Western imperialists. Throughout, he emphasizes the suffering on the part of all Asians, including the Japanese.

However, unlike other Asian and African countries, Hayashi argues that Japan is unique in having lost a sense of national consciousness as a result of being defeated in 1945. He attributes this loss to the historical perspective that came to dominate postwar Japan during the American-led occupation and the subsequent years of influence by progressive intellectuals such as Tsurumi Shunsuke (b. 1922), lead editor of the three-volume study of the *tenkō* phenomenon in wartime Japan (Shisō no Kagaku Kenkyūkai 1959: 117–22). Hayashi claims that when the Japanese empire collapsed in 1945, everything associated with it was denounced. Not only were wartime figures such as military men and politicians denounced and banished, but all the ideas and thoughts associated with wartime came to be denounced in the two decades following Japan's defeat. Thus, the modern Japanese nation-state itself came to be characterized as somehow inherently defective and harmful.

Hayashi is particularly scornful of postwar historians and educators like Ienaga Saburō (1913–2002), who portrayed modern Japanese leaders as having waged a "war of aggression" in line with the judgment of the International Military Tribunal for the Far East (Tokyo Trials) in the late 1940s. He rejects the labels "fascist" and "ultranationalist" for modern Japan and singles out prominent postwar intellectuals like Maruyama Masao (1914–1996) for having been infected by the "dementia virus of defeat," which "paralyzed their discerning minds" as they became "easily trapped by the magic and hypnosis of the prosecutors" of the Tokyo Trials (Hayashi 1974: 290). He argues that the Japanese people were *still* in a "dark valley" because of this version of history that had been forced on them during the occupation years. In his "affirmation," one of his main goals is to help his readers extricate themselves from what he calls the distorted historical perspective promoted during the early postwar years by the American General Headquarters (GHQ) and taken up by postwar progressives.

He blames these critics of Japanese modernization and nationalism for having fostered a general acceptance of the notion that the Japanese people should be ashamed of their modern history. This, he says, has created a populace that lacks the backbone and self-confidence to take pride in their own national traditions. For Hayashi, it was not enough that the Japanese people had made a full economic recovery from World War II by the early 1960s. In the wake of that success, he was now calling for a *spiritual* recovery of national self-confidence. In this regard, he notes the humiliation Japan endured when French President Charles de Gaulle referred to Prime Minister Ikeda Hayato (1899–1965) as a "transistor radio salesman" in 1960. Through this "theory of affirmation" Hayashi posits a corrective to the version of history that characterizes Japanese nationalism as something inherently and uniquely evil. Instead of highlighting Japanese aggression, Hayashi focuses on what he sees as the cooperative and helpful attitude and actions of Japanese Pan-Asianists like Uchida Ryōhei (see I:10), for example, in his discussion of Sun Yat-sen's political exile in Japan in the early twentieth century (see II:5 on Sun). In this way, he wants to stress the common agenda that Asians had at this time in support of revolutionary activities and movements for liberation and independence in the face of Western military might. In the process, one of Hayashi's strategies is to cite contemporary authors like Ashizu Uzuhiko (1909–1992), who shared his concern with Pan-Asianism in Japan's recent past, while also invoking the opinions of other Asians such as Sun Yat-sen, who saw the Russo-Japanese War (1904–1905), for example, as a "war of liberation." In this way, Hayashi shifts the characterization of Japanese military power as something inherently dangerous and threatening to its Asian neighbors into a force that instead has contributed to the liberation of Asia, as noted by one of the most highly regarded reformists in Asia in the face of Western expansionism, Sun Yat-sen. Such a scenario is meant to restore and instill a renewed sense of national pride and self-confidence among Hayashi's contemporaries, and it is this renewal of pride that remains at the center of contemporary historical revisionism in Japan in the twenty-first century.

In reaction to the critical view of Japanese imperialism that dominated the postwar Japanese academy and the public in general (Gluck 1993: 69–70), Hayashi also strove to complicate what he saw as an overly simplistic, formulaic narrative of modern Japanese militaristic aggression. He did this by trying to show the diversity of opinions that existed in Japan in the modern era, regarding the direction and nature of Japanese expansionism in other parts of Asia. For example, as included in the excerpt here, he notes how Uchida Ryōhei confronted Japanese government officials and military men over the level of Japanese interference with the activities of Chinese revolutionaries. Thus, he brings attention to such disputes among Japanese leaders as a way to counter the one-dimensional characterization of all Japanese aggressively plotting to eliminate the vibrant force of Chinese nationalism. Rather than necessarily seeing the Japanese and Chinese as adversaries in the modern age, Hayashi wants to restore to the historical record examples of mutual support and encouragement among the Japanese and their fellow Asians, tied as they were in their defensive posture against Western expansionism. In addition, Hayashi was eager to restore the historical reputation of certain Japanese ideologues, such as Kita Ikki, Ōkawa Shūmei, and Ishiwara Kanji (see I:27, II:4, and II:22), who were the focus of much scholarly attention after 1945. Whereas progressive scholars examined the lives and ideas of men like Kita Ikki in search of the roots of Japanese fascism and ultranationalism, Hayashi instead saw them as prophetic, tragic figures who should be revered for their commitment to charting the difficult course of Japanese modernization.

In this way, Hayashi's approach to modern Japanese history is fundamentally polemical and is part of a series of debates and disputes over the nature of modern Japanese relations with other Asian countries that continue unabated. Many of these debates focus on minute critiques of the empirical foundation of the other side's argument since Hayashi left himself open to accusations of blatantly distorting historical facts, such as his implication that Ōkawa Shūmei went mad during the Tokyo War Crimes Trials as a result of his treatment by the Americans instead of the actual cause, syphilitic dementia. Soon after Hayashi's perspective on the "100-year war" appeared in *Chūō Kōron*, Marxist scholars like Inoue Kiyoshi (1913–2001) mobilized to respond to what they saw as the glorification of Japanese militarism and the danger of the revival of Japanese militarism that was bound to follow in its wake. In the introduction to Inoue's 1966 *Nihon no "kindaika" to gunkokushugi* (Japan's 'Modernization' and Militarism), he contrasts previous works of his on Japanese modernization and militarism that were based on his own original research to this study, which is an explicit critique of writers like Hayashi who have "distorted true historical facts" in order to glorify Japan's militaristic past (Inoue 1966: 4). In the accompanying commentary to the 2001 reprint of *Affirmation of the Greater East Asia War*, Tomioka Kōichirō notes the contemporary significance of Hayashi's writing, given the popularity of authors like Nishio Kanji who have taken up many of the same historically controversial themes and issues as raised by Hayashi, such as the importance of Yasukuni Shrine in instilling patriotism and the problems associated with textbooks that they claim promote a "self-flagellating" historical perspective (Tomioka 2006). Such issues reflect the deep rifts that continue to divide academics and politicians in their commentaries on the nature of Japanese modernization and militarism. Not only do these issues divide the Japanese themselves, but they have also created divisions between the Japanese people and their Asian neighbors that have persisted to this day.

Source (translation from the Japanese original by Kristine Dennehy)
Hayashi Fusao (1974), *Dai Tōa Sensō Kōteiron* (Affirmation of the Greater East Asian War). Roman.

Genyōsha, Amur Society and Chinese Revolutionary Groups

It is a well-known fact that Sun Yat-sen, Huang Xing and other revolutionaries had strong connections to Japanese civilian patriotic associations. Sun Yat-sen's first political exile in Japan was in 1898. Through Miyazaki Tōten, Sun Yat-sen knew Inukai Tsuyoshi, Hiraoka Kōtarō and Tōyama Mitsuru, and with their cooperation and assistance, he planned to assist the independence movement of General Aguinaldo in the Philippines, etc., but all those plans failed. In 1904 he was in political exile in Japan again during the Russo-Japanese War. Ashizu Uzuhiko has written, "Sun Yat-sen saw the Russo-Japanese War as a war of liberation of Asia against Europe and thought it was a turning point in world history."

This was the time when the "Chinese Revolutionary League" was established at Uchida Ryōhei's home in Akasaka, Tokyo. It was the hotbed of 15,000 students studying abroad in Japan where they published the journal *Min pao* (People's News) and sent revolutionary ideas about overthrowing the Qing dynasty across the sea to the continent.

The Japanese government at the time (first Katsura Tarō Cabinet) saw the activities of the "Revolutionary League" as a threat. Tokutomi Sohō also attacked the "Republic ideology" but Tōyama Mitsuru declared, "Once China becomes a republic and is influenced by our national polity, they will look down on their own" and along with Inukai Tsuyoshi and others protected and encouraged the "Revolutionary League" as much as possible. Uchida strongly argued and persuaded the Japanese government and military leaders not to interfere with the Revolutionary Party. . . .

Manchuria and Japan's "Degeneration"

I don't agree with the view of theorists who claim that after the "annexation of Korea" Japanese imperialism degenerated from being the "pioneer of Asian liberation" to being the "tyrant and pillager of Asia." In terms of imperialism, Japan was already sufficiently *imperialistic* before the Meiji Restoration, from the time they were conscious of "Western powers' gradual move East." However, what I am talking about is different from the Leninist meaning of "imperialism" and has nothing to do with imperialism as the "highest stage of capitalism." It is, as meant by Nehru, the revelation and maturity of nationalism, from the vigor of people who seek independence and liberation. Mature nationalism changed into an expansionist policy and developed fangs and claws, meaning that first Taiwan and Korea suffered its damage, and then it was aimed at Manchuria. . . .

Japan Couldn't Stop

There is nothing as loathsome and foolish as someone pretending to be a sage in the aftermath of a fire. A sage is someone who can prevent a fire. A hero is someone who offers his own body to put out a fire that's started burning. However, over the last 100 years, Japanese people haven't been able to produce these sages or heroes. The reason for that is because the "East Asia 100-year war" is a big fire started from the outside, under the careful planning of Western countries, at various intervals, waiting for the right timing, it became an incendiary fire that spread from one to the next. Japanese people were not given the confidence to prevent this fire; in the midst of a constantly burning fire, they had to just fight against the fire itself. At times, it was like the mythical hero brandishing a sword, who had to cut down the dry brush burning around him. There were times when he wished that the wind would change direction so that the fire would move and burn in the direction of the neighboring village. There were also times when he himself would release the fire by using the reverse wind current. Because of that, he himself has even been criticized because he's been mistaken for an evil arsonist. I won't criticize the heroes who fought this incendiary fire. Many Japanese people burned to death. Even the heroes who survived after the fire was extinguished, almost all of them have extensive burns all over their body.

Let's leave it for another time to talk about the millions of soldiers who were wounded and died on the battlefront. In this essay, I have continued to talk primarily about ideology and ideologues. In this chapter, too, I have chosen three intellectuals [Ōkawa Shūmei, Kita Ikki, and Ishiwara Kanji] who appeared at the end of this era of 100 years of one continuous big fire. I would like to recollect the roles they played and their achievements which now seem to have withered away without bearing fruit. . . .

The Fate of Patriots

The postwar critics of Japan's defeat freely call them "the source of imperialism," "Emperor system fascists," "Asian invaders," "ultranationalists" and crown them with bad names and other such imported nonsense, but nobody can deny that they were also just as much idealists who dreamed and conceived of ideas for Japanese domestic reform and the development of the fate of the nation on the scale of Asia and the world. Moreover, almost all of them were "private citizens" far from the seat of power or "wanderers" (*rōnin*) and many of them lived in misfortune as failures and died of unnatural causes. . . .

The Misunderstanding of "Ultranationalism"

You can see the tragic nature of the "East Asia 100-year war" in the fate of the Japanese "ultranationalists" I've mentioned above. Their misfortune and burial is mainly due to *external* causes. That is the fate of the patriotic, revolutionary intellectuals of a small country who had to think and act while being surrounded on all sides by strong powers and were endlessly being threatened and attacked. Churchill, de Gaulle, and MacArthur, as well as Lenin and Stalin, all of them during the war, under the name of "wartime democracy" and "wartime communism" were "ultranationalists." But because they were victors in war they haven't been judged as villains but simply have been made into saints.

Nationalists in Japan from the Bakumatsu period [late Edo period, 1850s and 1860s] until the Shōwa period [1926–1989] have all been treated as accused defendants for the twenty years following defeat until today.

The lives of Ōkawa Shūmei, Kita Ikki and Ishiwara Kanji are tragic. Kita Ikki was sentenced to death. Ōkawa Shūmei went mad in the courtroom of the Tokyo Trials and after he left the psychiatric hospital he got sick and died in a secluded mountain village. Ishiwara Kanji witnessed the collapse of the ideal East Asian alliance and Manchukuo and squarely faced defeat. And from his sickbed he continued to denounce the farcical nature and illogic of the Tokyo Trials and died with a reputation as a crazy military man. . . .

The Need for Primary Source Research

Ōkawa and Kita did move at least one sector of Japanese people at the end of the "East Asia 100-year war" and formed the ideological background for the "Shōwa Upheaval." They did not succeed in their "work in the face of the enemy" but that is the shared fate of all prophetic thinkers. Prophets are not accepted in their own land. Actual history, in the details, does not follow the exact words of the prophet. But in the long term, their prophesies live on. . . .

CH. 18, "NATIONALISM HAS FANGS"

Too Soon to Debate Nationalism

Scholars and editors are making a big fuss about "neonationalism." I think it is a bit too soon for that. In Asian and African countries and in central and south America, the burning flames of nationalism are raging. In Japan too, there are many movements that are similar to this, but they're slightly different. The kind of nationalism that flares up from inside the blood vessels of the people, that moves people and makes them wildly enthusiastic to die for revolution and war, that doesn't actually exist in today's Japan. A long time ago in another age it existed but today that fire has been extinguished and quieted. Certainly there are trends and phenomena like the "Meiji Reverse Attack" (Kimura Tsuyoshi's term) and the "sudden increase in demand for Rising Sun flags" but these are the product of seven years of Occupation and GHQ's policies of weakening Japan and removing its backbone. More than ten years after this, it's a natural reaction to this truly vacuous situation.

There is also something called the A-A (Asia, Africa) Congress. Almost all revolutionary nationalism in India, Africa, South and North Vietnam, Indonesia, as well as Castro's Cuba which heads the central and South American countries, shows a clear slant toward communism and has stimulated the latecomer Japanese communists. . . .

Nationalism is not new or old

I do not take issue at all with those who advise to proceed forth while calculating national interest, but when national interest faces that of other countries, it becomes nationalism with fangs. All I would like to point out is that as those fangs get bigger, it's a fact that they grow into monsters called expansionism, ultranationalism and imperialism. . . . Japan was not alone in pursuing adventurism and forgetting the cold calculation of "national interest." That's because nationalism has fangs and claws.

Of course, politicians and leaders try to hide the fangs of nationalism. They commonly use flowery words like "justice" "morals" "enlightenment" "democracy" "liberation" and "communism" etc. to hide these fangs. Japanese people since antiquity have liked using fancy terms such as "righteous governance." This was not always just the influence of Confucianism. Ōkawa Shūmei discovered righteousness in Plato's "Republic," melded this with Confucianism and Buddhism and formulated his "Shōwa Restoration Theory" and "Theory of an Asian War of Liberation." However, there is no righteousness in actual politics and in war. Politics is always the rule of might and in war as well, those who actually use the rule of might become the conquerors and victors. The destruction and collapse of Japan's righteous ideology during the Greater East Asia War is an actual recent example of this. . . .

CH. 19, "JAPAN, ASIA AND THE WORLD"

The Need for a Pro-Japan Faction

From now on, what kind of attitude should Japan take toward Asia and the world? That is a political question, not a historical question. The future is made through the actions and struggles of human beings. Politicians organize and lead people and make the future by getting them to fight. For 100 years, Japan has waged a solitary struggle. When you look back on this as history, it is certainly not meaningless. You also can't call it reckless. Besieged by the colonization and aggression of the Western powers, no matter how great generals or politicians were, no other measures could have been taken. According to the government and military leaders at the time, there were also efforts to contain the Sino-Japanese War, and to avoid war with the United States and Britain, as many of the books being published these days prove. . . .

Withdrawal from "great domains"

Nationalism is not new or old. Japan's recovery is not just a recovery of industry, trade, roads, and taxes. It's unbearable that the prime minister is called a transistor radio salesman and he just stays silent like a broken radio. The time has come when we should erect the pillar of a national spirit and wave the flag of this spirit. However, when you think about the recovery of Japanese nationalism, you also have to think about your own fangs and claws that will grow.

Japanese people are now qualified and have the right to retire for a while from the historical stage, retire to "a mountain retreat," call upon the heavens and have a conversation with themselves. This is nothing to be done hurriedly. I don't know but it may take ten or twenty years to come back down again from the mountain. Now is the time for deliberation. It is time for self-fulfillment. People who are wounded and internally void, no matter how much they fly around the world, won't be of any use. First, we should retire to "a mountain retreat" to deliberate, store up internal power and ideas, and then proclaim them to Asia and the world. That's more than enough. Ten or twenty years is not more than a moment in history. Being "in a mountain retreat" is not a minus for the people.

Chapter Thirty-Five

Takeuchi Yoshimi: "Japan's Asianism," 1963

Christian Uhl

Takeuchi Yoshimi's (1910–1977) commentary for the first-ever collection of sources on Asianism (Takeuchi 1963a) is regarded as the point of departure for any serious analysis of the subject in present-day Japan. Yet, at the same time, the essay is itself an example of Asianist thinking.

Born in Nagano in 1910, Takeuchi studied Chinese literature at Tokyo Imperial University. A trip to China in 1932 stirred his interest in contemporary China. He was the only student in his 1934 cohort to graduate with a thesis on a contemporary subject—the writer Yu Dafu (1896–1945).

Takeuchi's opposition to traditional Japanese scholarship of China (*kangaku*) as well as to modern, Western-style Sinology (*Shinagaku*)—both positivistic, philological disciplines devoted to classical studies—manifested itself in the establishment of the Chūgoku Bungaku Kenkyūkai (Society for the Study of Chinese Literature). From 1935, it published its own journal, *Chūgoku Bungaku Geppō* (Chinese Literature Monthly). After a spell in China between 1937 and 1939, Takeuchi returned to Japan to work as a researcher at the Kaikyōken Kenkyūjo (Institute for the Study of the Islamic World).

At the end of 1941, Takeuchi published a manifesto that enthusiastically endorsed the attack on Pearl Harbor and hailed the declaration of the "Greater East Asian War" against the United States, the foremost Western imperialist power, as an act of atonement for Japan's aggression in China that marked its abandonment of the policy of imperialism. But by mid-1942 he had begun to show his dissatisfaction with the war situation by, for example, refusing to involve the Society for the Study of Chinese Literature in the First Conference of the Writers of Greater East Asia, a major government-sponsored propaganda event (see II:25). In 1943 Takeuchi's discontent led him to dissolve the Society and close down its journal. As a result of this act of defiance, Takeuchi was conscripted and sent to China. It was while he was there that his first book, *Rojin*, on the Chinese writer Lu Xun (1881–1936), a work that formed the cornerstone of his postwar career as a literary critic, was published in Tokyo in December 1944. Throughout the late 1940s and the 1950s Lu Xun enjoyed great popularity in Japanese intellectual circles, a vogue that amplified the influence of Takeuchi, who was recognized as the leading translator and interpreter of the Chinese writer's works. Moreover, Takeuchi caught the attention of the postwar reading public with his outspoken comments on various issues outside Chinese literature. In particular, he launched an uncompromising critique of the intellectual mainstream—for example, in his 1948 essay "'Kindai' to wa nani ka" (What Is "Modernity"?) and in his 1951 appeal for the creation of a "national literature" that would reflect the particular historical experience of the Japanese people instead of merely imitating the intellectual fashions imported from the West. And in 1959 he vocally opposed the revision of the U.S.-Japanese Security Treaty on the grounds that it would ally Japan with the United States, its former enemy, against China, the victim of Japanese aggression.

When in 1960 the government rammed the treaty revision through the Diet, Takeuchi resigned in protest from his university post and, together with Hashikawa Bunsō (1922–1983), founded the Chūgoku no kai (China Society) and launched *Chūgoku* (China), a journal dedicated to a "reconsideration of the problem of Sino-Japanese relations from a Japanese perspective." In the final years of his life Takeuchi devoted himself mainly to translating and annotating the *Collected Works of Lu Xun*, published in six volumes. The *Complete Works of Takeuchi Yoshimi*, which do not include his translations of Lu Xun and other modern Chinese writers, were published in seventeen volumes between 1980 and 1982.

His essay "Japan's Asianism" (Takeuchi 1963c: 94–156) was originally published under the title "Ajiashugi no Tenbō" (A Panoramic View of Asianism) as a commentary for the volume on *Asianism* in the series *Gendai Nihon Shisō Taikei* (Anthology of Modern Japanese Thought) (Takeuchi 1963a). It was the first academic attempt to address Asianism in a systematic and comprehensive way. The essay is a challenge to the unprepared reader, as it requires detailed knowledge of modern Japanese history. Moreover, Takeuchi's interpretation of the subject is based on philosophical premises that are not made explicit in the course of his argument and presuppose knowledge of his previous writings. Takeuchi himself acknowledged that, in order to stand as an independent work, his essay would require revision (cf. Takeuchi 1966: 428).

Takeuchi's main purpose in writing "Japan's Asianism" was to dissociate Asianism from fascism and thus to make possible a study of the subject that, he believed, would be more objective than the prevailing views of postwar scholars—notably Maruyama Masao, who considered Asianism to be one of three ideological pillars of Japanese fascism (Maruyama 1964). By arguing that the Asianist ideology of wartime Japan was, in fact, merely the hollow shell of a once rich and promising ideal, Takeuchi criticized Marxist, as well as liberal and modernist historiographies, which in various ways were all inspired by notions of progress and, as he complained, contaminated by the "poison of historicism." In the narrative offered by the "progressive" model, imperialist "Greater East Asian ideology" represents the apex of the evolutionary account of Asianist modes of thinking that, finally, with Japan's defeat in 1945, were all together overcome by the triumph of reason. Takeuchi challenged this model by means of a *non*genealogical and *dis*continuous counternarrative, a method that is also represented in the structure of Takeuchi's *Asianism* reader, which is divided into four sections—"prototypes" (*genkei*), "feeling" (*kanjō*), "logic" (*ronri*), and "rebirth" (*tensei*). According to Takeuchi, the idea of Asian solidarity emerged out of the political contradictions of early modern Japan, and the dominant characteristic of the Asianism of that period (the 1880s) was its oscillation between solidarity and aggression, which makes these aspects difficult to tell apart. This distinction became possible only later, in the years between the Sino-Japanese (1894–1895) and the Russo-Japanese wars (1904–1905), when the intellectual world split into leftist and rightist wings and the idea of Asian solidarity became the exclusive property of the latter. After Japan's defeat in 1945, Asianism was "reborn" because it was inseparably connected with the unsolved problems of modernity in Japan, or its "aporias," as Takeuchi put it elsewhere—that is, the impossibility of reconciling the contradictory notions of East and West, tradition and modernity, "national essence" (*kokusui*) and (Western) "civilization" (*bunmei kaika*), and so on (cf. Takeuchi 1958a: 146; 1958b: 65).

This is the message that Takeuchi conveyed in his concluding remarks concerning the ambiguous legacy of Saigō Takamori (1828–1877). Saigō played a crucial part in the overthrow of the Tokugawa shogunate and was a leading member of the Meiji government. But after his plan to invade Korea was rejected, he retired from politics and in 1877 led a rebellion against the central government. This "reactionary" rebellion, however, also marked the beginnings of the Freedom and People's Rights Movement, which some historians see as the first democratic revolutionary movement in the history of modern Japan. Takeuchi considers "Saigō's contradiction" as the first instance of the subsequently recurrent tension between the idea of "people's rights" (*minken*) and the "authority of the state" (*kokken*)—or, at a later stage, as a clash between the advocates of "Europeanization" (*Ōka*) and those who wanted to preserve "national essence" (*kokusui*).

Takeuchi characterized Japanese culture as a culture of "honors students." Its leaders, Takeuchi contended, are always anxious to be at the top of the class, the rest of which consists of a multitude of poor students—that is, the backward common people: "'It is our mission to guide these backward people, just as it is our mission to guide the backward Oriental people.' Such thinking represents the logical development of the honors student complex. . . . The roots of Japanese fascism lie in the very structure of Japanese culture" (Takeuchi 1948a: 150–51; 1948b: 67–68). "Japan is turning into Europe, becoming as European as possible; [this Europeanization] was conceived of as the path of its emergence . . . from being a *slave* to becoming a master." Takeuchi insisted, however, that master and slave were identical (Takeuchi 1948a: 158; 1948b: 72).

Takeuchi described an alternative attitude towards modernity when he defined what he called "Lu Xun's method." Lu Xun, Takeuchi noted, "never gave way and was not servile to anyone. He confronted the new era, then purified himself through 'resistance' and finally extracted this self from that era. . . . Yet this Lu Xun . . . was no different from before. Although some speak of progress in his thinking, such progress is really quite secondary to his unyielding self-assertion" (Takeuchi 1944: 10–11). The important notion here is that of "resistance" (*teikō*), a stance that is identified with what he calls a "literary perspective" (*bungaku no tachiba*), and it is Takeuchi's definition of "literature" that also brings to the fore his romantic mode of thinking. "Literature," in Takeuchi's terminology, signifies the subjective, emotional, immediate, sensuous, and concrete attitude toward the world and represents an individual's (or, in the case of "national literature," a nation's) self-expression and self-assertion. As such, the "literary perspective" is opposed to "scientific thinking," which is objective, reflexive, methodical, abstract, and universal and belongs to what Takeuchi, in contrast to "literature," calls "politics." This distinction between "literature" and "politics"—which was inspired by Nishida Kitarō's dialectic of "individual" and "universal" (Uhl 2009)—is also the key to a proper understanding of a second pair of concepts, "feeling" (*kanjō*) and "logic" (*ronri*), which form the core of Takeuchi's interpretation of Japanese Asianism. It was as a result of the lack of "resistance" (to Europe and the "world-historical process of modernization") that, in Japan, "feeling" and "logic" finally disintegrated, thus allowing the ideal of Asian solidarity to turn into an empty, abstract political ideology that supported European-style imperialist aggression against Japan's Asian neighbors. In other words, the problem does not lie with Asianism as such but with Japan's "honors-student" road to modernity that is oblivious to its own past.

The disintegration of "feeling" and "logic" in Japan was, according to Takeuchi, the result of an assimilation of European modernity, "which is not mediated by negation" (Takeuchi 1942: 427). However, to assume that for Takeuchi the East represents "feeling" and the West "abstraction" would be to fail to appreciate the complexity of his thought. Nowhere in his writings does Takeuchi conjure any kind of dualist essentialism. Instead, he regarded the East–West dichotomy as one of the "aporias of modernity," which he tried to grasp as a dialectical contradiction, the poles of which are mediated by "Oriental resistance." According to Takeuchi, "Europe and the Orient are contradictory notions, just as are the notions of the modern and the feudal." Europe, he insisted, "made the Orient possible," and the Orient made Europe what it was. "Without Oriental resistance Europe would be unable to realize itself. . . . In order for Europe to be Europe, it had to invade the Orient." Oriental resistance was a reaction against this penetration, and yet, as Takeuchi points out, it was precisely through such resistance that Asia succumbed to accelerating modernization. "Europe's invasion of the Orient resulted in the phenomenon of Oriental capitalism. . . . For Europe this was accordingly conceptualized as the progress of world history and the triumph of reason." Now, however, in other areas in Asia, though not in Japan, "it seems as though, through its continuing resistance, the Orient is creating something non-European, which is mediated by, and at the same time transcends the European" (Takeuchi 1948a: 130–33, 136; 1948b: 55–56, 58).

Since Takeuchi made no attempt to formulate a positive definition of Asia, to distinguish his stance from what is commonly understood by the term "Asianism" we should perhaps qualify his view as "utopian"—in the literal sense of the word "utopia," meaning "a place which does not exist." With this in mind and in light of Takeuchi's conviction that rescuing the past always requires a radical negation of the past, we are better equipped to get to grips with passages like the following: "The Orient must re-embrace the West, it must change the West itself in order to realize the latter's outstanding values on a greater scale. Such a rollback of culture or values would create universality. . . . When this rollback takes place, we must have our own values. And yet perhaps these values do not yet exist, in substantive form. Rather I suspect that they are possible as method. . . . This I have called 'Asia as method,' and yet it is impossible to state definitely what this might mean" (Takeuchi 1960a: 115; 1960b: 165).

Source (translation from the Japanese original by Christian Uhl)
Takeuchi Yoshimi, "Nihon no Ajiashugi" (Japan's Asianism), reproduced in *Takeuchi Yoshimi Zenshū* (Complete Works of Takeuchi Yoshimi), vol. VIII. Chikuma Shobō, 1980, 94–156.

WHAT IS "ASIANISM"?

In order to speak about Asianism one must first define the term. If one was dealing here with universal concepts such as democracy or socialism that are within the scope of common understanding, then there would be no need to begin with a definition. One could simply delve straight into the heart of the matter. However, the term "Asianism" is distinctive and in addition has numerous meanings. It means something different to everyone. So we have no choice but to narrow it down, as a first step.

Having said that, I have no intention of providing a final definition here, because I find it impossible to do so. . . . My final definition will probably not be settled on even when this volume is going to press. . . .

In my understanding, "Asianism" does not have any real content, but rather must be regarded as a tendency inherent in various distinct modes of thought. . . . While we can determine whether a certain way of thinking or a certain thinker at any given time was Asianist or not, clearly such evaluations change with changing circumstances and, for this reason, it is not possible to overlook the concrete situation at a time and to give a general definition. . . . I believe that all attempts to define [Asianism] as a concept are inevitably bound to fail. No matter how many definitions one produces, Asianism . . . does not lend itself to being grasped as an idea which fulfils a real function. Of course, one may say that this applies not only to Asianism, but in a sense to all kinds of thought. But in the case of Asianism this is a distinguishing characteristic.

Asianism is neither synonymous with expansionism nor with a policy of aggression. Neither is it completely synonymous with nationalism. . . . Nor is it the same as left-wing internationalism. But it occurs together in part with all of these and, in particular, it overlaps to a large extent with expansionism. Or, to put it more precisely: genealogically speaking, Asianism was the product of nascent expansionism after the Meiji Restoration. Expansionism, however, did not immediately lead to the development of Asianism. At first, it contained two opposing currents of thought: that of strengthening the authority of the state and that of strengthening people's rights. Later on, the two opposing currents became Europeanization and adherence to the national essence. Asianism arose from the tensions between these ill-matched twins.

I have gone to great lengths to show how difficult it is to define Asianism. However, . . . we have to acknowledge that an emotional disposition, a feeling, which can only be called Asianism, and certain modes of thinking which are grounded in this feeling, are apparent throughout the history of modern Japan and are emerging all the time. Now, contrary for example to democracy, socialism, fascism and the like—that is, to "officially sanctioned" ideas—Asianism as such contains no values of its own. . . . It always arises in association with other ideas. For that reason, it is not possible to trace the specific historical development of Asianism. The idea that it is possible to present a history of Asianism is based on a bias that is itself probably the product of the poison of historicism.

THE INTELLECTUAL EMPTINESS OF SELF-STYLED ASIANISM

The idea of the "Greater East Asian Co-Prosperity Sphere" during the Second World War in a sense marked the inevitable outcome of Asianism. In another sense, however, it represented a departure from Asianism, or rather a deviation from it. If one assumes that Asianism as a concept has any substance, and that it has developed historically, then one must conclude that the "Greater East Asian Co-Prosperity Sphere" was clearly the inevitable outcome of Asianism and that it perished as a system of thought with Japan's defeat. And, as a matter of fact, this view was predominant in the postwar period.

As I have tentatively noted above, because Asianism . . . always appears as a tendency in association with systems of thought that possess their own individuality, it does not have an independent existence. However, even making allowances for this, one must recognize a certain commonality inherent in its aspirations toward solidarity among peoples of Asia (regardless of whether it is used to serve aggression or not). This is the key attribute of Asianism in my minimum definition. And if that is the case, then the "Greater East Asian Co-Prosperity Sphere" was clearly a form of Asianism.

However, if one looks at the reality of it, it is possible to say that the "Greater East Asia Co-Prosperity Sphere" was a pseudo-idea that could only have arisen by suppressing all other systems of thought including Asianism. If an ideology is not productive, it cannot be called a genuine system of thought, and the ideology of the Co-Prosperity Sphere generated absolutely nothing. The bureaucrats who were proponents and propagators of this ideology, imposed by fiat from above, . . . simply spread the cloak of the "Greater East Asian Co-Prosperity Sphere" over everything. They held a "Greater East Asian Conference," issued a "Greater East Asian Declaration," [see II:27] and the like, but none of that had any real content.

The stifling of all thought was first directed at leftist thought, then was extended to liberalism and finally was gradually applied to the right wing. The ensuing crackdown affected both Nakano Seigō's Tōhōkai (Society of the East [see II:1]) and Ishiwara Kanji's Tōa Renmei (East Asian League [see II:22]). Because the idea of the Co-Prosperity Sphere owed its existence to the suppression of what could be regarded, in various degrees, as Asianist thought, from a certain point view it could be regarded as the extreme stage in depriving Asianism of any thought content. . . .

RE-DEFINITION OF THE PROBLEM

Here I must once again return to the subject of the [pan-Asianist] Genyōsha [see I:3]. That is because the question remains of explaining why in the twentieth century Asianism was represented only by the Genyōsha-Kokuryūkai [see I:3 and I:10]. . . . Some may of course argue that this view is wrong. Even I do not claim that all varieties of Asianism completely disappeared, with the exception of those represented by the Genyōsha-Kokuryūkai. The Miyazaki Tōten variety (as expressed in his *My Thirty-three Years' Dream* [see I:11]) has always persisted as a sentiment. The owner of the Nakamuraya [a restaurant in Shinjuku], [Christians and nationalists] Sōma Aizō [1870–1954], and his wife Kokkō [1876–1955 (I:24)] are a good example of this. Iwanami Shigeo [1881–1946] also represents an emotional Asianism that is not associated with Japan's expansionism. At the time of the China Incident [the initial stages of the war with China] he refused to pay his special tax to the military knowing full well that he would incur their wrath. However, when the Pacific War broke out, he stated at a gathering: "If it is to destroy the Anglo-Americans, then I am for it, too." . . . This kind of feeling was pervasive . . . among the masses, together with a feeling of contempt for the Chinese and Koreans, and it persists in a vague way down to this day. But this feeling has not been raised to [the level of] thought. In other words, there was no encounter between Miyazaki Tōten and [Okakura] Tenshin [I:7 and I:8]. The fact that this did not happen is the question I would like to address here.

As Asianists, Kita Ikki and Ōkawa Shūmei [see I:27 and II:4] represented a new kind of Asianism that emerged at the stage of imperialism. Kita took part in the Chinese revolution and dreamt in a unique way of the revolution's taking a course in opposition to Sun Yat-sen [see II:5]; once his dream was destroyed, he turned his energies to the reorganization of Japan. Ōkawa, on the other hand, although employed by the South Manchurian Railway, showed little interest in the China question. More accurately, he left China in the care of his people (behind the scenes he was also the leading orchestrator of the Manchurian Incident) and concentrated personally mainly on India and the areas west of it. . . . He was one of the pioneering [writers] who introduced Ghandi, Nehru, Pahlevi, Ibn Saud and Atatürk to the Japanese. He began to study Islam early on, and he did not limit himself to study alone but also helped to send Japanese students to Egypt's Al-Azhar University. In short, emotion separated itself from logic in the Asianism of that period, or, in other words, Asianist logic capitulated completely to the logic of aggression. All that remained were the most obnoxious parts of the Kokuryūkai's ideology. The question is why this happened and when. . . .

From the middle of the Taishō period [1912–1926] until the beginning of the Shōwa period [1926–1989], with right and left wings opposing each other, the right had the monopoly on Asianism while the left assumed the opposite position of proletarian internationalism. And then, with nationalism as an insurmountable problem, many defected from the left. What they returned to was in many cases Asianism or Saigō Takamori. . . .

One has to ask why Asianism was monopolized by the right in the period marked by a clear split between right and left. This surely had its origins at the end of the Meiji era, when Kita Ikki vacillated between the [socialist] Heiminsha (Commoner Society) and the Kokuryūkai. . . . Among the thinkers of that time, the disciple of Rousseau, Nakae Chōmin [1847–1901], and the Genyōsha's Tōyama Mitsuru [1855–1944; see I:3] had a relationship of mutual respect. They adopted an identical stance on the People's Rights Movement and the revision of the Unequal Treaties, and there was almost no difference between their views on East Asian politics. Although Tōyama was a supporter of imperial rule, Nakae did not reject the monarchy. And in supporting the war against Russia toward the end of his life, Nakae . . . followed the same route as the Genyōsha-Kokuryūkai. That was not the case with their respective disciples, Kōtoku Shūsui [1871–1911] and Uchida Ryōhei [1873–1937], in whose time [political] thought underwent a major split. . . .

After the Sino-Japanese War, Uchida travelled on foot from Vladivostok to Petrograd [*sic*] and back to investigate the domestic situation in Russia. He concluded that Russia was a despotic and barbaric state where freedom was suppressed and he realized that, as a result, it faced an imminent collapse. Back in Japan, he wrote *Roshia Bōkoku Ron* [On the Ruin of Russia], which, however, was banned immediately. . . . This took place in 1901, the same time as Kōtoku published his *Teikokushugi* [Imperialism], which, however, was not banned as it advocated pacifism. The government of the day held the view that war with Russia would be premature.

The Russo-Japanese War was a victory of civilization over barbarism—this is a logical extension of Fukuzawa Yukichi's understanding of civilization. However, this understanding contains also the seed of the later war-time idea of the "honorable death of one hundred million Japanese [*ichioku gyokusai*]." Japan at that time was a fully developed nation-state, and if the Russian threat was existential, then the affirmation of the war was surely legitimate. The problem here, however, lies with the question of the quality of "civilization."

During the Tokyo War Crime Trials [1946-1948] Uchida was posthumously charged with having been a man who opposed civilization. . . .

It is a fact that backward Japanese capitalism persisted until 1945 by repeatedly taking a form that concealed its internal defects through expansion overseas. Although the basic root of this phenomenon lay in the weakness of the people, on this fact hinges the most important question regarding Pan-Asianism at present—namely whether it is possible to discover occasions in history that could have prevented this form of capitalism from appearing. . . . It is, after all, problematic to discuss the new question of "Asian nationalism" that suddenly emerged after the war as if it was completely separate from the Asianism of the past, whether represented by Okakura, Miyazaki, Uchida or Ōkawa. . . .

THE DUAL CHARACTER OF SAIGŌ TAKAMORI

Probably because it is not sufficient to consider the problem of Asianism only within the parameters of the situation in the 1880s and the 1900s, we are ultimately forced to return to the even older dispute about the invasion of Korea. In other words, things boil down to the historical assessment of Saigō Takamori.

[The Canadian historian E. Herbert] Norman adopts a hostile attitude towards Saigō. This attitude is not limited to Norman, but is shared by Japan's progressive historians. In contrast, as we have already seen, the right extols Saigō as a symbol and sometimes makes him into an absolute. . . . But it is necessary to point out here that they do not limit their praise to the expansionist aspect of Saigō. . . .

It was not Saigō who was the counter-revolutionary, but the Meiji government that ousted him which had embraced counter-revolution. It was not the rightist faction of the Shōwa period that came up with this view, but it had already been formulated by Meiji nationalism. And it was only because the left failed to adopt it that it was taken up by the right. . . .

The question whether to regard Saigō as a counter-revolutionary or as a symbol of permanent revolution is not a question that can be easily settled. And yet Asianism cannot be defined in separation from this question. This means that the question can be approached from the opposite direction by means of Asianism. This is how I perceive our present intellectual position.

Part VI

PAN-ASIANISM, REGIONALIZATION, AND GLOBALIZATION, 1989–PRESENT

The end of the Cold War in 1989–1990 brought about a reshuffling in international relations. It is generally agreed that the collapse of the bipolar system gave a powerful stimulus to regionalist trends. The enlargement and institutional strengthening of the European Union and the Association of Southeast Asian Nations (ASEAN) led to renewed debate over the necessity for regional integration in East Asia. This in turn prompted a reexamination of the historical legacies of Pan-Asianism as an ideology of regionalism. The various contributions to this process of reexamination are introduced in this part.

As a specific policy, the ASEAN+3 cooperative network has been the most frequently discussed model for regional integration in East Asia (II:39). However, the ghosts of prewar rivalries over which country should lead the process of regional integration still haunt attempts to promote closer regional cooperation. Despite these obstacles, the past two decades have shown a resurgence of interest in Pan-Asianism in Japan and other parts of Asia. In Japan (at least before the economic bubble burst in the early 1990s), this reflected a newfound confidence after Japan had outperformed most Western countries as an economic powerhouse in the 1980s. This renewed confidence led (in some quarters) to a search for "Asian values" that would prove an alternative to "Western values" with their universalistic claims. It was argued that the economic success of Japan and other Asian countries was to be accounted for by superior Asian ways and traditions that were themselves the products of Asian culture (II:36 and II:37).

The first decade of the twenty-first century witnessed efforts to strengthen regional ties in East Asia, notably between Japan and Southeast Asia. Although arguments for regional cooperation were usually couched in economic terms, they were frequently reinforced by references to Asian commonalities.

In academia and journalism, retrospective attempts to justify World War II as a war of Asian liberation (see II:34) were in this period outweighed by analyses critical of Japan which nonetheless emphasize the importance of regional solidarity. Such critiques, written from an anti-Western and anti-American position, lambaste the "world domination" or hegemony of the United States and condemn Japan's role as an ally of America, perceived—implicitly or explicitly—as a betrayal of Asian ideals (II:40).

There are signs that, in recent years, the official position on Pan-Asianism has changed even in China and Korea (II:38 and II:41). A good example of this new attitude is represented by a high-ranking Chinese diplomat who, in an official address given in 2006, discussed the positive aspects of pan-Asian ideology—for over fifty years a taboo subject in China.

Chapter Thirty-Six

Ogura Kazuo: "A Call for a New Concept of Asia," 1993

Kristine Dennehy

Ogura Kazuo (b. 1938) followed the "elite course" of high-level Japanese government officials, with his graduation from the University of Tokyo Faculty of Law and subsequent entry into the Ministry of Foreign Affairs in 1962. He went on to obtain a degree in economics from Cambridge University and held a series of prominent posts, including ambassador to Vietnam, South Korea, and France and, more recently, president of the Japan Foundation. In the 1980s and early 1990s Ogura joined outspoken figures like Ishihara Shintarō (see II:37) in the debates over Japan's changing relationship with the United States in the wake of America's ongoing trade deficit and the rise of other Asian economies such as Singapore. He was a keen observer of the dynamics of trade friction between Japan and the United States since the 1960s and argued that a major contributing factor to these tensions was the American "lack of historical consciousness and the failure to understand other cultural traditions," combined with a sense of self-righteousness and "tendency for the American people to see themselves as crusaders for justice" that "borders dangerously close to a narrow-minded dogma which rejects anything not compatible with its own values and which lashes out against 'un-American' practices even when they exist in un-American locations" (Ogura 1983: 38–39). In this regard, Ogura's views are part of the polemical debates over the links between Japanese culture and its economic status. As James Fallows (1989) has argued in the United States, "Such tension over trade issues . . . arises from Japan's inability or unwillingness to restrain the one-sided and destructive expansion of its economic power."

While Ogura rejects what he calls the "myth of Western universality," with the growth of East Asian and Southeast Asia economies into the early 1990s, he claims that "Asia should now thoroughly absorb what the West has offered and develop a new set of universal values that it can transmit to the world"

(Ogura 1993). Like Ishihara and Mahathir, Ogura sees Asians as bound together by common cultural traits, such as discipline and order, and social values, as opposed to the decadence of Western individualism. Although he does not give an explicit definition of "Japanese-style management," Ogura touts these practices as worthy of export and universalization. A few years after the publication of Ogura's essay, Samuel Huntington (1927–2008), author of *The Clash of Civilizations and the Remaking of World Order*, singled out Ogura's recommendation for "the export of the social system of Asia, East Asia in particular," as a by-product of "Asian triumphalism" due to its economic success and categorically rejected "the elusive and illusory calls to identify the U.S. with Asia." Huntington continues, "Whatever economic connections may exist between them, the fundamental cultural gap between Asian and American societies precludes their joining together in a common home" (Huntington 1996: 108–9, 307).

In Ogura's articulation of his views on Pan-Asianism, he invokes the views and policies of other Asian leaders, such as Malaysia's Mahathir and Singapore's Lee Kuan Yew, as a way to stand up to the pervasive influence of American economic and cultural hegemony. In the case of Malaysia, the Look East policy took Japan as its economic and cultural model and reflected the active rejection of a Western model by Prime Minister Mahathir. Ogura, Ishihara, Mahathir, and Lee have all issued similar warnings to their respective national and regional audiences regarding the uncritical embrace of technology, industrialization, and individualism. All of them see these elements of modernity as associated primarily with the West, particularly the United States. They want to provide other options for economic development and regional cooperation and argue that "Asian" values of harmony are well suited to address the problems associated with industrialization and other aspects of modernization, such as the struggle to balance human needs with the preservation of the natural environment. While often undefined in precise terms, they agree that a particular Asian spirit must be fostered and combined with the material elements of modern life. Ironically, given both Lee's and Ogura's education at Cambridge, they also share a skepticism concerning the legacy of Western-oriented leadership in Asia, as seen in Ogura's claim that "the big issue for Asia from now on will not be how to modernize itself further so much as how to achieve global solutions for the problems that have led Western-style modernization and industrialization to a dead end . . ." (Ogura 1993).

In the excerpt reproduced here, Ogura's comments are reminiscent of the voices of the Asian leaders who gathered in Bandung in 1955 (see II:33), with their emphasis on the exploitative nature of Western global influence in the modern age of imperialism and the destructive legacy that has had all over

Asia. In this sense, their calls for post–World War II pan-Asian cooperation are inextricably tied to a critique of Western hegemony in the modern age, including a critical view of the modern nation-state as a political unit that drove global imperialist expansion following the industrial revolution. In his opening statement at Bandung, the Philippines delegate Carlos Romulo (1899–1985) pointed out the inadequacies of the nation-state in addressing the urgent problems of the nuclear age. He called for a "true interdependence of peoples" in contrast to the fervent nationalist sentiments that fueled "Europe's historic errors." The echoes of Bandung can be heard in Ogura's question that was posed as the year 2000 approached: "How is the rampant nationalism that has colored the modern history of Europe to be overcome as we prepare for the twenty-first century?" (Ogura 1993).

In Bandung, Indonesian President Sukarno and others saw themselves poised at a historic crossroads in the early stages of decolonization and offered a vision for a world order where Asian voices would be heard in international organizations in a coordinated, systematic kind of way. Decades later Ogura harkens back to these ideals with his recommendations for joint endeavors, such as common regulatory standards for industrial manufacturing and the environment as well as economic and cultural exchanges among Asians, particularly at the grassroots level. For, as he notes, "it is Asian people, not Asian elites, who will truly support the 'new' Asia" (Ogura 1993).

Source (English in the original)
Ogura Kazuo (1993), "A Call for a New Concept of Asia," *Japan Echo* 20:3 (Autumn 1993), abridged translation of "Ajia no fukken no tame ni," *Chūō Kōron* (July 1993), 60–73.

A MANUFACTURED "ASIA"

The concept of "Asia" was originally manufactured in the West, and over the course of history it has been laden with negative values. It has stood, for example, as a symbol of despotism and subservience to authority contrasting with Europe's liberty and equality. The same Asia that was laden with negative connotations and viewed as a threat to the West was also associated with wealth, pleasure, and dissipation, which made it a target for the West's acquisitiveness. Thus India, since it was a symbol of Asia's wealth, became a symbol of the glory of the British Empire. Nothing has been plundered by the nations of Western Europe more than the riches and resources of Asia, ranging from pepper to rubies. For a while, in fact, Asia may be said to have existed solely as the object of exploitation and plunder.

THE BIRTH OF A REAL ASIA

In the past few years, however, the concept of Asia, not manufactured but firmly grounded in reality, has emerged as a symbol with positive values for virtually the first time in modern history. Thanks to the remarkable economic development of Japan, South Korea, Taiwan, Hong Kong, the coastal regions of China, and the members of the Association of Southeast Asian Nations, trade and investment among these countries and regions have increased remarkably, and their interdependence has grown apace. The change is not limited to the economic front. In South Korea and the Philippines, democratic elections have been held, and the old political systems, which separated those in authority from the masses, have rapidly crumbled. Considerable progress has been made throughout East Asia in creating stable political setups to match the progress in economic development. A major change is also underway in the areas of culture and values. The "Asian" elements that have supported Japan's economic development (though there is the question of how accurately these can be defined) have come to serve as a model for the world; they are also one of the foundations of Malaysian Prime Minister Mahathir bin Mohamad's Look East policy. In every respect, the negative values that were for a long time associated with Asia are finally being replaced by positive ones. And in the midst of this shift, Asians are becoming engaged in a search for common directions and a common destiny in political as well as economic affairs.

MAKING USE OF ASIA'S TRADITIONAL SPIRIT

Given the emergence of a new Asian presence in the economic and political spheres (and of a concept of Asia that for the first time in modern history is associated with positive values), we in Asia must seriously search for values that we can present to the rest of the world as universal. In the process of this search, we must lend our ears not only to Okakura Kakuzo and Nitobe Inazo, author of Bushido, the classic exposition of the samurai spirit, but also to people like the Indian poet Rabindranath Tagore and Sun Yat-sen, the father of the Chinese revolution. In a book written shortly after a visit to Japan early in this century, Tagore delivered an indictment of the European nation-state as the opponent of humanity. He contrasted the civilization of Asia with that of Europe, saying that the former is "social" rather than political and that it is built on a variety of deep links with humanity. Tagore suggested that a spirit of humanity like that in Asia is flowing in the background of European civilization and argued that the humanity of the world should be saved from destruction through a linking of hands among kindred spirits. When Asia was economically and politically weak, comments like these tended to be seen as no more than self-serving, defensive rhetoric. At best they served as political tools for those Asians who were resisting Westernization. Now, however, Asia is in the process of building up its economic and political power, and in this context the ideas put forth by these distinguished figures from the past bear reexamination.

FOR AN ASIAN RESTORATION

One of the ideals that the new Asia should raise aloft is that of establishing personal control over desires in such a way as to achieve harmony between nature and humankind. A related aspect is that of finding a balanced approach to relations among human beings, including in particular the handling of family ties and the relationship between the individual and the group. To put it more concretely, the transmission of this ideal means the export of the social system of Asia, East Asia in particular. Asia should also transmit aspects of the everyday culture that serves as the background of this social system. We should pay more attention to the spirit that flows through such traditional pursuits as Japan's tea ceremony and flower arranging, China's cuisine and calligraphy, and Korea's songs and dances, because this is the spirit on which Asia's social system is built. The view of nature in haiku and the use of ingredients in Japanese cooking may also be said without exaggeration to be representative of a certain Asian spirit. Unfortunately, as a result of industrialization and Americanization, some of the precious cultural pursuits that were formerly linked closely to everyday life have turned into museum pieces or have become highly formalized activities carried out just for show.

BRINGING NON-ASIAN COUNTRIES INTO ASIA

Finally, the biggest obstacle to an Asian restoration is the wounds of the past. It will be difficult for Asia to take off and soar again unless it can get over the legacy of ill will caused by past invasions and strife; this legacy still clouds such relationships as those between Vietnam and China, Japan and China, and Japan and Korea. In order to eliminate the negative effects of old wounds, it goes without saying that Japan must make more efforts to further promote education and reflection on its history. But Japanese awareness and contrition alone will not suffice. If the scars of these old wounds are to become something of true meaning for the Asia to come, the countries that were injured will have to refrain from being prisoners of the past and adopt a future-minded posture. If Asia, which has become so Americanized culturally and economically, is to transmit its values powerfully to the rest of the world, it will have to do so not by working in opposition to the United States but rather by bringing the United States within its own sphere. One idea that deserves consideration is to hold summit meetings for the leaders of the Asia Pacific region; such gatherings could promote dialogue between the United States and Asia and help make the United States a full-fledged member of the Asian community. Prime Minister Mahathir's idea of an East Asia Economic Caucus could also prove worthwhile, providing that this grouping is positioned under a broad Asia-Pacific umbrella. The call for an Asian restoration must not be pursued in a way that excludes non-Asian countries; nor, in fact, is it being approached in that manner. The goal is rather that of bringing non-Asian countries into Asia, so to speak, and coexisting with them.

Chapter Thirty-Seven

Mahathir Mohamad and Shintarō Ishihara: "The Voice of Asia," 1995

Kristine Dennehy

The following excerpts are primarily from commentary by Ishihara Shintarō, the governor of Tokyo since 1999 and an outspoken critic of Japan's economic and strategic relationship with the United States, particularly in the wake of "Japan bashing" by American politicians in the 1980s. In this dialogue with the prime minister of Malaysia, Mahathir Mohamad, the two leaders joined together to criticize the legacy of European and American hegemony in the modern age and proposed instead a greater role for Japan as a model for a "flexible" kind of leadership among Asian nations. The Japanese title of the book, *"No" to Ieru Ajia*, translated as *The Asia That Can Say "No,"* is reminiscent of Ishihara's 1989 *The Japan That Can Say "No,"* a book that originally also included comments by Sony chairman Morita Akio, who shared Ishihara's frustration with American complaints about Japan's trade surplus and criticized Americans for their self-righteous attitude regarding human rights and fair trade practices. Like Hayashi Fusao (see II:34) before him, Ishihara is disheartened by the lack of pride and self-confidence among his compatriots, and he echoes Hayashi's attacks on postwar progressives who, he argues, have blindly accepted the notion that Japanese people should be critical of their own country's modern history and therefore fearful of the prospects for a future tied to Asia.

Ishihara originally gained fame as a novelist with the publication of *Taiyō no Kisetsu* (Season of the Sun, 1956; published in English as *Season of Violence*, 1966), which shocked readers with characters who rejected the values and proper demeanor of their elders. It sparked the "*Taiyō-zoku*" (sun tribe) phenomenon of postwar Japanese youth who emulated the fictional characters through their overtly sexual, violent, and antisocial behavior. The charismatic Ishihara subsequently joined the conservative Liberal Democratic Party and proved adept at tapping into and fostering the growing nationalist sentiments that accompanied Japan's increasing economic prosperity.

Both Ishihara and Mahathir stress the dichotomy between Eastern values and Western technical skills and argue that Japan is uniquely suited to be a model for other Asian nations eager to improve their material standard of living without compromising local cultural and social traditions. Mahathir first went to Japan in 1961 when the country was preparing for the 1964 Tokyo Olympics and was greatly impressed by the discipline and orderly nature of Japanese society. In the debates over so-called Asian values during the 1990s, Mahathir was critical of notions such as competition and individualism, which he associates with Western values, and argues that Asians need to work together to maintain and develop a distinct identity based on family-oriented social relations and social harmony (cf. Hashim 2000; Mahathir 2004). In the one section by Mahathir included here, he refers to the moral decline of Western families and society in general, represented by redefined notions of the family, including same-gender marriages. The other passages here highlight Ishihara's central areas of concern in the realms of economics, politics, and culture and provide a vision for an alternative path for Japan as a world leader, aligned in all these respects with other Asian nations.

Source (English in the original)
Mahathir Mohamad and Shintarō Ishihara: *The Voice of Asia: Two Leaders Discuss the Coming Century*. Trans. Frank Baldwin. Kōdansha, 1995. Originally published as *"No" to ieru Ajia* (The Asia That Can Say "No"). Kōbunsha, 1994.

I. Economic/Political Ties:

We are at a historic juncture. As Prime Minister Mahathir has noted, East Asia's rapid economic growth portends the future. The collapse of communism and the ebbing of the West mark the end of European modernism, long the dynamic force of global change. The Asian century is at hand.

Oswald Spengler's *The Decline of the West* (1918) prophesied what is now unfolding before our eyes: The West is reaping what it sowed. In the new era, East Asia, once so wantonly colonized and plundered, will sustain global prosperity.

Europe and the United States plainly hope, through the EU and NAFTA, respectively, to reassert their leadership of the global economy. Rejecting the Western brand of power politics—forcing concessions out of trading partners—East Asia seeks a shared prosperity through a flexible association. East Asia would not try to intimidate Europe or North America. But the United States is taking advantage of Asian tolerance and gradualism to block formation of a regional group here.

The end of the East-West ideological conflict has finally enabled Japan to start to disengage from the West. . . . Japanese are Asian, related to this region by blood and culture, and Japan is an Asian country. Again cognizant of the East, many Japanese sense the vitality of this region. Our interests lie more with Asia than with America.

Japan has come home to Asia, and our neighbors have gradually encouraged Tokyo to play a more active role, politically as well as economically. Although criticism continues that Tokyo's foreign policy is too attuned to U.S. priorities, trade flows—the movement of goods and services—have changed.

Prepared by decades of steady economic growth and investment in physical infrastructure and human resources, East Asia seized the opportunity. No matter how Washington tries to thwart the EAEC, Japanese offshore manufacturing is a fact of life. The Greater East Asia Co-Prosperity Sphere of World War II, backed as it was by the Imperial Army and Navy, had to be unwelcome. But now, though imperceptible to the untrained observer, Japan is building strong positive ties with East Asia.

Japan has returned to the East and we identify first and foremost with Asia. Of course, we cannot ignore our ties with the United States; the bilateral relationship is vital to both parties. Nevertheless, the time is approaching when the East should be our top foreign policy priority. To ignore the course of history and cling to the West would soon leave us excluded from East and West.

Global commerce—the spread of trade and reduction of tariffs—is an outgrowth of Western modernism. Yet in the nineteenth century free trade meant European merchants were free to sell things to the "natives." If the local people balked at opening ports or signing treaties of commerce, gunships and marines backed up the demand. Threats and force were integral to gaining market access. What Asians mean by freedom is very different from the way Europeans and Americans use the concept.

Americans have to understand that Asia is different from the West, has ancient traditions, especially compared with the United States, which did not even exist three centuries ago, and is enormously diverse.

To put it provocatively, we may have to form an Asian united front against Americanization. A vocal group of journalists and academics in the United States, dubbed the "revisionists," vilify Asia for having norms that were not made in the U.S.A. Japan's business practice and customs, for example, are dismissed as different and therefore wrong. We have to turn that argument against them by saying: "That's right. We're different. Why should Asians be the same as you?" It will take an Asian crusade to change Western attitudes into acceptance of cultural pluralism.

I am convinced the Asian era will be a time of peaceful coexistence. We are no threat to Europe or North America. We will not do what the West did to us. Unlike the colonial overlords who tried to convert indigenous peoples to Christianity, regardless of how powerful Asia becomes, we will never force our beliefs on others. It is not our way.

Now that Asians are working together to create a new economic co-prosperity sphere, it is far more useful to address what Japan's role should be and how we can accomplish it.

I use the word "co-prosperity" advisedly. Some people will associate it with the Greater East Asia Co-Prosperity Sphere, the wartime term used to rationalize aggression, or the propaganda slogan "eight corners of the world under one roof." I do not want to get bogged down in a sterile debate, accused of being an unreconstructed ultranationalist and so forth. What counts today is GNP, not the number of ballistic missiles a country has in hardened shelters.

The paramount reality of the mid-1990s—the retreat of the West and the increasing dynamism of Asia—presages a period of unprecedented prosperity for this region. By pouring as much investment and technology as possible into the region, Japanese can atone for the Pacific War and give substance to the Pan-Asian idealism of the 1930s. We would not be the board of directors for Asia, Inc., but pull our weight in solidarity with our Asian colleagues.

II. Cultural Affinities:

On my trips to Southeast Asia since the mid-1980s I have noticed many signs of the spread of Japanese popular culture. The year-long public television drama, "Oshin," a story about a young woman who personifies the traditional feminine virtues of selfless service and dedication, was broadcast in China and watched by 200 million people. The program was also very popular in Singapore, Indonesia, and Vietnam.

Our pop culture strikes a sympathetic chord across Asia. No hard sell is necessary; the audience is receptive. Underlying the empathy for Oshin, for instance, is an Asian work ethic very different from that of the West. Most Europeans and Americans would prefer a life of leisure, while Asians thrive on work. Westerners simultaneously hate and envy the idle rich. Not Asians. We feel sorry for a well-off man who has no calling. People say, "What a shame he hasn't got something worthwhile to do."

Many Western societies . . . are morally decadent. There is diminishing respect for the institutions of the family and marriage, and some even permit same-gender marriages. To us, that is not development. You must maintain cultural and moral values. We do not want to be just a rich country. (Mahathir)

The family is the spiritual foundation of Asia. Some Westerners retort that this was also true in the good old days in Europe but individualism weakened the family and that is already happening in Asia too. The skeptics even call Asian familism cultural backwardness. It sounds to me like an admission that they lost their core value, part of the Protestant ethic, in the course of modernization.

Family values are still paramount to most Asians. It is not that we are less individualistic or egotistical than Westerners, just that we assume a priori there must be an equilibrium between the individual and the larger society. We live in a social context. If Western societies are like an edifice made of bricks, each component separate and distinguishable, Asian societies are like nearly seamless concrete structures. We see ourselves as indivisible parts of the whole.

We are an Asian people, ethnically and culturally. Japan is not a unique, homogeneous country, as some argue. That is obvious from a glance at the faces in a crowded room. . . . Japanese are a heterogeneous people, shaped millennia ago by immigrants from Mongolia, the Korean peninsula, Southeast Asia and the South Pacific. The earliest Japanese were the Ainu, who still survive as a distinct ethnic group. . . . As this century draws to a close, we should come home to Asia, our heritage and our future.

From the temples of Kyoto to the Confucian veneration of family and learning, Japanese belong to Asia. Much of the time that identity goes unrewarded; we instinctively respond like other Asians. Mindful of our ancestry, we should deepen our ties with this region. We can accomplish far more with other Asians than in a "partnership" with Americans.

Chapter Thirty-Eight

Koo Jong-suh: "Pan-Asianism. Primacy of East Asia," 1995

Eun-jeung Lee

After the first discussions in Korea of the concept of an East Asian region at the end of the nineteenth and the beginning of the twentieth century ended in the discrediting of the concepts of regionalism and regional integration due to the instrumentalization of regional concepts for the sake of Japanese colonial rule in Korea and elsewhere (Shin 2005), it took almost a century for Korean intellectuals to rediscover "East Asia." The people of South Korea, too, became increasingly aware of the existence of "East Asia" during the first half of the 1990s, above all as a result of changing realities in the international situation surrounding South Korea, above all, the end of the Cold War. While the government of Kim Young-sam (1993–1997) strongly encouraged "internationalization," Korean companies expanded massively into China and Southeast Asia. At the same time, an influx of labor from other Asian regions, in particular China and Southeast Asia, was set in train. Under these new circumstances, debate over the notion of "East Asia" reemerged strongly in 1990s Korea (Shin 2005).

Koo Jong-suh's article "Pan-Asianism. Primacy of East Asia" is one of many contributions to the Korean debate on East Asia and regional integration that appeared in the mid-1990s as an expression of East Asian feelings of superiority at a time of much talk about the coming of "The Pacific Century." In South Korea, it is generally agreed that there were two reasons for the re-emergence of this debate during the 1990s. One was the end of the Cold War and East Asia's economic success (until the crisis of 1997); the other was the dissemination of the poststructuralist critique of modernity. Poststructuralism was introduced to South Korea at the end of the 1980s and quickly gained influence among intellectuals. Until then, Korean intellectuals had been strongly influenced by Eurocentric notions and the idea of modernity. Conceptually, "Asia" and "Korea" were considered as premodern constructs that ought to be discarded. Thus, the poststructuralist critique of modernity came as a deep shock. In particular, Edward Said's critique of "Orientalism" had a powerful impact on Korean intellectuals. An influential Korean intellectual, Yi Chin-o (1959–), commented, "For a long time we believed that the East was somewhat backward and worthless. Therefore we were quite depressed. [Thanks to Said], we now know that this was the historic result of Western hegemonic strategies to diminish and humiliate [our] culture. Now that we have drunk cold water and come to our senses, we turn to our tradition with hope" (Yi 2000).

This new self-assurance was enhanced by Samuel Huntington's thesis of a "clash of civilizations" that regarded "East Asia" as an independent civilization. To be sure, many Korean intellectuals critically scrutinized Huntington's thesis, among others president-to-be Kim Dae-jung (Kim 1994) and Han Sang-jin (2003), one of Kim's advisers. However, in their reactions and those of the wider public there was also a palpable sense of satisfaction that at long last Korea could no longer be ignored on the world stage—a notion we can also sense in Koo Jong-suh's article introduced here. On the other hand, by that time, Korea had already embarked on the path of democratization, and thus Huntington's thesis could no longer be used to legitimize an authoritarian regime as it was, for example, in Singapore or Malaysia, where supporters of authoritarian forms of government in the so-called Asian values debate asserted that Confucian ethics with its paternalistic view of society, far from being the cause of (former) Asian backwardness, had made a positive contribution to East Asia's social stability and economic success. Nevertheless, just as in Singapore, Malaysia, and other countries in the region, Huntington's thesis gave a boost to Korean self-confidence based on the idea of an autonomous East Asian civilization.

This boost in self-confidence was much stronger in Korea than in Japan or China. In an opinion poll held simultaneously in Seoul, Tokyo, and Beijing in October 1993, 300 young intellectuals (aged between thirty and forty-five) in each country were asked about their views on the future. When asked whether they believed that the paradigm of East Asian civilization could become a universal paradigm for the postmodern world, 90 percent of Korean respondents, 37.5 percent of Japanese, and 16 percent of Chinese replied in the affirmative (Delpai Research 1995). These differences can be explained in terms of the self-esteem derived from their respective countries' recent achievements and their resulting confidence in the potential of East Asian civilization.

In South Korea, debates on "East Asia" filled an ideological gap which the end of the Cold War had opened up. Certainly, this emergence of alternative discourses was not new. Throughout the twentieth century such debates had taken various forms, developing and receding at times of political upheaval. Salient examples are the discussions of Pan-Asianism in Japan before 1945 and of "East–West Culture" in China in the 1920s. Such discourses emerged whenever the weakness of Western civilization was attributed to Western belief in the supreme power of rationality. The Korean and East Asian debates on "East Asia" were no exception. They were alternative discourses in the sense that they were an antithetical construction that relied on the existence of a "West" in crisis. However, one should not underestimate the importance of these debates, in particular because they revived the notions of national and ethnic identity in East Asia and indeed the whole concept of identity formation. These debates not only were antithetical in character but also developed their own traditions over time. Thus, for decades in Korea the term "East Asian identity" was taboo, as it evoked memories of Japanese Pan-Asianism before 1945, an ideology that had been utilized to justify Japanese imperialism and territorial expansion. Even nowadays, Japanese and Chinese discourse on "Asia" generates a good deal of suspicion in Korea, as the Koo article reproduced here also shows.

As a result, the reemergence of such discourse in 1990s Korea, which included reference to the historical experience of Pan-Asianism, came as something of a surprise. The basic reason for the renewal of the debate was the peculiar Korean perception of "East Asia" as a useful tool for solving the "Korea problem." In this new "East Asia discourse," Korea was expected to occupy a central strategic position in East Asia. As China and Japan (in the Korean perception) had both risen to world-power status after the end of the Cold War, South Korea's regional influence had weakened, and Korean intellectuals and politicians were under pressure to find a new strategy for the new age. They claimed to have found it in the formation of an "East Asian community" and an "East Asian identity." Despite the obvious weaknesses of these concepts, they underlay the persistent vitality of the pan-Asian discourse in South Korea.

The participants in the Korean discourse on East Asia largely agree that the idea of an East Asian community under Korean leadership is a somewhat utopian notion. That this debate has nevertheless succeeded in gaining so much importance during the past decade is due to the participants' shared beliefs in its direct relevance to the question of the Korean peninsula. With few exceptions, the common assumption is that, in order to overcome the division of Korea, a regional concept of "East Asia" is needed as a new paradigm in politics. Since the country remains divided after the collapse of the Soviet Union and the end of the Cold War, the renewed debate on "East Asia" in Korea is seen as a means by which this division can be overcome. The article by Koo Jong-suh covers the full range of South Korean discourse on "East Asia" since the mid-1990s and is a typical example of a Korean perspective on the future of East Asian integration. Koo, a journalist specializing in international relations, worked over a long period for the daily newspaper *Joong-ang Ilbo*. Currently he is the director of the Research Institute for the History of Civilization in Seoul and one of the most important contributors to the debate on East Asia in newspapers and magazines. His views have had quite a strong political impact, particularly on the regional policies of the Roh Moo-hyun administration (2003–2008). Analyzing that government's northeastern Asian policies, it is clear that they were based on the academic debate over East Asia that emerged in the mid-1990s. In this sense, the discourse of East Asia in South Korea is an interesting example of an academic debate and its impact on politics.

Source (English in the original)
Koo Jong-suh, "Pan-Asianism. Primacy of East Asia." *The Monthly Joong-ang*, April 1995.

The world today is undergoing rapid changes. The Cold War world order, under which the international community was polarized between the Western and communist poles, has been dismantled. The ideological conflict between capitalism and communism is over, and a unipolar system, with the United States at its apex, has now emerged. It is the United States that presently commands the United Nations and is directing the new world order. . . . The United States is opposed to any change in the international status quo or a westward shift in the center of world power. The objective of U.S. world policy lies in retaining U.S. supremacy. One of its strategies calls for an active promotion of the Asia-Pacific Economic Cooperation (APEC) grouping. . . .

Pitted against this American effort are movements that seek to cement solidarity among Asian Nations. The most outstanding example of this is the EAEC (East Asian Economic Caucus), promoted by Malaysian Prime Minister Mahathir. The thrust of this movement lies in the formation of a purely Asian group for economic cooperation, leaving out the United States. Such an idea can be described as a manifestation of Pan-Asianism.

Pan-Asianism is the concept that Asians should free themselves from the domination, pressure and influence of Europe and the United States, whose culture and interests they do not share, and should unite and cooperate so that together they can preserve their culture and interests. This is an advocacy of Asian self-determination, an "Asia for Asians" movement. The concept stresses the need for Asians to approach and solve Asian problems themselves.

Movements advocating Pan-Asianism began during the period of Western expansion in Asia in the latter half of the last [the nineteenth] century, when European industrial powers mounted expansionist, colonial offensives in Asia. Prominent among these advocates were China's Sun Yat-sen and India's Jawaharlal Nehru. Japan's war-time drive for a "Great East Asia Co-Prosperity Sphere" could be considered one such Pan-Asianist concept. The movements led by Sun and Nehru failed because they could not enlist the support of countries other than their own. The Japanese concept of co-prosperity was nothing more than a façade for Japanese imperialist designs to occupy and rule other Asian countries. It was destined to fail, as indeed it did in the course of World War II.

Now that we are entering a new age, a Pan-Asianist movement should take a fresh approach. It should establish as its goal the preparation of Asians to meet the challenges of the new century, and it should be carried out in three stages.

The first should be a transitional, preparatory stage. In this stage, Asia would accept the US-led APEC setup. . . . In the second stage, Asians should consolidate their solidarity. In other words, they should create a continent-wide community made up of only Asian states, leaving out the United States and Oceanic countries. The union of regional groups in Southeast Asia, Northeast Asia and Western Asia would have to take place at this time. This could be realized on the strength of good neighbourly relations and competence built up during the first stage.

During the second stage, Asia will experience a great deal of tension and conflict in its relations with other continents. In particular, the United States, as the established hegemonic power, will apply constant pressure on Asia and try to create dissension among Asian countries to disrupt their efforts to establish independence and exclude outsiders. However, the outsiders will fail in their attempts to reverse the trend. Asia's independence is needed for Asians to prepare themselves for competing squarely with Europe and the Americas under a multipolar world order beginning in the 2020s. This second stage will cover two to three decades starting from around 2010.

In the third stage, East Asia will establish superiority over other regions. In other words, apart from Western Asia where diversity is prominent, East Asia should unite and try to become the world's center stage. It would be in this stage that Northeast Asia should merge with Southeast Asia to form an "East Asia Community". Under a multipolar setup, competition among the continents and among regional communities will intensify. The task for East Asia would be to establish its superiority in this stage, which would continue through the middle decades of the next century.

By going through these stages, East Asia would attain a position from which it could lead the world militarily, economically and culturally as a result of having become the most prosperous region in the world. This would complete the preparations to establish East Asian supremacy beginning at the end of the twenty-first century.

Broadly speaking, Asia consists of three different regions. First, there is Northeast Asia, comprising Korea, China and Japan. This is called the sphere of Confucian culture, Chinese characters or Chinese civilization. The second is South Asia, consisting of Southwest Asia and Southeast Asia, ranging from Pakistan and India in the west to the Philippines in the east. This region may be called the Indian civilization or Buddhist cultural sphere, though the region also has strong Islamic and Catholic elements. The third region is West Asia, ranging from Afghanistan to the Middle East and bordering the Mediterranean. This could be described as the Islamic or Arab civilization sphere, since, with the exception of Israel, most of the nations are Arab or Islamic states.

East Asia, comprising Northeast Asia and Southeast Asia, includes the Confucian states on the Western Pacific and a number of Buddhist nations. Among those nations, Korea and Vietnam share a delicate yet crucial role. Situated between China and Japan, Korea has traditionally played the role of bridge or mediator between the two countries. In other words, when the civilization on the continent had the upper hand, Korea passed it on to Japan and helped its civilization. Chinese characters and Buddhism passed through Korea into Japan. Algebra, painting and architecture were among those skills taught to the Japanese by Koreans. When maritime civilization has the upper hand, as it does now, Korea plays the role of transferring it to China. . . .

Though they are not neighbours, Korea and Vietnam share an important and unique mission for the future of East Asia. Korea needs to achieve reunification and, working with China and Japan, build a Northeast Asian community of cooperation. It is Korea's mission to achieve this goal. . . .

The hegemonic ambitions of China and Japan will be harmful in bringing about an age of East Asian supremacy. Their pursuit of hegemony is restrained somewhat by the United States, but is continuing nonetheless. East and Southeast Asian nations should join the United States in efforts to block their advance.

If China and Japan give up their ideas of pursuing hegemony and instead seek coexistence and share prosperity with the nations surrounding them, an age of East Asian primacy will come earlier and more easily. Asians should make a united effort to make this happen. The objective of the new Pan-Asianism is no less than moving Asia from marginal existence to a central presence.

Chapter Thirty-Nine

Japan and Southeast Asian Regional Integration: Prime Minister Koizumi in Singapore, 2002

Kristine Dennehy

The excerpts reproduced here are from a speech given by Japanese Prime Minister Koizumi Jun'ichirō (b. 1942) in 2002. Koizumi gave this speech in Singapore, which he visited with the objective of tightening Japan's relations with Southeast Asia. The speech represents a turning point in Japan's relationship with the countries of Southeast Asia in the post–World War II period. In the aftermath of the Asian financial crisis in 1997 and as a consequence of the 9/11 terrorist attacks on the United States in 2001, Koizumi's version of pan-Asian regionalism as promoted in this speech was predicated on a strong regional economic interdependence. It also reflected an emerging trend of cooperation in the area of "security" and "regional stability." At the same time, Koizumi also stressed the fundamental importance of the ties of the Association of Southeast Asian Nations (ASEAN) with the two other economic powerhouses in East Asia—China and South Korea—in addition to interregional links with the United States and Europe. While acknowledging the various levels of economic development and ongoing political reform in each Asian country, Koizumi asserted that they all shared the common values of democracy and market economy.

On the domestic front, Koizumi represented a new kind of charismatic, reform-oriented leadership compared to the old guard of the conservative Liberal Democratic Party (LDP), which had dominated postwar Japanese politics for decades. Promoting "regime change" and a "reform of the LDP," he became a highly popular prime minister in April 2001 with his strive for "reforms without sanctuaries," which targeted pork-barrel construction projects as well as the postal savings system, the reform of which was at the heart of Koizumi's domestic reform agenda.

Koizumi begins his Singapore speech with a reference to the Fukuda Doctrine of 1977, another pivotal moment in Japan's relations with Southeast Asian nations, following the decreased presence of the United States in Southeast Asia after the end of the Vietnam War. Despite Japan's ongoing close alliance with the United States, America's retreat from Indochina paved the way for greater Japanese autonomy in its relations with Singapore, Malaysia, Indonesia, Thailand, and the Philippines (the five original members of ASEAN). The Fukuda Doctrine specifically rejected Japan's playing a military role in Southeast Asia and emphasized that ties would be based on a relationship of mutual trust. It also asserted an equal relationship between Japan and ASEAN and noted their common interests in forging good relations with the other countries in Indochina. These specifications reflected the historical legacy of mistrust toward Japan because of Japanese expansionism and militarism in the region prior to Japan's surrender in 1945.

After France's defeat at Dien Bien Phu in May 1954, Cold War tensions led to American efforts to contain communism in Southeast Asia with the establishment in 1954 of the Southeast Asia Treaty Organization (SEATO), which was joined only by Thailand and the Philippines. In contrast to SEATO, ASEAN, formed in 1967 based on the principles of nonalignment, represented an explicit rejection of Cold War alliances. By the time of Koizumi's visit to Singapore, the five founding ASEAN members had been joined by Brunei Darussalam (in 1984, following its independence from Britain), Vietnam (1995), Myanmar and Laos (both in 1997), and Cambodia (1999). The term ASEAN+3, which came up in the early twenty-first century as an expression of an enlargement of regional integration in Southeast Asia by including Japan, the People's Republic of China (PRC), and the Republic of Korea. At this point in the early twenty-first century, Koizumi's stance was that cooperation among Asian countries must go hand in hand with affiliations to global institutions such as the World Trade Organization (WTO). For Koizumi, thus, the processes of regionalization and globalization are not exclusive but rather mutually reinforcing and complementary. They should take place simultaneously to serve the interests of Asian countries. The membership of both the PRC and Taiwan in a scheme of regional integration is mentioned as proof that such organizations provide a way to transcend economic and political rivalries left over from the twentieth century. He posited that Japan had a unique role to play in this kind of cooperation yet maintained a balance between identifying Japan as a leader in the region (with skills to offer in areas such as legal and bureaucratic reform) and noting the special talents of Southeast Asians, such as their English-language ability.

Furthermore, Koizumi highlighted the astounding economic achievements of Singapore. Singapore, like Hong Kong, Taiwan, and South Korea, was known in the 1970s and 1980s as one of the "Asian tigers" because of its status as a Newly Industrialized Economy (NIE). By 2002, Singapore, however, had surpassed this NIE threshold and concluded the first-ever free trade agreement with Japan, a sign that the two countries had become true partners in the economic realm. Conspicuously absent from Koizumi's remarks was any reference to the particular bond of so-called Asian values, such as those stressed in the 1990s by Singapore's former Prime Minister Lee Kuan Yew, which certain politicians in Japan refer to when constructing an anti-Western version of pan-Asian solidarity. Instead, Koizumi emphasized the particular urgency of contemporary issues such as global antiterrorism cooperation and declared that Japan had an "international obligation" to contribute both economically and politically, if not militarily, to these pressing issues. Such a claim was partly the result of criticism leveled at Japan during the 1991 Gulf War when its $13 billion contribution had been derided as "checkbook diplomacy." But it also dovetailed with widespread domestic support for the strengthening of Japan's Self-Defense Forces and the revision of Article 9 of the Constitution, which has served as a check on Japanese military activities abroad throughout the postwar era. Later in 2002, these trends continued to gain momentum with the increased sense that North Korea posed a serious threat to Japan because of its nuclear capabilities. In September 2002, Koizumi took the unprecedented step of meeting with Kim Jong Il in Pyongyang, where the "Dear Leader" of North Korea admitted to the abduction of a number of Japanese citizens in the 1970s and 1980s.

In his speech, Koizumi referred to the "paradigm shift" that had taken place since 9/11 and made an oblique reference to the links between poverty and terrorism in areas such as Mindanao in the Philippines and Aceh in Indonesia. Interestingly, he made no explicit reference to the Muslim populations in Mindanao or separatism in Aceh but implied that the political instability in these regions transcended religion and ideology and could be contained by improving the standard of living in economic terms. Koizumi's speech also reflected a stage in ASEAN's relationship with Japan that has largely overcome issues such as the demand for a Japanese apology for its actions during World War II or the need for Japanese politicians to reassure their Asian neighbors that they will not retread the road of militarism taken in the early twentieth century. Koizumi's call for cooperation between the Japanese Coast Guard and its ASEAN counterparts came on the heels of joint exercises with the Philippines in 2001 in an effort to combat piracy on the high seas. This is a representative example of the kind of transnational issues that Japan and other Asian countries are confronted with.

Source (English in the original)
Speech by Prime Minister of Japan Junichiro Koizumi, "Japan and ASEAN in East Asia: A Sincere and Open Partnership" (14 January 2002,

Singapore). Prime Minister of Japan and His Cabinet Website, http://www.kantei.go.jp/foreign/koizumispeech/2002/01/14speech_e.html (last accessed 30 March 2010).

Your Excellency, Prime Minister Goh Chok Tong,
Your Excellency, Deputy Prime Minister and Minister for Defence Tony Tan,
Ladies and Gentlemen,

I am greatly honored to give this speech here in Singapore, the final stop on my schedule of visits to the countries of ASEAN.

Singapore is a remarkable nation with remarkable people. Bursting through the constraints of size and resources, Singapore through sheer energy and willpower has created a tremendous place for itself in the world. Through its economic and diplomatic vitality, it contributes to the international community far in excess of what size alone would warrant. And so to the government and the people of Singapore, let me express my admiration and respect for your achievements.

I am told that Singapore is called the "Lion City." Maybe it has something to do with my hairstyle, but in Japan I am known as the "Lion Prime Minister." Perhaps that is why I am so delighted to be here in the Lion City.

Today I would like to speak about cooperation between Japan and ASEAN and my concept of how this cooperation can contribute to all of East Asia.

. . . Twenty-five years ago in 1977, then-Prime Minister Takeo Fukuda [1905–1995] made a speech in Manila, citing "equal partnership" and "heart-to-heart understanding" between Japan and ASEAN. . . .

In the quarter-century since the "Fukuda Speech," the global situation has undergone tremendous change. In Southeast Asia, peace has progressed with the resolution of conflicts in Indochina, resulting in the expansion of ASEAN to ten countries. Democratization and a market economy are also progressing in Asia. The People's Republic of China and Taiwan have joined the WTO. Furthermore, as a result of the terrorist attacks on the United States, we've seen a paradigm shift in security concepts, making patently clear the importance of working together for the sake of peace and stability.

. . . I believe that Japan has made a contribution in strengthening the countries of ASEAN. True to the old adage, "A friend in need is a friend indeed," Japan at the time of Asia's financial crisis played a role in easing that crisis. We viewed the situation not just as your challenge but as our own. I believe that Japan-ASEAN relations have reached a new level of maturity and understanding. In the 21st century, as sincere and open partners, Japan and ASEAN should strengthen their cooperation under the basic concept of "acting together—advancing together."

So, what are the areas where we should focus our cooperation as we "act together—advance together?"

First, by undertaking reforms in our respective countries, we will advance individually and jointly toward increased prosperity.

. . . Japan is ready to support ASEAN's serious efforts of reform. Specifically, Japan offers its cooperation to improve legislation, administrative capabilities and nation-building measures. . . .

Japan will continue to cooperate in such areas as Mekong Subregion Development so that Cambodia, Laos, Myanmar and Vietnam may accelerate their economic development. It is also important that we continue to cooperate in information and communications technology, which contributes to the integration of ASEAN. . . .

The second point is to continue and strengthen our cooperation for the sake of stability.

Instability is not always elsewhere. Sometimes it is at home. Factors for instability are also in the region. Japan for many years now has been the largest contributor of foreign aid in the world. In Southeast Asia, Japan would like to actively cooperate in reducing poverty and preventing conflicts, in such cases as Mindanao, Aceh and East Timor. In particular, by the spring of this year Japan will dispatch a Self Defense Force Engineer Unit to Peace-Keeping Operations in East Timor.

In recent years, Japan has begun to fulfill its international obligations, such as peace-keeping missions. We have dispatched Self Defence Forces to help in Cambodia, Mozambique, Zaire and the Golan Heights. And, in cooperation with the countries of ASEAN, we intend to make an even more active contribution to ensure regional stability here in Southeast Asia. . . .

Efforts towards democratization in Myanmar must also be accelerated, and this is an endeavor that we fully support.

Together, Japan and ASEAN must also tackle a variety of transnational issues such as terrorism, piracy, energy security, infectious diseases, the environment, narcotics and trafficking in people. . . .

A third area of cooperation between Japan and the countries of ASEAN relates to the future. I would like to propose initiatives in five areas.

One, we must focus on education and human resources development, which form the foundation for national development. I would like to dispatch a governmental mission to ASEAN countries to promote exchange and cooperation between universities. Some Japanese universities have already opened courses in English as well as Japanese language courses for students in ASEAN by utilizing the Internet. . . .

Two, I propose that 2003 be designated as the Year of Japan-ASEAN Exchange. We should present a number of ideas to stimulate exchanges in all areas, including intellectual and cultural. . . .

Three, I would like to propose an Initiative for Japan-ASEAN Comprehensive Economic Partnership. . . . The Japan-Singapore Economic Agreement for a New Age Partnership, which was signed yesterday, is an example of such economic partnership. . . .

Four, in order to pursue development in a new era, I propose the convening of an Initiative for Development in East Asia meeting. . . .

Five, I propose that Japan and ASEAN security cooperation, including transnational issues such as terrorism, be drastically intensified. . . . We must band together to eradicate the plague of piracy. In addition, I would like to strengthen cooperation between the Coast Guard of Japan and ASEAN counterparts. I also wish to promote regional cooperation in strengthening energy security, in light of the gap between the rapid increase of energy demand and lagging energy supply within Asia. . . .

Finally, let me turn to how cooperation between Japan and ASEAN should be linked to cooperation with all of East Asia. . . .

The first step is to make the best use of the framework of ASEAN+3. We should promote cooperation on the broad range of areas that I have been discussing today, in order to secure prosperity and stability in our region.

. . . An important challenge is strengthening economic partnership in the region. The Initiative for Japan-ASEAN Comprehensive Economic Partnership that I mentioned earlier will be an important platform for this purpose. I expect that the ASEAN-China Free Trade Area and moves toward economic partnership between ASEAN and Australia and New Zealand will make similar contributions.

. . . Through [accumulation] of this [concrete] cooperation, I expect that the countries of ASEAN, Japan, China, the Republic of Korea, Australia and New Zealand will be core members of such a community.

The community I am proposing should be by no means an exclusive entity. Indeed, practical cooperation in the region would be founded on close partnership with those outside the region. In particular, the role to be played by the United States is indispensable because of its contribution to regional security and the scale of its economic interdependence with the region. Japan will continue to enhance its alliance with the United States. Cooperation with Southwest Asia, including India, is also of importance, as is cooperation with the Pacific nations through APEC, the Asia-Pacific Economic Cooperation group, and with Europe through ASEM, the Asia-Europe Meeting. APEC and ASEM are important tools to link our region to other regions.

Through such efforts, the community I have described can take meaningful actions for regional cooperation. I believe that this in turn will benefit global stability and prosperity.

Chapter Forty

Nakamura Tetsu and the Peshawar-kai

Hatsuse Ryūhei

The source reproduced here is a protest raised by the Japanese physician Dr. Nakamura Tetsu against an attack by the U.S. Air Force on a civilian target that took place in Afghanistan on 2 November 2003. Two American helicopter gunships attacked a construction site where Nakamura's volunteers were working on excavating irrigation canals, having mistaken controlled explosions used by the Japanese in construction work for an attack by the Taliban. Fortunately, there were no casualties. Although it is a matter of debate whether Nakamura is a pan-Asianist, it is clear that his work in remote areas of Pakistan and Afghanistan is motivated mainly by his strong feeling of solidarity with Asian peoples, especially the oppressed among them, and his anger at perceived Western dominance over Asian politics, society, and culture.

Born in Fukuoka City in 1946, Nakamura obtained his medical degree from Kyushu University in 1973. Having heard, in 1982, a lecture by Iwamura Noboru (1927–2005), who had worked for many years in Nepal as a volunteer physician with the Japan Overseas Christian Medical Cooperative Service (JOCS), Nakamura decided to join JOCS. In May 1984 he was sent to the Mission Hospital in Peshawar in northwestern Pakistan, where he led the hospital's leprosy unit. Nakamura was also supported by a nongovernmental organization (NGO) called the Peshawar-kai, based in Fukuoka, which some of his friends founded in September 1983 while Nakamura was preparing for his departure for Pakistan.

Between 1984 and 1990, Nakamura worked chiefly within the framework provided by JOCS. At first, his major task was to treat leprosy patients. With financial support from the Peshawar-kai, he and his Afghan staff also started to provide medical treatment to Afghan refugees at camps on the northwestern frontier of Pakistan. To facilitate these activities, in January 1989 the Peshawar-kai established the Japan-Afghanistan Medical Service, which aimed to provide dispensary services for general—not just leprosy—patients in rural areas of Afghanistan. This violated the rules set by JOCS, which restricted the organization to providing manpower for missionary hospitals in developing countries but prohibited financial or material support. As a result, Nakamura was forced to resign from JOCS in 1990. In the 1990s, other Japanese arrived in Peshawar to work with Nakamura, who by this time was making efforts to extend his medical services to the rural poor in the mountainous areas of northeastern Afghanistan.

In October 1994, the Peshawar-kai established the Peshawar Leprosy Service, which was granted official status as a social welfare organization by the government of the North-West Frontier Province of Pakistan. In November 1998, in order to provide comprehensive support for its medical operations in the region, the Peshawar-kai opened its own seventy-bed hospital in Peshawar.

In 2000, a new stage of the Peshawar-kai's activities began when Nakamura and the association decided to launch a number of community development projects outside the field of medicine. Since then, a dozen or so Japanese volunteers have regularly been participating in projects in the region. The Peshawar-kai also launched a water supply project to provide clean water essential for the elimination of gastrointestinal infections. The project started with the digging of wells and then expanded to the restoration of abandoned *karez*—ancient underground canals—that are found in the area. By October 2001, the Peshawar-kai had helped local people dig more than 600 wells by providing them with financial, technical, and administrative support. In October 2001, when the United States started its bombing campaign against the Taliban in the aftermath of the terror attacks in the United States on 11 September 2001, the Peshawar-kai set up a "Funds for Life" program in Japan with the goal of providing food to Afghan refugees displaced by the bombing. In January 2002, by utilizing money left over from earlier fund-raising efforts, the organization launched the Green Ground Fund for Afghanistan.

However, the political and social situation of the Peshawar-kai volunteers based in Afghanistan deteriorated after September 2001. The Americans waged their "war on terror" against the Taliban in Afghanistan and pressured the Pakistani government to abandon its assistance to the Taliban and attack them instead. This led to the Taliban's supporters waging an armed struggle against the Pakistani government, causing chaos in the Peshawar region and undermining the basis of the Peshawar-kai's activities in Pakistan and Afghanistan. In April 2007, the Pakistani government ordered the Peshawar-kai to close its hospital by December 2009 and expelled Japanese doctors, nurses, and other medical support staff who worked there. In August 2008, Itō Kazuya, a fieldworker in agriculture in Afghanistan, was abducted and killed by a Taliban group. The deteriorating conditions forced all Japanese volunteers except Nakamura himself to leave Pakistan and Afghanistan in September 2008. The result is that more than half of the 1,500 wells built by the Peshawar-kai have now been abandoned. Notwithstanding such setbacks, in April 2009, Nakamura, together with Peshawar-kai members and local Afghans (many working as day laborers), completed a 24.3-kilometer irrigation canal after six years of extreme hardship. These canals irrigate 14,000 hectares of agricultural fields and provide a livelihood for more than 100,000 people.

What are the motives of Nakamura Tetsu and the Peshawar-kai? Nakamura sums up the basic principle behind his activities in the following slogan: "[We] go where others dare not go. [We] do what others dare not do" (Peshawar-kai 2009). Committed to human survival in the most basic conditions, Nakamura strives to be more practical than ideological, more flexible than rigid in fund-raising, and more idealistic than rational in his planning. Both his thinking and behavior demonstrate his concern with the implementation of human rights at the subsistence level endured by many Asian people, especially the socially and economically disadvantaged living in remote towns and villages. Thus, he has developed a strong sense of people-to-people solidarity, involving a respect for individual initiatives, which needs to be distinguished from political Pan-Asianism.

Nakamura's brand of Pan-Asianism has also found expression in his writings, an example of which is reproduced here. In Nakamura's understanding, both the bombing of a non-Western country and the subsequent recovery assistance offered it are based on the notion that Western modernity is a model for all societies to follow throughout the world. A non-Western country has to be bombed when it is judged not to have met Western standards of democracy, and only afterward is it given assistance for recovery so as to become "democratic" in the Western sense of the word. In both cases (destruction and reconstruction), the model proposed is not indigenous but exogenous since it comes from the West. In this way, Nakamura believes, the West oppresses the East in social and cultural terms as much as it oppresses it militarily, politically, and economically. It is this Western dominance in the social and cultural spheres that the Peshawar-kai has tried to overcome through its medical and communal activities.

Nakamura also criticizes the Japanese government's support for the Afghan War on the grounds that it hinders the activities of his NGO, which he takes pains to distance from the Japanese government. Yet, at the same time, he seems to be unaware of or unwilling to recognize the fact that the criticism he levels at the West applies also to his own activities, which, originating in Japan, could be interpreted as exogenous to Afghanistan. He emphasizes solidarity with Asia as the basis of his activities because like many other pan-Asianists he obviously believes (and indeed takes it for granted) that Asia constitutes a single entity, distinct and separate from the West. It is above all in that sense that he must be regarded as a pan-Asianist.

Source (English in the original)
Tetsu Nakamura, "Military Action Prompting Afghan Backlash." *International Herald Tribune/Asahi Shimbun*, 13 December 2003 (accessible online at http://www1a.biglobe.ne.jp/peshawar/eg/naka13dec03.html).

I am affiliated with the Peshawar-kai Medical Services (PMS), an organization currently helping to rebuild Afghanistan. On Nov. 2, while we were working to build an irrigation canal in Kunar province, U.S. helicopter gunships apparently mistook our blasting site for a ground-based attack. As a result, two choppers peppered the area with machine-gun fire, and the peaceful atmosphere that had been maintained at the site was destroyed in an instant.

Kunar is currently the focus of a steady buildup in U.S. military troop strength. The current level of local peace and order is the worst it has been in the 20 years I have spent there.

The poignant desire of Afghans, the vast majority of whom are farmers, is for food and a return to peace in their villages. Over the past four years, the eastern part of the country has suffered under an unprecedented drought, prompting the desertification of farmlands and the displacement of huge numbers of people.

Outside of the country, there is surprisingly little knowledge about how these displaced people have drifted into the big cities and now comprise one of the key factors behind the current deterioration of law and order. Our organization has sought to improve these conditions by digging wells—about 1,000 to date—and an irrigation canal is also under construction. This latest project aims to support the return to farming of well over 100,000 residents, thereby making a modest contribution to regional rebuilding and stability.

But a spate of accidental bombings by the U.S. military, linked to its mop-up operations against al-Qaida, has quickly managed to fuel residents' hostility against the American troops. As in Iraq, there are frequent attacks in Afghanistan, not only against the U.S. military, but also targeting United Nations agencies, the International Red Cross and overseas nongovernmental organizations (NGOs). These acts of aggression by local people have already caused some international bodies to withdraw. I imagine most Japanese find this difficult to understand, given that the groups traveled there with the original aim of offering humanitarian assistance.

This local backlash comes in response to the approach of linking rebuilding aid to military intervention, as well as the tendency to focus on the needs of outside countries, which causes such assistance to be far removed from the will of the people. At this point, the true sentiment of the Afghan people is that while the ruthless regime of the Taliban presented serious problems, the U.S. intervention is even more intolerable. Local people complain about how the Taliban has been replaced with American democracy, interpreting the situation simply as one repugnant system being cast out for another. Publicly expressing such sentiment, however, would simply earn them labels as al-Qaida collaborators.

In essence, violent intervention has failed to produce positive results. In other words, military troops are largely unnecessary in furnishing assistance for human survival and livelihood. The fact that before the recent incident, PMS had never once come under attack is evidence of this. In the recent accidental bombing, our organization was attacked not by "terrorists," but rather by the "justice of the international community." If the Japanese government aligns itself with this "justice" and dispatches "armed forces" in support of that stance in Iraq, hostility toward Japan will also erupt in Afghanistan. Under that scenario, there is no guarantee our organization would not be targeted, too.

We have already been forced to remove our Hinomaru [Rising Sun] flags and the word "Japan" from our vehicles, and we now repeatedly declare that our activities have no connection with the Japanese government. In peace, there is clearly a strength that exceeds that of military force. Tokyo's current tendency is to rebuke the very pacifism that has served as a core national platform in the postwar era as "unrealistic," while moving to approve not only the United States' exercising its military might, but also the dispatch of Self-Defense Forces.

In its ultimate implications, this leaning can only be labeled both risky and bizarre.

Chapter Forty-One

Wang Yi: "China's 'New Asianism' for the Twenty-First Century," 2006

Torsten Weber

With the rising political and economic power of China, a more proactive Chinese stance has emerged with regard to the claim to leadership in Asia. In this context, the value of Asianism has recently been "rediscovered" as a useful concept to appeal to an Asian commonality and to promote regional integration in East Asia. This "New Asianism" rests on a reevaluation of historical, mostly Japanese-led Asianism on the one hand and an affirmation of an implicitly China-centered cultural particularism on the other.

The academic groundwork for the current Chinese embrace of Asianism was laid by the historian Sheng Banghe, who, writing in the influential journal *Lishi Yanjiu* (Historical Research), in 2000, proposed a reevaluation of Japanese Asianism that extended thinking on the subject beyond the orthodox line—which hitherto had uniformly viewed Asianism as a Japanese ideology used to legitimize the conquest of China. Against this view, Sheng argued that some advocates of Japanese Asianism had initially promoted an "Asian alliance" (*Yazhou tongmeng*) and a concept of "Sino-Japanese mutual help and guidance" (*Zhong-Ri lianxie*) that was not directed against Asian countries but was rather a means of resistance against the Western powers (Sheng 2000: 125). A similar view was proposed by Wang Ping, a member of the Institute of Japanese Studies at the Chinese Academy of Social Sciences and frequent commentator on Sino–Japanese relations for the central organ of the Chinese Communist Party, the *Renmin Ribao* (People's Daily). Wang claimed that "Asianism cannot indiscriminately be labeled invasionism" and contended that the central argument in "Classical Asianism" had indeed been Asian solidarity (Wang Ping 2004: 17). For the twenty-first century, she proposed a "New Classical Asianism" that would take the form of nonexclusive regional cooperation (Wang Ping 2004: 366–67). Although Wang Ping claims to oppose avowals of "Asian values" and "Asian thought," or hegemonic hopes for an "Asian century," her perception of an Asian commonality draws explicitly on the traditional Chinese values of Confucianism and the assumed singular characteristics of "Chinese civilization" (*Zhonghua wenming*). In many respects, Wang Yi's call for a "Neo-Asianism for the twenty-first century" follows Wang Ping's line of argumentation.

Wang Yi was born in Beijing in 1953 and during the Cultural Revolution was banished to do physical work ("*xia fang*") in a rural area of China's northernmost province of Heilongjiang. After Mao's death in 1976, Wang returned to Beijing, where he studied at the Second Foreign Language Institute. In 1982, he entered the Ministry of Foreign Affairs and was appointed director of the Asia Bureau in 1995. Between 2001 and 2004 he served as vice minister in the Ministry of Foreign Affairs, a post he returned to in 2007. During his time as Chinese ambassador in Japan (2004–2007), Wang, who speaks excellent Japanese, gained a reputation as an expert on Japan. His efforts to improve Sino–Japanese relations have been widely praised by the media in both China and Japan.

Wang served as ambassador in Tokyo at a time of particularly tense relations between the two countries. During the premiership of Koizumi Jun'ichirō (2001–2006), Japan's relations with its Asian neighbors deteriorated to an unprecedented degree in the postwar period, largely because of the controversial visits of Koizumi and other members of his cabinet to the Yasukuni Shrine and disputes over Japanese history textbooks. In spring 2005, tensions between China and Japan led to massive and violent anti-Japanese demonstrations in China, and there were no mutual visits between Chinese and Japanese leaders from October 2001 until October 2006. Throughout this crisis, Wang Yi continually appealed to a Sino–Japanese commonality and put particular emphasis on the significance of past and present cooperation within Asia. Interestingly, he frequently resorted to language that resembled the Japanese Asianist rhetoric of the early twentieth century. In 2005, in a speech at Tokyo's Waseda University, he stressed that the "development of Asia in its entirety and the formation of an Asian consciousness" was necessary to accomplish the "revival of Asia" (*Ajia fukkō*). As in his article translated here, Wang explained that his vision of regional cooperation was premised on the idea of "reciprocal benefits and win-win relations" with other regions of the world. Nevertheless, like Wang Ping's "New Classical Asianism," Wang Yi's Neo-Asianism also assumes that Asian—in particular Chinese—virtues are unique.

Some weeks before the publication of Wang Yi's Asianism text in China's semiofficial *Waijiao Pinglun* (Foreign Affairs Review; Wang 2006b)—and only days after members of the Japanese Diet had once again visited the Yasukuni Shrine—Wang publicly put forward his vision of a "New Asianism" in Tokyo. In a speech titled "The future of Asia and the roles of Japan and China," he maintained that the gradual development of a "collective Asian consciousness" (*shūdanteki na Ajia ishiki*) in postwar Asia, as manifested in various types of "pan-Asian projects" (Association of Southeast Asian Nations [ASEAN], the Asian Cooperative Dialogue, and so on), heralded "a new Asianism for the twenty-first century" (Wang 2006a). This "New Asianism" should follow the principles of cooperation, openness, and harmony. Despite his repeated emphasis on equality, openness, and mutual benefits, Asia, as defined by Wang, is essentially an Asia centered on China—with "Chinese virtues" as its philosophical basis and China's rising economy as its engine of development. Consequently, the current Chinese adoption of Asianist rhetoric is being carefully monitored in Japan as a potential Chinese attempt at marginalizing Japan's role in Asia and promoting China to the position of regional spokesman and leader.

Source (translation from the Chinese original by Torsten Weber)
Wang Yi (2006b), "Sikao Ershiyi shiji de Xin Yazhouzhuyi" (Considering Neo-Asianism in the Twenty-First Century), *Waijiao Pinglun* (Foreign Affairs Review) 89, 6–10.

1 EARLY ASIANISM

In pre-modern Asia, there existed no clear geographical coordinates and intercontinental boundaries. Speaking in a general and traditional sense, the psychological limits of its people more or less comprised Northeast Asia, Southeast Asia, and Southern Asia. But in a broader and practical sense, geographically Asia also includes Central Asia, West Asia, and the region east of Russia's Ural Mountains. Asia's entire territory covers approximately 30% of the whole land area of the earth and includes approximately 60% of the total world population. While this article treats Asia in this broader sense, it also places special emphasis on the region understood in the traditional sense.

For a long period, Asia stood at the forefront of history and made some distinguished contributions to the human race. Among the four great ancient civilizations of the world, three are in Asia: China, India, and old Babylon. The three great religions of the world, Christianity, Buddhism, and Islam, all have their origins in Asia. Asia's classical Eastern philosophy continues to inspire human thought, and a number of outstanding inventions by Asians have influenced the progress of global civilization. Also, for a long time Asia was leading the world economy. As the data presented in Paul Bairoch's article "International Industrialization Levels from 1750 to 1980" [*Journal of European Economic History* 11: 2, Spring 1982, 269–333] demonstrate, at the beginning of the Industrial Revolution in the West, Asia accounted for two thirds of the world's GDP. In particular, China and India accounted for 32% and 24% respectively.

With the advent of the modern period, Asia fell behind as it could not keep up with the rapid tides of the Industrial Revolution and, confined to itself, the region gradually declined. In 1900, the combined GDP of China and India accounted for only 7.7% of the world total, while the six countries of Great Britain, France, Germany, Russia, Austria-Hungary, and Italy made up 54.5%, and the USA alone accounted for 23.6%. From the year 1510 onwards, when the Portuguese colonizers occupied Goa in India, almost all the Asian countries declined to various degrees as a result of becoming targets of invasion and colonization by the Western powers. Their peoples bore the tremendous sufferings inflicted by war and collective humiliation.

Confronted with invasion by the [Western] powers and with internal decline, members of the political and cultural elites of the various Asian countries began examining the position of Asia and that of their own countries from the perspective of international relations. Step by step they began connecting the fate of their own country with the future of Asia. Working from their respective positions, they formulated the ideal of Asianism (*Yazhouzhuyi*) and formed the movement known as "early Asianism".

We can divide early Asianism into roughly two periods. The first lasted from the Opium War [1839–1842] and the Japanese-American "Black Ships Incident" in the mid-nineteenth century [the "opening" of Japan by the United States in 1853–1854] until 1894, just before the Sino-Japanese War. In this period, a group of Japanese intellectuals took the lead in proposing the idea of an Asian alliance (*Yazhou lianhe*). They argued that Japan, China, and Korea were all members of an Eastern civilization (*dongfang wenming*) faced with increasing pressure from the advancing Western powers. Therefore, a Sino-Japanese alliance was desirable, and a triple alliance of Japan, China, and Korea also needed to be formed. At the same time, some important political figures and thinkers at the Qing [Ch'ing] court were making similar claims.

However, also at this very time, in Japan the domestic debate over national strategy came to a boil and eventually the argument for "leaving Asia, entering Europe," as represented by Fukuzawa Yukichi, prevailed. In 1889 and 1890 respectively, Japan promulgated an "Imperial Constitution" and instituted an "Imperial Diet." It adopted a political system based on a constitutional monarchy and imitated the "rich country, strong army" course characteristic of the Western powers. First of all, it directed its newfound aggression against Korea and China.

The second period lasted from the [beginning of the] Sino-Japanese War in 1894 to 1927 when the Japanese Prime Minister, Tanaka [Gi'ichi], called for an Eastern Conference (*Dongfang Huiyi*) and put forward his "Policy Outline on China," aiming at the invasion of China. In this period, the Western powers took a further step in their partition of the countries of Asia, in particular of China. Although Japan and the Western powers mutually colluded, they also checked each other. At the same time, Japan rapidly expanded its forces against Asia. Anti-Japanese resistance in Asia, particularly in China, intensified as the chief opposition to Japanese expansionism.

In the course of this process, in 1897 Japan established the Tōakai in Tokyo and the Dōbunkai the following year [*sic*]. Later, both merged into the Tōa Dōbunkai [all three organizations were in fact founded in 1898; see I:9] which became the chief center for Japanese research into Asian, particularly Chinese, issues and produced various relatively systematic ideologies of Asianism. At the same time, this early Asianism was increasingly diverted down a side road and gradually lost credibility as a tool of, and pretext for, the invasion and monopolization of Asia.

From the end of the nineteenth to the beginning of the twentieth century, early Chinese revolutionaries and thinkers such as Sun Yat-sen, Zhang Taiyan [Zhang Binglin, 1869–1936], Liang Qichao [1873–1929], and Li Dazhao also started to examine and elaborate Asianist thought from different perspectives. A number of intellectuals from India, such as Gandhi and Tagore, and others from Korea and Southeast Asia, subsequently added their contributions. Asianism became the common currency of the Asian political and intellectual world.

To sum up, the various forms of early Asianism share a number of common features:

First of all, it was a direct response to the oppression of the Western powers, which elicited the preliminary consciousness of ethnic nationalism and anti-colonialism.

Secondly, it was an intellectual and cultural phenomenon that followed the demise of the traditional East Asian international order. It forced the Asian elites to consider the reasons for the turn from prosperity to decay in their own countries, and in Asia in general, and it prompted a profound reconsideration of the common character of the destiny, interests, and culture of the countries affected.

Thirdly, it contained a relatively clear sense of resistance and exclusion. For example, right from the outset the Japanese scholar [politician and bureaucrat] Katsu Kaishū understood Asianism as "a coalition for a united resistance to the West."

Fourthly, Japan explored this option more vigorously than its neighbors, and at the same time nurtured and extended its strategic consciousness of the need to expand its influence abroad and to control Asia.

The development of early Asianism was never smooth, and the movement died prematurely. There were three main reasons for this outcome:

The first was the extreme weakness of the Eastern countries at that period, in particular as regards Asia's major power, China. It suffered from poverty and political weakness and this period is regarded as the most troubled in its history. Compared to the major world power blocs, Asia was very weak and it lacked the support of an adequate physical base for Asianism to flourish.

Secondly, the ideology of Asianism was formulated with relative haste and lacked theoretical direction. Also, it failed to elicit a sympathetic response from the leaders of the various Asian countries and, in particular, from the masses. Under the banner of Asianism, the demands of all sorts and varieties of narrow-minded ethnic nationalisms were combined.

Thirdly, Japan, the first [Asian] country to break away from the control of the [Western] powers and to embark on an industrial civilization, made the wrong choice and turned Asianism on its head. First, Japan opted for the doctrine of "leaving Asia, entering Europe," thus denying its own Asian identity. Following this, it associated itself with the Western powers and threatened the countries of Asia in a similar militaristic and aggressive spirit. Finally, it formed an alliance with international fascism and embarked on a path of militarism and aggression abroad, taking it beyond the point of no return. As early as 1919, Li Dazhao, one of the founders of the Chinese Communist Party, hit the nail on the head when he pointed out that "Japan's Greater Asianism is not a principle of peace, but of invasion; it is not the principle of national self-determination (*minzu zijue zhuyi*) but imperialism that annexes small and weak peoples; it is not Asian democracy but Japanese militarism."

In 1924, shortly before Dr. Sun Yat-sen fell ill and died, he made a famous speech in Kobe, Japan. At a crucial juncture of history, with his life-long political experience behind him, he issued a final warning to Japan (see II:5): "Japan to-day has become acquainted with the Western civilization of the rule of Might, but retains the characteristics of the Oriental civilization of the rule of Right. Now the question remains whether Japan will be the hawk of the Western civilization of the rule of Might, or the tower of strength of the Orient. This is the choice which lies before the people of Japan."

It is a pity that Japan paid no heed to the warnings and admonitions of both its neighbor and of the international community. Japan's militarism went ever further down the road of aggressive expansionism and brought disaster—not only to the peoples of Asia, but in the end it caused Japan itself to suffer heavy retribution.

2 THE TRANSITIONAL PERIOD

The period of nearly half a century from the end of World War II to the end of the Cold War was a period of transition for Asianism.

Following World War II, a large number of new countries in Asia and Africa which had broken away from colonial control once more raised the flag of regional alliance. Mao Zedong, Zhou Enlai, Nehru, Sukarno and other leaders vigorously advocated an Asian-African Assembly and released the profoundly influential Ten Principles of the Bandung Conference [1955]. The spirit of unity, collaboration, and of the putting aside of differences in the quest for commonality (*qiutong cunyi*) promoted by the conference gave the Asian countries a powerful collective boost and also prompted the re-emergence of Asianism. However, the Asian-African Assembly had a short life and renascent Asianism found itself stymied at its first step. The reasons for this were threefold:

Firstly, Asia was living under the shadow of the Cold War and the Asian countries were by and large split into two large confrontational camps, meaning that Asianism lacked a fundamental political consensus and a comprehensive ideology.

Secondly, although the Asian countries had broken away from foreign occupation and colonial control in rapid succession and had gained a new political life of their own, they constantly fought among themselves and their rates of economic growth varied considerably. Consequently, Asianism lacked a stable environment and material base on which to build.

Thirdly, there was the influence of factors operating within the major Asian countries and affecting their mutual relations. For a long time, China faced blocking and containment by America and other Western countries. For all practical purposes, it was excluded from the international system. Japan implemented the principle of economic priority and maintained political harmony with the USA. India mainly directed its energies toward South Asia and the non-aligned movement. For a long time, Sino-Japanese and Sino-Indian relations could not be normalized. Asianism lacked a leading force and more importantly, it lacked proper coordination between the major players.

From the 1970s onwards, Western Europe accelerated the process of political and economic integration and achieved a number of well-known and widely acknowledged goals. While on the global level the trend toward regionalization was still insignificant, it formed a major incentive to Asian countries. At the end of the 1970s, Japanese Prime Minister Ōhira Masayoshi [1910–1980] proposed the "idea of a Pacific Economic Sphere." Following the 1980s, the USA, Japan, Australia and other countries launched the Pacific Economic Cooperation Council (PECC), and promoted the organization for Asia-Pacific Economic Cooperation (APEC). The planning and realization of these transitional stages of regional cooperation set the stage for this new period of Asian cooperation and a new Asianism. . . .

4 THE FUNDAMENTAL STRUCTURE AND CHRONOLOGICAL IMPLICATIONS OF NEW ASIANISM

The objectives of New Asianism for the twenty-first century have been indicated by Chinese President Hu Jintao [1942–]. We must establish a harmonious Asia that works together in the political sphere, is economically even-handed and mutually beneficial, is marked by mutual trust and cooperation with regard to security, and cooperates freely in the areas of cultural exchanges and academic research. Whether or not the twenty-first century can formulate a new Asianism depends on the following factors: firstly, whether the Asian countries, in particular the countries of East Asia, can make a clean break with the past and begin afresh; secondly, whether Asia can continue to draw on its outstanding cultural and spiritual heritage; and thirdly, whether the road to Asian development continues to be smooth and whether it is widely recognized and accepted by the international community. . . .

. . . [I]n Japan justifications for Japan's aggression and attempts to excuse Japanese war crimes were still frequently voiced in public. While the vitality of a new Asianism depends on opening up and molding the future of Asia, its foundations will comprise the totality of the lessons taught by history as well as a basic consensus on the verdict of history. The more thoroughly this process of collective recognition can be accomplished, the firmer the intellectual basis of New Asianism will be.

Asia possesses a precious cultural heritage consisting of Confucianism and the best features of many different religions. Through long practice, Asians have formulated moral values and standards of behavior manifested in idioms such as the "unity of heaven and the people" (*tian ren he yi*), "harmony in difference" (*he er bu tong*), "insights from balance" (*zhong yong da guan*), and "honesty guards belief" (*cheng shi shou xin*). As in all other regions, Asia has now entered the new age of globalization and information. The vitality of the new Asianism will depend on whether it can equip this new era with a sense of meaning and purpose derived from this spiritual heritage, adapt this heritage to present and future developments, and promote the utilization of its gifts on the basis of the values of the past.

In terms of development, Asia has already achieved some remarkable successes but at the same time it is also confronted with a number of difficulties and challenges. Levels of development among the various countries in the region are extremely disproportionate. From time to time frictions arise among the regional powers, weapons of mass destruction are continuing to spread, and the threat of famine and natural disasters is always present. The vitality of a new Asianism depends on the integrated development and lasting stability of the region, the energetic advancement of cooperation across many different fields, and the integration and optimal allocation of natural resources. It also depends on the willingness to advance further down a new conceptual pathway that will continue to develop and be welcomed by countries within the region and by the international community.

What is the fundamental content of the new Asianism of the twenty-first century? . . .

Above all, this must be a cooperative Asianism. Cooperation is the constant theme of Asianism. If there is no cooperation among the Asian countries, it will be difficult to ensure the stability of peace in Asia. And if there is no cooperation between Asia and other regions of the world, Asia will be unable to realize the potential of its increasing international significance.

The aim of cooperation is the realization of common benefits and common development. Asia still has a population of some hundreds of millions of impoverished people. The gap between per capita incomes in the most prosperous and the least developed countries is still more than a hundredfold. . . .

The principle of cooperation is consistent with the Charter of the United Nations as the core international legal standard, comprising mutual respect for sovereignty and territorial integrity and mutual non-interference in internal affairs, and also including the peaceful settlement of international disputes and not resorting to force or threatening to do so. At present, all Asian countries lay emphasis on walking the path of peaceful development, and all are opposed to the ideology of hegemony. As a result, there are no major conflicts on the horizon. We should not regard neighboring countries as threats, but rather we should all regard the development of our neighbors as opportunities to pursue our own development.

As for the channels of cooperation, the main basis of regional cooperation is bilateral cooperation. Regional cooperation is both the main platform for the implementation of regionalism and also constitutes its theory. As the European experience makes clear, regional cooperation begins in the economic domain—gradually intensifying from the creation of a free-trade zone and customs union, to a common market, and then a currency and economic union, in addition to completing several stages of economic unification. After a relative maturity has been achieved economically, the process of unification on the political, social, diplomatic and security fronts can begin. East Asia and, indeed, all of Asia are at present still in the first stage of economic unification. We still have a very long way to go. The countries of East Asia have already set the goal of creating an East Asian Common Body (*Dongya Gongtongti*). This common body must first be a collective body based on economic values. At the same time it can also strengthen multi-level dialogue in such areas as culture, politics, society and security, begin any necessary cooperation and advance the quest for the common good.

The pattern of cooperation adopted must fit the special characteristics of Asia and must develop multiple initiatives. At present in Asia there already exist many regional or pan-regional multilateral organizations such as ASEAN, the South Asian Association for Regional Cooperation [SAARC], the Shanghai Cooperation Organization [SCO], 10+3 [ASEAN plus China, Japan, and South Korea], as well as East Asian summit meetings, the Six-Party Talks [over the North Korean nuclear weapons program], and the Asia Cooperation Dialogue [ACD]. . . .

The second [major principle] is that of an open Asianism. In physics, there is an important law—closed systems will inevitably heat up and self-destruct. However, open systems will continue operating for a long time without decay. A single country and a single region must in the same way replace the old with the new or spit out the old and accept the new. This will enable it to flourish and develop even more successfully. . . .

New Asianism must be an open regionalism, not relying on exclusion and protectionism, or pointing in one direction in particular. "Open" does not only mean mutual openness among countries within the region, but openness to other regions and also to the world. Asian cooperation, and particularly East Asian cooperation, requires the regular maintenance of relations with different regions, involving organizations such as APEC [Asia-Pacific Economic Cooperation, initiated in 1989], ASEM [Asia-Europe Meeting, started in 1996], and the Forum for East Asian-Latin American cooperation. The East Asian summit of 2005 held in Malaysia included India, Australia and New Zealand, and exemplified the open character of East Asian cooperation.

The United States of America has important interests and a traditional influence in Asia. While these interests have an historical basis, they are also objective realities in the present. Asian cooperation should strengthen communication with America and other countries outside the region, promote understanding and welcome the active role played by America and others for the stability and development of Asia. Traditional and recent arrangements for trade and security in Asia should not be seen as antagonistic, but as operating alongside one another, mutually tolerant, and competing in a positive spirit. China hopes that it and America will respect each other's interests in Asia and at the same time constantly develop new points of common interest.

The third [principle] is that of a harmonious (*hexie de*) Asianism. Eastern culture upholds the ideal of "harmony in difference," and emphasizes the belief that "it does no harm to hold up 10,000 things next to each other, and paths running in parallel do not run counter." Asia's greatest strength lies within the great framework of Eastern civilization, a setting of rich and varied diversity. The political and economic systems of the various countries are not all identical, and their historical and cultural backgrounds each have their own distinctive features. Also, there exist relatively large differences with regard to levels of development and talents. History shows that diversity is not in itself an obstacle to cooperation, but rather a force for cooperation. Much more importantly, it is the source of exchange, innovation, and creativity. Cooperation between Asian nations can and must respect the diverse characteristics found within our region, make a virtue of diversity and promote the development of diversification.

Attentive to the basic norms of international relations and universal human values, New Asianism must seek to respect differences of culture, religion, political systems, and forms of consciousness. And, furthermore, desiring peaceful co-existence among different countries, ethnic and other groups within the same region, it must pursue peaceful relations and harmony among member countries.

Over the past 50 to 60 years, the Asian countries have developed heterogeneously, adopting different political systems and democratic models. For example, those of China, Japan, Korea, India, and Singapore are by no means identical, but have each formed their own characteristics. These different patterns have their basis in the unique conditions and historical and cultural backgrounds of each country. At the same time, they also have their own unique vitality. To demand unilaterally the values associated with a particular model, or to attempt to force a homogeneous political system onto Asia has proven to fail historically, will lead nowhere in our present circumstances, and will also be difficult to justify in the future.

The new Asianism of the twenty-first century must be based on the massive changes that have occurred on the Asian mainland over the past 100 years, bearing in mind future directions for the development of Asia. Such development must be appropriate for the age of globalization and take the right direction in terms of historical progress. In this way, development will provide Asianism with a completely new context. To achieve this, we must take one further step and clarify the necessary roles and actions that the countries of Asia should undertake, and investigate ways of achieving the needed proactive coordination and interaction between Asia and the various extra-regional powers. In this way we can promote the healthy development of a New Asianism.

Chapter Forty-Two

Wada Haruki: "Maritime Asia and the Future of a Northeast Asia Community," 2008

Kyoko Selden and Mark Selden

Wada Haruki (b. 1938), Professor Emeritus of the Social Science Institute of Tokyo University and a leading historian of Russia as well as an authority on Korea and the Korean War, has been active in overcoming Japan–Korea tensions, promoting democracy in South Korea, and improving Japan–North Korea relations. He also played an important and controversial role in seeking Japanese apology and compensation for the wartime comfort women, serving as the final director of the Japanese government–supported Asian Women's Fund (Wada 2008a). Both his scholarship and his activism are rooted in a vision of a harmonious Asian community.

Wada has called for a regional solution to the conflicts that have afflicted northeastern Asia in light of the history of region formation in the era of colonialism, war, and bipolar conflict that scarred the region throughout the "long twentieth century." Since 1995 he has articulated a vision of a "common house of Northeast Asia" as a means to heal and unify a region that, in his expansive definition, includes China, Japan, North Korea, South Korea, Taiwan, Russia, and Mongolia and perhaps extends to Southeast Asia.

Wada distinguishes this conception from a number of other approaches to regional unity. These include Karatani Kōjin's (1941–) vision of a unitary world state that Wada believes could be achieved only through the "colossal violence" of another world war. It also includes major formulations crafted during the era of Japanese colonial empire by Tarui Tōkichi, Ishiwara Kanji, and Rōyama Masamichi (see I:5, II:22, and II:18). These approaches paved the way for a Greater East Asian Co-Prosperity Sphere as a vehicle for Japanese hegemony even prior to the attack at Pearl Harbor and Japan's conquest of much of East and Southeast Asia. Wada takes pains to clarify, then, his approach that both rests on the continued role of nation states and breaks with earlier formulations enshrined in Japanese aggression and colonialism.

The end of more than a century of warfare in East Asia with the defeat and withdrawal of United States forces from Indochina in 1975, and the end of the Cold War in Asia with the U.S.–China opening of 1970, especially the collapse of the Soviet Union in 1990, led Wada to the insight that the way could be open for regional solutions that transcend protracted experience with colonialism, war, and regional divisions. Other changes make it possible to contemplate what he calls a "Common House of Northeast Asia." These include democratization of South Korea, Taiwan, Mongolia, Russia, and Japan and the Association of Southeast Asian Nations plus three (ASEAN+3) initiative paving the way to greater accord between ASEAN and China, Japan, and Korea. This initiative has received increasing attention since the beginning of the twenty-first century, particularly as Japan, under a new Democratic Party administration, has attempted to strengthen its relations with China. Nevertheless, China, Japan, and South Korea each have their own vision of what ASEAN+3 and, perhaps, an expansion of free trade among the parties might look like. Equally important, the rise of an economically strong and more confident China transforms a situation in which Japan in the American embrace was the dominant northeastern Asian power. The change means that a common house of northeastern Asia, or indeed of northeastern and Southeast Asia and beyond, need no longer produce the fear that the conception is a thinly veiled ploy to secure Japanese hegemony or that of any single power. Indeed, a common house could make it possible for the region to act in concert to prevent domination by the United States in East Asia.

Although Wada does not allude to it, his vision for northeastern Asia also doubtless draws heavily on the formation and development of the European Union. By contrast, Hatoyama Yukio (1947–), Japan's Democratic Party prime minister (2009–2010), in his signature vision of a fraternal (*yūai*) society, draws explicitly on the experience of the European Union as an inspiration for a common northeastern Asia future. Both the *longue durée* experience of northeastern Asia and the character of ASEAN suggest, however, that any future northeastern Asian community is likely to differ in fundamentals in its core processes and institutional foundations from those of the European Union, perhaps retaining greater national autonomy with weaker common institutional ties and without an East Asian version of NATO, at least in the short run.

Wada points to other foundations for community. Among the most important is the existence of far-flung diasporas of Koreans and Chinese throughout East Asia, including those in China, Japan, Russia, Sakhalin, and Southeast Asia but also extending to Europe, North America, and beyond. The diasporas have already contributed to the economic development of northeastern Asia and could further help bind the region politically. For, whatever their present nationality, they are northeastern Asian in origin.

To be sure, deep legacies of mistrust and conflict remain throughout northeastern Asia. Among the most tenacious problems is that of a divided Korea and the (enduring) sixty-year U.S.–Korean War. Importantly there has been only an armistice but no peace treaty ending that war and continued U.S.–North Korean tensions and conflict over nuclear weapons as well as the specter of nuclear terror involving both the United States and North Korea. This volatile situation is exacerbated by North–South conflict. While Japan did not fight in Korea, Wada notes, it actively supported U.S. intervention, and indeed it took advantage of the U.S.–Korean War to jump-start Japan's postwar economic surge.

The road to a common house for northeastern Asia, in Wada's view, lies through meaningful apology and compensation of victims by aggressors, specifically Japan in China and Korea in the years 1895–1945, and the same applies to the United States in Vietnam and elsewhere. The problem is not that there have been no apologies. Wada points out that at various times—Japan for its invasion of China, most notably in the 1995 apology by Japan's Prime Minister Murayama Tomiichi (1924–) on the fiftieth anniversary of the end of the China-Japan War (Murayama 1995) and the U.S. Congress in its 1993 apology on the hundredth anniversary of the annexation of Hawaii (U.S. Public Law 103-150, 103rd Congress Joint Resolution 19, 23 November 1993)—aggressors have apologized for past actions (cf. Torpey 2003) with varying degrees of success in overcoming international tensions. For Wada, the combination of meaningful apology and compensation to victims can pave the way for more harmonious relations and ultimately to regional accord. The hundredth anniversary of Japan's annexation of Korea in 2010 provides an opportunity to resolve many outstanding issues in the relationship between colonizer and colonized and to strengthen political and cultural relations among two nations whose economic bonds are already strong.

Source (translation from the Japanese original by Kyoko Selden)
Wada Haruki, "Okinawa to Hokutō Ajia" (Maritime Asia and the Future of a Northeast Asia Community), *Ryūkyū Shinpō*, 7–9 January 2008.

I TRANSCENDING NATIONAL BOUNDARIES

We are now facing a critical situation. Not just Japan, but the world as a whole is in crisis. With America at the center, globalization is racing ahead, but there are also strong countercurrents with nationalism becoming stronger in various places. In the midst of war and terror, the threat of global warming is becoming clear to all. In this world, I believe that we should advance toward regionalism. In 2003 I hoisted this flag in a book entitled *The Common House of Northeast Asia—Declaration of a New Regionalism* published by Heibonsha.

We cannot live by denying the existence of states. However, it is necessary to relativize the nation state and to transcend state boundaries. This means that even as we belong to a state, we belong to a region and to the world. In 2006 Karatani Kōjin wrote a book called *Toward the World Republic*. But this proposal to go beyond states and aim toward a world republic is more dangerous than promising. If we think about the socialist Soviet Russia that came to an end, it was precisely aiming at a single world state. To turn humanity into a single state would require colossal violence. Moreover, the goal is unattainable. I think of the future of humanity as a league of regional communities (*chiiki kyōdōtai*). It can be said that regionalism is our utopia.

The idea of regionalism existed in the past. Japan has a failed history of trying to put regionalism into practice. The Greater East Union of Nations of Tarui Tōkichi [see I:5], who proposed a great united nation of the countries of Asian yellow peoples, ended in Japan's annexation of Korea. Out of the Manchurian Incident, Ishiwara Kanji's idea of an East Asian League [see II:22] was created. Amidst the Sino-Japanese War, the theory of an East Asia Community (1938) was proposed by Rōyama Masamichi [see II:18], who called for a regional economy of Japan, China and Manchuria. When these ideas reached a dead end, the concept of a Greater East Asia Co-Prosperity Sphere was born. This was one with the Greater East Asia War. The practice of regionalism was a billboard that covered aggression. So, with Japan's surrender, regionalism too came to be forgotten.

After experiencing the nation's defeat and the Korean War, Japanese people came to oppose the military. But at the same time, they depended on the United States. After the Asia-Pacific War, Asian peoples embarked on wars between communists and anti-communists. So in that period, regionalism could exist only as an anti-communist alliance and a military bloc of Northeast Asia. From that perspective, too, the Japanese people rejected regionalism.

However, in the late 1980s, the Cold War and state socialism ended, and in the 1990s new conditions were created in East Asia: China's economic development and South Korea's democratization were remarkable, while North Korea experienced a crisis. At this point, interest in regionalism emerged afresh.

ASEAN in 1997 invited China, South Korea and Japan to join a summit conference of ASEAN +3 out of which was born an East Asia Vision group. In 2001 it submitted a report called "We hope to create an East Asian Community (*kyōdōtai*) for peace, prosperity and progress." ASEAN leaders supported that dream-like concept and in 2005 an East Asia Summit was held. However, Japan and China were in conflict about who should participate.

The US, which was not invited, was dissatisfied, so the process has not been proceeding smoothly.

On the other hand, Northeast Asia has been strongly coming to the fore. In February 2003 South Korean Pres. Roh Moo-hyun, in his inaugural speech, talked about the advent of a new era of Northeast Asia and stated that a community of regional peace and prosperity is his dream, surprising the Korean people. . . .

Since 1995 I have been calling this the Common House of Northeast Asia (*Tōhoku Ajia kyōdō no ie*). The concept in which steps toward regional community begin from cooperation in peace and security is no longer a mere dream. It is a goal that the governments of the six countries pledge.

II WITHOUT RECONCILIATION THERE CAN BE NO COMMUNAL LIFE

Those who think seriously about Northeast Asia Community have no choice but to directly confront the area's special character. Its character is one of successive wars for 80 years from 1894 to 1975. . . .

The first fifty years of the eighty-year period was characterized by Japanese wars. . . .

Indeed, for half a century, Japan fought once or more than once with all neighboring countries to the West, North and East. Japan was always the attacker, and in the majority of cases, Japan was the aggressor. Those who were attacked and invaded were left with ineradicable scars and indelible pain. . . .

When the war ended on 15 August 1945, the Japanese military was dismantled, the emperor was stripped of military command, and Japan came to live under Article 9. However, the fact that Japan's war ended did not mean that the era of war in the area came to an end. Immediately, civil war began in China between Guomindang [Kuomintang, or Nationalist Party] and Communist forces and this lasted until 1949. In Indochina, too, the Vietminh of Ho Chi Minh fought the French.

In 1950 the Korean War began. The two states born in the South and the North, occupied separately by the United States and the Soviet Union, fought to achieve unification. But both sides failed to achieve reunification. The war became a US-China war fought on Korean soil. The Korean War achieved a moratorium in 1953, but did not go beyond that to sign a peace treaty. The Indochina War ended, but in 1960 Vietnam became anew the main theatre in the struggle between Communists and US-supported anti-Communists. . . .

Japan did not fight in these wars, but it supported the US and profited from them. The thirty-year war in Japan's neighborhood, involving national communism versus anti-communists and the US, ended for the US in Vietnam in 1975.

Dreadful memories of the eighty-year war and pains that continue today still tear apart the peoples of these areas. Assailants have to apologize, and the sorrow and pain of the victims have to be healed. Damages that can be rectified should be compensated, hatred must be conquered, and forgiveness given.

Throughout the thirty-year war, Japan was unable to criticize itself and apologize for its own wars. In 1972, the 27th year after the war, Japan expressed self-reflection (*hansei*) to the Chinese people over the damage it had wrought by the war.

In 1995 the fiftieth year since the war, Japan's Prime Minister Murayama [Tomiichi] spoke of self-reflection and apology for the fact that Japan had inflicted damage and pain by colonial rule and aggression. Concerning comfort women issues, in 1993, Chief Cabinet Secretary Kōno [Yōhei] (1937–) expressed reflection and apology.

In this, I think Japan made the minimum apologies that could become the basis for seeking reconciliation with the various countries in the area.

. . . The people of this region that was at war for eighty years aspire to total reconciliation. Only when everyone begins to walk in this direction will progress toward a common house for Northeast Asia be possible. The passion for reconciliation is an identity that unites this area.

III TOWARD A COOPERATIVE BODY THROUGH JOINING HANDS IN THE ISLANDS

Northeast Asian countries are extremely diverse and heterogeneous historically, politically, economically and culturally. Three countries have become parliamentary democracies (*gikaisei*) (Japan, South Korea and Taiwan), two are former communist countries (Russia and Mongolia), and in two (China and North Korea) the Communist Party still rules. It is difficult for such diverse countries of Northeast Asia to become a cooperative body. However, should that be realized, this would have epochal significance for overcoming the divisions of humankind. Something that binds Northeast Asia is the presence of Koreans who live in far-flung countries, notably Japan, China, Sakhalin, and the former Soviet Union, as diaspora as a result of an unfortunate history.

There are 2,400,000 Koreans in China, making possible the formation of a Korean autonomous region in Yanbian, where the largest number resides. The US has 2,050,000 immigrants from Korea. In Japan, including people from North and South, there are said to be 870,000 Korean residents, but if you add those who obtained Japanese citizenship, the number is at least one million. In the former Soviet Union, in and around Central Asia, there are 480,000 Koreans. As Southeast Asia is the world of the overseas Chinese (with smaller numbers in Northeast Asia), Northeast Asia is the world of the overseas Koreans.

Without neglecting their ethnic origins, thinking about the nations in which they currently live, they are a presence that shapes all Northeast Asia. They are Northeast Asians. In particular, more than 90% of Korean residents in Japan come from South Korea and they are members of Japanese society. They have relatives who migrated to North Korea, so they have body and heart split into three elements. Kang Sang-jung (1950–), a Korean resident intellectual in Japan, proposes a common house of Northeast Asia in the Japanese parliament committee. That, one can say, demonstrates the potential of Koreans as Northeast Asians.

. . .

What is noticed here is that the apology (*shazai*) resolution adopted by both houses of the US Congress on 23 November 1993 states that despite the fact that the United States and Hawaiian Kingdom had diplomatic relations for 67 years, in 1893 the American ambassador conspired to overthrow the kingdom and declare Hawaii an American protectorate. It quotes the protest by Queen Liliuokalani, which said that she gives up her political power in order to avoid bloodshed before the landing of US Marines. Further, the apology records that President Cleveland, when informed of this, did not approve the overthrow of the kingdom and demanded that the Queen be restored to her position despite the fact that those who supported the overthrow of the government had declared a Republic of Hawaii. Finally in 1898, President McKinley annexed Hawaii.

The US Congress, on the 100th anniversary of the illegitimate overthrow of the Hawaiian kingdom recognized that the sovereignty of the indigenous Hawaiians had been crushed and resolved that the US apologize and turn this apology into a basis for reconciliation with indigenous Hawaiians. President Clinton signed the resolution. Behind the President's signing the resolution stood the congressmen from Hawaii. Two of them were Hawaiian natives, and two were Japanese Hawaiians.

This is the America which has not taken the important action of apologizing for the Vietnam War. This makes us reflect on what attitude Japan should take toward its incorporation of the Ryukyu Kingdom and the annexation of Korea. The 100th anniversary of Korean annexation is coming in 2010.

Consolidated Bibliography

Unless otherwise stated, all Japanese titles are published in Tokyo and all Korean titles in Seoul.

Abdürreşid İbrahim (1910), *Alem-I Islam ve Japonya'da Intisari Islamiyet* (The Future of the Japanese from the Perspective of Religion). Istanbul: Ahmed Saki Bey Matbaasi.

Abe Hirozumi (1980), "Mori Kaku: Fuashizumu Taisei no Senku" (Mori Kaku: The Pioneer of the Fascist System), Andō Minoru et al., *Nihon Seiji no Jitsuryokusha* (Influential Figures in Japanese Politics), vol.2. Yūhikaku.

Aibara Shigeki (1998), "Konoe Atsumaro to Shina Hozenron" (Konoe Atsumaro and the Preservation of China's Territorial Integrity Principle). Okamoto Kōji (ed.), *Kindai Nihon no Ajiakan* (*Modern Japan's View of Asia*). Kyoto: Minerva Shobō, 51–77.

Aizawa Yasushi (1833), *Teki-ihen* (A Guide to Morals), reprinted in Aizawa Yasushi, *Shinron/Teki-ihen* (New Thesis/A Guide to Morals). Iwanami Shoten, 1931.

Akashi, Motojiro (1988), *Rakka Ryusui: Colonel Akashi's Report on His Secret Cooperation with the Russian Revolutionary Parties during the Russo-Japanese War.* Translated by Inaba Chiharu. Helsinki: SHS.

Akif, Mehmet (Ersoy) (2003), *Safahat* (Passages). Istanbul: Inkilap Kitabevi.

Ampiah, Kweku (2007), *The Political and Moral Imperatives of the Bandung Conference of 1955: The Reactions of the US, UK and Japan.* Folkestone: Global Oriental.

An Chung-gŭn (1910), "Tongyang Pyŏnghwaron" (A Discourse on Peace in East Asia), reprinted in Ch'oe Wŏn-sik and Paek Yŏng-sŏ (eds.), *Tongasia, Munje-wa Sikak* (East Asia, Problems and Points of View). Munhak-kwa Chisŏngsa, 1997, 205–15.

An Kyong-su (1900), "Nisshinkan Dōmeiron" (Argument for a Japanese-Chinese-Korean Alliance). *Nihon oyobi Nihonjin,* nos. 116–123 (8 parts).

Anderson, Benedict R. (1983), *Imagined Communities: Reflections on the Origin and Spread of Nationalism.* London: Verso.

Andō Hikotarō (1990), "Nihon Ryūgaku Jidai no Ri Daishō" (Li Dazhao during His Time as a Foreign Student in Japan). *Shakai Kagaku Tōkyū* 36:2, 347–72.

Ano, Masaharu (1997), "Yosuke Matsuoka: The Far-Western Roots of a World-Political Vision." *Oregon Historical Quarterly* 98:2, 164–204.

Aoe Shunjirō (1997), *Ishiwara Kanji* (Ishiwara Kanji). Chūō Kōronsha.

Aoe Shunichirō (1992), *Ishiwara Kanji* (Ishiwara Kanji). Chūō Kōronsha.

Arano Yasunori (2007), "Kinsei Nihon ni okeru 'Higashi Ajia' no 'Hakken'" (The 'Discovery' of 'East Asia' in Early Modern Japan). Kishi Toshihiko et al. (eds.), *"Higashi Ajia" no Jidaisei* (The Temporality of 'East Asia'). Keisuisha, 21–52.

Archer, Clive (2001), *International Organizations*. London and New York: Routledge.

Arendt, Hannah (1985), *The Origins of Totalitarianism*. San Diego: Harcourt.

Ariyama Teruo (1992), *Tokutomi Sohō to* Kokumin Shinbun (Tokutomi Sohō and the *Kokumin Shinbun*). Yoshikawa Kōbunkan.

Arrighi, Giovanni, Takeshi Hamashita, and Mark Selden (eds.) (2003), *The Resurgence of East Asia: 500, 150 and 50 Year Perspectives*. London and New York: Routledge.

Asiatic Association of Japan (Author Taraknath Das) (1918), *Isolation of Japan in World Politics*. Tokyo: Asiatic Association of Japan.

Association of Southeast Asian Nations (2009), "ASEAN Plus Three Cooperation." Official website of the Association of Southeast Asian Nations, Internet: http://www.aseansec.org/16580.htm (last accessed 1 June 2010).

Aydin, Cemil (2007a), "A Global Anti-Western Moment? The Russo-Japanese War, Decolonization and Asian Modernity." Sebastian Conrad and Dominic Sachsenmaier (eds.), *Conceptions of World Order, ca. 1880–1935. Global Moments and Movements*, 213–36. Basingstoke: Palgrave Macmillan.

—— (2007b), *The Politics of Anti-Westernism in Asia: Visions of World Order in Pan-Islamic and Pan-Asian Thought*. New York: Columbia University Press.

Banerjee, Taransankar (1977), *Sardar K. M. Panikkar: A Profile of a Historian: A Study in Modern Indian Historiography*. Calcutta: Ratna Prakashan.

Bayly, Christopher, and Harper, Tim (2007), *Forgotten Wars: The End of Britain's Asian Empire*, London: Penguin Books.

Beasley, William G. (1987), "Japan and Pan-Asianism. Problems of Definition." Janet Hunter (ed.), *Aspects of Pan-Asianism*. London: Suntory Toyota International Centre for Economics and Related Disciplines, London School of Economics and Political Science (International Studies 1987/II), 1–16.

Berger, Gordon M. (1977), *Parties Out of Power in Japan, 1931–1941*. Princeton, NJ: Princeton University Press.

—— (1979), "The Three-Dimensional Empire: Japanese Attitudes and the New Order in East Asia, 1937–1945." *The Japan Interpreter* 12:3–4, 355–83.

Bharucha, Rustom (2006), *Another Asia: Rabindranath Tagore and Okakura Tenshin*. New Delhi: Oxford University Press.

Bose, Rash Behari (Ras Bihari Bōsu) (1922), "Han Kaikyōshugi to Han Ajiashugi. Toruko Fukkō no Igi" (Pan-Islamism and Pan-Asianism—The Meaning of the Re-Emergence of Turkey). *Kaizō* 1922:11, 123–29.

Boyle, John Hunter (1972), *China and Japan at War, 1937–1945: The Politics of Collaboration*. Stanford, CA: Stanford University Press.

Brandt, Max von (1903), *Die Zukunft Ostasiens* (The Future of East Asia). Stuttgart: Strecker and Schröder (first edition 1895).

Brown, Giles (1948), "The Hindu Conspiracy, 1914–1917." *The Pacific Historical Review* 17:3, 299–310.

Brown, Roger H. (2007), "Visions of a Virtuous Manifest Destiny: Yasuoka Masahiro and Japan's Kingly Way." Sven Saaler and J. Victor Koschmann (eds.), *Pan-Asianism in Modern Japanese History: Regionalism, Colonialism and Borders*. New York: Routledge, 133–50.

——— (2009), "Shepherds of the People: Yasuoka Masahiro and the New Bureaucrats in Early Shōwa Japan." *Journal of Japanese Studies* 35:2, 285–319.

Caprio, Mark E. (2009), *Japanese Assimilation Policies in Colonial Korea, 1910–1945*. Seattle: University of Washington Press.

Chen Laixing and Yasui Sankichi (eds.) (1989), *Son Bun Kōen "Dai-Ajiashugi" Shiryōshū. Nihon to Chūgoku no Kiro* (Collected Sources Relating to Sun Yat-sen's Lecture "Pan-Asianism": The Crossroads of Japan and China). Kyoto: Hōritsu Bunkasha.

Cheung, Andrew (1995), "Slogans, Symbols, and Legitimacy: The Case of Wang Jingwei's Nanjing Regime." *Indiana East Asian Working Paper Series on Language and Politics in Modern China*, 6.

Chō Gun (Zhao Jun) (1997), *Dai-Ajiashugi to Chūgoku* (Greater Asianism and China), Aki Shobō.

Choi Hong-gyu (2004), *Sin Ch'ae-ho ŭi yŏksahak kwa minjok undong* (Historiography and the National Movement of Sin Ch'ae-ho). Inchi Publishing.

Cohen, Paul A. (1974), *Between Tradition and Modernity: Wang T'ao and Reform in Late Ch'ing China*. Cambridge, MA: Harvard University Press.

Coudenhove-Kalergi, Richard N. (1931), "Japans Monroe-Doktrin" (Japan's Monroe Doctrine) *Pan-Europa* 7:1, 256–63.

——— (1932), "Kyokutō Monrōshugi o Mitomeyo" (Let's Recognize the Far Eastern Monroe Doctrine). *Tairiku* no. 221, 19–22.

Crowley, James B. (1966), *Japan's Quest for Autonomy, 1930–1938*. Princeton: Princeton University Press.

——— (1971), "Intellectuals as Visionaries of the New Asian Order." James W. Morley (ed.), *Dilemmas of Growth in Prewar Japan*. Princeton, NJ: Princeton University Press, 319–73.

Da Yaxiyazhuyi yu xin Yaxiyazhuyi (Greater Asianism and New Asianism). *Guomin Zazhi*, 1 February 1919, reprinted in *Chenbao* (6 March and 21 March 1919) and in People's Press (ed.), *Li Dazhao Wenji* (Collected Writings of Li Dazhao), 1, no. 2 (1984), Beijing, 609–11.

Dai Ajia Kyōkai/Dai Tsuran Kyōkai (1922), *Dai Ajia* (Greater Asia). Dai Ajia Kyōkai.

Daniels, Roger (1977), *The Politics of Prejudice: The Anti-Japanese Movement in California and the Struggle for Japanese Exclusion*. Berkeley: University of California Press.

Das, Taraknath (1917a), "Ajia no Kyōisha wa Hatashite Nihon ka" (Is It Really Japan That Is a Menace to Asia?). *Nihon oyobi Nihonjin* 706 (1 June 1917), 68–75.

——— (1917b), *Is Japan a Menace to Asia?* Shanghai: no publisher.

——— (1936), *Foreign Policy in the Far East.* New York: Longmans, Green and Co.

——— (1944), *Indo Dokuritsuron* (On Indian Independence). Hakubunkan.

de Bary, William Theodore (ed.) (1960), *Sources of Indian Tradition.* New York: Columbia University Press.

de Bary, William Theodore, et al. (eds.) (1960), *Sources of Chinese Tradition.* New York: Columbia University Press.

Delpai Research (1995), "Tongasia Munmyŏng Chindan—Hanchungil Kongdong Yŏn'gu Kyŏlgwa Pigyo" (Diagnosis of Civilization in East Asia—Comparison of Research in China, Japan and South Korea). *Korea Forum* 21:14, 92–113.

Dennehy, Kristine (2007), "Overcoming Colonialism at Bandung, 1955." Sven Saaler and J. Victor Koschmann (eds.), *Pan-Asianism in Modern Japanese History: Regionalism, Colonialism and Borders.* New York: Routledge, 213–25.

Dignan, Don (1971), "The Hindu Conspiracy in Anglo-American Relations during World War I." *The Pacific Historical Review* 40:1, 57–76.

Dikötter, Frank (ed.) (1997), *The Construction of Racial Identities in China and Japan.* Honolulu: University of Hawai'i Press.

Doak, Kevin M. (1994), *Dreams of Difference: The Japan Romantic School and the Crisis of Modernity.* Berkeley: University of California Press.

Duara, Prasenjit (1998), "Transnationalism in the Era of Nation-States: China, 1900–1945." *Development and Change* 29:4, 647–70.

——— (1998) "Transnationalism in the Era of Nation-States: China, 1900-1945." *Development and Change*, 29:4.

——— (2001), "The Discourse of Civilization and Pan-Asianism." *Journal of World History* 12:1, 99–130.

——— (2003), *Sovereignty and Authenticity: Manchukuo and the East Asian Modern.* New York: Rowman & Littlefield.

Dufourmont, Eddy (2008), "Matsumura Kaiseki et l'Eglise du Japon (Nihon Kyōkai): Un Asiatisme Chrétien?" Christian Galan and Arnaud Brotons (eds.), *Japon Pluriel 7. Actes du Septième Colloque de la Société Française des Études Japonaises.* Paris: Picquier, 159–68.

Duus, Peter (1970), "Nagai Ryūtarō: The Tactical Dilemmas of Reform." Albert M. Craig et al. (eds.), *Personality in Japanese History.* Berkeley: University of California Press, 399–424.

——— (1971), "Nagai Ryūtarō and the 'White Peril,' 1905–1944," *Journal of Asian Studies* 31:1, 41–48.

——— (1995), *The Abacus and the Sword. The Japanese Penetration of Korea, 1895–1910.* Berkeley: University of California Press.

——— (2001), "The 'New Asianism.'" Arne Holzhausen (ed.), *Can Japan Globalize? Studies on Japan's Changing Political Economy and the Process of Globalization in Honour of Sung-Jo Park.* Heidelberg: Physica, 245–56.

Eizawa Kōji (1995), *"Daitō-A Kyōeiken" no Shisō* (The Ideology of the "Greater East Asia Co-Prosperity Sphere"). Kōdansha.

Esenbel, Selçuk (2002), "Japan and Islam Policy during the 1930s." Bert Edstrom (ed.), *Turning Points in Japanese History*. Manchester: Japan Library/Curzon Press, 180–214.

——— (2004), "Japan's Global Claim to Asia and the World of Islam: Transnational Nationalism and World Power, 1900–1945." *The American Historical Review* 109:4, 1140–70.

——— (2007), "The Legacy of the War and the World of Islam in Japanese Pan-Asianist Discourse: Wakabayashi Han's Kaikyō Sekai to Nihon. Rotem Kowner (ed.), *Rethinking the Russo-Japanese War 1904–05. Vol. 1. Centennial Perspectives*. Folkestone: Global Oriental, 263–80.

Esenbel, Selçuk, and Inaba Chiharu (eds.) (2003), *The Rising Sun and the Turkish Crescent: New Perspectives on the History of Japanese Turkish Relations*. Istanbul: Boğaziçi University Press.

Fairbank, John K., Edwin O. Reischauer, and Albert M. Craig (1989), *East Asia: Tradition and Transformation*. Boston: Houghton Mifflin Company.

Fallows, James (1989), "Containing Japan." *The Atlantic Monthly* (May 1989), 40–54.

Fletcher, William Miles III (1982), *The Search for a New Order: Intellectuals and Fascism in Prewar Japan*. Chapel Hill: University of North Carolina Press.

Forman, Michael (1998), *Nationalism and the International Labor Movement: The Idea of the Nation in Socialist and Anarchist Theory*. University Park: Pennsylvania State University Press.

Furukawa Takahisa (1998), *Kōki, Banpaku Orinpikku: Kōshitsu Burando to Keizai Hatten* (Imperial Calendar, the Expo and the Olympic Games: The Imperial Brand and Economic Development). Chūō Kōronsha.

Furuya Tetsuo (ed.) (1996), *Kindai Nihon no Ajia Ninshiki* (The Perception of Asia in Modern Japan). Ryokuin Shobō.

Gayle, Curtis Anderson (2003), *Marxist History and Postwar Japanese Nationalism*. London: RoutledgeCurzon.

Genyōsha Shashi Hensankai (ed.) (1917), *Genyōsha Shashi* (The Official History of the Genyōsha). Genyōsha Shashi Hensankai.

Ghose, Aurobindo (1972a), "Asiatic Democracy." *Bande Mataram*, 16 March 1908, 757–60.

——— (1972b), "India and the Mongolians." *Bande Mataram*, 1 April 1908, 812–17.

——— (1972c), "The Asiatic Role." *Bande Mataram*, 9 April 1908, 842–45.

——— (1972d), "Facts and Opinions." *Bande Mataram*, 31 July 1909, 230–31

——— (1972e), "Facts and Opinions." *Bande Mataram*, 9 October 1909, 247–58.

——— (1972a–1972e), Reprinted in Sri Aurobindo Birth Centenary Library (ed.) (1972), *Bande Mataram. Early Political Writings*, Vol. I. Pondicherry: Sri Aurobindo Ashram Trust.

Gluck, Carol (1993), "The Past in the Present." Andrew Gordon (ed.), *Postwar Japan as History*. Berkeley: University of California Press.

Go Toshi (ed.) (1944), *The Assembly of Greater East-Asiatic Nations*. The Nippon Times.

Goodman, Grant K. (1991), *Japanese Cultural Policies in Southeast Asia during World War Two*. New York: St. Martin's Press.

Goto, Ken'ichi (1997), *"Returning to Asia": Japan-Indonesia Relations 1930s–1942.* Ryūkei Shosha.

Gotō Ken'ichi (2007), "1930-nendai 'Ajia Kaiki' Ron to Dai Ajia Kyōkai: Sono Konnichiteki 'Imi' o Kangaeru" (The 1930s "Return to Asia" Debate and the Greater Asia Association: Considering Its Modern "Meaning"). Nishikawa Jun and Hirano Ken'ichirō (eds.), *Higashi Ajia: Kyōdōtai no Kōchiku* (East Asia: The Formation of a Community), Vol. 3, *Kokusai Idō to Shakai Hen'yō* (International Movements and Social Changes). Iwanami Shoten, 73–104.

—— (2008), "Hajime ni, Kaisetsu ni Kaete: Shōwa Senzenki Nihon to Dai Ajia Kyōkai," (Introduction, in Place of a Commentary: Japan in the Prewar Shōwa Period and the Greater Asia Association). Gotō Ken'ichi and Matsuura Masataka (eds.), Dai Ajiashugi *Kaisetsu Sōmokuroku* (*Dai Ajiashugi*: Commentaries and a Complete Catalogue), Ryūkei Shosha, 1–20.

Guan Wei (2003), "Lun Li Dazhao de Xin Yaxiya Zhuyi Jian tan Sun Zhongshan Da Yazhouzhuyi Zhi Bianqian" (On the New Asianism of Li Dazhao and the Transformation of Sun Yat-sen`s Great Asianism). *Beifang Luncong* 6, 51–55.

Gulick, Sidney Lewis (1905), *The White Peril in the Far East: an Interpretation of the Significance of the Russo-Japanese War.* New York: Fleming H. Revell.

Hamanaka, Shintaro (2009), *Asian Regionalism and Japan: The Politics of Membership in Regional Diplomatic, Financial and Trade Groups.* London: Routledge.

Hamashita, Takeshi (2008), *China, East Asia and the Global Economy*, edited by Linda Grove and Mark Selden. London: Routledge.

Han, Sang Jin (2003), "Theoretische Reflexionen über die Asiatischen Selbstbehauptungsdiskurse (Theoretical Reflections on Asian Discourse on Self-Assertion)." Iwo Amelung and Sven Saaler et al. (eds.), *Selbstbehauptungsdiskurse in China–Korea–Japan.* Munich: Iudicium, 325–52.

Hannaford, Ivan (1996), *Race: The History of an Idea in the West.* Washington, D.C., and Baltimore: The Woodrow Wilson Center Press and Johns Hopkins University Press.

Hanzawa Kōkan (1940), *Kōa Shokumin Kyōkasho* (Asia Development Textbook). Dai Nihon Tosho.

Hashikawa, Bunsō (1980), "Japanese Perspectives on Asia: From Dissociation to Coprosperity." Akira Iriye (ed.), *The Chinese and the Japanese. Essays in Political and Cultural Interactions.* Princeton, NJ: Princeton University Press, 328–55.

Hashim Makaruddin (ed.) (2000), *Politics, Democracy and the New Asia: Selected Speeches of Dr. Mahathir Mohamad, Prime Minister of Malaysia.* Selangor Darul Ehsan (Malaysia): Pelanduk.

Hatada Takashi (1969), *Nihonjin no Chōsen-kan* (Japanese Views of Korea). Keisō Shobō.

Hatano [Uho] (1912), *Asya Tehlikede* (Asia in Danger). Translated from Japanese by Mehmet Hilmi Nakawa and Abdürreşid İbrahim. İstanbul: Ahmed İhsan ve Şürekası.

Hatano Sumio (1996), *Taiheiyō Sensō to Ajia Gaikō* (The Pacific War and Asian Diplomacy). Tokyo Daigaku Shuppankai.

Hatsuse Ryūhei (1980), *Dentōteki Uyoku Uchida Ryōhei no Kenkyū* (A Study of Uchida Ryōhei, a Traditional Right Winger). Fukuoka: Kyushu Daigaku Shuppankai.

Hauner, Milan (1981), *India in Axis Strategy: Germany, Japan, and Indian Nationalists in the Second World War*. Stuttgart: Klett-Cotta.

Haushofer, Karl (1931), *Geopolitik der Pan-Ideen* (The Geopolitics of Pan-Ideas). Berlin: Zentral-Verlag.

Hay, Stephen N. (1970), *Asian Ideas of East and West. Tagore and his Critics in Japan, China, and India*. Cambridge, MA: Harvard University Press.

Hayashi Fusao (1974), *Dai Tōa Sensō Kōteiron* (Affirmation of the Greater East Asian War). Roman (reprinted as expanded edition Banchō Shobō 1975; reprinted Natsume Shobō, 2001).

Hazama Naoki (2001), "Shoki Ajiashugi ni tsuite no shiteki kōsatsu" (A Historical Inquiry into Early Pan-Asianism). *Tōa*, nos. 410–417 (2001–2002, 8 installments).

He, Jing (2006), *China in Okakura Kakuzō with Special Reference to His First Chinese Trip in 1893*. PhD diss., University of California, Los Angeles.

Heisig, James W., and John C. Maraldo (1995), *Rude Awakenings: Zen, the Kyoto School, and the Question of Nationalism*. Honolulu: University of Hawai'i Press.

Hinohara Shōzō (1884), "Nihon wa Tōyōkoku taru bekarazu" (Japan Must Not Be an Oriental Country). *Jiji Shinpō*, 11, 13, and 14 November 1884.

Hirai, Kazuomi (2005), "Sengo Shakai Undō no naka no Beheiren Undō no chiikiteki Enkai o Chūshin ni" (Citizen's Federation for Peace in Vietnam [Beheiren] and the Social Movements in Postwar Japan). *Hōsei Kenkyū/Journal of Law and Politics* 71:4, 355–87.

Hiraishi Naoaki (1994), "Kindai Nihon no 'Ajiashugi'" (The "Asianism" of Modern Japan). Mizoguchi, Yūzō et al. (eds.), *Sekaizō no Keisei* (Ajia kara kangaeru 5). Tokyo Daigaku Shuppankai.

Hirano Kuniomi (1863), *Seiban Sosaku* (Fundamental Measures for Expelling the Barbarians), reprinted in Hirano Kuniomi Kenshōkai (ed.), *Hirano Kuniomi Denki oyobi Ikō* (Biography and Posthumous Writings of Hirano Kuniomi). Shōzansha, 1980, 54.

Hirano Yoshitarō (1945), *Ajiashugi no Rekishiteki Kiso* (The Historical Foundations of Asianism). Kawade Shobō.

Hiranuma Kiichirō Kaikoroku Hensan Iinkai (ed.) (1955), *Hiranuma Kiichirō Kaikoroku* (The Memoirs of Hiranuma Kiichirō). Gaiyō Shobō.

Hohenzollern, William [Wilhelm von] (1922), "Memoirs of the Ex-Kaiser." *New York Times*, September/October 1922 (10 installments).

Holland, William L. (1955), *Selected Documents of the Bandung Conference: Texts of Selected Speeches and Final Communique of the Asian-African Conference, Bandung, Indonesia, April 18–24, 1955*. New York: Institute of Pacific Relations.

Horiuchi Bunjirō (1918), "Dai Ajiashugi to waga kokumin no shimei" (Great Asianism and the Mission of Our People). *Taiyō* 24:9.

Hosoi Hajime (1932), *Nihon no Ketsui* (Japan's Resolve). Nihon Yūben Taikai Kōdansha.

Hoston, Germaine (1984), "Marxism and Japanese Expansionism: Takahashi Kamekichi and the Theory of 'Petty Imperialism.'" *Journal of Japanese Studies* 10:1, 1–30.

Hotta, Eri (2006), "Rash Behari Bose and His Japanese Supporters." *Interventions* 8:1, 116–32.

—— (2007), *Pan-Asianism and Japan's War 1931–1945.* New York: Palgrave Macmillan.

Hughes, Thomas L. (2002), "The German Mission to Afghanistan, 1915–16." *German Studies Review* 25:3, 447–76.

Huntington, Samuel P. (1996), *The Clash of Civilizations and the Remaking of World Order.* New York: Simon & Schuster.

Hwang, Dongyoun (1998), "Some Reflections on War-Time Collaboration in China: Wang Jingwei and His Group in Hanoi." *Working Papers in Asian/Pacific Studies* 98-02.

Ichikawa Fusae, "Mite Kita Shin Shina" (The New China I Saw). *Fujō Shinbun*, no. 2080 (21 April 1940), 2, and no. 2081 (28 April 1940), 8.

Iida, Yumiko (1997), "Fleeing the West, Making Asia Home. Transpositions of Otherness in Japanese Pan-Asianism, 1905–1930." *Alternatives* 22, 409–32.

Inabe Kōjirō (2002), *Ikki to Reikichi: Kita Kyōdai no Sokoku* (Ikki and Reikichi: The Fatherland of the Brothers Kita). Niigata: Niigata Nippō Jigyōsha.

Inoue Hide, "Joshi Kyōiku no Dōkō" (Trends in Women's Education). *Kōa Kyōiku* 3:3 (1944), 18–24.

Inoue Hisakazu (2006), *Ajiashugi o Toinaosu* (Reconsidering Asianism). Chikuma Shobō.

Inoue Kiyoshi (1966), *Nihon no "Kindaika" to Gunkokushugi* (Japan's "Modernization" and Militarism). Shin Nihon Shinsho.

Inoue Masaji (1910), *Kyojin Arao Sei. Tsuketari Jūni Resshiden* (The Giant Arao Sei. Including The Lives of Twelve Patriots). Sakura Shobō.

—— (1944), *Kōa Gojūnen no Saka o Yojite* (Fifty Years in the Uphill Struggle to Raise Asia). Self-published.

Ishidō Kiyotomo (1985), "Tenkō ni tsuite" (Concerning Apostasy). *Undōshi Kenkyū* 16: 72–92.

Ishihara, Shintaro (1991), *The Japan That Can Say "No."* Translated by Frank Baldwin. New York: Simon & Schuster.

Ishiwara Kanji (1993), *Saishū Sensōron Sensōshi Taikan* (Treatise on the Final War and an Outline of War History). Chūō Kōronsha.

Itō Takashi (1978), *Taishōki "Kakushin"-ha no Seiritsu* (The Formation of the "Radical Faction" in the Taishō Era). Hanawa Shobō.

—— (1983), *Konoe Shintaisei: Taisei Yokusankai e no Michi* (The Konoe New Order: The Road to the Imperial Rule Assistance Association). Chūō Kōronsha.

—— (comp.) (2006), *Gendaishi o Kataru: Matsumoto Gaku* (Talking of Modern History: Matsumoto Gaku). Naiseishi Kenkyūkai Danwa Sokkiroku. Gendaishi Shiryō Shuppan.

—— (1989), "'Dai Ajiashugi' to 'Sanmin shugi.' Ō Seiei [Wang Jingwei] Kairai Seikenka no Shomondai ni tsuite" ("Greater Asianism" and "The Three People's

Principles." On Some Problems under Wang Jingwei's Puppet Government). *Yokohama Shiritsu Daigaku Ronsō* 40:1, 225–47.

Itō Teruo (ed.) (1990), *Ajia to Kindai Nihon: Han Shinryaku no Shisō to Undō* (Asia and Modern Japan: Anti-Invasionist Thought and Action). Shakai Hyōronsha.

Iwakura Tomomi (1875), "Tomomi Saido Kokusei o Hitsurokushi Goran ni Kyōzurukoto" (Tomomi Writes and Submits Another Proposal on the State Policy). Tada Kōmon (ed.), *Iwakura Kō Jikki* (Diary of Prince Iwakura), Vol. 2, (Kunaishō/Ministry of Imperial Household), 1906, 1270.

Jansen, Marius B. (1954), *The Japanese and Sun Yat-sen*. Cambridge, MA: Harvard University Press.

——— (1980), "Konoe Atsumaro." Akira Iriye (ed.), *The Chinese and the Japanese: Essays in Political and Cultural Interactions*. Princeton, NJ: Princeton University Press, 107–23.

——— (2000), *The Making of Modern Japan*. Cambridge, MA: Harvard University Press.

Jensen, Joan (1979), "The 'Hindu Conspiracy': A Reassessment." *The Pacific Historical Review* 48:1, 65–83.

Johnson, Chalmers (1964), *An Instance of Treason: Ozaki Hotsumi and the Sorge Spy Ring*. Stanford, CA: Stanford University Press.

——— (1993), "The State and Japanese Grand Strategy." Richard Rosecrance and Arthur A. Stein (eds.), *The Domestic Bases of Grand Strategy*. Ithaca, NY: Cornell University Press.

Kada, Tetsuji (1939), "The Theory of an East Asiatic Unity." *Contemporary Japan* July 1939 (VIII:5), 574–81.

Kajima Kenkyūjo (ed.) (1971), *Nihon Gaikōshi, 24-kan: Daitōa Sensō, Senji Gaikō* (History of Japanese Foreign Relations, Vol. 24: The Greater East Asian War, War Time Diplomacy). Kajima Kenkyūjo Shuppankai.

Kamachi, Noriko (1981), *Reform in China: Huang Tsun-hsien and the Japanese Model*. Cambridge, MA: Council on East Asian Studies, Harvard University.

Kamikawa, Hikomatsu (1939), "The American and Japanese Monroe Doctrines." *Contemporary Japan* 8:6, 740–50.

Kan Sō-ichi (Han Sang-il) (1984), *Nikkan Kindaishi no Kūkan: Meiji Nashonarizumu no Rinen to Genjitsu* (The Space of the Modern History of Japan and Korea: The Ideals and Reality of Meiji Nationalism). Nihon Keizai Hyōronsha.

Kaneko, Toshiya (2002), *Cultural Light, Political Shadow: Okakura Tenshin (1862–1913) and the Japanese Crisis of National Identity*. PhD diss., University of Pennsylvania.

Kang Sang-jung (2001), *Tōhoku Ajia Kyōdō no Ie o Mezashite* (Towards a Common House in Northeast Asia). Heibonsha.

Kanlidere, Ahmet (1997), *Reform within Islam: the Tajdid and Jadid Movement among the Kazan Tatars, 1809-1917*. Beyoğlu, Istanbul: Eren.

Kanokogi Kazunobu (1937), *Sumera Ajia* (Imperial Asia). Dōbun Shoin.

Karl, Rebecca (2002), *Staging the World: Chinese Nationalism at the Turn of the Twentieth Century*. Durham, NC: Duke University Press.

Katsube Mitake, Matsumoto Sannosuke, Ōguchi Yūjirō (eds.) (1972), *Katsu Kaishū Zenshū* (Collected Writings of Katsu Kaishū), Vol. 18. Keisō Shobō, 50.

Katzenstein, Peter, and Takashi Shiraishi (eds.) (1997), *Network Power: Japan and Asia*. Ithaca, NY: Cornell University Press.

——— (eds.) (2006), *Beyond Japan: The Dynamics of East Asian Regionalism*. Ithaca, NY: Cornell University Press.

Katzenstein, Peter, et al. (2000), *Asian Regionalism*. Cornell East Asia Series. Ithaca, NY: East Asia Program, Cornell University.

Kawahara Hiroshi (1979), *Shōwa Shisōshi Kenkyū* (The Study of Shōwa Intellectual History). Waseda Daigaku Shuppankai.

Kawai Yoshihiro (2006), *Yasuoka Masahiro no Kenkyū: Minponshugi no Keisei to sono Tenkai* (A Study of Yasuoka Masahiro: The Formation and Development of "People-as-the Base" Thought). Meisō Shuppansha.

Kawakami, K. K. [Kiyoshi Karl] (1919), *Japan and World Peace*. New York: Macmillan.

——— (1921), *What Japan Thinks*. New York: Macmillan.

Keene, Donald (1964), "Japanese Writers and the Greater East Asia War." *Journal of Asian Studies* 23:2, 209–25.

Kim Bongjin (2007), "Kindai Chōsen to Higashia Ajia Ninshiki" (Modern Korea and Asian Consciousness). Kishi Toshihiko et al. (eds.), *"Higashi Ajia" no Jidaisei* (The Temporality of "East Asia"). Keisuisha, 53–90.

Kim Dae-Jung (1994), "Is Culture Destiny? The Myth of Asia's Anti-Democratic Values." *Foreign Affairs*, November–December, 189–94.

Kim, John Namjun (2007), "The Temporality of Empire: The Imperial Cosmopolitanism of Miki Kiyoshi and Tanabe Hajime." Sven Saaler and J. Victor Koschmann (eds.), *Pan-Asianism in Modern Japanese History: Regionalism, Colonialism and Borders*. New York: Routledge, 151–67.

Kingston, Jeffrey (2004), *Japan's Quiet Transformation: Social Change and Civil Society in the Twenty-First Century*. London: RoutledgeCurzon.

Kita Ikki (1921 [1915]), *Shina Kakumei Gaishi* (An Unofficial History of the Chinese Revolution), Daitōtaku, reprinted in Kita Ikki (1959), *Kita Ikki Chosakushū* (Collected Works by Kita Ikki), Vol. 2. Misuzu Shobō, 1–213.

——— (1919), *Kokka Kaizōan Genri Daikō* (Outline of a Plan for the Reconstruction of Japan), Yūzonsha, reprinted in Kita Ikki (1959), *Kita Ikki Chosakushū*, Vol. 2. Misuzu Shobō, 215–81.

——— (1959), *Kita Ikki Chosakushū* (Collected Works of Kita Ikki), Vol. 2. Misuzu Shobō.

Kita Ikki, Ōkawa Shūmei, and Mitsukawa Kametarō (2008), *Ajiashugishatachi no Koe 3: Yūzonsha to Kōchisha, aruiwa Kokka Kaizō e no Kokoromi* (Pan-Asianist Voices, Vol. 3: The Yūzonsha and the Kōchisha, or An Attempt at State Reform). Shoshi Shinsui.

Kita Reikichi (1917a), "Gokai Saretaru Ajiashugi" (Misunderstood Asianism). *Tōhō Jiron* 2:7, 8–10.

——— (1917b), "Waga Kuni no Daishimei" (The Great Mission of Our Country). *Tōhō Jiron* 2:12, 19–21.

——— (1918), *Hikari wa Tōhō Yori* (The Light from the East). Dai Nihon Yūbenkai.
——— (1941), *Haigeki no Rekishi* (The History of Rejection). Dairi Shobō.
Kitaoka Shin'ichi (1988), *Gotō Shinpei. Gaikō to Vision* (Gotō Shinpei. Foreign Policy and Vision). Chūō Kōronsha.
Kiyofuji Kōshichirō (ed.) (1981), *Ten'yūkyō* (The Band of Heroes Assisted by Heaven). Kōryū Shorin (reprint).
Kobayashi Hideo (1995), *"Nihon Kabushikigaisha" o Tsukutta Otoko: Miyazaki Masayoshi no Shōgai* (The Man Who Created "Japan Inc.": The Life of Miyazaki Masayoshi). Shōgakukan.
——— (2005), *Mantetsu Chōsabu* (The Research Department of the Southern Manchurian Railway Co.). Heibonsha.
Kodera Kenkichi (1916), *Dai Ajiashugiron* (Treatise on Greater Asianism). Hōbunkan.
Koizumi, Junichiro, Prime Minister of Japan (2002), "Japan and ASEAN in East Asia: A Sincere and Open Partnership" (14 January). Prime Minister of Japan and His Cabinet website, http://www.kantei.go.jp/foreign/koizumispeech/2002/01/14speech_e.html (last accessed 30 March 2010).
Kojima Shinji et al. (eds.) (1974), *Chūgokujin no Nihonjinkan Hyakunenshi* (Hundred Years' History of Chinese Views of the Japanese). Jiyū Kokuminsha.
Kokuryūkai (1934), *Nikkan Gappō Kinentō Shashinchō* (Monument to the Union of Japan and Korea). Kokuryūkai Honbu.
——— (1966a), *Nikkan Gappō Hishi* (Secret History of the Union of Japan and Korea). Hara Shobō (first published 1930 by Kokuryūkai Shuppanbu, ed. by Kuzuu Yoshihisa).
——— (ed.) (1904), *Seiro Annai* (Guidebook to Conquering Russia). Futendō.
——— (ed.) (1966b), *Tōa Senkaku Shishi Kiden* (Biographies of Pioneer East Asian Patriots), 3 vols., Hara Shobō (first published 1933–36 by Kokuryūkai Shuppanbu, ed. by Kuzuu Yoshihisa).
Kokuryūkai Honbu (1924), Kokuryūkai Kakuchō Shuisho (Program for an Expansion of the Kokuryūkai), reprinted in Uchida Ryōhei Monjo Kenkyūkai (ed.), *Uchida Ryōhei Kankei Monjo*, Vol. 7, Fuyō Shobō, 20f.
——— (ed.) (1904), *Kokuryūkai Mankan Shinzu* (Kokuryūkai's New Map of Manchuria and Korea). Kōbunkan Yoshikawa Hanshichi.
Kokuryūkai Shuppanbu (ed.) (1918), *Ajia Taikan* (Overview of Asia). Kokuryūkai Shuppanbu.
Komagome Takeshi (1994), "'Manshūkoku' ni okeru Jukyō no Isō: Daidō, Ōdō, Kōdō" (Tenets of Confucianism in Manchukuo: The Great Way, the Kingly Way, the Imperial Way). *Shisō* 841, 57–82.
Kondō Kuniyasu (1979), "Kaisetsu" (Commentary). Nishi Junzō (ed.), *Genten Chūkoku Kindai Shisōshi*, Vol. 3 (A History of the Foundations of Modern Chinese Thought). Iwanami Shoten, 3–26.
——— (1981), *Chūgoku Kindai Shisōshi Kenkyū* (Studies in Modern Chinese Intellectual History). Keisō Shobō.
Konoe Atsumaro (1898a), "Dōjinshu Dōmei, Tsuketari Shina Mondai Kenkyū no Hitsuyō" (An Alliance of the Same Race and the Necessity of Studying the Chinese Question). *Taiyō,* 24:1 (1 January 1898), reprinted in Konoe Atsumaro Nikki

Kankōkai (ed.), *Konoe Atsumaro Nikki*, supplement. Kajima Kenkyūjo Shuppankai, 1969, 62–63.

——— (1898b), "Teikoku no Ichi to Gendai no Seijika" (The Position of Our Empire and the Politicians of Today). *Tōa Jiron* 1 (December), 5–7.

Konoe Atsumaro Nikki Kankōkai (ed.) (1968–1969), *Konoe Atsumaro Nikki* (The Diaries of Konoe Atsumaro), 6 vols. Kajima Kenkyūjo Shuppankai.

Konoe Fumimaro (1918), "Eibei Hon'i Heiwashugi o Hai Su" (A Call to Reject the Anglo-American Centered Peace). *Nihon oyobi Nihonjin* 746 (12 December), 23–26.

——— (1981), *Sengo Ōbei Kenbunroku* (Travels in Post-War Europe and the United and States). Chūō Kōronsha (first edition Gaikō Jihōsha, 1920).

——— (1937), "Manchukuo, Precursor of Asiatic Renaissance and the Government by Wang-Tao (Kingly Way) Based on Theocracy." *Contemporary Manchuria* 1:2, 1–17.

Koo Jong-Suh (1995), "Pan-Asianism. Primacy of East Asia." *The Monthly Joongang*, April.

Koschmann, J. Victor (1997), "Asianism's Ambivalent Legacy," in Peter J. Katzenstein and Takashi Shiraishi (eds.), *Network Power: Japan and Asia*. Ithaca, NY: Cornell University Press, 83–110.

Kurbangaliev, M. (1924), "Ajia no Roshia ni okeru Uraru Arutai Minzoku" (The Ural-Altaic Peoples in Russian Asia). *Manmō* 10, 20–32.

Kuroki Morifumi (2002), "Ueki Emori no Taigai Shisō (1)" (On the Foreign Thought of Emori Ueki [1]). *Fukuoka Kokusai Daigaku Kiyō* 7, 15–27.

——— (2005), "Kōakai no Ajiashugi" (The Asianism of the Kōakai). *Hōsei Kenkyū* (Kyūshū Daigaku) 71:4, 247–87.

——— (2007), "The Asianism of the Kōa-kai and the Ajia Kyōkai: Reconsidering the Ambiguity of Asianism." Sven Saaler and J. Victor Koschmann (eds.), *Pan-Asianism in Modern Japanese History*. London: Routledge, 34–51.

Kuroki Morifumi and Masuzawa Akio (eds.) (1993), *Kōa-kai Hōkoku/Ajia Kyōkai Hōkoku* (Bulletin of the Kōakai, Bulletin of the Ajia Kyōkai). Reprint, 2 vols. Fuji Shuppan.

Kushner, Barak (2006), *The Thought War: Japanese Imperial Propaganda*. Honolulu: University of Hawai'i Press.

Laffan, Michael Francis (2003), *Islamic Nationhood and Colonial Indonesia: The Umma below the Winds*. London: RoutledgeCurzon.

Lee, Chong-sik (1985), *Japan and Korea: The Political Dimension*. Stanford, CA: Hoover Institution Press.

Lee, Peter et al. (eds.) (2000), *Sources of Korean Tradition*. New York: Columbia University Press.

Li Cai-hua and Suzuki Tadashi (2007), *Ajia to Nihon: Heiwa Shisō toshite no Ajiashugi* (Asia and Japan: Asianism as an Ideology of Peace). Nōbunkyō.

Li Narangoa (2007), "Universal Values and Pan-Asianism: The Vision of Ōmotokyō." Sven Saaler and J. Victor Koschmann (eds.), *Pan-Asianism in Modern Japanese History: Colonialism, Regionalism and Borders*. London: Routlege, 52–66.

Li Quanxing (ed.) (1994), *Li Dazhao Yanjiu Cidian* (Dictionary for Research on Li Dazhao). Beijing: Hongqi Chubanshe.

Mackie, Jamie (2005), *Bandung 1955: Non-Alignment and Afro-Asian Solidarity.* Singapore: Editions Didier Millet.

Maeno Ryōtaku (1777), *Kanreihigen* (Humble Opinion from Limited Observation), reprinted in Numata Shirō et al. (eds.), *Nihon Shisō Taikei, Vol. 64: Yōgaku* (Survey of Japanese Thought, Vol. 64: Western Science). Iwanami Shoten, 1973.

Mahathir Mohamad (2004), *Achieving True Globalisation.* Interview and composition by Kohei Hashimoto. Selangor Darul Ehsan (Malaysia): Pelanduk.

Mahathir Mohamad and Shintarō Ishihara (1995), *The Voice of Asia: Two Leaders Discuss the Coming Century.* Translated by Frank Baldwin. Kōdansha, 1995. Originally published as *"No" to ieru Ajia* (The Asia That Can Say "No"), Kōbunsha, 1994.

Mannheim, Karl (1953), *Essays on Sociology and Social Psychology*, edited by Paul Kecskemeti. London: Routledge and Kegan Paul.

Mantetsukai and Shimano Saburō Denki Kankōkai (eds.) (1984), *Shimano Saburō* (Shimano Saburō). Hara Shobō.

Mark, Ethan (2006), "'Asia's' Transwar Lineage: Nationalism, Marxism and 'Greater Asia' in an Indonesian Inflection." *Journal of Asian Studies* 65:3, 461–93.

Maruyama Masao (1964), "Nihon Fuashizumu no Shisō to Undō" (The Thought and Movement of Japanese Fascism), Maruyama Masao, *Gendai Seiji no Shisō to Undō* (The Thought and Movement of Modern Politics). Miraisha, 29–87.

——— (2002), "Fukuzawa Yukichi no 'Datsuaron' to sono Shūhen" (Fukuzawa Yukichi's *Datsuaron* and Its Context). *Maruyama Masao Techō* 20, 1–42.

Maswood, S. Javed (ed.) (2001), *Japan and East Asian Regionalism.* London: Routledge.

Matsui Iwane (1933), "Dai Ajiashugi" (Greater Asianism). *Kingu*, May Issue Supplement "Jikyoku Mondai: Hijōji Kokumin Taikai" (The Problems concerning the Current Situation: A People's Rally in Times of Emergency), 2–9.

Matsumoto Gaku (1933), "Nippon Bunka Renmei no Teishō: Daigo Intaa (Nihon Seishin Intaa) ni Tsuite" (A Call for a Japan Culture League: On the 5th International [The International of the Japanese Spirit]). *Kokui* 14, 3.

——— (1940), "Eastern Culture and Its Peculiar Features." *Cultural Nippon* 8:4, 1–15.

Matsumoto Ken'ichi (2000), *Takeuchi Yoshimi "Nihon no Ajiashugi: Seidoku* (Careful Reading of Takeuchi Yoshimi's "Japan's Asianism"). Iwanami Shoten.

Matsumura Masayoshi (1987), *Pōtsumasu e no Michi. Kōkaron to Yōroppa no Suematsu Kenchō* (The Road to Portsmouth. The Yellow Peril and Suematsu Kenchō during His Time in Europe). Hara Shobō.

Matsuoka Yōsuke (1941a), Address by the Foreign Minister of Japan before the 76th Session of the Imperial Diet, 21 January 1941. *Contemporary Japan*, February.

——— (1941b), *Kōa no Taigyō* (The Gigantic Task of Raising Asia). Naikaku Insatsukyoku/Daiichi Kōronsha.

Matsuura Masataka (2007a), "Han-Ajiashugi ni okeru 'Indo Yōin'" (The Indian Factor in Pan-Asianism). Ishida Ken (ed.), *Bōchō Suru Teikoku, Kakusan Suru Teikoku* (The Growing Empire, the Disintegrating Empire). Tokyo Daigaku Shuppankai, 3–53.

——— (ed.) (2007b), *Shōwa-Ajiashugi no Jitsuzō* (The True Picture of Shōwa-Period Asianism). Kyoto: Minerva Shobō.

——— (2010), *Taiheiyō Sensō wa naze Okita no ka: Han-Ajiashugi no Seiji Keizaishi* (Why Did the Pacific War Come About? The Political and Economic History of Pan-Asianism). Nagoya: Nagoya Daigaku Shuppankai.

Matsuzawa Tatsuo (1939), "New Chosen." *Contemporary Japan*, June, 455–64.

Matsuzawa Tetsunari (1979), *Ajiashugi to Fashizumu* (Asianism and Fascism). Renga Shobō Shinsha.

Mazumdar R. C. (1927), "Introduction." *Ancient Indian Colonies in the Far East*, Vol. I. Champa: The Punjab Sanskrit Book Depot and Lahore, i–xxiv.

McCormack, Gavan (2000), "The Japanese Movement to 'Correct' History." Laura Hein and Mark Selden (eds.), *Censoring History: Citizenship and Memory in Japan, Germany, and the United States.* Armonk, NY: M. E. Sharpe.

McWilliams, Wayne C. (1975), "East Meets East: The Soejima Mission to China, 1873." *Monumenta Nipponica* 30:3, 237–75.

Meisner, Maurice (1967), *Li Ta-Chao and the Origins of Chinese Marxism.* Cambridge, MA: Harvard University Press.

Miki Kiyoshi (1938), "Tōa Shisō no Konkyo" (The Basis of East Asian Philosophy). *Kaizō*, December, 8–20.

Minichiello, Sharon (1984), *Retreat from Reform: Patterns of Political Behavior in Interwar Japan.* Honolulu: University of Hawai'i Press.

Mitani Hiroshi (1997), *Meiji Ishin to Nashonarizumu* (The Meiji Restoration and Nationalism). Yamakawa Shuppansha.

Mitsukawa Kametarō (1921), *Ubawaretaru Ajia* (Stolen Asia). Kōbundō Shoten (reprinted 2007 by Shoshi Shinsui).

——— (1935), *Sangoku Kanshō Igo* (After the Triple Intervention). Heibonsha (reprinted 1977 by Dentō to Gendaisha and 2004 by Ronsōsha).

Miwa Kimitada (1973), "Ajiashugi no Rekishiteki Kōsatsu" (Historical Examination of Asianism). Hirano Ken'ichirō (ed.), *Nihon Bunka no Hen'yō.* Kōdansha, 385–461.

——— (1990), "Japanese Policies and Concepts for a Regional Order in Asia, 1938–1940." James W. White, Michio Umegaki, and Thomas R. H. Havens (eds.), *The Ambivalence of Nationalism: Modern Japan between East and West.* Lanham, MD: University Press of America, 133–54.

——— (1999), *Kakusareta Perii no "Shirahata"* (Perry's Hidden "White Flag"). Sophia University Press.

Miyadai Shinji (2004), *Ajiashugi no Tenmatsu ni Manabe* (Learn from the Development of Asianism!). Jissensha.

Miyagawa Torao (1972), *Okakura Tenshin.* Tokyo University Press.

Miyagi Taizō (2001), *Bandon Kaigi to Nihon no Ajia Fukki* (The Bandung Conference and Japan's Return to Asia). Soshisha.

Miyai Kanejirō (1925), *Dai Ajia Renpō no Kensetsu* (The Construction of a Greater Asian Federation). Ajia Shinbunsha.

Miyamoto Moritarō (1984), *Shūkyōteki Ningen no Seiji Shisō: Abe Isoo to Kanokogi Kazunobu no Baai* (The Political Thought of Religious Men: The Case of Abe Isoo and Kanokogi Kazunobu). Bokutakusha.

Miyazaki Masayoshi (1938), *Tōa Renmei Ron* (On the East Asian League), Kaizōsha.

Miyazaki Ryūsuke and Onogawa Hidemi (eds.) (1971), *Miyazaki Tōten Zenshū* (Complete Works of Miyazaki Tōten), Vol. 2. Heibonsha.

Miyazaki Tōten (1902), *Sanjūsannen no Yume* (Thirty-Three Years' Dream). Kokkō Shobō.

—— (1915), "Rikkōho Sengen" (Election Manifesto), reproduced in *Miyazaki Tōten Zenshū* (Complete Works of Miyazaki Tōten), Vol. 2, Heibonsha, 1971, frontispiece.

—— (1919), "Tokyo yori" (From Tokyo, 1919), *Miyazaki Tōten Zenshū* (Complete Works of Miyazaki Tōten), Vol. 2, Heibonsha, 1971, 128.

—— (1982), *My Thirty-Three Years' Dream: The Autobiography of Miyazaki Tōten*. Translated, with an introduction by Etō Shinkichi and Marius B. Jansen. Princeton, NJ: Princeton University Press.

Miyazaki Tōten, Kayano Nagatomo, and Kita Ikki (2008), *Ajiashugisha no Koe 2: Kakumei Hyōronka aruiwa Chūgoku Kakumei e no Kan'yo to Satetsu* (Pan-Asianist Voices, Vol. 2: Critics of Revolution or Engagement and Failure in the Chinese Revolution). Shoshi Shinsui.

Mizoguchi Yūzō et al. (eds.) (1993–1994), *Ajia kara Kangaeru* (Asian Perspectives). 7 vols. Tokyo Daigaku Shuppankai.

Mizuno Naoki (1996), "1920-nendai Nihon: Chōsen, Chūgoku ni okeru Ajia Ninshiki no Ichidanmen: Ajia Minzoku Kaigi o Meguru Sangoku no Ronchō" (Japan in the 1920s: One Aspect of Asia Awareness in Korea and China. Debates Concerning the Conference of Asian Peoples in the Three Countries). Furuya Tetsuo (ed.), *Kindai Nihon to Ajia Ninshiki* (The Perception of Asia in Modern Japan). Ryokuin Shobō, 509–48.

Mizushima Naofumi (1978), *Sugita Junzan Ō Shōden* (Short Biography of the Venerable Sugita Junzan). Fukui: Yasuda Shoten/Himawari Shoten.

Mori Kaku (1941), "Hijōji no hijō shudan" (Extraordinary Means for Extraordinary Times). *Diamond*, July 1932, reprinted in Yamaura Kan'ichi, *Tōa Shintaisei no Senku: Mori Kaku*. Mori Kaku Denki Hensankai, 1941, 26–29.

Mori Rintarō (Ōgai) (1904), *Kōkaron Kōgai* (An Outline of the Yellow Peril). Shun'yōdō.

Morishima Michio (2000), *Collaborative Development in Northeast Asia*. Basingstoke: Palgrave Macmillan.

Mukherjee, Tapan (1997), *Taraknath Das: Life and Letters of a Revolutionary in Exile*. Calcutta: National Council of Education in Bengal.

Mulgan, Aurelia George (2009), "Hatoyama's East Asia Community and Regional Leadership Rivalries." Internet: East Asia Forum, http://www.eastasiaforum.org/2009/10/13/hatoyamas-east-asia-community/ (last accessed 1 June 2010).

Murayama Tomiichi (1995), "Statement by Prime Minister Tomiichi Murayama 'On the Occasion of the 50th Anniversary of the War's End' (15 August 1995)." Internet: *Ministry of Foreign Affairs*, http://www.mofa.go.jp/announce/press/pm/murayama/9508.html (last accessed 1 March 2010).

Muro Kiyoshi (1999), *Tōjō Utsubeshi: Nakano Seigō Hyōden* (Tōjō Must Be Struck: A Critical Biography of Nakano Seigō). Asahi Shinbunsha.

Murobuse Kōshin (1926), *Ajiashugi* (Asianism). Hihyōsha.

Mutō Shūtarō (2003), "Hirano Yoshitarō no Dai Ajiashugiron" (Hirano Yoshitarō's Theory of Greater Asianism). *Ajia Kenkyū* 49:4, 44–59.
Nagai, Ryūtarō (1913), "The White Peril." *The Japan Magazine*, 39–42.
——— (1920), *Kaizō no Risō* (The Ideal of Renovation). Seikadō.
——— (1937), "Ajia saiken no seisen" (Holy War for the Reconstruction of Asia). *Nihon Bunka* 10 (November), 27–42.
——— (1944), *Nagai Ryūtarō shi Kōa Yūbenshū* (Speeches of Nagai Ryūtarō concerning the Raising of Asia). Ryūginsha.
Nagami Shichirō (1942), *Kōa Ichiro: Inoue Masaji* (Inoue Masaji: Path to a Prosperous Asia). Tōkō Shoin.
Naimushō Keihokyoku Hoanka (1926), *Zen Ajia Minzoku Kaigi Tenmatsu. Tsuketari Puratappu no Torai* (The Circumstances of the Conference of Asian Peoples. Addendum: The Arrival of Pratap). Gaimushō Gaikō Shiryōkan (Diplomatic Record Office of the Ministry of Foreign Affairs of Japan), Gaimushō Kiroku (Diplomatic Records), MT I.4.6.0.1-1, Minzoku Mondai Kankei Zakken (Miscellaneous Matters Relating to the Question of Asian Nationalities), Vol. 2: Ajia Minzoku Mondai (The Question of Asian Nationalities).
Najita, Tetsuo (1971), "Nakano Seigō and the Meiji Restoration in Twentieth-Century Japan." Morley, James (ed.), *Dilemmas of Growth in Prewar Japan*. Princeton, NJ: Princeton University Press.
Nakagawa Hidenao (2006), "Atarashii Ajiashugi" (A New Asianism). Abe Shinzō et al., *Nitchū Taiwa* (Japanese-Chinese Dialogue). Genron NPO.
Nakajima Takeshi (2005), *Nakamuraya no Bōsu: Indo Dokuritsu Undō to Kindai Nihon no Ajiashugi* (The Bose of the Nakamuraya: The Indian Independence Movement and the Asianism of Modern Japan). Hakusuisha.
——— (2009), *Bose of Nakamuraya: An Indian Revolutionary in Japan*. New Delhi: Promilla & Co. Publishers in association with Bibliophile South Asia.
Nakamura Naomi (1991), "Tokutomi Sohō no 'Ajiashugi'" (Tokutomi Sohō's "Asianism"). *Shakai Kagaku Kenkyū* 37:2, 415–37.
Nakamura Tetsu (2003), "Military Action Prompting Afghan Backlash." *International Herald Tribune/Asahi Shimbun*, 13 December (accessible online at http://www1a.biglobe.ne.jp/peshawar/eg/naka13dec03.html).
Nakano Seigō (1917), "Bōkoku no Sanga" (The Mountains and Rivers of a Fallen State), *Sekai Seisaku to Kyokutō Seisaku* (Global and Far Eastern Policy). Shiseidō Shoten.
——— (1942), "Kono Issen: Kokumin wa ika ni Tatakaubeki ka!" (This One War: How the People Should Fight!), Tōhōkai, Tokyo, January, 13–16.
Nakano Yasuo (1988), *Ajiashugisha Nakano Seigō* (The Pan-Asianist Nakano Seigō). Aki Shobō.
Nakashita Masaharu (1996), *Shinbun ni Miru Nitchū Kankeishi: Chūgoku no Nihonjin Keieishi* (Sino-Japanese Relations as Seen through Newspapers: China's Japanese-Run Newspapers). Kenbun Shuppan.
Nakatani Takeyo (1985), "Matsui Taishō to Dai Ajiashugi. Jo ni Kaete" (General Matsui and Greater Asianism. In Place of a Preface). Tanaka Masaaki (ed.), *Matsui*

Iwane Taishō no Jinchū Nisshi (General Matsui Iwane's War Diary). Fuyō Shobō, 4–6.

——— (1989), *Shōwa Dōranki no Kaisō: Nakatani Takeyo Kaikoroku* (Recollections of the Upheavals of the Shōwa Period: The Memoirs of Nakatani Takeyo). 2 vols., Tairyūsha.

Nicolaevsky, B. (1949), "Russia, Japan, and the Pan-Asiatic Movement to 1925." *The Far Eastern Quarterly* 8:3, 259–95.

Nihon Bunka Chūō Renmei (ed.) (1938), *Nihon Bunka Dantai Nenkan* (The Year Book of Japan's Cultural Bodies), Nihon Bunka Chūō Renmei.

Nish, Ian (2005), "Suematsu Kencho: International Envoy to Wartime Europe," *Discussion Paper no. IS/05/491*. The Suntory Centre. Suntory and Toyota International Centres for Economics and Related Disciplines.

Nishihara Yukio (1980), *Zenkiroku Harubin Tokumu Kikan: Kantō-gun Jōhōbu no Kiseki* (Complete Records of the Harbin Special Service Agency: Traces of the Kwantung Army's Intelligence Section). Mainichi Shinbunsha.

Nitta Kiyo (1971), *Sawayanagi Masatarō. Sono Shōgai to Gyōseki* (Sawayanagi Masatarō. His Life and Work). Seijō Gakuen Sawayanagi Kenkyūkai.

Norman, E. Herbert (1944), "The Genyosha: A Study in the Origins of Japanese Imperialism." *Pacific Affairs* 17:3, 261–84.

Northedge, F. S. (1986), *The League of Nations: Its Life and Times, 1920–1946*. Leicester: Leicester University Press.

Oates, Leslie Russell (1985), *Populist Nationalism in Prewar Japan: A Biography of Nakano Seigo*. Sydney: Allen and Unwin.

Obi Toshito (ed.) (1962a), "Dai 20-kai [Ozaki Hozumi] Jinmon Chōsho" (The 20th [Ozaki Hozumi] Interrogation Report). *Zoruge Jiken* (Sorge Incident), Vol. 2, Gendaishi Shiryō (Sources on Modern History), Vol. 2, Misuzu Shobō, 197–210.

——— (ed.) (1962b), "Ozaki Hotsumi no Shuki (1)" (Ozaki Hotsumi's Memorandum, part 1), *Zoruge Jiken* (Sorge Incident), Vol. 2, Gendaishi Shiryō (Sources on Modern History), Vol. 2. Misuzu Shobō, 1–25.

——— (ed.) (1962c), "Rishaado Zoruge no Shuki (1)" (Richard Sorge's Memorandum, part 1), *Zoruge Jiken* (Sorge Incident), Vol. 1, Gendaishi Shiryō (Sources on Modern History), Vol. 1. Misuzu Shobō, 139–70.

O'Connor, Peter (2004–2005), *Japanese Propaganda: Selected Readings*. Folkestone: Global Oriental and Tokyo: Edition Synapse.

Office of Strategic Services (1944), "Japanese Attempts at Infiltration among Muslims in Russia and Her Borderlands," *O.S.S./State Department Intelligence and Research Reports, I. Japan and Its Occupied Territories during World War II*. R&A Report no. 890.2.

Oguma Eiji (1995): *Tan'itsu Minzoku Shinwa no Kigen* (The Myth of the Homogenous Nation). Shin'yōsha.

——— (1998), *"Nihonjin" no Kyōkai* (The Boundaries of the "Japanese"). Shin'yōsha.

——— (2002), *A Genealogy of "Japanese" Self-Images*. Melbourne: Trans Pacific Press.

——— (2007), "The Postwar Intellectuals' View of 'Asia.'" Sven Saaler and J. Victor Koschmann (eds.), *Pan-Asianism in Modern Japanese History: Regionalism,*

Colonialism and Borders. New York: Routledge, 200–212 (revised version accessible online at http://www.japanfocus.org/-Oguma-Eiji/2350).

Ogura Kazuo (1982), *Nichi-Bei Keizai Masatsu: Omote no Jijō Ura no Jijō* (US-Japan Economic Tension: The Publicly Known Circumstances and the Behind-the-Scenes Circumstances). Nihon Keizai Shinbunsha.

——— (1983), *Trade Conflict: A View from Japan*. Japan Economic Institute.

——— (1993), "A Call for a New Concept of Asia." *Japan Echo* 20:3 (Autumn 1993) (abridged translation of "Ajia no Fukken no tame ni," *Chūō Kōron*, July 1993: 60–73).

——— (1999), "Creating a New Asia." *Japan Echo* 26:3 (March–April).

Ohsawa, J. G. (1954), *The Two Great Indians in Japan. Sri Rash Behari Bose and Netaji Subhas Chandra Bose*. Calcutta: Sri K. C. Das for Kusa Publications.

Oka, Yoshitake (1983), *Konoe Fumimaro*. University of Tokyo Press.

Okakura Kakuzo [Tenshin] (1920), *The Ideals of the East, with Special Reference to the Art of Japan*. London: J. Murray (originally published in 1903, accessible online at http://www.archive.org).

Okakura Kakuzō (1981), *Okakura Tenshin Zenshū* (Complete Works of Okakura Tenshin), Vol. 8, edited by Kumamoto Kenjirō et al. Heibonsha.

——— (1984), *Okakura Kakuzō Collected English Writings*. Heibonsha.

Okakura Tenshin (1940a), *The Awakening of the East*, with notes and an introduction by Akira Asano. Seibunkaku (originally published in 1905).

——— (1940b), *The Awakening of Japan*, edited with notes by Hiroshi Muraoka. Kenkyūsha (originally published in 1904, accessible online at http://www.archive.org).

Ōkawa Shūmei (1913), "Nihon Bunmei no Igi oyobi Kachi" (The Significance and Value of Japanese Civilization). *Tairiku* 3 (September), 22–32.

——— (1916), "Kokuminteki Risō Juritsu no Kyūmu" (The Urgent Task of Establishing a National Ideal). *Michi*, February, 35–40.

——— (1943), *Kaikyō Gairon* (A General Outline of Islam). Keiō Shobō.

——— (1961), *Anraku no Mon, Ōkawa Shūmei Zenshū* 1 (The Gate to Comfort, Complete Works of Ōkawa Shūmei). Iwasaki Shoten, 724–865.

——— (1993), *Fukkō Ajia no Shomondai* (Various Problems of Asia in Revival). Chūō Kōronsha (originally published in 1922 by Daitōkaku).

Ōmae Ken'ichi (1994), *Ajiajin to Nihonjin: Mahatiiru Marēshia Shushō to no Taiwa* (Asians and Japanese: A Dialogue with Mahathir, the Prime Minister of Malaysia). Shōgakukan.

Otabe Yūji (1981), "Nihon Fuashizumu Keisei to 'Shin Kanryō': Matsumoto Gaku to Nihon Bunka Renmei" (The Formation of Japanese Fascism and "the New Bureaucrats": Matsumoto Gaku and the Japan Culture League). Nihon Gendaishi Kenkyūkai (ed.), *Nihon Fuashizumu (1): Kokka to Shakai* (Japanese Fascism [1], State and Society). Ōtsuki Shoten, 79–117.

Ōtani Kōzui (1939), *Ōtani Kōzui Kōa Keikaku* (Ōtani Kōzui's Plan to Raise Asia). 3 vols., Yūkōsha.

Ōtsuka Takehiro (1995), *Ōkawa Shūmei* (Ōkawa Shūmei). Chūō Kōronsha.

Ōuchi Chōzō (1934), "Konoe Kazan-kō to Tōa Dōbun Shoin" (Prince Konoe Kazan and the Tōa Dōbun Shoin). *Shina* 25:2/3, 143–47.

Ōyama Ikuo (1916), "Dai Ajiashugi no Unmei Ikan" (What Is the Fate of Greater Asianism?). Ōyama Ikuo: *Ōyama Ikuo Chosakushū* (Collected Works by Ōyama Ikuo), Vol. 1. Iwanami Shoten, 1987, 134–52.

Pané, Sanoesi (1930), "De Boodschap van India" (The Embassy of India). *Timboel* 4:8–9, 112–13.

Panikkar, K. M. (1953), *Asia and Western Dominance: A Survey of the Vasco Da Gama Epoch of Asian History, 1498–1945*. London: George Allen & Unwin.

Peattie, Mark R. (1975), *Ishiwara Kanji and Japan's Confrontation with the West*. Princeton, NJ: Princeton University Press.

Peshawar-kai (2009), *About Us*, http://www1a.biglobe.ne.jp/peshawar/eg/annai.html (accessed 21 May 2009).

Pierson, John D. (1980), *Tokutomi Soho, 1863–1957: A Journalist for Modern Japan*. Princeton, NJ: Princeton University Press.

Pratap, Mahendra (1947), *My Life Story of Fifty-Five Years*. Dehradun: World Federation.

Reynolds, Douglas R. (1986), "Chinese Area Studies in Prewar China: Japan's Tōa Dōbun Shoin in Shanghai, 1900–1945." *Journal of Asian Studies*, 45:5, 945–70.

——— (1989), "Training Young China Hands: Tōa Dōbun Shoin and Its Precursors, 1886–1945." Peter Duus, Ramon H. Myers, and Mark R. Peattie (eds.), *The Japanese Informal Empire in China, 1895–1937*. Princeton, NJ: Princeton University Press, 210–71.

——— (1993), *China, 1898–1912: The Xinzheng Revolution and Japan*. Cambridge, MA: Harvard University Press.

Richard, Michel Paul (1987), *Without Passport: The Life and Work of Paul Richard*. New York: Peter Lang Publishing.

Richard, Paul (1917), *To Japan*. Privately published; text in four languages, French (Au Japon), Chinese (translated by Matsudaira Yasukuni), Japanese (by Ōkawa Shūmei), and English (by Mirra Richard).

——— (1920), *The Dawn over Asia*, translated from the French by Aurobindo Ghose. Madras: Ganesh & Co., Publishers.

Romulo, Carlos (1956), *The Meaning of Bandung*. Chapel Hill: University of North Carolina Press.

Rōyama, Masamichi (1934), "The Meaning of the Manchukuo Empire." *Contemporary Japan*, 3:1, 27–33.

——— (1938), "Tōa Kyōdōtai no Riron" (Theory of East Asian Cooperative Body). *Kaizō*, November, 6–26.

——— (1941), *Foreign Policy of Japan: 1914–1939*. Westport, CT: Greenwood Press Publishers.

Rozman, Gilbert (2004), *Northeast Asia's Stunted Regionalism*. Cambridge University Press.

Saaler, Sven (2002), *Pan-Asianism in Modern Japanese History: A Preliminary Approach*. Tōkyō: Deutsches Institut für Japanstudien (DIJ Working Paper 02/4).

——— (2005), *Politics, Memory and Public Opinion. The History Textbook Controversy and Japanese Society*. Munich: Iudicium.

——— (2007), "The Construction of Regionalism in Modern Japan: Kodera Kenkichi and His 'Treatise on Greater Asianism' (1916)." *Modern Asian Studies* 41: 1261–94.

——— (2008a), "The Russo-Japanese War and the Emergence of the Notion of the 'Clash of Races' in Japanese Foreign Policy." John Chapman and Inaba Chiharu (eds.), *Rethinking the Russo-Japanese War, Vol. 2*. Folkestone: Global Oriental and University of Hawai'i Press, 274–89.

——— (2008b), "Taishō-ki ni okeru Seiji Kessha. Kokuryūkai no Katsudō to Jinmyaku" (Political Societies in the Taisho Era: The Activities and the Social Network of the Kokuryūkai). Inoki Takenori (ed.), *Demokurashii to Chūkan Dantai—Senkanki Nihon no Shakai Shūdan to Nettwaku* (Democracy and Intermediary Organizations—Social Organizations and Networks in Interwar Japan). NTT Shuppan, 81–108.

Saaler, Sven, and J. Victor Koschmann (eds.) (2007), *Pan-Asianism in Modern Japanese History: Colonialism, Regionalism and Borders*. London: Routledge.

Said, Edward (1995), *Orientalism*. London: Penguin Books.

Sakai Tetsuya (2007), *Kindai Nihon no Kokusai Chitsujoron* (The International Order of Modern Japan). Iwanami Shoten.

Sakeda Masatoshi (1978), *Kindai Nihon ni okeru Taigaikō Undō no Kenkyū* (A Study of the Movement for Hardline Foreign Policy in Modern Japan). Tokyo Daigaku Shuppankai.

Sakurai Yoshiyuki (1964), *Meiji to Chōsen* (Meiji [Japan] and Korea). Sakurai Yoshiyuki Sensei Kanreki Kinenkai.

Sakuramoto Tomio (1995), *Nihon Bungaku Hōkokukai* (Patriotic Association for Japanese Literature). Aoki Shoten.

Sanbō Honbu (ed.) (1985), *Sugiyama Memo* (The Sugiyama Memorandum), Vol. 2. Hara Shobō.

Sareen, T. R. (2004), "Subhas Chandra Bose, Japan and British Imperialism." *European Journal of East Asian Studies* 3:1, 69–97.

Sarkar, Benoy (1916), *Chinese Religion through Hindu Eyes: A Study in the Tendencies of Asiatic Mentality* (originally published in Shanghai in 1916, reprinted by Oriental Publishers & Distributors, Delhi, 1975), 245–80.

——— (1922), *The Futurism of Young Asia and Other Essays on the Relations between the East and the West*. Berlin: J. Springer.

Satō Dōshin (1999), *Meiji Kokka to Kindai Bijutsu—Bi no Seijigaku* (The Meiji Nation State and Modern Fine Arts—Political Science of Aesthetics). Yoshikawa Kōbunkan.

Sawayanagi Masatarō (1917), "Bunkateki Han-Ajiashugi o Teishō su" (I Advocate Cultural Pan-Asianism). *Shin Nippon* 7/3.

——— (1919a), *Ajiashugi* (Asianism). Daitōkaku.

——— (1919b), "Asianism." *The Japan Magazine*, August, 141–44.

——— (1927), "The General Features of Pacific Relations as Viewed by Japan." *News Bulletin* (Institute of Pacific Relations), 1: 24–27.

Sawayanagi Reijirō (1937), *Waga Chichi Sawayanagi Masatarō* (My Father Sawayanagi Masatarō). Toyama Shobō.

Schmid, Andre (2002), *Korea between Empires 1895–1919*. New York: Columbia University Press.

Sheng Banghe (2000), "19 Shiji Yu 20 Shiji Zhi Jiaode Riben Da Yazhouzhuyi" (Japanese Asianism in the Transitional Period from the 19th to the 20th Century). *Lishi Yanjiu* 3: 125–35.

Shi Guangshang (2006), "Ajia Keizai no Mirai to Nitchū no Keizai Kyōryoku" (The Future of the Asian Economy and Sino-Japanese Economic Cooperation). Abe Shinzō et al., *Nitchū Taiwa* (Japanese-Chinese Dialogue). Genron NPO.

Shi Jiafang (2002), *"Tongwen Tongzhu" de Pianju. Ri wei Dongya Lianmeng Yundong de Xingwang* (The Fraud of "Same Culture, Same Race." The Rise and Fall of Japan's Fake East Asian League Movement). Beijing: Shehui Kexue Wenxian Chubanshe.

Shillony, Ben-Ami (1981), *Politics and Culture in Wartime Japan.* Oxford: Clarendon Press/Oxford University Press.

Shimada, Kenji (1990), *Pioneer of the Chinese Revolution: Zhang Binglin and Confucianism.* Translated by Joshua A. Fogel. Stanford, CA: Stanford University Press.

Shimano Saburō Denki Kankōkai (ed.) (1984), *Shimano Saburō: Mantetsu Soren Jōhō Katsudō no Shōgai* (Shimano Saburō: A Life in the Intelligence Service of the South Manchurian Railway against the Soviets). Hara Shobō.

Shimazu, Naoko (1998), *Japan, Race, and Equality: The Racial Equality Proposal of 1919.* London: Routledge.

Shin, Gi-Wook (2005), "Asianism in Korea's Politics of Identity." *Inter-Asia Cultural Studies* 6:4, 616–30.

——— (2006): *Ethnic Nationalism in Korea: Genealogy, Politics and Legacy.* Stanford, CA: Stanford University Press.

Shindō Eiichi and Hirakawa Hitoshi (eds.), (2006), *Higashi Ajia Kyōdotai o Sekkei Suru* (Construction of an East Asian Community). Nihon Keiyai Hyōronsha, 2006.

Shisō no Kagaku Kenkyūkai (ed.) (1959), *Kyōdō Kenkyū: Tenkō* (Cooperative Research: Conversion), Heibonsha, Vol. I.

Sima, Josef (1974), "On the Character of the So-Called Pan-Mongol Movement after 1911." *Archiv Orientalni* 42:4, 97–119.

Sin Il-ch'ol (1981), *Sin Ch'ae-ho ŭi Yŏksa Sasang Yŏn'gu* (A Study of the Historical Thought of Sin Ch'ae-ho). Korea University Press.

Sin Yong-ha (1984), *Sin Ch'ae-ho ŭi Sahoe Sasang Yŏn'gu* (A Study of the Social Thought of Sin Ch'ae-ho). Hangil Publishing.

Singh, Bhubhindar (2002), "ASEAN's Perceptions of Japan: Change and Continuity." *Asian Survey* 42:2, 276–96.

Smith, Warren W. (1959), *Confucianism in Modern Japan: A Study of Conservatism in Japanese Intellectual History.* The Hokuseido Press.

Snyder, Louis (1984), *Macro-Nationalisms. A History of the Pan-Movements.* Westport, CT: Greenwood Press.

Sŏ Chaep'il Kinyŏmhoe (ed.) (2003), *Sŏ Chaep'il Kwa kŭ Sidae* (Sŏ Chaep'il and His Times). Samhwa Press.

So Wai-Chor [Su Wei Chu/So I Sho] (2007), "Ō Seiei [Wang Jingwei] to Dai Ajiashugi" (Wang Jingwei and Greater Asianism). Matsuura Masataka (ed.) (2007), *Shōwa Ajiashugi no Jitsuzō. Teikoku Nihon to Taiwan, "Nanyō," "Minami Shina"* (The True Picture of Shōwa Asianism. Imperial Japan and Taiwan, the Southern Islands, and Southern China). Kyoto: Minerva Shobō, 182–204.

Sokarno (1955), "Sokarno, President of the Republic of Indonesia at the Opening of the Asian-African Congress in Bandung, Indonesia, on 18 April 1955," The Ministry of Foreign Affairs, Republic of Indonesia (ed.), *Asia-Africa Speaks from Bandung*. Djakarta: Ministry of Foreign Affairs, 19–29.

Son Bun [Sun Yat-sen] (1974), "Dai-Ajiashugi." Kojima Shinji et al. (eds.), *Chūgokujin no Nihonjinkan Hyakunenshi* (Hundred Years' History of Chinese Views of the Japanese). Jiyū Kokuminsha, 158–63.

Stalker, Nancy K. (2006), "Suicide, Boycotts and Embracing Tagore: The Japanese Popular Response to the 1924 US Immigration Exclusion Law." *Japanese Studies* 26:2, 153–70.

——— (2008), *Prophet Motive: Deguchi Onisaburō, Oomoto, and the Rise of New Religions in Imperial Japan.* Honolulu: University of Hawai'i Press.

Steinhoff, Patricia G. (1991), *Tenkō Ideology and Societal Integration in Prewar Japan*. New York: Garland.

Storry, Richard (1957), *The Double Patriots: A Study of Japanese Nationalism.* London: Chatto and Windus.

Sudo, Sueo (2002), *The International Relations of Japan and South East Asia: Forging a New Regionalism*. London: Routledge.

Sugimori Hisahide (1963), *Tsuji Masanobu* (Tsuji Masanobu), Bungei Shunjū Shinsha.

Sugita Teiichi (1916), "Waga Gaikō to Tōyō Renmei" (Our Foreign Policy and the Oriental League). *Nihon oyobi Nihonjin* 674 (11 February), 25–30.

——— (1920), "Address on the Occasion of the Founding of the League for the Equality of Races, 1919." Paul Richard, *The Dawn over Asia.* Madras: Ganesh & Co. Publishers, 90–92.

——— (1924), "Dai Ajia Gasshōron" (An Argument for Uniting Greater Asia). *Tōyō Bunka* 8: 7–13.

Suh Sung (2005), "Japanese Neo-Nationalism and an Idea of East Asian Community." *Inter-Asia Cultural Studies* 6:1, 609–15.

Sun Ge (2000), "How Does Asia Mean?" *Inter-Asia Cultural Studies* 1:1, 13–47, and 1:2, 319–41.

——— (2003), "The Habit of Thinking." *EMPIRE. A Symposium on the Emerging World Order*. Internet: http://www.india-seminar.com/2003/529.htm (last accessed 1 May 2010).

Sun Yat-sen (1923), "Inukai Tsuyoshi ate Shokan" (Letter to Inukai Tsuyoshi). Kojima Shinji et al. (eds.), *Chūgokujin no Nihonjinkan 100 Nenshi* (Hundred Years' History of Chinese Views of the Japanese). Jiyū Kokuminsha, 1974, 153–58.

——— (1941), "Pan-Asianism." *China and Japan: Natural Friends—Unnatural Enemies*, Shanghai: China United Press, 141–51.

Suyematsu, Baron (Suematsu Kenchō) (1905), *The Risen Sun*. London: Archibald Constable & Co.

Swale, Alistair (2003), "Tokutomi Sohō and the Problem of the Nation-State in an Imperialist World." Dick Stegewerns (ed.), *Nationalism and Internationalism in Imperial Japan: Autonomy, Asian Brotherhood, or World Citizenship?* London: RoutledgeCurzon, 69–88.

Szpilman, Christopher W. A. (1998a), "Conservatism and Its Enemies in Prewar Japan: The Case of Hiranuma Kiichirō and the Kokuhonsha." *Hitotsubashi Journal of Social Studies* 30:2, 101–33.

——— (1998b), "The Dream of One Asia: Ōkawa Shūmei and Japanese Pan-Asianism." Harald Fuess (ed.), *The Japanese Empire in East Asia and Its Postwar Legacy*. Munich: Iudicium, 49–63.

——— (2002), "Kita Ikki and the Politics of Coercion." *Modern Asian Studies* 36:2, 467–90.

——— (2004), "Fascist and Quasi-Fascist Ideas in Japan, 1918–1941." Bruce E. Reynolds (ed.), *Japan in the Fascist Era*. New York: Palgrave Macmillan, 73–106.

——— (2007), "Between Pan-Asianism and Nationalism: Mitsukawa Kametarō and His Campaign to Reform Japan and Liberate Asia." Sven Saaler and J. Victor Koschmann (eds.), *Pan-Asianism in Modern Japanese History: Colonialism, Regionalism and Borders*. London: Routledge, 85–100.

Tajima Nobuo (2007), "Son Bun no 'Chū-Doku-So Sangoku Rengō' Kōsō to Nihon, 1917–1924" (Sun Yat-sen's Idea of a "Chinese-German-Soviet Alliance," 1917–1924). Hattori Ryūji et al. (eds.), *Senkanki no Higashi Ajia Kokusai Seiji*. Chūō Daigaku Shuppanbu, 3–52.

Takaki, Yasaka (1932), "World Peace Machinery and the Asia Monroe Doctrine." *Pacific Affairs* 5:11, 941–53.

Takamure Itsue (1940), "Shin Shina no Kensetsu to Nihon Fujin" (The Establishment of a New China and Japanese Women). *Josei Tenbō* 14:4 (April), 5.

Takegoshi [Takekoshi] Y[osaburō] (1919), "The Future of Japan." W. H. Morton-Cameron (comp.), *Present-Day Impressions of Japan: The History, People, Commerce, Industries and Resources of Japan and Japan's Colonial Empire, Kwantung, Chosen, Taiwan, Karafuto*, Vol. 1. London: The Globe Encyclopedia, 83–89.

Takeuchi Yoshimi (1942), "Tabi Nikki Shō" (Extracts from My Travel Diary), reprinted in *Takeuchi Yoshimi Zenshū* (Complete Works of Takeuchi Yoshimi), Vol. 14. Chikuma Shobō, 1980, 395–428.

——— (1944), *Rojin* (Lu Xun), reprinted in *Takeuchi Yoshimi Zenshū* (Complete Works of Takeuchi Yoshimi), Vol. I. Chikuma Shobō, 1980, 1–175.

——— (1948a), "Kindai to wa Nani ka (Nihon to Chūgoku no Baai)" (What Is Modernity? The Case of China and Japan), reprinted in *Takeuchi Yoshimi Zenshū* (Complete Works of Takeuchi Yoshimi), Vol. IV. Chikuma Shobō, 1980, 128–71.

——— (1948b), "What Is Modernity? The Case of China and Japan." Richard F. Calichman (ed.), *What Is Modernity? Writings of Takeuchi Yoshimi*. New York: Columbia University Press, 2005, 53–81.

——— (1958a), "Kindai no Chōkoku" (Overcoming Modernity), reprinted in *Takeuchi Yoshimi Zenshū* (Complete Works of Takeuchi Yoshimi), Vol. VIII. Chikuma Shobō, 1980, 3–67.

——— (1958b), "Overcoming Modernity." Richard F. Calichman (ed.), *What Is Modernity? Writings of Takeuchi Yoshimi.* New York: Columbia University Press, 2005, 103–47.

——— (1960a), "Asia as Method." Richard F. Calichman (ed.), *What Is Modernity? Writings of Takeuchi Yoshimi.* New York: Columbia University Press, 2005, 149–65.

——— (1960b), "Hōhō toshite no Ajia" (Asia as Method), reprinted in *Takeuchi Yoshimi Zenshū* (Complete Works of Takeuchi Yoshimi), Vol. V. Chikuma Shobō, 1980, 90–115.

——— (ed.) (1963a), *Ajiashugi* (Asianism). Chikuma Shobō (Gendai Nihon Shisō Taikei, Vol. 9).

——— (1963b), "Ajiashugi no tenbō" (The Prospect of Asianism), in Takeuchi Yoshimi (ed.), *Ajiashugi* (Asianism) (Gendai Nihon Shisō Taikei, Vol. 9), Chikuma Shobō.

——— (1963c), "Nihon no Ajiashugi" (Japan's Asianism), reprinted in *Takeuchi Yoshimi Zenshū* (Complete Works of Takeuchi Yoshimi), Vol. VIII. Chikuma Shobō, 1980, 94–156.

——— (1966), "Kaisetsu" (Commentary), reprinted in *Takeuchi Yoshimi Hyōronshū, Vol. III: Nihon to Ajia* (Collection of Takeuchi Yoshimi's Essays, Vol. III: Japan and Asia). Chikuma Shobō, 421–31.

——— (1969), "Ōkawa Shūmei: Profile of Asian Minded Man." *The Developing Economies* 7:3, 367–79.

Takeuchi Zensaku (1948), "Meiji Makki ni okeru Chūnichi Kakumei Undō no Kōryū" (The Exchanges between the Chinese and Japanese Revolutionary Movements in the Late Meiji Period). *Chūgoku Kenkyū* 1948:5, 74–95.

Takushoku Daigaku Sōritsu Hyakunenshi Hensanshitsu (ed.) (2002–2005), *Tanaka Ippei.* Takushoku Daigaku, 5 vols.

Tanaka Ippei (1924), *Isureamu to Dai-Ajiashugi* (Islam and Asianism). Self-published.

Tanaka Keiichi (ed.) (1996), *Shibata Shūzō Nikki* (Diaries of Shibata Shūzō). 2 vols. Heibonsha.

Tanaka Sōgorō (1930), *Tōyō Shakaitō Kō* (Thoughts on the Eastern Socialist Party). Ichigensha.

——— (1971), *Kita Ikki: Nihon no Fasshisuto no Shōchō* (Kita Ikki: The Symbol of Japanese Fascists), Expanded Edition, San'ichi Shobō.

Tanaka, Stefan (1993), *Japan's Orient—Reading Pasts into History.* Berkeley: University of California Press.

Tang Zhijun (ed.) (1977), *Zhang Taiyan Zheng Lun Xuan ji* (Collected Works on Zhang Taiyan's Political Writings). Beijing: Zhonghua Shuju, Vol. 1.

——— (1991), "Guanyu Yazhou Heqin hui" (On the Asiatic Humanitarian Brotherhood). Wuchang Xinhai Geming Yanjiu Zhongxin (ed.), *Xinhai Geming yu Jindai Zhongguo; 1980–1989 Nian Lunwen Xuan.* Wuhan: Hubei Renmin Chubanshe.

Tang, Leang-Li (ed.) (1941), *China and Japan: Natural Friends, Unnatural Enemies.* Shanghai: China United Press.

Tankha, Brij (ed.) (2009), *Okakura Tenshin and Pan-Asianism: Shadows of the Past.* Global Oriental.

Tano Daisuke (2009), "Yoka no Sūjiku. Sekai Kōsei Kaigi to Nichidoku Bunka Kōryū" (The Axis of Leisure. The World Welfare Congress and Japanese-German Cultural Exchange). *Geshihite* 2, 21–39.

Tarling, Nicholas (1992), "'Ah-Ah': Britain and the Bandung Conference of 1955." *Journal of Southeast Asian Studies* 23:1, 74–111.

Tarui Tōkichi (1893), *Daitō Gappōron* (Arguments on Behalf of the Union of the Great East), reprinted in *Fukkoku Daitō Gappōron* (Chōryō Shorin/Wakatsuki Shoten, 1975).

Thompson, Richard Austin (1978), *The Yellow Peril, 1890–1924*. New York: Arno Press.

Tikhonov, Vladimir (2002), "Korea's First Encounters with Pan-Asianism Ideology in the Early 1880s." *The Review of Korean Studies* 5:2, 195–232.

Tōa Renmei Kyōkai (ed.) (1940), *Tōa Renmei Kensetsu Yōkō* (Prospectus for Constructing the East Asian League). Ritsumeikan Shuppanbu.

Tōjō Hideki (1943), "Taishō o Haishi Tatematsurite—Kōa no Seigyō kono Issen (Revering the Imperial Edict: This One War [Is] the Holy Task of Raising Asia). *Seinen* 27:1 (1 January), 38–39.

Tokugawa Yoshichika (1973), *Saigo no Tonosama: Tokugawa Yoshichika Jiden* (The Last Lord: The Autobiography of Tokugawa Yoshichika). Kōdansha.

Tokutomi Iichirō (1917), "Japan's Mighty Mission," in Taraknath Das, *Is Japan a Menace to Asia?* Shanghai: no publisher, 153–59.

Tokutomi Sohō (1913), "Jimu Ikkagen" (An Opinion on Current Issues), reprinted in Tokutomi Sohō (1974), *Meiji Bungaku Zenshū* (Complete Collection of Meiji Literature), Vol. 34. Chikuma Shobō, 301–14.

Tomioka Kōichirō (2006), *Shin Daitōa Sensō Kōteiron* (A New Affirmation of the Greater East Asian War). Asuka Shinsha.

Torpey, John (ed.) (2003), *Politics and the Past: On Repairing Historical Injustices.* Lanham, MD: Rowman & Littlefield.

Tōyama Mitsuru, Inukai Tsuyoshi, Sugiyama Shigemaru, and Uchida Ryōhei (2008), *Ajiashugisha no Koe 1: Gen'yōsha to Kokuryūkai, aruiwa Kōdōteki Ajiashugi no Genten* (Pan-Asianist Voices, Vol. 1: The Gen'yōsha and the Kokuryūkai, or: The Origin of Activist Asianism). Shoshi Shinsui.

Tsuji Masanobu (1950), *Ajia no Kyōkan: Tatakai o Tsūjite Mita Chūgoku* (Empathy with Asia: The China I Saw through My Struggle). Atō Shobō.

Tsukui Tatsuo (1956), *Uyoku Kaigan: Chūkyō to Nikkyō* (The Opening of the Right Wing's Eyes: The Chinese Communist Party and the Japanese Communist Party). Takubunkan.

Tsunoda, Ryusaku et al. (eds.) (1958), *Sources of Japanese Tradition*. New York: Columbia University Press.

Uchida Rōan (Roansei) (1917), "Gakujutsuteki Han-Ajiashugi" (Academic Pan-Asianism). *Taiyō* 23:4, 65–75.

Uchida Ryōhei (1918), "Jo" (Preface). Kokuryūkai Shuppanbu (ed.), *Ajia Taikan* (Overview of Asia). *Kokuryūkai Shuppanbu*, 1–4.

——— (1920), "The Asian Review and the Kokuryu-kai." *The Asian Review* 1:1, 3–5.

Uchida Ryōhei Monjo Kenkyūkai (ed.) (1992), *Kokuryūkai Kankei Shiryōshū* (Collection of Sources Relating to the Kokuryūkai), Vol. 1. Kashiwa Shobō.

Uhl, Christian (2009), "Displacing Japan: Takeuchi Yoshimi's Lu Xun in Light of Nishida's Philosophy—and Vice Versa." *Positions: East Asia Cultures Critique* 17:1, 207–38.

Ukita Kazutami (1918), "Shin Ajiashugi" (New Asianism). *Taiyō* 24:9, 2–17.

Umetsu Jun'ichi (2006), "Tokutomi Sohō to 'Chikara no Fukuin': *Shōrai no Nihon* kara *Jimu Ikkagen e*" (Tokutomi Sohō and "The Gospel of Power": From *The Future of Japan* to *An Opinion on Current Issues*). *Seigakuin Ronsō* 19:1, 16–31.

Utsunomiya Tarō Kankei Shiryō Kenkyūkai (ed.) (2007), *Nihon Rikugun to Ajia Seisaku. Rikugun Taishō Utsunomiya Tarō Nikki 3* (The Japanese Army and Asia Policy. The Diary of Army General Utsunomiya Tarō, 3). Iwanami Shoten.

Valliant, Robert B. (1974), "The Selling of Japan: Japanese Manipulation of Western Opinion, 1900–1905." *Monumenta Nipponica* 29:4, 415–38.

Wada Haruki (2003), *Tōhoku Ajia Kyōdō no Ie: Shinchiikishugi Sengen* (North Western Asian Common Homestead: The Declaration of a New Regionalism). Heibonsha.

——— (2008a), "The Comfort Women, the Asian Women's Fund and the Digital Museum." Internet: *JapanFocus*, http://japanfocus.org/-Wada-Haruki/2653 (last accessed 1 March 2010).

——— (2008b), "Okinawa to Hokutō Ajia" (Maritime Asia and the Future of a Northeast Asia Community). *Ryūkyū Shinpō,* 7–9 January.

Wada Mamoru (1990), *Kindai Nihon to Tokutomi Sohō* (Modern Japan and Tokutomi Sohō). Ochanomizu Shobō.

Wakabayashi, Bob Tadashi (1986), *Anti-Foreignism and Western Learning in Early-Modern Japan: The New Theses of 1825*. Cambridge, MA: Harvard University Press.

Wakabayashi Nakaba [Han] (1937), *Kaikyō Sekai to Nihon* (The World of Islam and Japan). Dainichisha.

Wang, C. C. (1934), "The Pan-Asiatic Doctrine of Japan." *Foreign Affairs* 13:1, 59–67.

Wang Jingwei (1940), "Minzuzhuyi yu Da Yazhouzhuyi" (Nationalism and Greater Asianism). *Da Yazhouzhuyi* (Greater Asianism), 1:4 (November), 1–5.

Wang Ping (2004), *Jindai Riben de Yaxiyazhuyi* (Modern Japanese Asianism). Beijing: Shangwu Yinshuguan.

Wang Yi (2006a), "Ajia no Shōrai oyobi Nitchū Ryōkoku no Yakuwari" (The Future of Asia and the Roles of Japan and China). Internet: http://jp.chineseembassy.org/jpn/sgxx/t282546.htm (last accessed 4 October 2009).

——— (2006b), "Sikao Ershiyi Shiji de Xin Yazhouzhuyi" (Considering Neo-Asianism in the Twenty-First Century). *Waijiao Pinglun* (Foreign Affairs Review) 89: 6–10.

Watanabe Kyōji (2006), *Hyōden Miyazaki Tōten* (Critical Biography of Miyazaki Tōten). Shoshi Shinsui (first edition by Yamato Shoten, 1976).

Weber, Torsten (2009), "'Unter dem Banner des Asianismus': Transnationale Dimensionen des japanischen Asianismus-Diskurses der Taishō-Zeit (1912–1926)" (Under the Banner of Asianism: The Transnational Dimensions of Japanese Discourse on Asianism in the Taishō Era [1912–1926]). *Comparativ. Zeitschrift für Globalgeschichte und Vergleichende Gesellschaftsforschung* 18:6, 34–52.

Wilson, George M. (1969), *Kita Ikki: Radical Nationalist in Japan*. Cambridge, MA: Harvard University Press.

Wilson, Sandra (2005), "The Discourse of National Greatness in Japan, 1890–1919." *Japanese Studies* 25:1, 35–51.

Wong, Yong-tsu (1989), *Search for Modern Nationalism: Zhang Binglin and Revolutionary China, 1869–1936*. Hong Kong: Oxford University Press.

Worringer, Renée (2006), "Pan-Asianism in the Late Ottoman Empire, 1905–1912." Camron Michael Amin, Benjamin C. Fortna, and Elizabeth B. Frierson (eds.), *The Modern Middle East: A Sourcebook for History*. Oxford: Oxford University Press, 331–38.

—— (ed.) (2007), *The Islamic Middle East and Japan: Perceptions, Aspirations, and the Birth of Intra-Asian Modernity*. Princeton, NJ: Markus Wiener Publishers.

Yamagata Bantō (1820), *Yumenoshiro* (A Castle of Dreams), reprinted in Tominaga Nakamoto and Mizuta Norihisa (eds.), *Nihon Shisō Taikei, Vol. 43: Yamagata Bantō* (Survey of Japanese Thought, Vol. 43: Yamagata Bantō), Iwanami Shoten, 1973, 223, 433.

Yamamoto Shigeki (2001), *Konoe Atsumaro: Sono Meiji Kokkakan to Ajiakan* (Konoe Atsumaro: His Views on the Meiji State and Asia). Kyoto: Minerva Shobō.

Yamamuro Shin'ichi (1993), *Kimera: Manshūkoku no Shōzō* (Chimera: A Portrait of Manzhouguo). Chūō Kōronsha (translated into English as *Manchuria Under Japanese Dominion* by Joshua Fogel, Philadelphia: University of Pennsylvania Press, 2005).

—— (2001), *Shisō Kadai toshite no Ajia* (Asia as an Intellectual Theme). Iwanami Shoten.

—— (2005), *Nichiro Sensō no Seiki* (The Century of the Russo-Japanese War). Iwanami Shoten.

Yamanokuchi Kōichi (1996), "Kokuryūkai: Uchida Ryōhei no Dōkōkai Katsudō (The Kokuryūkai: The Activities of Uchida Ryōhei in the Dōkōkai). *Nihon Hōsei Gakkai Hōsei Ronsō* 32: 155–65.

Yamaura Kan'ichi (1941), *Tōa Shintaisei no Senku: Mori Kaku* (Mori Kaku, the Pioneer of the East Asian New Order). Mori Kaku Denki Hensankai.

Yasko, Richard A. (1973), *Hiranuma Kiichirō and Conservative Politics in Pre-War Japan*. PhD diss., University of Chicago.

Yasuoka Masahiro (1922), *Fukkō Ajia no Shisōteki Konkyo* (The Ideological Basis for a Revived Asia). Yūzonsha Shōsatsu no. 2, November.

—— (1933), "Seiji Tetsugaku yori Mitaru Gendai Nihon: Sekai Topikku" (World Topics: Contemporary Japan from the Perspective of Political Philosophy). *Kōen* 234, Kigen 2, 593.

—— (1938), "Shina Jihen no Shisa suru Kongo no Kyōyō Mondai" (The Future of the Matter of Personal Cultivation as Indicated by the China Incident). *Kinkei Gakuhō* 12: 1–22.

—— (1943a), *Daitōa Kyōeiken no Shidōsha taru beki Nihonjin no Kyōiku* (Education for Japanese Capable of Being Leaders of the Greater East Asia Co-Prosperity Sphere). Keimeikai.

—— (1943b), *Naigai Jisei no Konpon Mondai* (Fundamental Issues of Current Domestic and Foreign Political Trends). Chōsa Hōkokusho no. 15. Nihon Gaikō Kyōkai.

Yeo Lay Hwee (2006), "Japan, ASEAN, and the Construction of an East Asian Community." *Contemporary Southeast Asia* 28:2, 259–75.

Yi, Chin-o (2000), Orientalisŭm-kwa Oksidentalisŭm-ŭl Nŏmŏsŏ (Beyond the Orientalism and Occidentalism). Onŭl-ŭi Munye Pip'yŏng, Internet: http://home.pusan.ac.kr/~jino/Jeosul/gt02.htm (last accessed 31 March 2010).

Yō Teruko (2007), "Kanokogi Kazunobu ni okeru Nihon Seishin to Nachizumu" (The Japanese Spirit and Nazism in Kanokogi Kazunobu). Mochida Yukio (ed.), *Kindai Nihon to Doitsu* (Modern Japan and Germany). Minerva Shobō.

Yokoi Shōnan (1860), *Kokuze Sanron* (Three Theses on State Policy), reprinted in Satō Shōsuke et al. (eds.), *Nihon Shisō Taikei, Vol. 55: Watanabe Kazan, Takano Chōei, Sakuma Shōzan, Yokoi Shōnan, Hashimoto Sanai* (Survey of Japanese Thought, Vol. 55: Watanabe Kazan, Takano Chōei, Sakuma Shōzan, Yokoi Shōnan, Hashimoto Sanai). Iwanami Shoten, 1971, 450–51.

Yonehara Ken (2003), *Tokutomi Sohō: Nihon Nashonarizumu no Kiro* (Tokutomi Sohō: Japanese Nationalism at a Crossroads). Chūō Kōronsha.

Yonetani Masafumi (2006), *Ajia/Nihon* (Asia/Japan). Iwanami Shoten.

Yoshimi Yoshiaki (1987), *Kusa no Ne no Fashizumu* (Grass-Roots Fascism). Tokyo Daigaku Shuppankai.

Young, Louise (1998), *Japan's Total Empire: Manchuria and the Culture of Wartime Imperialism*. Berkeley: University of California Press.

Zachmann, Urs Matthias (2007), "Blowing Up a Double Portrait in Black and White: The Concept of Asia in the Writings of Fukuzawa Yukichi and Okakura Tenshin." *Positions: East Asia Cultures Critique* 15:2, 345–68.

—— (2009), *China and Japan in the Late Meiji Period: China and the Japanese Discourse on National Identity, 1895–1904*. London: Routledge.

Zen Ajiakai (1917), *Kokusaikan ni okeru Nihon no Koritsu* (The Isolation of Japan in International Relations). Zen Ajiakai.

Zhai Xin (Teki Shin) (2001), *Tōa Dōbunkai to Chūgoku: Kindai Nihon ni okeru Taigai Rinen to sono Jissen* (The Tōa Dōbunkai and China: The Ideal and Practice of Foreign Relations in Modern Japan). Keiō Gijuku Daigaku Shuppankai.

Zhang Weixiong (1999), *Bunjin Gaikōkan no Meiji Nihon: Chūgoku Shodai Chūnichi Nihon Kōdan no Ibunka Taiken* (The Meiji Japan of the Literati-Diplomats: The First Chinese Diplomatic Mission to Japan and Its Experience of a Foreign Culture). Kashiwa Shobō.

Zhongnan Diqu Xinhai Geming Shi Yanjiuhui (ed.) (1980), *Xinhai Geming Shi Cong Kan* (Materials on the History of the Xinhai Revolution), Vol. 1. Beijing: Zhinghua Shuju.

Zhou Huaren, (1940), "Da Yazhouzhuyi yu Sanminzhuyi" (Greater Asianism and the Three People's Principles). *Da Yazhouzhuyi* (Greater Asianism), 1:2 (September), 11–15.

Zumoto Motosada (1927), "Japan and the Pan-Asiatic Movement." *News Bulletin* (Institute of Pacific Relations), 8–15.

Index

List of Contributors to Volume 2

Roger H. Brown is professor of Japanese history and U.S.–Japan relations at Saitama University, Japan. He is the author of "Visions of a Virtuous Manifest Destiny: Yasuoka Masahiro and Japan's Kingly Way" (included in *Pan-Asianism in Modern Japanese History*, 2007) and "Shepherds of the People: Yasuoka Masahiro and the New Bureaucrats in Early Showa Japan" (*Journal of Japanese Studies,* Summer 2009).

Kristine Dennehy is an associate professor of history at California State University, Fullerton. Her recent publications include "Resident Korean Labor 'Movements' in Postcolonial Japan: Cinematic and Literary Representations in Hayafune Chiyo's *Foundry Town* (*Kyūpora no aru Machi*) and Yang Sogil's *All Night* (*Yoru o Kakete*)" (*Contemporary Women's History in Asia*, 2009).

Prasenjit Duara is Raffles Professor of Humanities at the National University of Singapore. He received his PhD from Harvard University. His publications include *Rescuing History from the Nation* (1995), *Sovereignty and Authenticity: Manchukuo and the East Asian Modern* (2003), and *The Global and Regional in China's Nation-Formation* (2009).

Eddy Dufourmont is associate professor of modern Japanese history and thought at University Michel de Montaigne Bordeaux 3. His publications include a translation of Nakae Chōmin's *A Discourse by Three Drunkards on Government* and articles on the Japanese thinkers Nakae Chōmin and Yasuoka Masahiro.

Curtis Anderson Gayle is associate professor at Japan Women's University, Tokyo. He has published *Marxist History and Postwar Japanese Nationalism* (2003) and *Women's History and Local Community in Postwar Japan* (2010).

Jung-Sun N. Han is assistant professor at the Graduate School of International Studies, Korea University, where she teaches modern Japanese history. She has published "Rationalizing the Orient" (*Monumenta Nipponica*, 2005) and "Envisioning a Liberal Empire" (*Journal of Japanese Studies*, 2007).

Hatsuse Ryūhei is professor of Japanese history, Kyōto Women's University. His numerous publications include *Dentōteki Uyoku Uchida Ryōhei no Kenkyū* (A Study of Uchida Ryōhei, a Traditional Right Winger, 1980), *Kokusai Seijigaku* (International Politics, 1993), and *Esunishitii to Tabunkashugi* (Ethnicity and Multiculturalism, 1996).

Eri Hotta, an independent scholar based in New York, received her doctorate in international relations from Oxford, where she taught for four years and where she was also a junior research fellow until 2005. She has since held several visiting research and teaching posts in the United States and Japan. Her book *Pan-Asianism and Japan's War 1931–1945* was published in 2007.

Eun-jeung Lee, professor of Korean studies at the Free University of Berlin, was previously an Alexander von Humboldt Foundation fellow and a Japan Foundation fellow. Her publications include *Anti-Europa: Die Geschichte der Rezeption des Konfuzianismus in Europa* (Anti-Europe: The History of the Reception of Confucianism in Europe, 2003).

Stefano von Loë, who was a research fellow at Tokyo University between 1998 and 2000, is a PhD candidate at the Department of History and East Asian Languages, Harvard University.

Ethan Mark is university lecturer in modern Japanese history at Leiden University, Netherlands. His works include *Appealing to Asia: Nation, Culture, and the Problem of Imperial Modernity in Japanese-Occupied Java, 1942–1945* (PhD dissertation, Columbia University, 2003) and "Asia's Transwar Lineage: Nationalism, Marxism, and 'Greater Asia' in an Indonesian Inflection" (*Journal of Asian Studies*, 2006).

Mutō Shūtarō, senior scholar at Fudan University in Shanghai, was formerly research fellow at the Japan Society for the Promotion of Science. He is the author of *Kindai Nihon no Shakaikagaku to Higashi Ajia* (The Social Sciences in Modern Japan and East Asia, 2009).

Li Narangoa is associate professor at the Australian National University. Formerly a researcher at the Nordic Institute of Asian Studies (Copenhagen), she is the coeditor of *Imperial Japan and National Identities in Asia 1895–1945* (2003) and *Mongols from Country to City: Floating Boundaries, Pastoralism and City Life in Mongol Lands* (2006).

Sven Saaler, associate professor of modern Japanese history at Sophia University in Tokyo, was formerly head of the Humanities Section of the German Institute for Japanese Studies and associate professor at the University of Tokyo. He is the author of *Politics, Memory and Public Opinion* (2005) and coeditor/coauthor of *Pan-Asianism in Modern Japanese History* (2007) and *The Power of Memory in Modern Japan* (2008).

Michael A. Schneider is professor of East Asian history and chair of the Asian Studies Program at Knox College, Galesburg, Illinois. He has also served as an exchange professor and visiting scholar at Waseda University. He has published a number of articles on Pan-Asianism and Japanese colonial policy in Korea.

Kyoko Selden, who taught Japanese language and literature at Cornell University until 2008, is the translator of Honda Katsuichi's *Harukor: An Ainu Woman's Tale* (2000), the cotranslator of Kayano Shigeru's *Our Land Was a Forest: An Ainu Memoir* (1994), and the coeditor of *The Atomic Bomb: Voices from Hiroshima and Nagasaki* (1997).

Mark Selden is a senior research associate in the East Asia Program at Cornell University and Bartle Professor of History and Sociology at Binghamton University. His numerous publications include *The Yenan Way in Revolutionary China* (1971, 1995), *China, East Asia and the Global Economy* (coauthor, 2008), and *Chinese Society: Change, Conflict and Resistance* (coeditor, 2009).

Christopher W. A. Szpilman, professor of modern Japanese history at Kyushu Sangyo University, Fukuoka, received his PhD from Yale University. He is the coeditor of Mitsukawa Kametarō's Diaries (2011) and of a new revised edition of Kita Ikki's *National Polity and Pure Socialism* (in Japanese, 2007) as well as the author of a number of articles on Japan's prewar right wing and conservatism.

Brij Tankha is professor of modern Japanese history, Department of East Asian Studies, University of Delhi. His publications include *Shadows of the Past of Okakura Tenshin and Pan-Asianism* (editor, 2008) and *A Vision of Empire: Kita Ikki and the Making of Modern Japan* (2003).

Christian Uhl is professor of Japanese intellectual history, Department of South and East Asian Languages and Cultures, Ghent University, Belgium. His publications include "Displacing Japan: Takeuchi Yoshimi's Lu Xun in Light of Nishida's Philosophy—and Vice Versa" (*positions*, 2009) and *Who Was Takeuchi Yoshimi's Lu Xun* (in German, 2003).

Torsten Weber, research associate in the project "Asianisms in the 20th Century" at Jacobs University Bremen (Germany), previously held research and teaching positions at the universities of Leiden and Heidelberg. He is the author of various articles on modern Asia discourse and is currently completing a monograph on transnational Asianism discourse in interwar Japan.

www.ingramcontent.com/pod-product-compliance
Lightning Source LLC
Chambersburg PA
CBHW060130280326
41932CB00012B/1472